The Eastern Frontier

CHARLES E. CLARK

THE
EASTERN
FRONTIER

The Settlement of

Northern New England

1610-1763

ALFRED A. KNOPF   NEW YORK   1970

For Margery

Preface

To most students of the American past, amateur or professional, the phrase "colonial New England" calls forth a cluster of associated images. Pilgrims at Plymouth. The solemn signing of the Salem church covenant. Boston's John Winthrop presiding sternly but prayerfully over the Massachusetts Court of Assistants. Stubborn Roger Williams and uppity Anne Hutchinson, both infected by more than a touch of mysticism. Interminable sermons and cold feet in the meetinghouse. The village common. Brooding dark brown Tudor houses outnumbered after a time by stark white saltboxes and finally by cheerful Georgians. Haughty, self-satisfied merchants with lace trimmings, convinced that divine grace and worldly treasure exist in direct proportion. Industrious goodmen and goodwives in homespun. Solemn-faced children, worried about their souls.

The trouble with such images is not that they are false (though some of them are exaggerated), but that they are incomplete. Taken together, they recall a way of life for which our limited vocabulary supplies the inevitable label "Puritanism." This way of life, moreover, is associated so thoroughly with "colonial New England," especially in the seventeenth century, that the distinction between it and the region is often made fuzzy indeed.

The picture is currently undergoing salutary revision, but the "New England" of both the traditional and revised accounts ended, at least through most of the seventeenth century, approximately at the Merrimack River. The settlers of that corner of America which became New Hampshire and Maine differed from southern New Englanders in place of origin, motives for settlement, religion, politics, temperament, and way of life. These differences, and those of geography, resulted in a regional distinction between northern and southern New England that was as marked as the time-honored separations that are usually observed between New England and the Middle Colonies, and between the Middle Colonies and those of the Chesapeake. Readers, therefore, will occasionally find me referring unabashedly to the land beyond the Merrimack as a "region."

This very difference is reason enough for a detailed examination of colonial society from the Merrimack to, say, Penobscot Bay. One cannot hope for a total comprehension of "colonial New England" if he fails to understand that it was not in the beginning all of a piece. The most obvious and, I think, most important purpose of this study, therefore, is simply to describe, for its own sake, the origins and development of this "different" society approximately to the end of the American colonial period.

My investigation, however, for all the uncomplicated nature of the impulse that launched it, has led to something more than bare description and narrative. Though I conducted it as a study neither of the "frontier" nor of "imperialism," but simply of northern New England, I found that both these rather time-worn concepts offered such compelling utility in shaping what I conceive to be the true story of the social and cultural development of the region that it was impossible to ignore them.

The society of northern New England did not remain utterly distinct from the society south of the Merrimack indefinitely. Given the power, the vigor, and the size of the province that lay to the south, it was probably inevitable that the magistrates and ministers of Massachusetts would entertain imperial and missionary ambitions with respect to the land and the people of New Hampshire and Maine. The absorption of territory and the imposition of an essentially alien culture that resulted from these ambitions form one of the organizing themes of this study. However, the "Puritan conquest," as I have called it, was by no means either complete or entirely successful. I believe that its partial failure helps to illuminate not only the role of the "frontier" in American history, but also the nature of the "colonial" experience in general.

I have aimed primarily at writing a social (though not "sociological") history—that is, a study of a people, their way of living, their problems, their social organization, their cultural accomplishments, and, so far as possible, their distinctive character and ways of thought. When I have thought it necessary, however, I have not hesitated to include a narrative of economic, political, and institutional developments sufficient to clarify and place in perspective the growth of the society I have sought to portray. The task was complicated by the diversity of the people. The study crosses not only colonial boundaries, but social and cultural lines as well. Its subjects include urban dwellers as well as pioneers, villagers as well as country farmers, merchants as well as fishermen and woodsmen, Ulstermen as well as Englishmen, and Anglicans and Presbyterians as well as Congregationalists and heathens.

Though I have sought to record with proper emphasis the most conspicuous names in the colonial history of the region, such as those of Sir Ferdinando Gorges and Captain John Mason, the Reverend John Wheelwright, John and Benning Wentworth, and Sir William Pepperrell, I have felt that my purpose could be best served by stressing the sort of lives that were led by people who were more representative of the societies under study. Thus the reader will find that prominent places have been assigned to men and women of whom he may never have heard, such as Matthew Patten, the farmer and diarist of Bedford, New Hampshire; Thomas Chute, the tailor and founder of New Marblehead, Maine; Nicholas Gilman, the eccentric revivalist of Durham, New Hampshire; and Moses Pearson, the Old Light merchant, landowner, justice, sheriff, militia officer, and clerk of practically everything in Falmouth, Maine.

It was with some reluctance that *The Eastern Frontier* was settled upon as a title. Contrary to what some readers may feel the title suggests, I have made no conscious effort to argue for or to elaborate upon any particular general theory of historical causation, including the famous one advanced seventy-seven years ago by Frederick Jackson Turner. Whatever interpretations are found in the following pages emerged, I like to think, not from doctrine but from the logic of the evidence itself.

Just as I find it prudent to dismiss the "ideological" implications that some readers may find in the use of the term "frontier," I think it wise to point out that the word as it is used in the title is intended to be broadly rather than narrowly construed. I have paid little attention to the "frontier" phenomenon as such, whether one means a frontier of place—that is, the forward line of settlement—or a frontier of function, such as fishing, lumbering, agriculture, or urban commerce. I have made an attempt to distinguish between the sort of tentative community that characterized the pioneering, unformed stage of forward settlements in the wilderness and the permanent rural agricultural communities that often replaced them if the pioneers succeeded in their initial work. Beyond that, however, my concern has been with a particular, rather large and diverse area on the map, and with the variety of people who lived there—not with a process abstractly defined. The term "Eastern Frontier" is intended to describe this region in the seventeenth and eighteenth centuries, conveying a sense of its initial remoteness from the more settled parts of America and of its nature as a northeastward extension of New England society. I pondered a number of alternate descriptive phrases. Applied to the entire region over a span of more than a century and a half, none of them seemed to do the job as well.

As in any book about New England, the word "town" is used prominently and repeatedly, and demands explanation for those whose understanding of the word as I have used it is not second nature. The town, first of all, was and remains the fundamental unit of local political organization in both the northern and southern parts of the region. In that sense, it was and is a body politic, a municipal corporation, the whole body of freeholders or voters residing and exercising their political rights and duties within a prescribed geographic area divided from adjoining municipalities by political boundaries. The town was and is also, by common usage, the geographic area over which the municipal corporation exercises jurisdiction. In the seventeenth and eighteenth centuries, the term "town" was *not* ordinarily used in New England, and is not used in this book, to refer to an area of compact settlement. When necessary to distinguish compactly settled parts of the town, if they existed, from the rural or undeveloped parts of it, I have used the term "village" or, when more appropriate because of minute size, "hamlet." In a footnote to Chapter IX, when the problem first arises, I have tried to distinguish between the political term "town" and the proprietary term "township."

I have tried to be scrupulously accurate in rendering quotations, but for the sake of consistency and clarity I have employed a modified version of what the editors of the *Harvard Guide to American History* call the "expanded method." I have used the letters *i, j, u,* and *v* in accordance with modern usage, and changed the thorn (commonly written *y* in the seventeenth and eighteenth centuries) to *th*. Superior letters have been lowered, the appropriate letters have been substituted for diacritical marks, and the ampersand has been replaced with *and.* In the case of abbreviations, I have supplied the missing letters when they are omitted from the middle of a word but not when they were left off the end of a word. In those cases, I have supplied a period at the end of the abbreviation even when the manuscript does not. I have not meddled with punctuation except when I have felt it absolutely necessary for clarity or when the writer plainly intended a dash to indicate a full stop. In those few instances, I have substituted the period. Dates prior to September 14, 1752, are rendered Old Style with double year designations between January 1 and March 25.

The most necessary and most pleasant of any author's tasks is the acknowledgment of his dependence upon others. The greatest single debt that I have incurred in the preparation of this study is to Professor Carl Bridenbaugh, who suggested back in 1963, while I was studying at Brown University and casting about for a dissertation topic in colonial history, that I might be the one to investigate the neglected area of northern New England. Under his tutelage, I completed the dissertation, profiting at every step from his large fund of scholarship, wisdom, wit, and understanding. Later, when I had expanded upon the original research and recast the material into something like its present form, Professor Bridenbaugh again read the manuscript with his customary acute eye for stylistic and factual errors. To him and to my colleague at the University of New Hampshire, Donald M. Murray, who also read virtually the entire manuscript with the critical eye of a practicing artist, are largely due whatever literary merit the work may possess. Professor Murray, I must add, devoted to the text time and mental effort far exceeding the call of either duty or friendship. Later, my colleague in history at New Hampshire, Professor David F. Long, performed the valuable service of reading the proofs, thus saving me from several errors, both mechanical and substantive.

Work on this study during the dissertation stage was facilitated enormously by the Committee of Management of the John Carter Brown Library, which honored me with one of that library's valuable fellowships. Equally vital to the subsequent preparation of the book was a National Endowment for the Humanities Fellowship from the National Foundation on the Arts and the Humanities. I am likewise grateful to Professor Samuel A. Stone, who while a dean at Southeastern Massachusetts Technological Institute, now Southeastern Massachusetts University, was kind enough to nominate me for this important grant, and to my colleagues in the Department of History and the administration of the University of New Hampshire, who, under unexpected circumstances, willingly made the adjustments necessary to permit me to take advantage of it during my first year on the university faculty. I have also been assisted with grants from the Central University Research Fund, administered by the Research Council of the University of New Hampshire.

To list, or even to recall, all of those individuals who have provided help, advice, encouragement, and insights would, of course, be impossible. However, I do wish to single out for recognition several persons and staffs who occupy conspicuous places in my recollection of the six years during which, in one way or another, I have lived with this project. Some of them may not know for what precise reason they are listed; suffice it to say that I do not necessarily regard all of the most valuable contributions as those that are most easily defined.

My thanks go to the staff of the John Carter Brown Library in the years 1964 and 1965, especially Glenn B. Skillin, Mrs. Joseph Hardy, and Miss Jeannette D. Black; the staff of the Maine Historical Society in 1964, 1965, and 1968, especially Miss Elizabeth Ring, Miss E. Marie Estes, Mrs. Alvah H. Small, and, again, Mr. Skillin; John H. Lindenbusch, formerly of the New Hampshire Historical Society; Miss Dorothy M. Vaughan of the Portsmouth Public Library; Donald H. Margeson of the Portsmouth Athenaeum; Geoffrey P. Moran of Bradford Junior College, formerly of "Strawbery Banke, Inc."; the staff of the Dimond Library at the University of New Hampshire, especially Hugh C. Pritchard; Professor William G. McLoughlin of Brown University; Professor Dickinson W. Adams of Southeastern Massachusetts University; Dean H. Trevor Colbourn and Professor Darrett B. Rutman of the University of New Hampshire; Charles W. Eastman, Jr., my graduate assistant in 1969 and 1970; John W. Gibson, who took the photographs; Derek Terreson, the artist who produced the maps and sketches; Mrs. Albert W. Snow, who contributed to my morale by praising the manuscript even as she typed it; and Jane N. Garrett, a most congenial editor.

I must add a special note of gratitude to my parents, the Reverend Clarence H. Clark and Beatrice Wright Clark, who not only provided encouragement and enthusiasm but also instilled in me from boyhood a fond attachment to the region whose study I have undertaken here and a sympathetic awareness, not to be found in manuscripts or artifacts, of the distinct, extra-sharp flavor that has long belonged to those who have worked the soil, fished the waters, and cut the trees north of the Merrimack. I should be remiss, too, if I failed to acknowledge that my children, Marilyn, Douglas, Jonathan, and David, have been understanding in yielding time to this book that they would have preferred that their father spend in other ways.

None of the many scholars, librarians, and friends who have helped me and given advice in this undertaking is, of course, in any way responsible for its errors or shortcomings. The interpretations and conclusions—and the mistakes—are in every case my own.

As is customary, I have reserved mention of my wife until the last. The dedication to her is only an imperfect symbol of all that we have suffered and celebrated together during the making of this book.

C.E.C.

Durham, New Hampshire
Thanksgiving, 1969

Contents

Illustrations

DesBarres's view of Portsmouth, 1770's (?)
(courtesy of the John Carter Brown Library)

DesBarres's chart of Falmouth Harbor, 1770's
(courtesy of the John Carter Brown Library)

Maps and Town Plans
in the Text

Chronology

1607   Unsuccessful attempt to establish a permanent colony at Sagadahoc under the sponsorship of Sir John Popham.

1607   Settlement of Jamestown, Virginia.

1610   Probable beginning of the first year-round settlement of English fishermen at Monhegan Island.

1620   Settlement of the Plymouth Colony.

1622   Grant of territory between the Merrimack and Kennebec Rivers to Sir Ferdinando Gorges and Captain Robert Mason by the Council for New England.

1623   Settlement of colonies at Dover Point and at the mouth of the Piscataqua.

1625   Accession of Charles I.

1629   Division of the Gorges-Mason holdings at the Piscataqua River.

1630   Beginning of the "great migration" of Puritans to New England and the settlement of Boston under John Winthrop and the Massachusetts Bay Company.

1631   Beginning of Robert Trelawney's fishing and trading colony at Richmond Island.

1635   Death of Mason.

1638   Founding of Exeter under John Wheelwright after his expulsion from Massachusetts Bay.

1638   Settlement of Hampton by Newbury people under Stephen Batchelor.

1638–1639 John Josselyn's first visit to Black Point (Scarborough).

1641 Absorption of Dover and Portsmouth by Massachusetts.

1642 Beginning of the English Civil War.

1643 Absorption of Exeter by Massachusetts.

1647 Death of Gorges.

1649 Execution of Charles I and proclamation of the English Commonwealth.

1651 Beginning of attempts by Massachusetts to annex Maine.

1658 Successful completion of the Massachusetts campaign to secure the capitulation of all settlements in Maine and "Lygonia."

1660 Restoration of royal government in England under Charles II.

1664–1666 King's Commissioners in New England.

1665 Establishment by Commissioners of royal government in Maine.

1667–1671 John Josselyn's second visit to Black Point.

1668 Re-establishment of Massachusetts authority in Maine.

1671 Congregational church gathered in Portsmouth under Joshua Moodey.

1675–1677 King Philip's War.

1677 Purchase of the Gorges propriety by Massachusetts.

1680 Establishment of the royal province of New Hampshire.

1685 Accession of James II.

1686 Establishment of the Dominion of New England under Sir Edmund Andros.

1688 Glorious Revolution and accession of William and Mary.

1689 Overthrow of the Dominion of New England; temporary return of New Hampshire to the jurisdiction of Massachusetts.

1689–1697 King William's War (War of the League of Augsburg).

1691 New Massachusetts provincial charter.

1692 Re-establishment of royal government in New Hampshire.

1698   Arrival of Samuel Moody at York.

1702   Accession of Queen Anne.

1702–1713 Queen Anne's War (War of the Spanish Succession).

1705   Appointment of Jonathan Bridger as surveyor general of pines and timber.

1713   Schism in the Portsmouth church.

1713   Revival of the Massachusetts "Committee of Eastern Claims and Settlements" and designation of five abandoned Maine towns for resettlement.

1714   Accession of George I.

1714   Beginning of extralegal resettlement of Falmouth.

1715   Beginning of extralegal resettlement of North Yarmouth.

1716   Construction of the Macpheadris mansion in Portsmouth.

1717   Appointment of John Wentworth as lieutenant governor of New Hampshire.

1718   Incorporation of Falmouth.

1719   Settlement of Nutfield (later Londonderry) by Ulster Scots under James MacGregor.

1722   Appointment of the Committee for the Resettlement of North Yarmouth.

1722   Incorporation of Londonderry by New Hampshire.

1722–1725 "Dummer's War" with the "eastern Indians."

1725   Arrival in Falmouth of Thomas Smith.

1726   Peace treaty at Casco Bay with the "eastern Indians" and establishment by Massachusetts of provincial truckhouses for trade with the Indians.

1727   Accession of George II.

1727   Ordination of Thomas Smith and gathering of the First Parish Church in Falmouth.

1727   Arrival in Falmouth of Thomas Westbrook as mast agent.

1727   Minor earthquake arouses temporary religious excitement.

1728   Arrival in Falmouth of Moses Pearson.

1728, 1734 Granting of the "Narragansett townships."

1732   Building of Queen's Chapel, Portsmouth.

1732   Compromise agreement settling differences between the "old" and the "new" proprietors of Falmouth.

1733   Incorporation of North Yarmouth.

1735   Granting of the first "Canada townships."

1735–1740   The great epidemic of "throat distemper."

1736   Appointment of Arthur Browne as missionary to Portsmouth by the Society for the Propagation of the Gospel.

1738   Settlement of New Marblehead by Thomas Chute.

1740–1748   King George's War (War of the Austrian Succession).

1740–1748   Nicholas Gilman's tumultuous career in Durham.

1740   Settlement of Township Number 4 (later Charlestown).

1740   First visit of George Whitefield.

1741   Settlement of the Massachusetts-New Hampshire boundary and appointment of Benning Wentworth as governor of New Hampshire.

1742   Second visit of George Whitefield.

1744   Third visit of George Whitefield.

1746   Purchase of the Mason claim in New Hampshire by the "Masonian Proprietors."

1750   Arrival in Falmouth of George Tate as mast agent.

1750   Founding of the Library Society of Portsmouth.

1752   Governor Benning Wentworth's final victory over the New Hampshire Assembly.

1752   Settlement of Walpole by Benjamin Bellows.

1755–1763   French and Indian War (Seven Years' War).

1756   Founding of the *New-Hampshire Gazette*.

1760   Surrender of Canada.

1760   Accession of George III.

1762   Incorporation of Windham (formerly New Marblehead).

1763   Peace of Paris and establishment of the Proclamation Line closing off westward expansion.

PART

I

NOTES

FOOTNOTE NUMBERS IN THE TEXT
REFER TO BIBLIOGRAPHICAL NOTES
LIKELY TO BE OF INTEREST ONLY TO SCHOLARS.
THESE ARE PLACED AT THE BACK OF THE BOOK AND
MAY BE SAFELY IGNORED BY
THE GENERAL READER.

CHAPTER I

The Forest and the Sea

1

North of the Merrimack soared the tall pines. From the craggy sea-coast to the granite-tipped mountains, and in the broad uplands beyond the northeastern reaches of the Appalachian chain, the land lay gloomy, chaste, and still. A vast green umbrella, fresh-scented and innocently stirring, shut out the sun.

In 1524, as Giovanni da Verrazano, exploring for France, scudded before the southwest wind and squinted intently toward this coast over his port gunwale, only the lakes and rivers, a few barren peaks, and rare natural meadows broke the awesome dark green monotony of the forest. By 1624, a handful of scattered Englishmen had squatted on the coast, but the forest remained inviolate. By 1724, despite civilized man's talent for destruction, the wilderness was there still. But much of it within human reach had been altered, for the English had now begun the ravishment of *Pinus strobus*, the queen of the northern forest.

The white pine, pliant and supple, yielded readily to the colonists' lust for a cheap building material, but above all suited perfectly the demand for tall, straight masts for British men-of-war. Before the harvest, many of its specimens were magnificent. The largest on record, cut down near the Merrimack in southern New Hampshire, measured seven feet, eight inches across the butt, and some giants have been recorded as much as 250 feet tall.[1] More commonly they grew to about a yard through and a hundred feet high. They grew so close together that they could not sprout any substantial limbs for the first eighty feet or so,[2] the better for smooth masts and clear boards, and they grew tall and straight in search of sunlight.

Though the white pine dominated the forest, it shared its domain with other trees. Pitch pine also abounded. So did spruce, fir, and hemlock. Hardwoods grew liberally among the more numerous conifers, and sometimes appropriated a patch of forest to the exclusive use of several species of maple, birch, oak, and ash. During the eons before white men brought steel axes to the forest, thousands upon thousands of tall trees had competed for growing room. As the successful ones reached their full growth, their branches merged high above the leaf- and needle-covered mould to form a shady cover. This process discouraged the kind of dense undergrowth that chokes the cut-over or burned-over woodlands of a later day. There were low vines and shrubs, some with briars and berries, and saplings, only one of which in perhaps a thousand would reach full maturity. Mosses clung to the soaring trunks and to the rocks and boulders that studded the hilly forest floor. Mushrooms and ferns erupted here and there, perhaps from around a rotting tree trunk, which in its turn fertilized the dank and stony black soil from which it had sprung a century or more before. But a moose or a black bear or a man could make his way through the forest with little difficulty.

The forest ended at the sea. With rare exceptions, a brine-washed border of striated ledge or a brief sandy beach stretched across the few hundred yards between woods and water. Occasionally, a wooded promontory might stand high enough above the reach of the tide that the only separation between forest and sea would be a vertical one.

This coast is one of the most spectacular in the world; to the mariner, much of it is forbidding. Captain John Smith thought the "high craggy clifty Rocks and stony Iles" of the region made it "a Country rather to affright than delight one." Nevertheless, its fecundity and sheltered anchorages impressed him greatly. "How to describe a more plaine spectacle of desolation, or more barren, I know not," the captain wrote after a coasting voyage from Penobscot Bay to Cape Cod in 1614, "yet are those rocky Iles so furnished with good Woods, Springs, Fruits, Fish and Fowle, and the Sea the strangest Fish-pond I ever saw." [3]

To Samuel de Champlain, exploring the coast a decade earlier, its beauty had been more impressive than its desolation. He gave the name *Isle des Monts Deserts* to the hundred square miles of bald mountains that loom out of the sea east of the Penobscot country. In Penobscot Bay, he viewed the wooded Camden Hills and sailed up the bay to the mouth of the Penobscot River, which he found guarded by "numerous islands, rocks, shoals, banks, and breakers on all sides, so that it is marvelous to behold." By careful navigation, he finally managed to enter the river itself. There he saw "beautiful islands, which are very pleasant and contain fine meadows," and admired the broad, deep blue river and the "very pleasant countryside" as he made his way upstream as far as the falls at modern Bangor. Champlain had the good fortune of making this part of his voyage in September, when the air is clearest.[4]

Next to Champlain's *Isle des Monts Deserts,* the most spectacular portion of the coast probably consists of about a dozen fingers of land that probe into the Atlantic between Penobscot Bay and Casco Bay. In the heart of this country, the majestic Kennebec, having hurried a hundred and fifty miles through the wilderness from Moosehead Lake, mingles in Merrymeeting Bay with the Androscoggin, which rises in the White Mountains. The combined rivers, which the natives called the Sagadahoc but which white men have generally known as the lower reach of the Kennebec, then make their broad, placid way to the sea between the two largest peninsulas. At the hidden mouth of this river, Sir John Popham's men tried and failed to plant the first permanent English colony in America in 1607.

Casco Bay, filled with islands and bounded by an irregular shoreline, lies southwest of the Kennebec region. On a sparkling autumn day, the great bay presents a spectacle of majesty and serenity that Verrazano compared to the harbors and channels of the Adriatic Sea.[5] When the lifting fog of midsummer reveals only a few of the islands nearest the shore, it appears to one standing on the mainland that he is gazing into an interminable misty succession of dark-green islands and gray channels, alternating endlessly in an enchanted watery labyrinth.

Into Casco Bay, which provides the best harbor north of the Piscataqua, empty three relatively small but historically important rivers. The stream that became known as Royal's River in North Yarmouth had plenty of spots that could be dammed with pine timbers to create a mill site, and thus helped determine the shape of that settlement. Southwest of Royal's River, the Presumpscot flows into the bay from Sebago Lake. Along the eastern shores of this beautiful but treacherous inland sea dwelt Indians, jealous for their invaded homeland, who figured prominently in the New Englanders' attempts to build inland settlements in the eighteenth century. The Presumpscot served as a transportation lane to the interior, a source of fish and water power, and a means of floating masts and timber to the port of Falmouth. The third river is the Fore, the largest of the three in breadth and depth but only a few miles long, important chiefly as a harbor.

The seventy-five miles of coastline from Casco Bay to the mouth of the Merrimack run smoothly and regularly compared with the fantastic indentations and outcroppings to the east. The crescent-shaped sandy border of Saco Bay curves from Cape Elizabeth to the mouth of the Saco River, smaller than the Penobscot and Kennebec but broader and much longer than the Presumpscot, also used as a route for inland settlement and a source of power. Smaller rivers indent the gently concave coastline for the next twenty-five miles southwestward. The mouth of one of them in particular, the York, provides a small but satisfactory protected harbor. Here in 1623, Christopher Levett thought there "may be a good plantation seated," not only because of the harbor but also because recently departed Indians already had cleared and planted land.[6]

The York River and its harbor mark the beginning, historically if not geographically, of the Piscataqua country. Not surprisingly, the Piscataqua became the site of the first successful permanent settlements in northern New England. The river and its estuaries transform the eighteen miles of New Hampshire seacoast into more than a hundred miles of saltwater shoreline. From about 1623, this area never lacked some form of English settlement.[7]

Eight rocky peaks of a submerged chain of hills peep from the sea ten miles out from Piscataqua Harbor. European fishermen undoubtedly anchored at this cluster of islands long before their charm so captivated Captain Smith in 1614 that he named them after himself.[8] Just why the English began in 1622 or earlier to replace the name of "Smith's Isles" with "the Isles of Shoals" remains a mystery; perhaps it was because Smith's title implied a proprietary claim, and he was then losing favor with the Council for New England. In any case, nobody but John Smith and Dutch mapmakers ever called the islands by the captain's name after 1623.* Captain Smith, normally an intensely practical man, indulged himself in a rare moment of rapture

* In 1624, the Council divided its territory on paper among its twenty patentees, leaving to Smith only these islands, of which the Council had claimed possession. About 1630, Smith bitterly described his "share" as "a many of barren rocks, the most overgrown with such shrubs and sharp whins [thorny bushes] you can hardly pass them; without either grass or wood but three or four shrubby old cedars." He had changed his tune since 1614. Philip L. Barbour: *The Three Worlds of Captain John Smith* (Boston, 1964), pp. 391–2. See also John S. Jenness: *The Isles of Shoals*, 2nd edn. (New York, 1875), pp. 35, 39, 52.

when he first described the beauty of the little islands. Christopher
Levett, landing there in 1623, took a more hardheaded view when he
took pains to note that he "neither could see one good timber tree,
nor so much good ground as to make a garden." Levett's forthright
assessment of the islands was gravely commercial: "The place is found
to be a good fishing place for six. Shippes, but more can not well be
there: for want of convenient stage-roome. . . . The Harbour is but
indifferent good." [9]

Twenty miles of sandy beaches and tidal marshes stretch from
Piscataqua harbor to the mouth of the Merrimack. The river flows
110 miles from its origin in the picturesque lake country of New
Hampshire to the sea at Newburyport. A sand bar and shallow water
at the mouth close it to ocean shipping, but the river and its valley,
like the Connecticut to the westward, became a busy route for inland
settlers, who took salmon from its waters and built mills on its
tributaries. From its source, the Merrimack takes a south-southeasterly
heading, flowing generally toward Boston. At Nashua, it begins a great
horseshoe curve to the left, touching the bottom of the curve at Lowell
and then reaching to the northeast. Finally, it straightens out on a
generally easterly heading until it reaches the sea. The early notion
that the river flowed eastward throughout its length, rather than for
only a few miles near its mouth, induced the English authorities to
fix the Massachusetts boundary, they thought conveniently, three
miles north of the Merrimack. The subsequent struggle over the interpretation of this boundary profoundly affected the political history
of northern New England until the middle of the eighteenth century.

The coastline from Mount Desert Island to the mouth of the
Merrimack is 270 miles long, almost ten times that distance if you
count the shores of all the bays and inlets. A string of submarine
banks and shoals, highlands on the ancient margin of the continent
drowned by the Atlantic ages ago, lies a few miles offshore from Cape
Cod to Nova Scotia. The shoal waters teemed with swarms of fish.
Great cod and halibut lurked lazily along the shallow bottom to feed
on tiny sea creatures. Huge schools of finger-length herring darted to
and fro above the shoals, and hordes of shining mackerel rippled the
surface. The catalogue of species is almost endless, from the great
staple varieties of the North Atlantic to the exotic and the useless.
The offshore shoals were the major feeding grounds, but millions of
flounder, hake, and mackerel strayed closer to shore, where shellfish
littered the bottom, and the eerie lobster stalked in search of prey

and the fleeting crab scuttled silently across the ocean floor. With spears and hand nets, the coastal Indians easily took as much of this immense supply of food as they needed to live. With hooks, lines, and drag nets, the intruding Europeans mined the wealth of these waters for profit.

The white man took his first courageous bite of the Maine lobster on June 4, 1605, when Captain John Waymouth's men, in James Rosier's words, "tooke Cod and Hadocke with hooks by our ship side, and Lobsters very great: which before we had not tried." [10] Exclaiming over the plenty he discovered here in 1614, Captain Smith wrote, "You shall scarce find any bay, shallow shore or Cove of sand, where you may not take many Clamps [clams] or Lobsters, or both at your pleasure, and in many places load your Boat if you please, nor Iles where you finde not Fruits, Birds, Crabs, and Mustels, or all of them; for taking at low water Cod, Cuske, Hollibut, Scate, Turbut, Mackerell, or such like are taken plentifully in divers sandy Bayes, store of Mullit, Bases, and divers other sorts of such excellent fish as many as their Net can hold; no River where there is not plenty of Sturgion, or Salmon, or both, all which are to be had in abundance observing but their seasons." [11]

In every colony from Maine to Georgia, the English first planted their fields, their gardens, and their cities in the coastal lowlands. The broad tidewater flatlands of the South nurtured a plantation economy, and the sluggish rivers that wound through them offered inland avenues for the ships that bore English goods to the planters and cotton to London. In northern New England, the lowlands are narrow, and in the Penobscot region and eastward, where the mountains touch the sea, they virtually disappear. The belt between the coast and the great Appalachian barrier—Mount Katahdin and a chain of lesser peaks in Maine and the White Mountains in New Hampshire—never exceeds eighty miles and is often as little as fifty or sixty miles wide. The belt itself is nearly everywhere a succession of hills and valleys, sometimes gently rolling but often sufficiently rugged to test the vigor and enterprise of even the strongest and most determined pioneer. The fall line is close to the sea, so no skipper could take his ocean vessel into the interior, even in those rare places where the seaward ends of such rivers as the Penobscot and Kennebec beckoned invitingly.

Though waterfalls and rapids and the rocky hills of the piedmont raised obstacles to inland travel, sometimes almost within sound of the crashing surf, they also gave the settlers of northern New England an advantage unknown on the wide coastal plain of the South. At the same falls where an inland-bound traveler had to leave his ship and begin to carry a canoe, the settlers built dams and water wheels which powered rasping vertical saws even within the boundaries of such coastal townships as North Yarmouth, Falmouth, Saco, York, and Kittery. Forests and waterfalls together in the very midst of the first pockets of coastal settlement meant the almost immediate rise of a lumber industry.

It was almost as hard to travel along the coast by land, especially east of Casco Bay, as to push inland. Try to explore the ragged contours of the Maine coast by automobile today and you realize that for many of the earliest decades, a visit between even some very close neighbors would have been out of the question except by boat. To live on this shoreline, therefore, was to know isolation, and to feel the persistent pull of the sea.

The forest, the fish, the hills, the waterfalls, the harbors and bays, and the islands combined to encourage the first settlers to make their living in two basic ways: by cutting trees for lumber, timber, staves, and naval stores, and by going to sea to fish or to trade. Shipbuilding, the product of America's earliest and most obvious industrial merger, began soon after the two basic parent industries had taken firm hold.

On the other hand, neither the rocky coast nor the wooded hills of the interior offered any particular encouragement to agriculture. The soil, though fairly fertile, is stony and difficult to plow and to hoe, even after the strenuous task of clearing it of trees is done. The contours of the land and the granite ledges and boulders that dot the landscape confine gardens, meadows, and grain fields to small, irregular patches, and each spring thaw yields a new crop of rocks and stones to be carried and dumped on the nearest rude stone wall before plowing and planting can begin. The growing season is limited—a full month shorter, for example, than in Rhode Island, Connecticut, and southern Massachusetts. The icy winds and snows of winter swoop down across the north country from Canada in early December; often they do not retreat until the middle or the end of March. During these bitter months, a pioneer family spent most of its energy plugging chinks in the walls of its tiny cabin of hewn logs, splitting firewood, and during the long nights moving numbed legs and feet in bed under a bearskin cover—all in a perpetual losing effort to stay warm. Winter, in short, demanded too much for survival to allow for productive farm work, at least until after the settlers could build barns and warm, permanent frame houses. It is a tribute to the men rather than to the environment that by 1760, the dominant feature of the economic and social life of the region had become agriculture.

Northern New England offered attractions to settlers besides fish and standing timber. One of them, paradoxically, was climate. The delicious fragrance of spring, the mild, dry breezes of summer, and the crisp brilliance of autumn were to spirited men and women more than sufficient to offset the inconvenience of a severe winter. The clear, refreshing air, a complement to the bold scenery of the coast, the lakes, and the mountains, was surely one attraction to the wilderness of Maine and New Hampshire and one contribution to the physical and psychic health of the inhabitants. In the midsummer of 1734, a member of the large entourage that accompanied Governor Jonathan Belcher on a diplomatic errand to the eastern Indians reported rapturously: "All that Coast appears to be full of commodious Rivers, Bays, Harbours, Coves, and delightful Islands; the most agreeable Part of the *Massachusetts Province,* both for Scituation, Fishery, Lumber-Trade, and Culture [!]; and highly worthy of the Publick Care." [12] The clear skies and tangy breezes of the season had set off the rugged landscape to its best advantage, moving the reporter in the same way that other explorers had been moved a century before. Even the morning fog, heavy with sea smells, altering the scenery as it thickens or lifts, masking from sight the source of the gull's scream, holds a mysterious attraction to all in man that is poetic and contemplative. Another such advantage was the fresh, cold water in thousands of lakes, brooks, and underground springs.

The region contained some mineral as well as timber wealth, such as bog iron, quartz, and feldspar. Practically none of several attempts to exploit such resources economically succeeded in colonial times. The colonists did, however, make some use of the huge supply of granite. Most builders worked primarily with wood because they could use it more cheaply and easily than stone, but they found that with a steel drill and hammer, gunpowder, and wooden wedges swollen with water, they could remove blocks of granite from the ledges and haul them away on ox-drawn sledges to use for foundations, cellar walls, doorsteps, fenceposts, paving, and fortifications.

For meat and furs, the forests offered moose, deer, bear, beaver, muskrat, mink, raccoon, wildcats, and gray squirrels. The salt marshes and bays of the seacoast were alive with ducks and geese during the fall migrating season, and partridges and wild turkeys rustled through the forests and fields throughout the summer and fall. Like most of the American wilderness at the beginning of colonization, northern New England, though it had a flavor of its own, was a rich land.

2

In the age of discovery, explorers in the vicinity concentrated on the coastline from the Kennebec eastward. English and French mariners of the sixteenth century looked toward the northern edge of the continent for a passage to the Orient. Nearly all of them who visited the coast of New England, therefore, approached the region from the northeast. Verrazano was the exception. The Europeans' occasional contact with the vague region on the "back side" of Nova Scotia produced the legend of "Norumbega," the name given to a supposedly rich country and native capital, the northern equivalent of the fabulous kingdoms of the Aztecs and the Incas, in the vicinity of the Penobscot River.[13]

Gradually, however, as the areas of national interest in North America became defined, the English concentrated their northern colonization efforts generally to the south of Cape Ann, and the myth of Norumbega was, in due course, dispelled. From about 1630 on, it was principally from Massachusetts rather than from across the sea that the region north of the Merrimack attracted the interest of Englishmen. Until late in the eighteenth century, therefore, most significant social development in the region took place southwest of the Kennebec. After the settlement of Massachusetts Bay, the chief importance of northern New England was no longer as a mysterious promise to the west of Nova Scotia, but as a buffer zone, source of fish and timber, and goal of expansion to the northeast of Massachusetts. Thus Norumbega became, in the homely plain style of the Puritans, "the eastern parts."

The first Englishmen north of the Merrimack were fishermen, far removed in purpose and spirit from the more sober-minded main body of New England settlers to the south. The story of the region's development from about 1630 to the American Revolution can be told pretty much in terms of its slow absorption into what might be called "greater Massachusetts." This was true in a political sense, except that the province of New Hampshire finally survived as a distinct jurisdiction under the rule of a remarkably able and affluent minority faction, but it was even more true in a cultural sense. That a viable society emerged from the rude commercial beginnings of the early seventeenth century is due in very great measure to an exercise in imperialism by the civil and spiritual fathers of Massachusetts Bay.

But the story is not quite that simple. As in most colonial experiences, this was not simply a matter of duplicating the society of Massachusetts, with its Puritan institutions and values unmodified, in the northern wilderness. Modifications were necessary—special adaptations to unique conditions—to save this colonial venture from utter failure. And so the society of northern New England, as it took shape during the century or so before 1775, came to possess an identity of its own, fused from the interacting, often competing influences of Puritan imperialism, the independent, materialistic, and frequently hedonistic tendencies of the first settlers, and, wildly appealing though it was, a hostile natural environment.

CHAPTER II

Our Main End Was
to Catch Fish
1610–1680

1

The stocky, tough men who first settled the craggy islands and the sand and salt marsh harbors hidden among the granite walls of the Maine and New Hampshire coast lived to fish and trade, not to pray. Their homes had been the brawling seaports of western England, not the Puritan strongholds of East Anglia. Cotton Mather, who had a call to evangelize all New England, recognized better than most of his clerical colleagues this fundamental difference between the lusty fishermen of the eastern parts and the sober colonists of his own Massachusetts Bay. In 1702, he told a story of a Massachusetts minister, new to the homiletical challenge of converting men whose gods were fish and pine. The parson finally rounded up some curious listeners and began to exhort the congregation to walk in the paths of righteousness and piety so that they would not "contradict the main end of Planting this Wilderness," which in his view, of course, was the pure worship of an austere, wrathful Jehovah. Suddenly a fisherman blurted out, right in the middle of the sermon, "Sir, you are mistaken, you think you are Preaching to the People at the Bay; our main End was to catch Fish." *

* *Magnalia Christi Americana* (London, 1702), p. 15. Nathaniel Adams, the early chronicler of Portsmouth, has given another version of the same anecdote, this one presumably set in a later generation and in New Hampshire rather than in Maine. Here, the minister scolded his listeners for having "forsaken the pious habits of your forefathers, who left the ease and comfort which they possessed in their native land, and came to this howling wilderness to enjoy without molesta-

For years—and perhaps generations—before the Pilgrims debarked at Plymouth, grizzled, horny-handed English sailors from the shires of Cornwall, Dorset, Somerset, and Devon had fished the banks northeast of Cape Ann and even set up temporary bases for drying fish and repairing boats and nets along the coast. Finally someone dared to camp there year round instead of just during the fishing season. No one knows who tried it first, or just where, but there is evidence of tiny settlements at Monhegan Island in 1610, Damariscove and Pemaquid in 1614, Winter Harbor in Saco Bay in 1616, the Isles of Shoals in 1622, Piscataqua in 1623, Spurwink near Cape Elizabeth in 1625, Richmond's Island in 1627, and Pejepscot (now Brunswick) and Penobscot in 1628.* [1]

The English merchants who controlled the fishing and trading expeditions to the northwestern Atlantic soon saw the advantages of

---

tion their pure principles of religion." The response from the pew is supposed to have been, "Sir, you entirely mistake the matter; our ancestors did not come here on account of their religion, but to fish and trade." *Annals of Portsmouth* (Portsmouth, N.H., 1825), p. 94.

* Detailed and exact information about the earliest fishing settlements must await the painstaking work of anthropologists and historical archaeologists. There is an interesting restoration project now underway at Pemaquid, a small peninsula near the mouth of the Pemaquid River near Monhegan and Damariscove Islands where Samoset, the Wawenock chieftain, probably learned enough English from fishermen and traders to be able to address the astonished Pilgrims at Plymouth in their own language in the Spring of 1621. Pictures and descriptions of artifacts uncovered at the site are contained in a booklet by Mrs. Helen B. Camp, who began the excavations in 1965, *Pemaquid Lost and Found* (Ancient Pemaquid Restoration Booklet Series, 1967). Further historical background on the colony and information about the restoration project is handily available in a newspaper-style publication of Ancient Pemaquid Restoration entitled *The Pemaquid Story*. Aside from the Pemaquid project, which is primarily commercial, the study of the earliest settlements of the region remains undone. I am grateful to the following scholars for explaining to me the relatively skimpy state of knowledge about these settlements and for suggesting the procedures that might be followed to correct the deficiency: Mr. Wendell Hadlock, director of the William A. Farnsworth Library and Art Museum, Rockland, Maine; Dr. John L. Cotter, Chief of Archaeological Research, Northeast, in the National Park Service; Professor Howard R. Sargent of the Department of Anthropology, Franklin Pierce College; and Professor Dean R. Snow of the Department of Sociology and Anthropology, State University of New York at Albany. Scientific archaeological and anthropological research is as much outside the competence of the present author as it is of most of his colleagues in the historical profession. One can hope, however, that the time is not far distant when members of the archaeological and anthropological disciplines will, in a joint effort with historians, make these important colonies as well known and as thoroughly understood as such other pioneer settlements as Plymouth and Jamestown.

keeping their workmen at a permanent American base near the fishing grounds. The three to four months out of every year that the fishermen had absorbed sailing to and from England could now be spent on the banks, and more of the costly, risky transatlantic voyages could now be devoted wholly to cargo. In the off-season, the sturdy young fishermen could cultivate the fur trade with Indians eager for cheap bright beads, woolen coats and blankets, iron tools and fishing hooks, guns, and liquor. They could cut the cost of supporting the expeditions by growing some of their own food, and they could dry and pack the fish for shipment more efficiently by building permanent processing plants and making their own casks and hogsheads from the trees that grew near the shore. They could even build their own fishing boats, and might eventually try building ships. The possibilities were almost endless, and when a few of the first adventurous fishermen proved that they could survive the winter on the Maine or New Hampshire coast, the profit-hungry mercantile companies of western England eagerly poured more of their resources into strengthening the bases they had begun and founding new ones. The risk was great, but a few of these colonies survived long enough to return their sponsors a handsome profit.

Moreover, the investors were risking only money. The workmen they recruited to spend what might well have been the rest of their lives on the desolate shore of an unknown land were risking far more. Without comforts, without adequate protection from the bitter winter cold or possible enemies, without the solace of a vigorous religious faith, and without women, these men cut whatever tenuous family and community connections they may have had in the commercial ports of the West Country and staked their lives on the certainty of high adventure and the possibility of a share in great profits. Men such as these live for the moment, not for eternity.

Gradually, a sprinkling of the colonies began to acquire some of the fundamentals of a stable community. Somehow—we do not know the exact circumstances—a few women began to appear in the rough fishing hamlets, having sailed either with their husbands or to join men who had come before. Pemaquid, which had started as a feeble trading post, received a patent in 1630 and became a thriving town. A colony began at Sheepscott in 1630 and grew in seven years to fifty families. By then, settlements had started at South Berwick, York, and Saco, and the wives of some of the leading members and a few servant girls had come to join the fishing and trading establishment at Richmond Island.[2] With but few exceptions, however, the coast of northern New England in the early seventeenth century remained very much a man's world, and showed it.

Captain John Smith thought of the effort to populate this coast with English fishermen as a moral and patriotic calling that would strengthen the economy and naval abilities of the nation and the backbones of Englishmen, who faced physical dissipation and spiritual decay if they stayed at home. He foresaw a sort of fishermen's yeoman republic, where all hands would devote their mornings to the communal fishery and split up for the rest of the day so that each man could "tread and plant the ground he hath purchased by the hazard of his life." * Had the fishermen and their employers shared Smith's vision as completely as the founders of Massachusetts shared John Winthrop's vision of a "city on a hill," the society of northern New England might have profited from a unifying ideal as powerful as that of the Puritans. It never happened. Instead, it remained for the Puritans to civilize the eastern parts by conquest.

At the mouths of the Piscataqua and York Rivers, the proprietors of New Hampshire and Maine laid the foundations of their two provinces. To comprehend fully the emergence of the Portsmouth oligarchy on the one hand, and the conquest of Maine by Puritan Massachusetts on the other, we must single out for special notice these two visionary landlords and their influence on the early coastal settlements.

Sir Ferdinando Gorges, the proprietor of Maine, and Captain John Mason, the proprietor of New Hampshire, inherited the sixteenth-century tradition of men such as Sir Humphrey Gilbert, Sieur de Monts, and Sir John Popham, who had conceived of American settlement as an undertaking by aristocrats intending to become lords of vast new feudal domains. This was especially true of Gorges, who had been a partner with Popham in the short-lived venture at Sagadahoc and never abandoned his dream of a personal empire in the New World, complete with medieval trappings. Mason, a generation younger than Gorges,

---

* In *New England's Tryalls* (London, 1622), Smith argued that by settling New England, the English would be able, on a highly efficient basis, to win the lucrative European market for fish. He emphasized not only the profits that would result from such a trade, but also "the increase of shipping and of Mariners," which would strengthen the nation both commercially and militarily. In *The Generall Historie of Virginia, New England, and the Summer Iles* (London, 1632), he developed his full theory of the development of New England fishing and agricultural communities by what would have amounted to a mixture of industrial socialism and staunch individual enterprise. See esp. pp. 216 and 221.

less gentle in birth, and more commercial-minded, had a more realistic conception of what American settlement could accomplish and more practical notions of how to go about it.* But he started out as a partner with Gorges, and shared with the older man part of the same anachronistic dream.

In 1620, Gorges got from the Crown a new patent reincorporating the old Plymouth Company as the "Council established at Plymouth . . . for the planting, ruling, ordering and governing of New England in America."[3] Gorges became president and Mason secretary of the new Council, which received from James I a grant of all the lands in America between the fortieth and forty-eighth parallels (Philadelphia to central Newfoundland) from sea to sea.[4]

In 1622, the Council granted to Gorges and Mason all the territory between the Merrimack and the Kennebec from the coast to the "furtherest heads" of the two rivers. According to their patent, the partners intended to call their propriety the Province of Maine—the first use of this designation in any official document.[5] The grantees must have had second thoughts, however, for they finally named their domain "Laconia," after a company of merchants they headed.[6]

The year after the grant to Gorges and Mason, the Laconia Company outfitted and sent to the Piscataqua a small group of men under two London fishmongers, Edward and William Hilton, with instructions to set up a colony that would send fish back to England. Earlier in the year, David Thomson, acting for three merchants of Plymouth under a separate grant from the Council for New England, had started another little base overlooking the swift current at the mouth of the river. Thomson soon found an island in Massachusetts Bay that he liked better than his site on the west side of the Piscataqua. He moved there, leaving part of his colony behind. It fell into the hands of Mason as a matter of course. The Hiltons settled at Dover Point, an attractive, defensible point of land formed by the merging waters of the Piscataqua and picturesque Great Bay, a few miles from the river's mouth. Their men built drying stages and began to catch and cure fish. Neither the Hiltons' colony nor Thomson's abandoned men at Odiorne's Point prospered during the first few years,

---

* Unlike Gorges, Mason had been in the New World, having served as governor of Newfoundland between 1615 and 1621. He conducted a thorough exploration of that colony and made a very acceptable map of the island, which was published in William Vaughan's *Golden Fleece* (London, 1626), a tract promoting the settlement of Newfoundland. He also wrote a pamphlet of his own on the same subject. For brief biographical treatments of Gorges and Mason, see the *Dictionary of National Biography*.

but they did survive, and were in fact able to send provisions to the starving Plymouth colony.[7]

Gorges and Mason divided their holdings in 1629, drawing the line down the middle of the Piscataqua.[8] Mason came to own the large house that Thomson's men had built at Odiorne's Point, likely of stone, and an adjoining estate of three or four thousand acres.* He also took firm charge of the organization of both tiny colonies on the Piscataqua. He put an "agent" in command of each, Captain Walter Neal at the "lower" colony and Captain Thomas Wiggin at Dover Point. Under this commanding officer he placed about ten "stewards," each of whom had charge of one of the several divisions of the colony's business. The most important steward was the one responsible for the fishery. At the "lower" colony, this vital job went to Edward Godfrey, an old colonial hand who later served as governor of Maine during the brief period that province was under royal control. Godfrey commanded a flotilla of six large shallops, five smaller sailing craft, and thirteen skiffs. Other stewards headed such departments as the salt works, the sawmill, trade, building, and farming. These higher ranking colonists also included a surgeon but apparently not a chaplain. The commonalty of the lower colony, designated "servants," included about eight Danes, whom Mason recruited to saw lumber and make potash. An inventory of 1635 indicates that Mason kept his isolated employees well supplied with the necessities of living, industry, and defense—including some of the earliest cattle imported to America.[9]

When Mason died in 1635, his American holdings were valued at £10,000. In his will, he left the manor house, which he had named "Mason Hall," to a grandson, Robert Tufton, and most of the rest of his New Hampshire estate to another grandson, John Tufton, on the condition in each case that the grandson adopt the surname Mason. Only Robert lived to maturity. He fulfilled the condition of the legacy and inherited all of Mason's New Hampshire holdings. But he claimed them only after a lapse of time during which the stewards and servants of the Piscataqua colonies appropriated the land and other property to themselves. The resulting controversy colored New Hampshire politics for several generations. The merchant oligarchy of Portsmouth, whose fortunes were founded in part on this confiscation, fought

---

* Adams: *Portsmouth*, p. 11. Since neither remnants of the building nor conclusive documentary evidence has yet been found, the long-accepted tradition that the house was built of stone awaits verification.

both Masons and Puritans in their successful struggle to control the province half a century later.[10]

The Puritans of Massachusetts Bay were no friends of Mason. Both he and Gorges wanted the King to revoke the Massachusetts charter and appoint a royal governor for all of New England. John Winthrop even went so far as to ascribe Mason's death to divine "mercy." [11]

Sir Ferdinando, if only because he lived longer than Mason, was an even more bitter enemy of the saints. In 1634, Gorges presented to Charles I a detailed plan for the government of New England. Under it, a single "lord governor, or lord lieutenant" would have ruled all New England in the name of the King. The territory would have been divided into provinces with royal appointees governing in each. The governor would have had a number of impressively named assistants, including "one lord bishop."

Astounding as this forgotten chapter of New England history may seem in light of the familiar success story of the Puritan oligarchy, it should come as no surprise that the absolutist, high church Stuart King, plagued as he was at home by the challenge of religious dissent and whiggish parliamentarians, accepted Sir Ferdinando's welcome suggestion. In 1635, he made Gorges "lord governor" of New England. The Council for New England cooperated with the scheme by surrendering its charter in order to nullify the patent it had granted to the Massachusetts Bay Company. It was about this time that Mason died, and the ship that was to have brought Gorges to his long-sought viceroyalty was wrecked in the launching.[12] These and other frustrations delayed the fulfillment of the grand plan. Massachusetts continued on her independent way, and the Royal government became increasingly preoccupied with the disastrous chain of events in England. In the end the idea seems simply to have died.

Gorges, however, still had one string to his bow. He had his Maine, a province as yet unspoiled by religious zealots or opponents of royal power. It lay nearly vacant between the Piscataqua and the Kennebec, ready for the realization of his feudal dreams. Besides providing him a handsome fief, he thought, his province* might serve as a base for a flanking movement against the dangerous, rapidly

---

* Named either after the French province of which Henrietta Maria, the young consort of Charles I, was feudal proprietor, or simply to formalize the distinction that had long been made between the many islands in the region and "the maine," or mainland.

developing institutions of Massachusetts.[13] The Council for New England, which had granted the province to Gorges, was now defunct; his patent had no legal basis. But in April, 1639, the King himself confirmed Gorges's grant, established the Church of England in Maine, and conferred upon Sir Ferdinando practically unlimited powers.

Gorges drew up an elaborate plan of government for the few tiny coastal settlements in this wilderness. He divided his land into "bailiwicks," "hundreds," and "parishes," and planned to establish the seat of his government, which he hoped would eventually encompass all New England, at Agamenticus, which he christened "Gorgeana." He erected this pathetic little fishing hamlet on the York River into a city and episcopal see with a complement of forty-three municipal officers, probably more than half the male population. Sir Ferdinando could not go to Maine to take personal charge at once, so he sent his nephew, Thomas Gorges, as deputy governor, placing him at the head of a seven-member council.[14]

Civil war in England halted emigration to the colonies and affairs at home became far more pressing than those in America, even to so single-minded a proprietor as Sir Ferdinando. Massachusetts, Plymouth, Rhode Island, and Connecticut continued to flourish as virtually independent commonwealths; the settlements of Maine remained tiny and primitive. Gorges apparently never meddled in the administration of his council, and he never saw the land that for twenty-seven years had been his central vision. One wonders how he would have taken the shock of reality if he had. Mercifully, his death came in 1647, before he could see the kingdom of England itself tumble down around the royal chopping block. The old knight died at 82, possibly still full of glorious dreams but utterly incapable of effectively managing his domain in New England even if the state of English affairs had permitted it.

Sir Ferdinando's America was a land of misty dreams rooted in England's feudal past. His grandiose plans for "Gorgeana" were as tragically oblivious to the changing political, social, and economic realities of a turbulent England as they were ludicrously unsuited to the Maine wilderness. The England of Gorges's declining years belonged to hardheaded, shrewd investors, practical administrators, and calculating politicians—the rising merchant class. Men of this new class, of Mason's generation or younger, favored with inherited or acquired wealth but unrestrained by the institutions and ideologies of the past, stood the best chance of capitalizing on the fish, the pines, and the good trading location of the New Hampshire and Maine coast.

Robert Trelawney was such a man. His commercial colony at Richmond Island provided him not with a vision, but with hard cash. Though larger and more successful than most, the Trelawney enterprise, in its workmen and their activities, was typical of the sparse settlements that dotted the coast from the Piscataqua to the Penobscot.

Trelawney was the son of a successful merchant of Plymouth, the center of the fishing and trading interests of western England. He was born in 1598 and came to maturity just as the plans and investments of such companies as the Council for New England were beginning to have results. At home on the docks and in the taverns and warehouses of this bustling seaport, now beginning to stretch its influence into some of the strangest corners of the earth, the young man took over the family business when his father died in 1627. Increasingly, he concentrated upon American interests. With Moses Goodyear, another prominent Plymouth merchant, Trelawney secured from the Council for New England in 1631 a patent for the use of the land bordering Casco Bay, including the right to build drying stages and store fish on the nearby islands.[15] Trelawney and Goodyear dispatched as their agent the "grave and discreet" John Winter, who later married Trelawney's daughter,[16] to establish possession of the territory against some previous claimants and set up a permanent fishing base. The station was also to serve as the western terminal of a transatlantic trading venture.

Winter chose for the headquarters of his operation a flat, unwooded island about a mile long and three-quarters of a mile wide, lying a few hundred yards off the southeast tip of Cape Elizabeth, then called Spurwink, just outside Casco Bay. Spurwink, accessible by fording at low tide and a short row at high tide, had been claimed by a hardy independent fisherman and trader named George Cleeve, who had built a small house there. But no matter. Winter's crew of thirty brawny fishermen were more than a sufficient force to evict Cleeve and send him a few miles eastward to the later site of Falmouth, and to resist the enforcement of an order by one of Gorges's ineffectual courts to restore the territory to Cleeve.[17] The small protected harbor between Winter's fishing headquarters on Richmond Island and the mainland farm at Spurwink provided an ideal anchorage for the ships that brought supplies to the colony and took fish to Europe.

On the island near the harbor, Winter's men, more accustomed to ships than houses, built what must have seemed to them an entirely logical kind of accommodation. Probably using boards they had brought from England, they put up a two-story wooden structure forty feet long and eighteen feet wide. The lower level, which contained a storeroom and a large kitchen "for our men to eat and drinke in," may have had walls of stone because it seems to have been partly underground. One can imagine the crew of boisterous, bored young seamen spending the long winter evenings here by firelight around long dining tables, gulping down their home-brewed beer, repeating endlessly the same repertory of bawdy songs and stories, and intensifying the constant battle of wits until a session of rough raillery ended in a fist-fight.

When too sleepy or drunk to continue, they staggered upstairs to the upper level, which the builders probably thought of as the main deck. In one of the two second-story "Chambers," each man had his narrow bunk, boarded in to make a private sleeping compartment. The bunks, which Winter called "Close borded Cabbins," were ranged along the sides of the sleeping room, one above the other. In the other "chamber," Winter kept the ship's sails and the colony's store of dry goods. When his wife and daughter and a maid joined the colony a few years later, the Winters and their fat, "sluttish" servant slept there among the sails and boxes of clothing. The building had a large "Chimnay" fitted with two ovens, of which Winter once wrote affectionately, "We Can brew and bake and boyle our Cyttell [kettle] all at once in him." Hard by this land-based vessel, Winter's men built a smaller building to house the mortar, handmill, and sieve used for preparing corn and malt, the essential ingredients of the winter supply of bread and beer.

The colony's few husbandmen lived on the mainland at Spurwink, across the narrow channel. They slept in Cleeve's deserted house and planted corn and pumpkins nearby in a palisaded garden of four or five acres. The only other structure was a shelter for the pigs, which thrived on corn, acorns, and clams, and increased through intensive breeding efforts to a foraging herd of about seventy in the summer of 1634 and to ninety by 1635.[18]

Winter's crew, supplemented by new recruits whom Trelawney sent over from time to time, had grown to forty-seven men by 1637 and about sixty by 1638.[19] Aside from the handful of farmers who tended their crops and swine only to provide food for the colony, they all worked in the fishery, handled cargoes, and helped run Winter's extensive trading activities.

Winter sent his shallops to sea after fish whenever the weather permitted, regardless of the season. Even in bitter January, if there were no storm to keep the boats in the harbor, the men bent their aching fingers around the heavy oars or clumsily worked stiff halyards and sheets. They felt the icy north wind cut through their heavy canvas clothing as frozen salt spray pelted their lips and congealed on their unkempt whiskers. Braced against pitching gunwales, they pulled in cod, haddock, pollock, and hake on frozen handlines and dumped the wriggling, slimy bodies around their feet into the bottoms of their boats. Back at the island, they salted down their catches in casks as "cor" (corned) fish. In warm, dry weather, they spread the gutted fish out to dry in the sun on raised wooden racks called stages before packing them in barrels or hogsheads to be sold by the "quintal," or hundredweight. The best fish went to Catholic France and Spain, whose merchants returned wines and salt directly to the colony or extended credit to Winter's sponsors in England.[20] Winter found a market for the poorer qualities of fish in Massachusetts and Virginia.[21]

Trade was almost as important a part of the enterprise at Richmond Island as fishing. The initial idea was to exchange English goods such as clothing, trinkets, and liquor for furs with the Indians. Winter found the Indian trade disappointing, however. Few of the natives lived close enough to Richmond Island to deal with him conveniently, and several trading stations to the east were competing both with his own and with interloping traders from Virginia and from the Dutch and French colonies. As a result of the scramble among white men for beaver furs, the Indians began to understand their value to Europeans and to demand appropriate prices.[22] The colony did a thriving business, however, in "sacke," "aquavita," and other spirits with the hard-drinking fishermen who populated other English settlements along the coast. These customers often paid for their liquor in pelts, which they had procured from Indians. Winter also sold clothing and liquor to his own men and deducted the cost from their wages.[23]

Several times a year, Winter's workmen gladly welcomed the interruption in their routine that came with the arrival of a ship from Trelawney's Plymouth docks, such as the "Barke of 300 Tuns, laden with Island Wine, and but 7 men in her, and never a Gun," which spoke the vessel carrying John Josselyn to New England in June, 1638.[24] The colony imported a varied lot of merchandise from Trelawney in exchange for furs and for the credit gained in the European fish trade. A shipment of September, 1638, is more typical than the all-liquid cargo of the previous June: biscuits, malt, hops, pickled beef and pork, "aquavite," * vinegar, cider, gloves and clothing, leather, cloth, traces for an "Asse plough," tobacco, nets and fishline, hooks, sails, nails, oats, hay, tar, boards, a new shallop, and other items. The oats and hay were to feed the six asses that Trelawney had ordered the ship's master to take on board at the Isle of Mayo in Ireland. Winter found them unsatisfactory as draft animals. There were no horses anywhere in the vicinity at this time, but the colony eventually acquired some cattle and a few goats.[25]

Trelawney had recruited nearly all of his Richmond Island employees in Devonshire, bound them for three years, and put them on a fixed wage ranging from two to fourteen pounds per year, which they received in addition to their transportation, shelter, a specified amount of food and clothing which they could supplement if they wanted to by buying more from the colony's store out of their pay, and a small share in the fishing profits. Unlike the indentured servants who later worked off their passage to America in Virginia and Pennsylvania, many of these men had no intention of staying in America after their terms expired; they engaged themselves for a term of work for wages in exactly the same way a sailor might sign on for a ship's voyage. Winter had some trouble with runaways, most of whom were in debt to the colony for provisions when they disappeared.[26]

About 1636, the colony acquired a minister, the Reverend Richard Gibson. He came at the request of Trelawney's brother Edward, who had joined Winter in Maine and, apparently as a result of observing the moral character of the Massachusetts Puritans, acquired a measure of piety. About four years after he came, Gibson, an Anglican, accepted an invitation to serve the newly organized church in Portsmouth. He must have left gladly.

Things went poorly for him from the time he disappointed Winter by choosing Mary Lewis for his wife instead of Winter's daughter

---

* Although the medieval alchemist's term "aqua vitae" eventually came to be used loosely to refer to almost any distilled beverage such as brandy or whisky, it probably had a more precise meaning in the early seventeenth century. By the fifteenth century, the term, which originally meant almost pure alcohol, referred in England specifically to the brandy distilled from yeast-fermented barley. After the discovery of the New World, a similar brandy, also called "aqua vitae," was often made from fermented Indian corn. Since the shipment of September, 1638, originated in England, the casks of "aquavite" undoubtedly contained brandy made from a base of barley. See the *Oxford English Dictionary*, s.v. "aqua vitae," and esp. T. K. Derry and Trevor I. Williams: *A Short History of Technology from the Earliest Times to* A.D. *1900* (New York, 1961), pp. 62, 68.

Sarah. In September, 1640, he and Mary went into the somewhat in-effectual court at Saco to sue John Boynthon for slander. The defend-ant had called Gibson "a base priest, a base knave, a base fellow," and his bride "a base whore, an impudent whore, a base strumpett" who "had or should have had a bastard three yeares since." Mr. Gib-son complained, with admirable understatement, that by these public accusations he and his wife were "greatly prejudiced in their reputa-tion and the plaint. Richard much disparaged in his ministery." The court found for the plaintiffs, but instead of the £500 damages they asked, awarded the minister and his maligned wife less than six and a half pounds.[27] The message that the Gibsons were not wanted must have come across clearly. In any case, they were soon gone.

The Trelawney operation flourished until about 1640, when im-migration to America began to fall off because of the looming show-down in England between King and Parliament. With the decline in immigration came a decline in money, which meant the loss of some of Winter's market in Massachusetts, Virginia, and along the Maine coast. The radical faction cast Trelawney out of Parliament and then into prison. In 1644, he died. The next year, Winter also died, and the whole enterprise fell into the hands of Robert Jordan, the Anglican minister who had succeeded Gibson in Maine and married Winter's daughter. Jordan now abandoned the church for business and colonial politics during the period that the Massachusetts Bay colony was be-ginning to extend its influence north of the Merrimack.[28]

During the 1630's, Sir Ferdinando's feeble government in the Province of Maine exerted little influence over the lives of the colonists at Richmond Island or anywhere else on the coast. In 1639, Winter complained of general poverty and lawlessness in the region. His own situation was far from happy, what with the rigorous climate, the failure of the fur trade, and unruly and runaway servants. But at Rich-mond Island there were for a time food and shelter, subsidized from England when necessary, and a strong arm at the local helm. Else-where, Winter reported to his employer:

> every man is a law to him selfe. Yt is a bad kind of livinge to live
> in a place where is neather law nor government amonge people.
> The people about these parts ar very poore, for I Cannot Con-
> ceave what the[y] Can have out of the Country to by them
> Clothes. The bever trade doth faile which was their Cheffest stay
> for buy them Cloths. The wolves do kill their goates and swine,

wherin the[y] had a good hope to gaine som thinge about them. Now the[y] Can hardly keep so many to find them meat. Som Indian Corne the[y] sell at harvest tyme, but ar faine to buy againe before harvest Comes againe, and som have no bread in 2 moneths before . . . their Corne be ripe, for wants of meanes to buy yt, yett the[y] will not worke under 18 or 20d. a day, and though the[y] have but 2 daies worke in a weeke.[29]

In his discouraged state, Winter failed to mention the two hopeful elements in this dismal situation. One was that fishing remained profitable and promised to continue that way for anyone with the proper equipment, skill, and means to send his wares to a market. The other was that the coastal settlers had just begun the gainful exploitation of the forest.

In 1635, Richard Williams and Peyton Cooke, "Gent.," formed a partnership at Saco for making clapboards.[30] Winter hired some carpenters to build a ship of native materials, and in 1639 he loaded a cargo of pipe staves which he had bought from workmen at Casco Bay.[31] Edward Trelawney proposed in 1635 that the Richmond Island colony try producing clapboards and staves. Whether or not Winter adopted the suggestion, it is certain that these products began to be shipped from northern New England about that time or even earlier.[32] Most authorities believe that the first water-powered sawmill in America was built near York, perhaps as early as 1623. And in 1634, the first cargo of New England pine masts arrived in England, though the systematic supply of the Royal Navy from the Piscataqua was still eighteen years in the future.[33]

A hard-working man who was willing to forsake practically all the comforts of normal life could indeed find a way to make a living along the eastern coast. But there were many obstacles, and existence was often precarious at best. Life in poor, unregulated communities settled by men looking for adventure and profit rather than for other motives generally was lived in the crude and uninhibited manner that one might expect. One of Sir Ferdinando's early associates, Dixy Bull, turned, without changing his theater of action, from trading along the northern New England coast to piracy.[34]

Few of the coastal dwellers were criminals, but the kind of wholesome society that Captain John Smith had expected from industrious fishermen and tillers of the soil failed to emerge. When Massachusetts took charge of Maine in the 1650's, its people were hardly prepared for the enforcement of laws based upon a more sober view of man's duty and destiny.

2

From the first generation of West Country sailors who fished and traded along the northern New England coast sprang descendants, physical and spiritual. Like their fathers and predecessors, they were common, coarse, practical, sturdy, and independent. Not given either to elegant dreams or to theological speculation, they were never rich but hoped to discover the means to a reasonable abundance in this life and possibly in some cases, a measure of bliss in the next. They possessed neither the distinguished and opulent backgrounds of ambitious schemers such as Popham and Gorges nor the underlying religious motivation of the Puritans.

In time, a few of them became transmuted into an aristocratic ruling class. Upon others, the Bible Commonwealth impressed its spirit and its laws. Despite such mutations, the men and women who were the raw materials of the more refined societies of a later day retained some of the lusty pragmatic traits that the men of Devonshire and Cornwall had brought to America and nurtured on a hostile coast. During the middle and waning years of the seventeenth century, one could still look at some of the offshore fishing colonies such as the booming Isles of Shoals and find the raw materials in their unrefined state.

By 1670, the Isles of Shoals were studded with fishermen's huts built of sod, rocks, or boards and shingles brought over from the mainland. On the rocks along the shores lay hundreds of wooden racks, or "flakes," on which the fishermen spread out their fish to dry in the sun, and nearby were stacked the piles of weathered hoops and oak staves from which they assembled their barrels and hogsheads. Everywhere, nets and sails lay spread to soak up the warm sun and constant sea breeze in the perpetual fight against dampness and mildew. Some of the fishermen owned rude "fish houses," or foul-smelling shacks next to the shore for the storage of their gear and fish barreled for shipment. Pinnaces and shallops rode at anchor in the tiny coves and harbors and small rowboats dotted the gravelly beaches and ledges beside the water.

Smuttynose Island, one of the largest of the islands at the northern end of the group and the most heavily populated before 1680, was also called Church Island because it contained a brick chapel occasionally used for Anglican services. On one point of Star Island, which lay on the New Hampshire side of the province boundary that ran through the cluster of tiny islands, a small stone fort overlooked the harbor. Scattered among the primitive huts of Smuttynose and Appledore were a few substantial frame houses comparable to the average mainland dwelling. Smuttynose boasted a full-fledged tavern, which probably differed from the many shacks where fishwives and their daughters informally dispensed ale and flirted with the thirsty fishermen only in that one could find a bed there and buy a meal as well as a drink. Hog Island even had a bowling alley and a brewery.[35]

The colony at the islands had then reached its all-time peak of population and prosperity. About five hundred persons, including a disproportionate number of ruddy young bachelors, lived there around the year. As many as 1,500 fishermen made the islands their headquarters at the height of the season.[36] The entire legal population during part of the seventeenth century was male. Some early authority, in a ludicrous attempt to curb prostitution, simply banned all women from the islands.* The prohibition, which the Shoals fishermen had violated almost from its institution both honorably and otherwise, was repealed officially in 1650. The Maine General Court at Gorgeana ordered, somewhat reluctantly, "that as the fishermen at the Isles of Shoals *will* entertain womanhood, they have liberty to sit down there, provided they shall not sell neither wine, beare, nor liquor." [37]

Either because or in spite of this magnanimous gesture to "womanhood," life at the islands seems not to have been marked by great domestic felicity. Joan Ford, a fishwife, was whipped in December, 1665, and again shortly afterward, the first time for "calling the constable Hornheaded rogue and Cowhead rogue" and the second time for "reviling and abusing" both the constable and her neighbors with "very evil speeches." [38] The frequency with which women of the Shoals were presented as "scolds" between 1665 and 1669 supplies painful evidence of the kind of shrill billingsgate that competed with the screaming of the circling gulls in shattering the idyllic calm of the little islands.[39]

The islanders were frequently drunk. Many of them were prosecuted for this crime in the 1660's during the first flush of enthusiasm

---

* "A Description and Historical Account of the Isles of Shoals," Massachusetts Historical Society *Collections,* 1st Ser., VII (1801), 250–1; John S. Jenness: *The Isles of Shoals,* 2nd edn. (New York, 1875), pp. 131–3. There is no known record of this fascinating ruling, and therefore it is not possible to know by what body, or even under what jurisdiction—most likely an early Maine court under the proprietorship of Gorges—it was made. That there was such an order seems beyond doubt, because in 1647 attempts were made to revive and enforce it, and a Maine court, while refusing to enforce the obsolete order, did not question its existence.

with which the Maine courts tried to enforce Massachusetts laws,[40] but business was too brisk to continue to handle. The courts tried nobody from the Shoals for drunkenness between 1680 and 1692.[41] William Hubbard delighted in fleshing out his history of New England with moralistic anecdotes about fishermen and sailors of the Shoals and the Piscataqua who were drowned while in their cups.[42] Cotton Mather, who knew about life at the islands, must have been thinking about them as well as other eastern fishing colonies when he warned in *The Fishermans Calling* that Satan had induced too many fishermen to become "slaves of the *Bottel.*" [43]

Occasionally an islander was haled into court for offenses common in the other eastern communities during the seventeenth century—assault, "reviling" and cursing, and breach of the Sabbath. In proportion to the population at the Shoals, however, this happened rarely. Cases of fornication and other sexual offenses formed a major part of the docket of the Maine courts of the period, but the islanders seem to have been exempt from prosecution in this field. It stretches credibility to imagine that it was because the hard-drinking, quick-tempered lonely young bachelor fishermen, the vitriolic fishwives, their fighting husbands, and their daughters who came to age in an atmosphere of unchurched brawling squalor lived by a sterner morality than the people of Kittery, York, and Wells. To enforce the law on an island twelve miles from the nearest court was never convenient and not always practical.

Such peace as obtained at the islands was enforced more often by the local fishing master than by the often-maligned constable appointed by the mainland court. When turbulent fishing crews swelled the population, the leading employers assumed the authority of magistrates by invoking ancient precedent. This procedure, which had become institutionalized under the name of the "Newfoundland law," had promoted all the peace and order that the temporary fishing bases of the sixteenth century ever knew. Such assumption of authority now had no legal sanction, but the mainland magistrates, lacking experience in handling rough crowds, gladly left such matters in the relatively competent hands of the fishing masters. The unofficial rulers of the islands understood, as no inexperienced dignitary ever could, how far they had to stretch the ordinary standards of law and civility in order to keep the unruly mob from falling into complete anarchy.[44]

An island fisherman's most important property right was the space he claimed for drying and packing fish and storing and repairing his gear. "Flake room" must have been claimed originally by squatter's right and defended by fist and club.* As late as 1662, Thomas Seavy charged John Diamond in court with "strikeing of him and takeing possession of his fishing Rowme after Itt was delivered him by execution." The court was puzzled as to how to deal with matters that had always been settled by a different kind of due process. The magistrates finally decided for the militant Diamond, ruling "that former possession of fishermen att the Yles of Shoals stands good in Law." [45]

Before 1680, most of the population at the Isles of Shoals lived on Smuttynose and Appledore, on the Maine side of the province boundary. In that year, the Crown separated New Hampshire from Massachusetts and made it into a new royal province. At about the same time, Massachusetts, after a period of doubt, secured permanent control of Maine. Though the islanders were cool to outside authority in any form, they left little doubt about their preference of jurisdictions when in the early 1680's they began to move in large numbers to Star Island, on the New Hampshire side of the line. Puritan courts, laws, and meetinghouses were not for them—or so they thought at that point.[46]

After that, the Maine magistrates occasionally tried to exercise a more stable kind of authority over the islanders who stayed on their side of the boundary. In response to a complaint from Roger Kelly about the "inconveniencys" resulting from the "want of some setled authority," the General Assembly of Maine ordered in 1682 that three leading citizens of the province "repayre to said Yslands" and call a town meeting for the election of local officers.[47] Several other times during the 1680's, the Maine authorities directed Courts of Session to be held on Smuttynose, not only for "tryall of Actions," but also "to make diligent Inquiry into the state of the people, and to require their Attendance to their dutys to his Majestys authority established in this province according to law." [48]

At one of these special sessions in 1684, Nicholas Bickford, an in-

---

* "Flakes" and "stages" served the same purpose: drying fish in the sun. The difference was that stages were elevated. There are far fewer references to stages than to flakes and "flake room" in the seventeenth-century fishing community at the Isles of Shoals, though stages seem to have been more common elsewhere. This may be because stages took up more space, which was extremely precious on the little islands, or perhaps because the timbers or poles upon which stages were erected had to be brought over in boats from the mainland. Contemporary drawings of stages usually picture the drying platforms at about the level of a man's chest or waist. John Josselyn enumerated among the duties of the "shore man" attached to each fishing shallop in the 1660's washing the fish "out of the salt" and drying it "upon hurdles pitcht upon stakes breast high." John Josselyn: *An Account of Two Voyages to New England* . . . (London, 1674), p. 211.

dentured servant, was sentenced to pay a twenty-shilling fine or receive thirteen lashes for "profaine swearing, and multipliing of oaths." The court also ordered Walter Randall, clerk of the writs for the islands, to account for drawing of defective summonses and warrants; appointed a grand juryman; and fined the same Nicholas Bickford and his master, Roger Kelly, "for abuseing the wife of Phillip Odihorne, by uncivill Actions, as footeing upon her, and dragging of her about in an unseemely manner." [49] In the few civil actions decided at the Shoals, the judges occasionally ordered payment in fish.[50]

Despite such attempts to enforce the law at the islands, society remained in much the same disordered state. When a court at Wells convicted Roger Kelly's wife Mary of defamation in 1681, it ordered her to acknowledge her offense "at some publique meeteing at the Yles of shoales." Recognizing the small likelihood of any such meeting being held in the near future, the court provided as an alternative that she make her confession at the next court held on Smuttynose.[51] The residents of Appledore and Smuttynose sent deputies to the General Court in Boston only once in the seventeenth century; the men at Star Island equally ignored their duty to elect representatives to the New Hampshire General Assembly. Nor did the Star Islanders pay any attention to the assessment of province rates.[52]

Though they were indifferent to law and order, the islanders possessed in abundance, by New England standards, the virtues of charity and compassion. In 1653, the men at the Shoals collected £56 on their own initiative for the support of a maimed fisherman. The Maine court praised their "charitable minds and good will" and appointed a two-man committee to look after the victim.[53] Whether his neighbors approved of the court's interference in the matter was not recorded. The same court may have recognized this hearty propensity again in 1671 when it provided for a unique "free Contribution" to be made by the islanders every Sunday for "the supply of their necessitys of poor, sicke, aged and deceased [diseased] or decreped persons." [54]

In 1677, an appeal went throughout New England to raise ransom money for some captives of the Indians from Hatfield, Massachusetts. The Shoals men, though safe from Indian attacks and unfamiliar with this particular variety of hardship, contributed liberally. The amount they collected exceeded what was raised in the bustling seaport of Salem. They shared their charitable disposition with others in northern New England. On this occasion, the contribution of Portsmouth was second only to that of Boston. Of the forty-six towns from which money was received, Dover was among the half-dozen most generous.

The residents of poverty-stricken Kittery gave as much as the people of much larger and more prosperous Lynn.[55] The same generous inclination was at work some years later when the freeholders of Portsmouth voted a large annual contribution to Harvard College.[56]

Though far from zealous, the eastern fishermen as a group were not necessarily hostile to religion. Even at the Isles of Shoals, an Anglican parson or two who had dared to try the hard and discouraging life of a missionary to the eastern fishermen paid occasional visits prior to 1640. During these years, someone had built the small brick chapel that by the 1680's had all but fallen down. The first full-time clergyman at the islands was Richard Gibson, whom we met at Richmond Island. He stayed at the Shoals in 1641 and 1642 after serving briefly at Portsmouth and before the Massachusetts authorities sent him back to England. After Gibson left, the Reverend Joseph Hull of Agamenticus, who had occasionally read the service at the islands before Gibson's arrival, resumed his sporadic visits.[57]

The Anglican influence at the islands, which had probably never been especially strong anyway, soon met the formidable challenge of the encroaching saints from the Bay. About 1650, the Reverend John Brock, a Puritan minister, was settled at the Shoals. He preached every Sabbath and gave frequent weekday lectures for the next twelve years. The succession of ministers was unbroken until 1775, when the few remaining islanders were dispersed by the War for Independence.[58] In 1685, a Maine court cited the inhabitants of Appledore and Smuttynose for failing to maintain an adequate meetinghouse. In the same year, however, the recently naturalized New Hampshiremen built a shingled meetinghouse twenty-eight by forty-eight feet, with belfry and bell, on the highest point on Star Island.[59]

In 1705, the minister at the Shoals was being supported partly from the mainland. The Massachusetts General Court voted, characteristically, to provide £14 of his salary if New Hampshire would furnish another £6. The New Hampshire assembly, long since free of political control from the Bay, nevertheless complied with this early piece of incentive legislation.[60] Its terms were contrived, it would seem, to be so easily met that they could not be refused. With this kind of imperialistic genius, Massachusetts saved the eastern parts from the devil—and probably for civilized society.

As the center of the great fishery in the Gulf of Maine, the colony at the Isles of Shoals, brawling, lawless, and squalid as it was, surpassed most of the northern New England settlements in population and business. During its most thriving years, from about 1640 to

1680, Portsmouth developed rapidly into the leading seaport of the region, and the hamlets of Kittery, York, and Wells grew steadily and took permanent root under the influence of Massachusetts. To the east, the economy and the society remained extremely primitive—so much so that all the tiny settlements east of Wells were easily wiped out by the Indians during King Philip's War from 1675 to 1677. In attitudes and style of life, the settlers from Saco to the Kennebec resembled the men at the Shoals, though their lives were much lonelier and not always completely dependent upon fishing.

John Josselyn, an English traveler with an eye for detail and a gift for writing about it, described life in the easternmost settlements after visiting his brother Henry, a gentleman adventurer to America who first became one of Mason's stewards at Piscataqua and then an early and tenacious settler at Black Point, part of modern Scarborough. Josselyn's two visits to America were separated by almost thirty years.

During his first stay on the Maine coast in 1638 and 1639, while the Richmond Island enterprise flourished about a league to the northeast, the settlement at Black Point was little more than a clearing in the wilderness for a few buildings, a small flock of goats, and one shallop. It was one of the "few scattered plantations, with as few houses" that Josselyn had observed during his coastal voyage from Boston.[61]

Nothing impressed the visitor more than a body of extravagant local folklore that the lonely settlers invented and improved upon while gathered about one another's hearths on stormy nights. His diary contains several of these tall stories, one about a great sea serpent "quoiled up like a Cable upon a Rock at *Cape-Ann*," and another about a merman who gushed purple blood when a fisherman chopped off its hand in Casco Bay.[62] At the end of Josselyn's first visit to Maine, when he sailed from Richmond Island at six in the morning, "several of my friends came to bid me farewell, among the rest Captain *Thomas Wannerton* who drank to me a pint of kill-devil *alias* Rhum at a draught." [63]

During his second trip to Black Point, when he stayed from 1667 to 1671, the mature Josselyn had time to observe the northern New Englanders more analytically. He divided the residents of Maine into three occupational groups: magistrates, husbandmen or planters, and fishermen. "Of the magistrates," he wrote, "some be Royalists, the rest perverse Spirits, the like are the planters and fishers, of which some be planters and fishers both, others meer fishers." [64] By "perverse Spirits," he probably meant those who wanted to return to the control of Massachusetts, but he might have applied the phrase more aptly to those who were content to let the province slip into anarchy. Josselyn noted that the Maine settlements contained but few "handicraftsmen" and no shopkeepers at all, and described the utter reliance of the easterners upon profiteering merchants of Massachusetts for English manufactured goods, and even for most of their meat and produce.[65]

He reported varying degrees of industry among the "planters" and fishermen, and thought the land offered a decent return to conscientious workmen who spent their time "providing for their Cattle, planting and sowing of Corn, fencing their grounds, cutting and bringing home fuel, cleaving of claw-board and pipe-staves, fishing for fresh water fish and fowling." Though "the diligent hand maketh rich," he moralized, "if they be of a droanish disposition as some are, they become wretchedly poor and miserable, scarce able to free themselves and family from importunate famine, especially in winter for want of bread." After offering this traditional explanation of the well born for the troubles of the poor, Josselyn took pains to report that most of the farmers "have a custom of taking Tobacco, sleeping at noon, sitting long at meals sometimes four times in a day, and now and then drinking a dram of the bottle extrao[r]dinarily." [66] He thought they generally ate well, enjoying "as good fish, Beef, Pork, Mutton, Fowl and fish as any is in the whole world besides." Some of the "planters" got indentured servants from England. If they were retained after their time expired, they cost their employers the large sum of £15 or £20 per year in corn, cattle, and fish. More commonly, servants took up a piece of cheap land for themselves when free of their indentures.[67]

The fishermen whom Josselyn met in the late 1660's were probably much more typical of the coastal fishery than Trelawney's hired hands at Richmond Island thirty years before. Instead of working for wages, they combined into crews of about nine men each, went to sea in a shallop under the command of a master, sold their catches to a merchant, and divided the proceeds at the end of each voyage. By then the New Englanders had found a market for the "refuse," or poorer quality fish, in the West Indies, where it was fed to the black slaves on the sugar plantations. The best, or "merchantable" fish still went to southern Europe.

According to Josselyn's jaundiced report, the eastern fishermen almost universally squandered their shares, which amounted to £8 or £9 a man for a voyage of several weeks, on the brandy, rum, wine, and tobacco that was put ashore by "walking taverns," as he described the barks from Massachusetts that called at the fishing colonies. Merchants frequently put in at the peak of the season and gave the men "a Taster or two, which so charms them, that for no perswasions that their imployers can use will they go out to Sea, although fair and seasonable weather, for two or three days, nay sometimes a whole week till they are wearied with drinking, taking ashore two or three Hogsheads of *Wine* and *Rhum* to drink off when the Merchant is gone." [68]

The Royal Commission of 1664–6 made an even more incriminating report of the eastern fishermen, who, the commissioners complained, "never had any government among them; most of them are such as have fled from other places to avoid justice. Some here are of the opinion that as many men may share a woman as they do a boat, and some have done so." [69]

Such were the founders of northern New England.

CHAPTER III

The Puritan Conquest
1638–1658

1

The fishermen and woodsmen of northern New England were exceptions to the rule that in the seventeenth century Europeans took possession of America in the name of God. In this respect, they contrasted sharply with their closest neighbors. Religious zealots to the north and south soon began to cast the shadows of their conflicting faiths between the Merrimack and the Kennebec. For some European princes and explorers, the cause of Christianity had merely provided convenient sanctions for making war and expanding trade and territories. To the Jesuits of Canada and the Puritans of Massachusetts, however, religion was not an excuse but the real motive. Their fervor itself powered changes in history.

The French missionaries dealt mainly with the natives. They supplied the eastern Indians, already indignant and frightened over the English seizure of their hunting and fishing grounds, with religious sanctions and the encouragement of holy men in their wars against New England. Red men half-Christianized by ardent Jesuits later became the French shock troops in the long struggle with England for North America. In this struggle, northern New England was almost a continual battleground. To a large extent, war molded the history of this region during the colonial period. There was an earlier, even more potent formative influence: the conquest of Maine and New Hampshire by the Puritans of Massachusetts.

The conquest took several forms: social, economic, political, and military. It was resisted at some stages and places, and actually requested at others. At still others, it seems simply to have happened. It was not entirely successful. The political annexation of New Hampshire by Massachusetts, except for the sharing of governors, failed to last through the seventeenth century. By the middle of the eighteenth century, a group with ideals and a spirit alien to Puritanism had taken charge of the society of Portsmouth and completely dominated the government of the province. In Maine, political dominion became complete, and, for our purposes, permanent. Under wilderness and wartime conditions, however, and in the face of uncongenial tendencies in the original settlers, the Puritan conquerors could realize their social goals only in places and in part.

Despite all this, they achieved remarkable success. The realization of many of the imperial schemes of Massachusetts Bay helps illustrate the development of that extraordinary colony as a virtually independent commonwealth. The extent to which the conquerors were able to export a moral and social system scarcely designed for popular appeal or easy acceptance demonstrates the vitality of Puritanism as a cultural force in the seventeenth and eighteenth centuries. In the face of obstacles of many kinds, and despite the possible cynicism of ambitious magistrates and morally and spiritually inadequate ministers, it was religious men from Massachusetts, by and large, who civilized the northeastern wilderness.

2

Early in the seventeenth century, much of even the most accessible part of northern New England was uninhabited. In most of the settlements, the unbridled nature of society contrasted vividly with life in the well-regulated towns of Massachusetts. Such conditions naturally attracted the attention of some of those unhappy residents of the Bible Commonwealth who came to need a religious haven. Thus it was an Antinomian exile from Massachusetts who introduced the institutions and spirit of Puritanism into northern New England.

The Reverend John Wheelwright, son of a middle-class family of the eastern English coast, had played football at Cambridge with Oliver Cromwell. After his eviction from a Lincolnshire vicarage, he gained notoriety as a Puritan leader. Excluded from all the established pulpits in the land, he made his way in 1636 to Boston, New England, the home of his brother-in-law, William Hutchinson, and William's dangerously mystical wife, Mistress Anne. Both Wheelwright and his more famous sister-in-law challenged the New England orthodoxy of the day, resulting in a theological debate over Antinomianism, as the "heresy" was called by its detractors. The issue, however, soon became political rather than religious, for John Winthrop regarded heterodoxy as seditious, tending to undermine the established civil and ecclesiastical authority in the Bay Colony. The General Court at length agreed with him and banished both Mrs. Hutchinson, who had divided the Boston church, and Wheelwright, who had become identified as a leader of the popular Antinomian faction early in his pastorate in Braintree, where he was installed soon after his arrival in Boston. Upon their expulsion in the fall of 1637, Wheelwright and his sister-in-law went separate ways, she to Rhode Island and he to New Hampshire, each with a coterie of followers.[1]

About twenty families went with Wheelwright. At least seven of them were headed by Wheelwright partisans who had been disaffected from the religious establishment in Massachusetts and followed him voluntarily. The rest were recent arrivals from Lincolnshire, former friends or relatives of Wheelwright and the Hutchinsons who had had the misfortune to land in Boston after the passage in 1637 of America's first immigration law. As a direct result of the Antinomian crisis, the Massachusetts General Court excluded any new arrival from more than a few weeks' residence in the Bay Colony unless with the specific approval of a Councilor or two other magistrates. These new arrivals, because of their connection with the most notorious subversives then in the colony, obviously were not acceptable. Indeed, it was precisely against their expected arrival that the law had been enacted.[2] Among this Lincolnshire group that accompanied Wheelwright was William Wentworth, whose descendants provided the core of the Portsmouth merchant oligarchy and dominated the politics and commerce of New Hampshire for much of the eighteenth century.[3]

Emery Battis has made an interesting distinction between the group that went with Wheelwright to New Hampshire and Anne Hutchinson's pilgrims to Rhode Island:

> When it came time for them to abandon their homes and go elsewhere, seven men elected to follow Pastor Wheelwright northward to New Hampshire. The choice suggests a difference in the degree of their disaffection. Not only was Wheelwright ultimately to prove less radical than Mrs. Hutchinson in his definition of the Covenant of Grace, but five of the men who joined him received formal dismission from the church of Boston. This indicated that they were regarded as being in good spiritual standing and were thus authorized to join another church or, if need be, to organize their own. It is also noteworthy that this small group

included none of Mrs. Hutchinson's most active supporters, nor did it include any of the more eminent and affluent participants in the [Antinomian] movement.[4]

Wheelwright spent the winter at Strawberry Bank, then went with his fellow exiles to the falls on the Squamscot River, where they built their town of Exeter. Like Roger Williams, Wheelwright insisted upon establishing his title to the land by buying it from the Indians. In this instance, there was a more compelling reason than one's sense of righteousness. New Hampshire, since the death of Mason in 1635, had been without any central government. Wheelwright could not, therefore, appeal to any New Hampshire authority for the grant of a township, and he did not want to appeal to Massachusetts. The Exeter men bought a tract of land from some local sagamores in April, 1638.* They organized a church, installed Wheelwright as pastor, built a meetinghouse, and laid out a burying ground. To provide some basis for government, the thirty-five male church members (several followed the original twenty to Exeter after the settlement was begun) signed a compact, similar to the one drawn up by the Pilgrims on board the *Mayflower,* in which they acknowledged their allegiance to the King and agreed to live quietly and peaceably together "in all godlyness and honesty." In accordance with the agreement, they then elected magistrates and passed some simple laws. Within a short time, the Exeter colony had lands under cultivation, gristmills in operation, a working local government, and a flourishing church.[5]

At about the same time, a few religious eccentrics fled from Massachusetts to Dover. Captain John Underhill, whom Governor Winthrop had brought to Boston to train the militia, became an outspoken partisan of Antinomian doctrines and signed a petition against the General Court for its treatment of Wheelwright. Still worse, he was suspected of having trusted his privately received assurance of free grace to the extent of indulging fearlessly in adultery. Admonished by the church and banished by the Court, Underhill made his way to Dover in 1639. He served briefly as governor of that tiny colony and helped supervise the gathering of a church.

This was the second attempt to found a religious institution at Dover, and it proved as unsatisfactory as the first. The company of

---

* It was accepted for many years that Wheelwright had bought land from the Indians at Exeter during an early visit to New England before he moved permanently to America. The supposed deed is printed as Appendix I in Jeremy Belknap: *The History of New-Hampshire* (Dover, N.H., 1812), I, 289–91. Most modern authorities doubt its authenticity.

Bristol merchants that owned two-thirds of the patent for "Northam," as the colony was known during its early years, had sold out in 1633 to a company headed by two Puritan peers, Lord Say and Sele and Lord Brooke. Thomas Wiggin, the chief agent of the company, had been well recommended to Governor Winthrop by an English correspondent, and Winthrop referred on one occasion to the arrival at "Pascataquack" of "one Mr. Leverich, a godly minister." This was the Reverend William Leveridge, who preached for about two years in the little meetinghouse that Wiggin's men built when the colony came under Puritan control. In the middle 1630's Leveridge had to move south for lack of support. There had been no organized church either during his stay or during the brief ministry of his successor, George Burdett.

With Burdett, the people of Dover, several of whom had been sent by the new proprietors and undoubtedly had serious views of religion, had been introduced to the very human sort of minister with which they became all too familiar over the next few years. Burdett had entertained worldly ambitions and worked his way into favor with a faction that was powerful enough to install him as governor in place of Wiggin. From his position of both civil and spiritual authority, he had carried on a private correspondence with Archbishop Laud in which he criticized the Massachusetts government. When this correspondence was discovered, he had moved to York, where the prevailing attitude toward Massachusetts was more like his own. A short time later, a Maine court convicted him of adultery, after which he returned to England. This unsavory episode had ended Dover's contact with religious institutions until the arrival of Captain Underhill.[6]

The first minister of the congregation that was gathered during Underhill's regime was Hansard Knollys. From 1636, when as a Separatist he renounced his orders in the Church of England, to his death while serving as a Baptist minister in London in 1691, Knollys made a career of religious radicalism.[7] When Underhill sponsored his move from Boston to Dover in 1638, the minister seems to have been going through an Antinomian phase, or at least his beliefs were interpreted that way by the subversive-hunting clergy and magistracy of Boston. His pastorate at Dover was a riotous one. Like Burdett, he wrote back to England to complain that the Massachusetts government was arbitrary and that New England lacked real religion. Someone intercepted a copy of the letter and sent it to Winthrop. To keep his peace with the Massachusetts oligarchy, Knollys went to Boston to make a public confession and retraction. In 1640, Thomas Larkham, a former minister of the Church of England who had found even less to his taste in the doctrine and discipline of the Massachusetts churches than in those of the established Church at home, left Boston for Dover. Aiming to take Knollys's place in the ministry, he rounded up enough support to force the pastor to step down. Knollys was reinstalled when Larkham's scandalous private life became known, but the reinstated champion fell from local grace almost immediately when he was discovered in the bed of his maid the night after he had excommunicated Larkham—for, among other things, unchastity.

The whole affair was attended by riots, fines, excommunications, and, at one point, an armed but harmless meeting between the two parties, the members of one of which appeared in what passed for martial array. This last bit of melodrama, fortunately, came to nothing more than a request from Larkham for intervention by the governor of the Portsmouth colony. The Portsmouth magistrate, though presumably lacking jurisdiction outside his own "lower colony" at Strawberry Bank, forced Knollys and Underhill to submit to a sort of drumhead court-martial, which convicted them both of starting a riot. Underhill in turn petitioned for intervention from Massachusetts, which came in the form of a committee of two ministers who decided that both sides had been at fault. They persuaded the Knollys-Underhill faction to revoke Larkham's excommunication and the Larkham faction to withdraw the fines and banishment which the Portsmouth governor had imposed upon the rioters.*

---

* Belknap: *N.H.*, I, 41–5; "Biographical Sketch of Col. Winthrop Hilton" in John Farmer and Jacob B. Moore, eds.: *Collections, Topographical, Historical, and Biographical, Relating Principally to New Hampshire*, I (December 1822), 243; Thomas Hutchinson: *The History of the Colony and Province of Massachusetts-Bay*, ed. Lawrence Shaw Mayo (Cambridge, Mass., 1936), I, 94–5. Knollys has had his defenders. Among them was the Reverend J. Newton Brown of Exeter, New Hampshire, who tried in 1837 to rescue his reputation from the harsh interpretations of Winthrop, Belknap, Hubbard, and Hutchinson, and presumably the account in Farmer's and Moore's *Collections* of 1822 cited above. His treatment of the incident involving the maid is a bit strained and clumsy: "Both Winthrop and Belknap say, that 'a discovery was made of his failure in point of chastity'; and that he himself acknowledged before the church that he had been guilty of improper 'dalliance' towards two young women that lived in his family; and that, on this account, he was dismissed by the church, and removed from Dover. Admitting all this to be true, (and more than this was once true of so good a man as David) his criminality seems to have been much exaggerated by Hubbard and others." Brown offers as arguments for Knollys's innocence his own statement that he returned to England at the request of his aged father, his appearance as plaintiff in an action of slander in a New Hampshire court in 1641 (never prosecuted because he returned to England), the unconscious prejudice likely in historians of different religious views from those of Knollys, and Cotton Mather's description of Knollys in the *Magnalia* as a "godly Anabaptist"

This attempt at reconciliation probably would not have ended the matter except that the long-suffering people of Dover, to their great relief, were soon rid of all three of the principal actors. For his indiscretion with his maid, Knollys was dismissed from the pastorate in 1640, and he returned to England.[8] Underhill, whom Larkham had accused of having tried to persuade the Dover people to submit to Massachusetts authority in order to gain personal favor with Winthrop and the Saints, returned the same year to Boston. There he confessed both his errors and his sins, and was restored to communion with the Boston church. He soon found freer air, however, in New Netherlands, where he spent the rest of his life in the military service of the Dutch.[9] Larkham, who like Knollys had scandalized the community by his loose morals, returned to England in 1641.[10]

Meanwhile, the Massachusetts General Court had granted permission in 1638 to fifty-six Puritans, most of whom had come to Massachusetts from East Anglia, to move from Newbury across the Merrimack and begin a township at nearby Winnecunnet, the later site of Hampton.[11] Two years earlier, the Court had authorized the men of Newbury to build a house there in order to assert a claim to the rich grazing lands in the broad salt marshes of Winnecunnet.[12] At this stage, in the face of actual settlement by Massachusetts men, it made no practical difference that the claim conflicted both with the terms of Mason's patent and with Wheelwright's deed from the Indians. Moreover, the Massachusetts authorities now began to re-examine their own charter, and in 1639 sent surveyors to discover the northernmost point of the Merrimack. By a construction of the charter which agents of the colony later disavowed, the Massachusetts magistrates hoped to establish that point as the basis of their northern boundary.[13]

In granting the new township at Winnecunnet, the General Court designated a committee of three prominent Massachusetts men to assist in laying out the town and to apportion land to the residents, "so as nothing shall be done therein without alowance from them, or 2 of them."[14] At first, this special committee had all the powers normally vested in the town government. Not until a year after the settlement began did the legislature give the town, later named Hampton, the power to elect officers, make rules, and send a deputy to the General Court. The nonresident committee, which the Court evidently looked

---

who had "a respectful character in the churches of this wilderness." "Memoir of Hanserd Knollys, M.A.," New Hampshire Historical Society *Collections*, V (1837), 177–9.

upon as a board of trustees to act as proprietors, retained the power of laying out land.[15] The General Court followed a similar procedure a century later when it was overseeing the resettlement of the Maine towns abandoned during the Indian wars. The appointment of non-resident committees to supervise the establishment of eastern towns, therefore, seems to have been introduced at this point as a feature of Massachusetts colonial policy.

Hampton, like Exeter, was founded by an exiled minister and his followers. But the Reverend Stephen Batchelor's troubles with the authorities involved conduct rather than doctrine. Hampton, like Dover, therefore, owes its origin in part to the misadventures of an errant clergyman. Batchelor was a former minister of the Church of England who had been silenced at home for nonconformity. After a brief voluntary exile in Holland, he had sailed to Massachusetts with a handful of his church members in 1632. He went immediately to Lynn and formed his followers into a church, accepting as additional members anyone else in town who cared to join. Scarcely four months elapsed before the beginning of a long period of bickering about whether Batchelor's church, which he had gathered without the usual Puritan formalities, was a true one. More seriously, questions arose about Batchelor's private conduct, though he had been seventy-one years old when he landed in America. A council of ministers confirmed the legal status of the church, but not before the General Court had silenced Batchelor's preaching "until some scandles be removed." The old minister arrived in Newbury in the summer of 1638 after being forced to leave Lynn for trying to form a second church there, and then received permission to lead the settlement at Winnecunnet, where the gathering of a church was among the first orders of business.[16]

In the rejuvenating air of New Hampshire, the venerable pastor soon found himself fighting, not always successfully, the same sort of temptation that one gathers had led to some of his earlier troubles. In 1641, at the age of eighty, Batchelor, in the words of John Winthrop, "did solicit the chastity of his neighbour's wife." The woman informed her husband, whereupon the minister was charged with the offense in court and faced an inquiry by his church. He at first denied the charge to the satisfaction of both the church and the magistrates. His conscience gained the upper hand just prior to the next Communion, however, and he confessed voluntarily "that he did intend to have defiled her, if she would have consented." The church members at first forgave, but later excommunicated him. They were divided over whether to readmit him until the matter was referred to a group of magistrates and elders, who persuaded the church to restore him to membership, but not to the pulpit.[17]

Neither the community of saints nor the world of women had heard the last of Batchelor. The church at Exeter, a few years later, would have had him for its pastor had not the Massachusetts General Court intervened. In 1650, at Portsmouth, he married a third wife, Mary, and was fined for not having published his intentions beforehand. The marriage was so unsuccessful that a court found it necessary to order the couple to live together. Possibly for this reason, Batchelor sailed alone the following year to England, where, aged ninety, he took his fourth wife. Mary was still the old man's lawful wife and was still very much alive. Having moved by now to Kittery, she was sentenced by a York County court in 1651 to receive thirty-nine stripes and be branded with the letter "A" six weeks after bearing a child of George Rogers. In 1656 she petitioned the General Court, unsuccessfully, for a divorce from her runaway husband. The virile clergyman died near London in his hundredth year.[18]

While Exeter flourished and the people of Dover and Hampton struggled with embarrassing problems of the ministry, the settlers at the mouth of the Piscataqua thrived on a wealth they had appropriated after the death of John Mason and worried lest their late proprietor's heirs would one day threaten their happy state. Though there probably was not a Puritan among them, they may have been inclined to look upon the relatively strong government of Massachusetts as a likely source of protection against possible land claims by the heirs of Mason.[19] The fear of the Mason family may well have smoothed the way for agreement by the men of Strawberry Bank and Great Island to a plan for annexation to Massachusetts, which took place in 1641.

The colony at the river's mouth, later named Portsmouth, lacked a legal basis for incorporation as a town, but governed itself under an agreement similar to the Exeter combination. In 1640, Francis Williams, the governor, and nineteen other inhabitants granted fifty acres for a "glebe" to two men designated as "church wardens" of the parish. At the same time, they appropriated money for a parsonage and a chapel, and chose the Reverend Richard Gibson as their minister. Their terminology and choice of Gibson, the Richmond Island priest whom the Massachusetts authorities later drove out of New England, mark this settlement as distinctly Anglican in whatever religious sentiments its people had.[20]

Gibson was still in the pulpit when the Massachusetts General

Court ordered on October 9, 1641, "with the consent of the inhabitants of the said ryver," that all the persons settled at "the ryver of the Pascataquack" were "accepted and reputed under the government of the Massachusetts, as the rest of the inhabitants within the said jurisdiction are." [21] The Court seems to have regarded Dover and the future Portsmouth as a single colony. There is no record of negotiations between the men of Strawberry Bank and Massachusetts, as there is in the case of Dover, but that settlement clearly was to be included in the extended jurisdiction, and seems readily to have acquiesced. The governor of the "lower colony" was appointed one of the magistrates of the court of quarter sessions for the new Piscataqua district.[22]

It is not clear whether the negotiations that led to the absorption of Dover and Portsmouth were initiated by Massachusetts or by the men of New Hampshire. We do know, however, that three committees from Dover proposed to the General Court in 1639 that that settlement be annexed to Massachusetts. A committee representing the Bay Colony, which was at that moment attempting to extend its claim well to the north, agreed instantly. After a year of negotiations, the patentees of the colony at Dover ceded to Massachusetts the jurisdiction over their holdings but not the title to the land.[23]

If, in fact, the inhabitants of Dover took the first steps toward the annexation, the reasons for it are not difficult to find. Underhill displayed his eagerness for at least a measure of Massachusetts control, probably for personal reasons, in his successful petition for intervention in the ecclesiastical dispute of 1640. Underhill was an eccentric, and undoubtedly a sefish one. In Dover, however, unlike Portsmouth, there were a number of serious Puritans who by 1640 must have been thoroughly disenchanted with ministers such as Burdett, Knollys, and Larkham. Their experience with this remarkable succession certainly provoked wistful glances at the well-ordered communities of Massachusetts. The Puritan group at Dover, then, led by the influential Edward Hilton and Thomas Wiggin, favored an alliance with Massachusetts as a solution to the troublesome religious life of the community.

The means by which Mason's one hundred former "stewards" and "servants" at Strawberry Bank and Great Island were included in the transaction, apparently without significant protest, are less clear. However, the advantages of coming under the protection of a relatively strong government must have been manifest. Even aside from their concern over possible claims to their appropriated property by the heirs of Mason, they needed institutions for defense and internal order, which would have been difficult to provide on their own. The Reverend Mr. Gibson opposed the exercise of Massachusetts power after the annexation, but whether he had voiced opposition beforehand is uncertain. Sometime before he left Portsmouth, he sent an open letter to Larkham at Dover. In it, according to Winthrop, "he did scandalize our government, oppose our title to these parts, and provoke the people, by way of arguments, to revolt from us." In 1642, the General Court ordered him to appear to answer for this act of near treason and for presuming to baptize and marry people at the Isles of Shoals. The Court dismissed the charges when the harried priest announced that he planned to return shortly to England.[24] Either Gibson spoke too late or he lacked enough influence to prevent the peaceful absorption of Portsmouth as well as Dover.

In 1642, the General Court made an important concession to the majority at the Piscataqua plantations, and to religious liberty in the eastern parts. It provided that former freemen in those towns should continue to exercise their civil rights, whether or not they were "at present" church members.[25] Thus Massachusetts showed her willingness to sacrifice an important feature of her own system if necessary to expand her dominion. In being exported to a new environment, the Puritan ideal underwent its first relaxation. The words "at present," however, strike one as arrogant. They seem to imply that after sufficient enlightenment under the wholesome rule of Massachusetts, all those at Piscataqua deemed sufficiently worthy would, as a matter of course, gather themselves into a "church way" after the orthodox manner.

After 1641, Exeter remained the only New Hampshire town outside the Bible Commonwealth. Its independence was short-lived. Because of its relative prosperity and ordered community life, the town attracted new settlers; as it grew in population, Wheelwright's immediate followers lost their majority. For about two years after the peaceful fall of the Piscataqua colonies, the men of Exeter were divided over whether to capitulate. To many people, the advantages of being under such a government were obvious. Wheelwright, however, was under sentence of banishment. If Exeter should come under Massachusetts jurisdiction, he would have to move again. Against this possibility, two of Wheelwright's associates had prepared another refuge by arranging with Thomas Gorges, the deputy governor of the Province of Maine, for a grant of land and the right to settle at Wells. By May, 1643, Wheelwright's men could no longer resist the tide. Twenty-two Exeter men, only one of whom had been a close associate of Wheelwright, petitioned the General Court to be taken within its jurisdiction. The vote to grant the petition, "Whereas Excetter is found to bee within our patent," came on September 7, 1643. Political dominion of New Hampshire by Massachusetts, to last for forty years, was complete.[26]

3

Wheelwright, with some of his original followers, fled to Wells, where he started another wilderness community by building a garrison house of hewn logs, gathering a church, and erecting a sawmill. His stay there was only temporary, because the General Court revoked his banishment in 1644 after he had written servile confessions to the Court and to Governor Winthrop. He accepted the pastorate at Hampton in 1647, but left during the period of the Protectorate to live for a time in England. He returned to New England in 1662, and served as pastor at Salisbury until his death in 1679.[27]

A series of conflicting grants, purchases, modifications, and reinterpretations had rearranged property lines in such a way that at the time of Wheelwright's flight to Wells, there were four discernible jurisdictions east of the Piscataqua. All that was left of Gorges's Province of Maine ended at the Kennebunk River, which empties into the sea about ten miles northeast of Wells. Between the Kennebunk and the Kennebec lay the Province of Lygonia, which the Council for New England had carved from Gorges's patent in 1630 and granted to a group that called itself a "company of Husbandmen." Sir Alexander Rigby had bought the patent in 1643 and made George Cleeve, who had moved to Casco Bay from Spurwink under harassment from Trelawney's agent at Richmond Island, the chief magistrate of the province with the title of deputy president. Between the Kennebec and the Penobscot was the Sagadahoc territory, and between the Penobscot and the St. Croix was contested land occupied, where it was occupied at all, by Frenchmen.[28]

Thomas Gorges, who governed Maine under the proprietorship of Sir Ferdinando, returned to England about 1643 to take part in the Civil War, which was also claiming the attention of his aging uncle. He left the people of Maine to such government as they could manage, entrusting to Edward Godfrey, who was an early settler of Agamenticus, Mason's former fishing "steward" at Piscataqua, and a former mayor of Gorgeana, the care of the Gorges interests. He and the officers of the propriety tried to operate within the unwieldy framework of Gorges's charter, sustained only by the hope that the Lord Proprietor, backed by the Crown, would before long be able again to make his strong will felt in this lonely Royalist outpost.

For six years, the people of Maine lived with virtually no government and an ever-ebbing hope for the survival of their province. The purchase of the Lygonia patent by Rigby, whose political sympathies were with the Puritans of England, was discouraging enough. Then, beginning in 1647, came rumors that Sir Ferdinando was dead. These were confirmed in 1649, which was about when New England learned that the mother country no longer was a kingdom. Godfrey and the other provincial officers responded to this disastrous turn of affairs by calling an assembly at which the people of Kittery, Gorgeana, and Wells agreed to govern themselves under the privileges of Gorges's charter. They elected Godfrey governor, and named the appointive officers who had assisted him to the positions they had held previously.[29]

On October 16, 1649, the new legislature gave liberty to "all gode people within the Jurisdiction of this province who are out of a Church way and be orthodox in Judgment and not scandalous in life" to "gather themselves into a Church estate, provided they do it in a Christian way. . . ." Each church so gathered was to have the privilege of electing and ordaining all its officers, "provided they be able, pious, and orthodox." [30]

What is one to make of this action by the legislature of a nominally Anglican province? Charles M. Andrews viewed it as a significant step toward religious liberty, comparable to similar statements in Maryland and Rhode Island. It stands, he said, "in striking contrast with the official attitude of the Puritan colonies." [31] What is really striking about it, however, is not so much its contrast with the Puritan attitude toward diversity in religion as its expression of the Puritan view, modified from the strictest version though it was, of the church. One of the provisions of the act was that the gathering of churches under it must be accomplished "with the due observation of the rules of Christ revealed in his worde." Such a concern unquestionably reflects Puritan thought, as does the provision for congregational election and ordination of officers. The phrase "able, pious and orthodox" is straight out of the Massachusetts statute books, except that the Bay Puritans generally used "learned" rather than "pious."

Granted that the act was a short step toward religious liberty, it would seem to have been a liberty specifically for congregationalism.

Perhaps the Maine authorities hoped that by this act, they would display a cooperative attitude toward Parliament, and preserve the province from tampering or extinction. This would have been consistent
with Godfrey's policy of accommodation to the new government in
England. It is also suggestive, however, that the act was passed at
the precise time that the Cambridge Platform, that definitive statement of the Puritan view of the source of church authority and the
scriptural means of ecclesiastical government and discipline, was being
circulated among the churches of Massachusetts for their approval.[32]
In the absence of more satisfactory proof, one can only say that the
Maine act of 1649 contains substantial internal evidence of Puritan
influence from southwest of the Piscataqua.

Again, however, the eastern version of Puritanism became attenuated as compared to the pristine Massachusetts model. The concern
here seems to have been merely for the organization of churches, perhaps in the interest of good order, perhaps ultimately, in someone's
mind, in the interest of preparing the way for a Puritan conquest.
Membership, therefore, was not limited, as in the churches of Massachusetts, where a principal concern was the *purity* of churches, to
"saints by calling." Indeed, where in Maine would one look to find
one, except possibly among the handful of Wheelwright's former followers in Wells? Instead, the Maine legislature, presuming to establish
its own standards for membership in a congregational church, opened
the privilege to "all gode people" who were "orthodox in Judgment
and not scandalous in life."

In Lygonia, a smoldering feud between Cleeve, the chief magistrate, and other officeholders such as Henry Josselyn and the Reverend
Robert Jordan was muddling public affairs. Cleeve was republican
in temperament and favored the Puritan cause in England. Josselyn
and Jordan had sympathized with Gorges in Maine and the Crown
back home, and disliked the new propriety. In 1650, Rigby, the
proprietor, died unexpectedly in England. Josselyn and Jordan openly
sought an arrangement that would end the Rigby family's authority;
Cleeve sailed for England with a petition asking Parliament to confirm
it. Cleeve also took with him a petition from Godfrey asking for a
charter of government for Maine.[33] During his two-year absence,
Massachusetts began the campaign to annex Maine and Lygonia.

Previously encouraged by the confusion in Lygonia and by intel-
ligence of a growing sentiment for annexation in Maine, the General
Court acted in 1651 in response to a report of Godfrey's petition to
Parliament. The Court directed separate letters to the government and

the people of Maine, asserting its claim to jurisdiction over all territory south of a line drawn three miles north of the northernmost point of the Merrimack. Three commissioners dispatched for the purpose failed to secure the consent of the people of the three Maine towns, but on a second trip to Maine in 1652, they publicly proclaimed the Massachusetts claim and absolved the people of allegiance to Godfrey and his government. Godfrey and his council issued a counterproclamation, which proved less convincing than the claims and persuasive arguments of the commission from Massachusetts. In the same year, the General Court sent two surveyors to the head of the Merrimack. They fixed the northern boundary of Massachusetts at 43°43′12″N. When the line was extended eastward, it came out in the middle of Casco Bay.[34]

Meanwhile, Rigby's son, under the influence of Cleeve, had addressed a letter to the Josselyn-Jordan faction in Lygonia forbidding any further "private and secret combinations" and declaring all official acts subsequent to the death of his father to be "utterly void." Thus Lygonia was left completely without government. This was a state of nature similar to the one Massachusetts had discovered when she absorbed New Hampshire. The difference here was that both Cleeve and his royalist opponents continued to resist annexation for some time.

From November, 1652, to July, 1658, commissioners of the General Court visited the settlements from Kittery to Casco Bay, securing signed articles of submission and constituting courts and town governments. The three towns in Maine and the Lygonia settlements of Saco and Cape Porpoise submitted at the beginning, but not until 1658, after a prolonged losing debate by Cleeve, Josselyn, and Jordan against the scattered majority in northern Lygonia, did the commissioners complete their task. On July 13, after securing the signatures of twenty-nine persons, including the principal opponents, the commission constituted Black Point, Blue Point, and Stratton's Island the town of Scarborough, and the settlements at Spurwink and Casco Bay the town of Falmouth.[35]

As each successive town capitulated and became a part of the newly created York County jurisdiction during these six years, the Massachusetts commissioners carefully selected the former leaders of the community, including the opponents of annexation, for office in the town government and county courts. Thus Godfrey, Josselyn, Jordan, and Cleeve, who led the resistance to the last, all took their places in the Yorkshire magistracy along with such former leaders as

Nicholas Shapleigh, Edward Rishworth, Abraham Preble, Samuel Wheelwright, and George Munjoy.[36] The designers of Massachusetts colonial policy matched their aggressiveness with great wisdom.

In this way, Massachusetts first established her dominion over Maine. For practical purposes, the conquest was a permanent one, though at several times during the next few decades, the hold of the Bay on her eastern colony was either in doubt or actually loosened. During the period from 1649 to 1658, Maine lost forever her character as the primitive feudal domain of an ineffectual princely proprietor and became instead the frontier outpost of a Puritan society.

CHAPTER IV

From Servants to Oligarchs

1635–1692

1

When the pervasive government of Massachusetts slipped smoothly into the political vacuum along the west bank of the Piscataqua in 1641, no one in either province had reason to suppose that the union between New Hampshire and the Bay would not be permanent. At the time, there were nothing but advantages for such a connection on both sides. The Puritan commonwealth was satisfying its urge for imperial expansion and fulfilling its divine mission to Christianize and civilize all New England. The thriving little settlement at Great Island and Strawberry Bank—Mason's former "lower colony"—was beginning to develop a bustling trade, which could supplement the economy of a province that depended upon commerce rather than compete with it. The General Court would be in a much better position to deal with remaining traces of royalism and prelacy that threatened the unity and harmony of the region, such as the troublesome Richard Gibson. For their part, the men of New Hampshire cared little for religious contention. Puritan rule might bring minor annoyances for some, but that was of small account compared to the peace, order, and above all the protection of their property that would come from being a part of a vigorous commonwealth. At this point, the men of the Piscataqua had little interest in governing themselves. They were interested in getting rich.

Captain John Mason had given them the chance. He had outfitted his colony well with shiploads of arms and ammunition, clothing, tools for blacksmiths, coopers, carpenters, and masons, food, naval stores, boats, fishing gear, and cattle. With his financing, the "servants" of the colony had built houses to live in, cleared land, and planted crops. Thomas Warnerton, one of the leading "stewards," lived in the "great house" at Strawberry Bank, which soon became the center of the Piscataqua settlement. There was another large fortified house with outbuildings about sixteen miles upriver at Newichawanneck (now the Salmon Falls River), near the Hiltons' colony, where Mason's Danish servants had built a water-powered sawmill and gristmill. At Odiorne's Point at the mouth of the river, on the three-thousand-acre estate attached to "Mason's Hall," the big stone house built by David Thomson in 1623, others of Mason's men collected sea water in large shallow pans and scooped up stores of salt when the water evaporated. On Great Island, across a small harbor from Strawberry Bank and overlooking the river channel, Mason had financed the erection of a substantial fort and armed it with brass cannon. He had even sent over twenty-two women to his men, who lived well, some of them presumably happily, on the supplies and capital he had poured into his colony from England.[1]

The outlook for Mason had been bright. He had invested enthusiastically and heavily, but his plantations were well established and could soon be self-supporting. There had been every prospect that his employees would soon be reaping handsome returns for him from their fishing and lumbering. Then, in November, 1635, he died. His widow was executrix of the will and entitled to the income from all his estates until John and Robert Tufton came of age. The colonists waited, their minds whirling with schemes and dreams of wealth, to see what she would do. After two years, she decided, in effect, to abandon the New Hampshire enterprise.[2] Robert, who alone of the proprietor's grandsons lived to claim his patrimony, was still thirteen years away from his majority. In any case, the commotions in England would have prevented him from pressing his claim until after the Restoration.

The hundred or more settlers at the Piscataqua were on their own. Captain Francis Norton, a steward at Strawberry Bank, drove Mason's herd of about a hundred head of yellow Danish cattle overland to Boston, where he sold them for £2,500, pocketed his fortune, and settled in Cambridge. Forty years later, Nathaniel Boulter and John Redman vividly recalled the strange sight of a great drove of large lowing cows and oxen raising the dust of the lone woods road through the infant settlement of Hampton as Norton and a few companions urged them toward Boston.[3] Thomas Warnerton gathered up as many weapons and stores as he could take to Port Royal in Acadia, where he sold them to the French. He was killed in the process.[4] The Waldrons of Dover conspired with Sampson Lane, a former steward who stepped in after the death of Warnerton to claim possession of the "great house" and the thousand acres of prime riverfront property at Strawberry Bank that went with it, to appropriate the brass cannon at Great Island and ship them away, presumably for cash, on one of Lane's ships. The woodsmen and millhands at Newichawanneck divided up the land there among themselves, built dwellings of their own, and allowed the large garrison house to slip into ruins.[5] Gradually, all of Mason's land and other property on the Piscataqua became divided up among his settlers and was either sold or put to personal use.[6]

Certainly this was a spectacular act of mass plunder, but it ought to be judged fairly. While the disarming of the fort and Norton's selfish cattle-rustling may well have overstepped the bounds of propriety, the rank and file of Mason's colony had little choice but to make the best of a disastrous and utterly unexpected turn of events. Mrs. Mason tried briefly to keep the colony going, but decided in the end that the expense of maintaining it was too much. Her employees pressed her for back wages. Undoubtedly she owed Norton the most of all. Finally, she decided to give it up. She sent word to her servants, in Belknap's words, "that they must shift for themselves." This they did, some of them handsomely.

About the time Massachusetts took over the jurisdiction of New Hampshire, a few of the most energetic and contriving of the men at the Piscataqua, some of them new arrivals, began to shape the colony's economic future and establish their own dominant positions. Building partly on the abandoned wealth of the Mason family and partly on their own resources, this handful of ambitious men forged a base of economic and social power that would one day give them a position of political authority as well. They may not have known it then, but the Cutts, the Waldrons, and the Vaughans built the foundation of the future Portsmouth oligarchy about 1640 when they began the serious development of the Piscataqua trade. As the Wentworths and their associated clans were to do decades later, these three leading families eventually became allied by marriage—a most effective technique for the concentration of wealth and power, one which became a New Hampshire tradition.

John, Richard, and Robert Cutt were sons of a Welsh merchant who, after moving his family to Bristol in Gloucestershire, later sat in Cromwell's Parliament. Attracted by the American fishery, the three brothers emigrated to the Piscataqua region at least as early as 1640. Robert soon went to the West Indies to make his fortune, but John and Richard found the fish and lumber industries at the Isles of Shoals and Piscataqua a sufficient inducement to stay.[7]

William Vaughan, also a Welshman, came to New Hampshire from London, where he had been trained in business and the social graces by Sir Josiah Child. In 1668 he married the daughter of Richard Cutt.[8] Richard Waldron, scion of a good family in Warwickshire who had come to Dover as a youth to see the country in 1635, bought land during his visit, returned to marry an English gentlewoman, and brought her back to Dover. There he built mills, acquired property and ships, and prospered. His son, Richard Waldron, married successively daughters of John Cutt and William Vaughan.[9]

These New Hampshire mercantile careers began with fishing and expanded rapidly into the lumber trade. By 1650, shipyards on both sides of the Piscataqua were producing fishing smacks and other small vessels, and in 1665, more than twenty sawmills were operating on the river and its various branches.[10] In the absence of controls from England, the merchants of the Piscataqua developed a brisk ocean trade. Some of their ships sailed to the West Indies laden with lumber, staves, and trash fish and returned with cargoes of rum and molasses. Others headed across the sea, bound for southern Europe with the better grades of fish, and brought salt, wine, and brandy back to New Hampshire. This trade nourished the rapid growth of shipbuilding, which had the great advantage of an unparalleled supply of nearby materials. Beginning in 1652, the Royal Navy began to send ships to the Piscataqua for pine masts during the first Dutch war, and Portsmouth remained the center of the mast trade until it moved to Falmouth, Maine, in the 1720's. In 1671, ten cargoes of white pine masts left Piscataqua harbor for Britain.[11]

During his first trip to the Piscataqua country in September, 1687, Samuel Sewall visited the sawmill at Salmon Falls near Dover, then rode into a nearby swamp "to see a Mast drawn of about 26 Inches or 28; about two and thirty yoke of Oxen before, and about four yoke by the side of the Mast, between the fore and hinder wheels. 'Twas a very notable sight."[12] The mast was apparently slung by chains, according to the usual practice, from two axles, each connecting a pair of immense wheels, large enough to be drawn over rocks, stumps, and gullies—in this case by seventy-two powerful oxen.

Entries into the harbor during a ten-month period in 1680–81 amounted to forty-seven vessels, including twenty-two ships, eighteen ketches, two barks, and five smaller craft.[13] In addition to ocean commerce, the Portsmouth merchants carried on a healthy coasting trade, mostly with Boston. Portsmouth and Boston vessels generally sailed from the Piscataqua with cargoes of wood products such as boards, staves, "trunnells" (tree nails, or wooden pegs), planks, and oars. They returned with corn, wool, wheat, flour, hides, beef, pork, indigo, and "parcels of English goods." [14]

The acts of trade and navigation, even had they been enforced during the years when New Hampshire and much of the rest of New England were being ruled from Boston rather than from London, would have had little effect on the prosperity of Portsmouth's developing merchant class. The laws affected no important feature of their trade, although there is evidence that the Piscataqua merchants were not averse to selling an occasional cargo of masts to the Dutch or importing contraband goods directly from Europe.[15]

To what extent the Piscataqua merchants depended upon illicit trade is not clear, but it could hardly have brought in a significant share of their profits. Until 1680, however, the port had no customhouse,[16] and the merchants and shipmasters grew accustomed to full freedom. Naturally, therefore, when Edward Randolph's deputy collector, Walter Barefoote, opened an office at Strawberry Bank and announced that all vessels must enter and clear under his supervision, resentment ran high.

This was perhaps the first reaction at the Piscataqua to the colonial policy of the Restoration as it affected New Hampshire. More fundamental, and more significant to the future power of the oligarchy was the actual separation of the four towns from Massachusetts and the establishment of a separate government. Although the merchants were at first suspicious of this royal act—for good reason—the erection of the royal province of New Hampshire supplied the occasion for building a political and social stronghold upon the solid foundation of wealth, class solidarity, and aggressive leadership that the first families of the region had already laid.

Broadly considered, the separation of New Hampshire from Massachusetts and the establishment of a royal government and a collector of customs at the Piscataqua was part of the ministry's attempt to regain control over all the colonies for the benefit of the entire imperial system. Robert Tufton Mason had supplied a more concrete reason for the separation, as we shall see, but one of the great objects of Restoration policy was to strip Massachusetts as much as possible of the power and degree of independence that the strong-minded Puritan oligarchy of Boston had managed to acquire during a half-century of imperial neglect. In setting up a separate government for New Hampshire, the Crown attempted to meet one of Randolph's many complaints about Massachusetts: that she had assumed many powers of sovereignty that she did not legally have, including the extension of that supposed sovereignty into neighboring jurisdictions. Presumably, too, the ministry saw that removing an important port from the refractory Bay Colony might have a salutary effect upon the enforcement of the navigation laws.

The immediate cause of the separation was the revival by Captain Mason's heir of his claim to his grandfather's property in New Hampshire. Upon the accession of Charles II, Robert Tufton Mason, a relative of Edward Randolph, had gone into the English courts to begin the long legal battle for his American lands. At a hearing on Mason's claim before the Lords Chief Justices of the King's Bench and Common Pleas in 1677, the agents of Massachusetts disclaimed ownership of the lands claimed by Mason and admitted, after nearly forty years of rule in New Hampshire, that the northern boundary of the Bay Colony's jurisdiction extended no further than three miles north of any point on the Merrimack. Massachusetts thus withdrew from what promised to be a great land controversy from which, under the circumstances, she could not hope to benefit. At the same time, she left the four towns of New Hampshire without a government.

The judges reported to the King that they could not rule on the right of ownership, since the tenants were not there to defend themselves. They and Mason's counsel agreed that Mason had no right of government within the lands he claimed, only a possible title to ownership. The Attorney General then ruled that, because no court in England was competent to judge the matter, the differences between Mason and the colonists over the use of the New Hampshire lands must be tried on the ground in question.

In view of all this, a new jurisdiction, in which the King might direct the mode of trial and appeal, became necessary. Charles put Mason in legal possession of the lands he claimed, but bound him not to charge retroactive rents, and to pass title to the present tenants and their heirs in return for an annual quit-rent. If any tenant should refuse these terms, the President and Council of the new province were either to settle the difference or submit the evidence and their opinions to the King in Council. The commission for the new government passed the royal seal on September 18, 1679, and took effect on the following January 1.[17]

2

To this point in history, if anywhere, we can trace the emergence of the New Hampshire oligarchy as a self-conscious, self-assertive group. With the removal of their province from the jurisdiction of Massachusetts a fact, the accustomed freedom of their commerce threatened by the Crown, and the free use of their lands challenged by Robert Mason, the first families of New Hampshire now made clear their intention of taking unquestioned charge of this provincial society. To the merchants, it was even more important than defending their lands that they assume unqualified supervision of the regulation of commerce, upon which their wealth depended. They thus fought Randolph and Barefoote before they fought Mason, and for the time being it was expedient that they remain friendly to Massachusetts.

At the head of the new government, the King placed the wealthiest or otherwise most conspicuous men of the province. The venerable John Cutt, who with his brother Richard had acquired most of Strawberry Bank in the division of the Masonian holdings and was now one of the most successful merchants in Portsmouth, as the Bank and its surroundings had been named in 1656, was made President. To the Council, Charles named William Vaughan, Richard Martyn, and Thomas Daniell of Portsmouth, John Gilman of Exeter, Christopher Hussey of Hampton, and Richard Waldron of Dover. He gave the Council authority to add three other members of its own choosing. The President and Council exercised executive and judicial powers and had some control over the acts of the popularly elected Assembly.[18]

Vaughan had received a stylish London upbringing and was now one of the wealthiest merchants in Portsmouth. Martyn, described by Belknap as "of good character, and great influence," had taken a leading role in procuring a minister for Portsmouth. Daniell, the son-in-law of President Cutt's brother Richard, had in 1671 built a tavern which served for many years as the center of the official and social life of Portsmouth and the province. The other three councilors were the leading men of their communities. Waldron, one of the first settlers of Dover, had become especially distinguished as a civil and military leader.[19]

Belknap, whose Puritan bias one must always take into account, nevertheless was probably correct in his assertion that most New Hampshiremen, including the President and Council, accepted the order for the erection of a separate government only reluctantly. This was more especially the case since it was the hated Randolph who, on January 1, 1679/80, brought the order to Portsmouth. There seemed a plain connection between the establishment of the new government and an anticipated assault on property long held by squatters.*

Whatever their attitude toward separation from Massachusetts, the new governors eagerly undertook their duties. When Randolph, as collector of customs for New England, seized a ketch in the execution of his office, the master, Mark Hunking of Portsmouth, sued for damages before the President and Council and recovered thirteen pounds. In Belknap's words, Randolph "behaved on this occasion with such insolence, that the council obliged him publickly to acknowledge his offense and ask their pardon."

President Cutt and the Council then directed their new-found authority toward Barefoote, the deputy collector for Portsmouth. They fined him ten pounds for "having in an high and presumptuous manner set up his majesty's office of customs without leave from the president and council; in contempt of his majesty's authority in this place; for disturbing and obstructing his majesty's subjects in passing from harbour to harbour, and town to town; and for his insolence in making no other answer to any question propounded to him but 'my name is Walter.' " Having denied Randolph's and Barefoote's authority, the New Hampshire magistrates issued orders and appointed officers of their own for the enforcement of the laws of trade. Again in 1682, the Council bound Barefoote and two of his assistants to good behavior after they had seized a vessel "under pretence of his majesty's name, without the knowledge or the authority of the province, and without shewing any breach of statute though demanded." [20]

Mason's prosecution of his land claims under the new government was no more successful than Randolph's attempts to enforce the navigation laws. At every opportunity, the Council resisted Mason's attempts to collect his rents. Mason's "stewards" aroused universal hostility at the beginning of the new regime by demanding rents from

---

* Jeremy Belknap: *The History of New-Hampshire* (Dover, N.H., 1812), I, 143–5. This historian, whose thorough scholarship, careful documentation, and lucid style provide us with a monument among early colonial histories, rejects unceremoniously William Douglass's assertion that the men of New Hampshire wanted the new government for reasons of defense. See also Thomas Hutchinson: *The History of the Colony and Province of Massachusetts-Bay*, ed. Lawrence Shaw Mayo (Cambridge, Mass., 1936), I, 96.

several landholders and threatening to sell their houses for payment. In December, 1681, Mason himself arrived in Portsmouth with a royal order requiring the Council to admit him as one of their number. The Council complied, and Mason, styling himself "lord proprietor," joined his stewards in their unsuccessful attempts at rent-collecting.

Petitions for protection against the collectors flowed into the Council from each of the four town governments and from some individuals. The Council published an order prohibiting further attempts at collection, which it ruled to be irregular, and announced that all the many complaints would be sent to the King. Mason responded to this insult by refusing to sit with the Council, whereupon the Council threatened to prosecute him for neglect of duty. The lord proprietor next issued, on his own authority, a summons to the President and some of the councilors to appear before the King within three months. The Council issued a warrant for Mason's arrest, charging him with usurpation of authority. At this point, Mason ended the farcical exchange by running off to England.[21]

The new government, having confounded the principal purpose for which it had been established, lasted but two years. But the Portsmouth merchant class had tasted political power. The day was near when these men and their successors would be pleased to count themselves among the supporters of the royal prerogative and would act with far less hostility toward officers of the Crown. The day was coming, too, when the ties that now bound the budding aristocracy in unnatural alliance with Puritan Massachusetts were to be loosened, and the divorce finally solemnized by the erection of a proper Anglican church. For now, it was enough that economic power had been joined for a moment with official authority, and that the group that had wielded both had proved itself capable of effective leadership and deserving of the community's esteem.

3

The decade that followed was a turbulent one, in old England and New. In 1682, Mason procured the appointment of Edward Cranfield, a royal officeholder in England, as lieutenant governor and commander-in-chief of New Hampshire. To him, Mason mortgaged the whole province in return for an annual payment of £150. Envisioning a rich return in quit-rents despite Mason's obvious failure, Cranfield arrived in Portsmouth in October bearing his commission, which named the

same Council as before, including Mason, with the addition of Barefoote and Richard Chamberlayne.[22]

The new governor suspended Waldron and Martyn within six days
of his arrival, but later reinstated them. In 1683, he dissolved the
Assembly. Edward Gove, an assemblyman from Exeter, tried to lead
an armed revolt against the governor, whom he denounced as a
traitor for having taken this unprecedented (but legal) action. For the
first time, the New Hampshire oligarchy lined up with the prerogative
men against the popular faction. Waldron was the judge and Vaughan
and Daniell were assistants of the special court that convicted Gove
of high treason, although tradition says the old judge wept as he read
the grisly sentence under which the ineffectual rebel was to be hanged,
drawn, and quartered. To what was probably the immense relief of
almost every New Hampshireman, Gove was sent across the sea to the
Tower of London instead and finally pardoned and returned home.[23]

This first alliance between the blooming oligarchy and the cham-
pions of royal authority was short-lived. Cranfield aimed all his efforts
at securing profits from Mason's lands, and eventually replaced the
councilors with men who could better help him do it. In 1685, however,
the King replaced Cranfield with Barefoote, the deputy governor, who
held office only until the establishment of the Dominion of New England the following year.[24]

The men of New Hampshire generally favored the New England
rebellion of 1689 against the rule of Sir Edmund Andros, during which
Mason, a member of his council, had died. Upon the dissolution of
the Dominion, however, they were left with neither a government nor
instructions from the new King and Queen. At the suggestion of some
of the former councilors, who by now were looked to as the natural
leaders of the province, the four towns elected delegates to a convention with authority to set up a provincial government. The convention's
solution was a petition to be taken again under the government of
Massachusetts, to which the Bay Colony readily consented. The
annexation took place at once, pending an announcement of the royal
pleasure.

This arrangement ended abruptly in 1692, when William and
Mary appointed a new royal governor for New Hampshire. He was
Samuel Allen, a London merchant who had bought title to the New
Hampshire lands from John Tufton Mason's two sons. Allen stayed in
London and sent his son-in-law John Usher, who had been treasurer
of the Dominion under Andros, to take charge at Portsmouth as lieu-
tenant governor.[25]

From then until American independence, New Hampshire was governed as a separate royal province, except that between 1698 and 1741 she shared with Massachusetts the same succession of royal governors. Under her royal governors, New Hampshire prospered, her oligarchy flourished, and her capital developed from plain beginnings into an impressive center of distinguished architecture and pleasant provincial society.

CHAPTER V

Growing Pains
1660–1713

1

During the first years of the reign of William and Mary, the governments and jurisdictions of the various New England colonies took on their permanent form except for the resolution of the important question of the Massachusetts-New Hampshire boundary. While New Hampshire became a separate royal province, the Maine settlements became indisputably a part of Massachusetts. During the Stuart Restoration, however, the issue had been in doubt. Even more doubtful was the extent to which the fishermen and woodsmen of the eastern coastal frontier would ever become truly absorbed into a society that was governed by different attitudes and different values.

Under the influence of the heirs of Mason and Gorges, the Restoration government tried to strip Massachusetts of her control of both her northern satellites. The first attempt came in Maine, which probably contained more royalists at this stage than New Hampshire. But during a brief period of ineffective royal government between 1665 and 1668, the defenseless settlements of the Maine frontier were threatened for the first of many times with the possibility of attack by the Indians and the French.[1] Certainly some Maine men still favored the Gorges interests and others had smarted under the relatively strict moral code that the Massachusetts courts had tried hard to enforce. They were probably outnumbered, however, by men who had enjoyed the relative prosperity, order, and protection that they had experienced under the rule of the Bay. Thus a new commission of the General Court had little difficulty in re-establishing her judicial and military institutions in Yorkshire in 1668. The following year, the people of Maine sent three delegates to the General Court.[2]

In 1677, Massachusetts ended further doubt about her title and jurisdiction over Maine by buying all rights to the propriety from Gorges's heir for £1,250. The King was furious, but the title of Massachusetts was better than ever.[3] In 1680, the General Court, acting as the proprietor of Maine, established a government for the province under the terms of Gorges's charter.[4] When Massachusetts lost her own charter in 1684, her connection with Maine remained unbroken, but during the brief period before the establishment of the Dominion of New England, the eastern province slipped into virtual anarchy. The provincial charter of 1691 made the old Plymouth colony, Maine, and the Sagadahoc territory all parts of Massachusetts, and so they remained for 130 years.[5]

For the two generations following the establishment of Massachusetts authority in Maine in 1658, while the merchants of Portsmouth marshaled their resources and ingenuity to mold a ruling class, the leaders of most of the Maine settlements struggled gamely to tame their rough society. Even armed with the awesome authority of the Great and General Court, they faced a discouraging task—at times, it seemed, a hopeless one. Those who sought to civilize the Maine coast—to make it culturally as well as politically a part of Puritan Massachusetts— had to contend not only with unrestrained habits of long standing, but also with those eternal enemies of order and social stability, war and its degenerating and demoralizing consequences.

Of the fifteen or twenty settlements that dotted the Maine and New Hampshire coastline late in the seventeenth century, at least a third still lived by fishing. In a few of these, such as the tiny fortified coastal hamlets at Sagadahoc and Black Point, the colonists had made tentative advances in farming, and the rough inhabitants of some of the mainland fishing stations far to the east were still trading with the Indians for furs.[6] In the more southwestern communities, beginning in a small way at Casco Bay, Saco, and York but most impressively at the Piscataqua, the settlers had begun to supplement their fishing and subsistence farming by cutting timber and producing naval stores.[7]

In 1660, Samuel Maverick listed three sawmills on the Newichawanneck, the north branch of the Piscataqua (later named Salmon Falls River), two more at the head of Cocheco Creek, and several each at Oyster River (Durham) and Exeter. Most of the masts sent to England had been cut along the east or Maine side of the Newichawanneck near Mason's original sawmill, but good ones could be found in abundance at Cocheco and Oyster River, both then in the New Hampshire town of Dover. "Mutch Tarr," he wrote of Cocheco, "hath been made on that Creeke side." * By 1665, the Piscataqua region had more than twenty sawmills.[8]

Portsmouth was rapidly becoming a prosperous commercial town whose merchants exported in 1671 some 20,000 tons of boards and pipe staves, 10,000 quintals of fish, ten shiploads of masts, and several thousand furs. Her imports for the same year, as listed by Robert Tufton Mason, included 300 tons of wine and brandy, 200 tons of "goods from the Leeward Islands," and 2,000 tons of salt. By the 1690's, shipbuilding had become a flourishing industry at the Piscataqua.[9]

At the same time, the island fishing bases such as Monhegan and the Isles of Shoals were declining. In the seventies, the fishmasters had begun to send their fleets to more fruitful fishing grounds as far eastward as the banks of Cape Breton and Newfoundland. The Shoals, in particular, thus lost the advantage of being in the very midst of the most-used fishing grounds. Moreover, fishing voyages to the east were now often combined with trading at Newfoundland, and the islands were poor places to load cargoes of farm and forest products from the mainland.[10] The fishing fleets, therefore, tended increasingly to sail from such ports as Piscataqua and Casco Bay, and many of the islanders moved to the mainland.

In contrast to Portsmouth and the other relatively prosperous towns along the Piscataqua, most communities in Maine at the end of the seventeenth century were scenes of poverty and, in some cases, desolation. Lacking the sound economic basis of a Boston or a Portsmouth in the first place, the small beginnings that the Maine settlements had made by 1690 were wiped out by the depredations of King William's War. In all of Maine and in the more remote communities of New Hampshire, life was profoundly shaped for several generations by the very real threat, which on occasion became grim reality, of unannounced house burnings, mass slaughters, forced marches through the snowbound forest to Canada, tortures, and baby killings.

Had the Maine towns been settled compactly and adjacent to one another, according to the Puritan ideal that was supposed to govern

* *Briefe Description of New England* (written in 1660 and published in Boston in 1885), pp. 9–10. Maverick preceded Winthrop's Puritans to the Boston area by six years and lived in New England most of his life. He opposed the independent course of the Massachusetts government and served as a member of the King's Commission of 1664–6. (Preface to *Briefe Description* by John Ward Dean, pp. 3–4.)

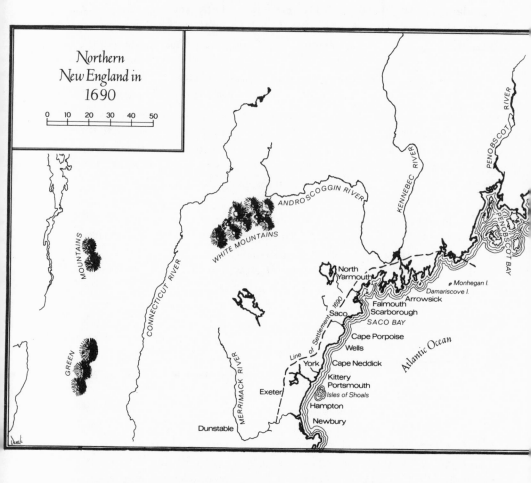

the settlement of Massachusetts, they might have been less vulnerable
to Indian attack than they were, despite their locations on the frontier.
But the settlers had lacked the sense of community that came with
close religious and social ties, and had felt no necessity for the consolidated arrangement by which the Puritans to the south tried to
foster moral and civic responsibility, church attendance, and public
education. After the Indian wars became commonplace, new settlers
in Maine and the interior of New Hampshire considered the needs of
defense when they built their towns, but in the seventeenth century,
most of the settlements were characterized by dispersion. Nearly all
of them had been settled by individuals or families acting as such, not
by ready-made communities. Each householder pursued his own ends,

generally farming, fishing, trading, or a combination of these. He procured a tract of land, sometimes by squatter's right but more frequently by purchase or grant from some large patentholder, and built his isolated house with little regard to nearness to his neighbors.

The sporadic warfare along the Maine coast during King Philip's uprising between 1675 and 1677 taught some lessons, but only in Wells did the settlers take them seriously enough to keep their town intact during the much more serious hostilities of King William's and Queen Anne's Wars between 1689 and 1713.

In Kittery, across the Piscataqua from Portsmouth, a tentative line of isolated farmhouses and tiny clusters of fishermen's huts straggled twenty miles up the river and even up such smaller streams as Spruce and Sturgeon Creeks. In 1690, a party of French and Indian raiders swooped down on the upper part of this township of 125 square miles and picked off the scattered families one by one. After each isolated slaughter, the family's house, built with such difficulty in the forest, was burned to the ground. In all, eighty-eight unsuspecting men, women, and children died.[11] The neighboring settlement of York stretched for several miles along the eastern bank of the Agamenticus, or York River. It was somewhat better prepared than Kittery, since about five two-story garrison houses built sturdily of hewn logs were scattered among the smaller framed cottages and farmhouses, and there was even a massive stone gaol, built near the meetinghouse of the shire town in 1653 to comply with Massachusetts law. Each of the garrison houses could be defended by about thirty men, and if warned in time, the surrounding families could take cover in them and be relatively safe. But on a cold January morning in 1692, the enemy took the settlement by surprise. There was no time to hide. Indians and Frenchmen slaughtered seventy-five persons and marched over a hundred more through the snow to Canada—a full half of the town's population. Before they left, they burned every building in the settlement except the meetinghouse, the gaol, and the palisaded garrison houses.[12]

Similar scenes had taken place to the east, most recently at Wells, which was spread along a road running parallel to the shore but was protected by seven good garrison houses and the only effective local militia organization in Maine,[13] and at Falmouth, which consisted of scattered farmhouses on Falmouth Neck and on a few of the islands of Casco Bay. After the capture of Fort Loyal at Casco Bay in 1690, the only Englishmen remaining east of Wells were a few soldiers in

Fort William Henry at Pemaquid, and that final stronghold was wiped out during a renewal of hostilities in 1696.[14]

The Treaty of Ryswick ended the war between the French and the English in September, 1697, and the New Englanders made a separate peace with the Indians in 1699.[15] During the summers of 1699 and 1700, some of the eastern landowners who had escaped the enemy and gone for refuge to Portsmouth or Boston resettled their former holdings at Falmouth, Scarborough, Saco, Cape Porpoise, and Cape Neddick. The brief peace during which they began the laborious process of rebuilding was an uneasy one, in both Europe and America. The eastern Indians, apparently stirred by rumors that the English planned a surprise attack on their tribes, began again to lurk about the white settlements in war paint. This put the Maine towns once more on a wartime footing, complete with night watches and a mobilized militia.

In an attempt to win the natives to the English side, emissaries and missionaries from Massachusetts visited the eastern tribes, with some success. Gradually, the tension eased, and there was hope for a more thorough resettlement of the abandoned towns. During the war of 1689–97, however, the raiders had destroyed mills, fences, roads, and, most seriously, deeds. To hasten a resettlement that would be as free as possible from land controversies, the General Court established in 1700 a committee on eastern claims. This body of seven was to examine all titles and claims to land in the deserted area and report its findings to the General Court.[16]

Scarcely had the committee begun its complicated task when the death of King William and the accession of Queen Anne in 1702 precipitated the long-brewing War of the Spanish Succession. The events in Europe had coincided with boundary disputes between the French and the English in America, competition between the two nations for influence among the eastern Indians, and serious controversy over fishing rights in the western Atlantic. After the declaration of war in Europe, Governor Dudley of Massachusetts and the chiefs of the Maine tribes made a treaty of friendship at Casco Bay in June, 1703. Six weeks later, however, the Indians, again under French influence and for the second time in fourteen years, laid waste the few English settlements between Casco and Wells. Not until after 1713 did New Englanders again attempt to settle this region.[17]

Between 1675 and 1713, scarcely a settlement, from the remotest northeastern outpost at Pemaquid to Hampton, remained physically untouched by French and Indian raiders. Scarcely a man emerged free from some devastating effect of war upon his family, fortune, or person. No social institution remained unaffected. The official records of the period, whether of town meeting, selectmen, court, provincial council, legislature, or governors, provide forceful reminders that war and its effects demanded an overwhelming share of public and private attention. The fact that northern New England was a battleground during almost forty years surrounding the turn of the eighteenth century and again between 1744 and 1760 determined in great part the region's landscape, its economics, its social development, and its politics.

York, Kittery, and Wells were the only settlements in Maine that remained inhabited at all throughout the period from 1689 to the Peace of Utrecht in 1713. In those three townships, and in the villages of New Hampshire outside Portsmouth, sporadic raids took many lives. Even in the quietest times, the danger of attack was nearly constant. The worst raid was the massacre that severely crippled York in 1692. Durham, New Hampshire, on the Oyster River, took a damaging blow from the Indians in 1694, and the settlers at Wells, though better prepared, were victims of a similar attack at the outbreak of Queen Anne's War in 1703.

At the cost of disrupting useful employment and normal social life, the townspeople on the severely contracted eastern frontier deserted their small farmhouses for garrison life. Once they knew the devastating cost of ignoring the danger, each family repaired to the nearest garrison house, which was usually under the military command of the owner. The family lived with others in the house or, more frequently, in one of several temporary huts erected just outside the house but within the stockade. In daylight, men and women might work in their own fields, if they were not too distant. The men, however, frequently scouted, guarded, and performed other military duties —supplementing, if the town was fortunate, a garrison of five or ten men furnished by the province.[18]

The contraction of the eastern frontier, which lasted for a quarter of a century except for the brief attempts at resettlement in 1699 and 1700, was the most immediate and obvious result of King William's and Queen Anne's Wars. Many of the refugees, their possessions destroyed or abandoned, somehow made their way to Boston, where they added to the capital's growing problem of caring for the poor.[19] On petition from the town of Lynn, the General Court twice voted funds to support Onna Thomas, "a poor helpless Widow, driven in from the Eastern Parts, in the late War." But on the third petition, in 1720, the House cut off the flow of province aid, leaving the Widow Thomas to the mercy of the Lynn town fathers or of charitable friends and neighbors.[20] There is no reason to suppose that this town was alone among the smaller Massachusetts communities in providing a haven, willingly or otherwise, for one or more war refugees.

The social and psychological effects of the wars upon the settlers of the northern communities that remained intact, but in a state of virtual siege during much of the period, are incalculable. Though it was usually possible to defend the garrison houses successfully, there was no way to protect the surrounding countryside and undefended dwellings from destruction. To work in the fields or in the woods was unsafe in most cases, and, in any event, the able-bodied men usually had other duties. Except for the few merchant-shipowners at Portsmouth and Kittery who prospered under wartime economic conditions, northern New Englanders became very poor.

The disruption of normal domestic life that resulted from garrison living encouraged departures from ordinary social conduct, even by Maine standards. During the winter of 1695, Alice Metherell, a notorious tart who five years before had borne the child of "Black Will," one of the few slaves in the eastern parts, found the Curtis garrison at Wells a happy frolicking place. She shared a room with John Thompson of Kittery, even though, in the words of one of many witnesses to the affair, "most of the people that did belong to the garrison did Lie in there Litle houses nere the garison." This arrangement bothered some of the guards and scandalized two or three older women—not, apparently, because it was unprecedented for persons to share a room in this manner, but because the ill-famed Alice was soon discovered to be pregnant again, and they feared Thompson would have to take the blame. Alice had a husband whose whereabouts do not appear in the records, but to nobody's surprise but Thompson's, Alice named her roommate as the father. Her testimony, combined with that of many others, convinced the court.[21]

The nature of Indian warfare, with its swift, silent attacks, its ambuscades, its disregard of age and sex, and its deliberate cruelties, must have promoted a special terror and inspired a special hatred of the natives—matched only, perhaps, by the growing resentment of the red men themselves over the clearly unjust and ceaseless encroachments on their hunting grounds and way of life by people who, unlike the French, displayed little interest in their welfare. Imagine the reaction of Captain Convers and his fifteen men at Wells who were forced in the spring of 1692 to watch helplessly from their garrison house while a band of Indians disposed hideously of an English prisoner

The province gaol at York, built in 1653. Note the large section of stone masonry.

The McIntire garrison house overlooking the York River in the "Scotland" section of York, Maine. The walls are built entirely of horizontal courses of hewn timbers, dovetailed at the corners. The clapboard sheathing is to keep the timber walls from rotting. The original windows, probably of the casement style, were considerably smaller than those pictured. The bulkhead cellar door is also a relatively recent addition.

Seventeenth-century house in Portsmouth, constructed about 1664 by Richard Jackson, a shipbuilder. The wings at the ends were added at a later date. At the rear of the house, not shown, the roof sweeps almost down to ground level.

The Captain John Sherburne House, preserved at the "Strawbery Banke" restoration project in Portsmouth. The western half, to the left of the photo, was built about 1695; the house was doubled in size by the addition of the right-hand half between 1700 and 1703.

Early Georgian house built in Portsmouth by Captain Archibald Macpheadris in 1716. Not only was the house far in advance of its Portsmouth contemporaries in style, but the brick construction was extremely rare in the period throughout northern New England, where wooden building materials abounded.

The Chase House, a dignified early Georgian structure at "Strawbery Banke," Portsmouth, probably built between 1730 and 1740.

Gambrel-roofed house built in Portsmouth about 1758 by Captain Gregory Purcell, now known as the "John Paul Jones House."

Governor Benning Wentworth's country seat at Little Harbor near Portsmouth, originally built about 1690. Wentworth kept remodeling it and adding rooms during his occupancy from 1750 until his death in 1770.

The framed house built for the Reverend James MacGregor by his parishioners in Londonderry soon after the township was settled in 1719. The other settlers lived at first in temporary log houses. A few of Mr. McGregor's neighboring farmers began to build houses similar to this one in the early 1720's.

The house of Matthew Patten of Bedford, built in 1738. Undoubtedly this became the most numerous type of northern New England farmhouse between 1760 and 1775. The barn was somewhat removed from the house.

The home of George Tate, Falmouth mast agent, built in the Stroudwater section of Falmouth overlooking the mast landing on the Fore River in 1755. Note the unusual treatment of the roof and the third-story windows, resulting in what is known as an "indented gambrel roof."

The farmhouse of the Reverend Timothy Walker of Penacook (now Concord, New Hampshire), illustrating occasional attempts to introduce architectural style and dignity to the countryside and frontier. Mr. Walker erected the shell of the house between 1733 and 1735, making it contemporaneous with several very similar houses in Portsmouth. The interior was not finished, however, until 1764.

Reconstruction of the timbered fort and stockade at Township Number 4 on the Connecticut River (now Charlestown, New Hampshire). The hills and trees beyond the fort are across the river, in Vermont. During King George's War, the entire community lived in hastily erected huts within the stockade.

A view of Portsmouth, apparently sketched in the 1770's, from Joseph F. DesBarres: The Atlantic Neptune *(London, 1780). The view is from an island in the Piscataqua just off Strawberry Bank. The spires belong to the South meetinghouse, left, Queen's Chapel, center, and the North meetinghouse, right.* Courtesy of the John Carter Brown Library.

A pilotage chart of Falmouth Harbor prepared in the 1770's for the use of the Royal Navy and published in Joseph F. DesBarres's The Atlantic Neptune *(London, 1780). The principal settlement of Falmouth, the center of the modern city of Portland, is shown on Falmouth Neck. Note the extensive system of roads leading northward from Falmouth Neck and in Purpooduck (modern South Portland), across Fore River from the Neck.* Courtesy of the John Carter Brown Library.

named James Diamond. In plain sight of the garrison but just out of
musket range, the savages first stripped Diamond, then castrated him,
sliced between his fingers and toes, covered his body with gashes into
which they thrust firebrands, and left him, blazing and bleeding, to
die.[22] Men who had lost wives and children in Indian raids commonly
nourished a spirit of murderous revenge for the rest of their lives.

The people of the frontier towns tried during the wars to maintain
as best they could the bases of normal community life as well as their
defenses. The correspondence between Maine towns and the Massachusetts authorities during the first half of the eighteenth century
reflects to a striking degree the concern for peopling the settlements
with permanent inhabitants. In at least one instance, some of the leading men of York thought it more important that a potentially useful
citizen should have the opportunity to found a family in their town
than that he continue to strengthen their roving scouting parties. They
petitioned Governor Dudley in 1711 to release Samuel Sewall, lately of
Newbury, from regular military duties in view of previous service and
because "he desires to build, to marry, to Settle at York, having received a Grant of Land to incourage his settling with us, he being a
good tradesman, a good Commonwealthsman, a good Soldier of Christ,
as well as of Your Excellencies." [23] One wonders, however, whether the
town fathers would have been quite as solicitous of one who was not a
nephew of the eminent Judge Samuel Sewall of Boston (whose son was
married to Governor Dudley's daughter) and the brother-in-law of the
town's popular minister, the Reverend Samuel Moody. [24]

Although political connections between Maine and New Hampshire
had ended by the time of King William's War, the New Hampshire
authorities anxiously eyed the state of defenses in Maine, which took
the worst blows. In turn, Massachusetts aided New Hampshire when
it seemed necessary. On March 30, 1693, the Provincial Council of
New Hampshire authorized the lieutenant governor to "aide and assist
them with what strength the nature of this Province will afford" upon
any application for help from "the neighboring County of York or
Province of Maine." [25] The same spring, the governor of Massachusetts,
to the great consternation of the New Hampshire Council, withdrew
the Massachusetts troops that had spent the winter in New Hampshire.[26] The following year, however, Massachusetts again sent sixty
soldiers to her neighboring province.

During these years, the people of New Hampshire outside of prospering Portsmouth felt the pressures of war and poverty in a manner
similar to that of the settlers of Maine, who on the whole were more

seriously affected. The New Hampshire Assembly, responding to a request from Lieutenant Governor John Usher for higher taxes, promised to raise enough to pay the provincial debt and to meet a proposal from Massachusetts to send sixty soldiers into New Hampshire for six months if New Hampshire would supply their food and ammunition and a third of their pay. The legislators jumped at this chance to reinforce their frontiers "against our French and Indian enemy, of whose invasion there is great cause to fear." On the other hand, the Assembly refused to vote supplies for repairing the fort at Great Island, which, understandably, seemed less necessary to the representatives of farmers from Dover, Exeter, and Hampton than to the merchants of Portsmouth. The assemblymen complained to Usher that "the Province is not capable to raise supplies for those ends, the rate now being the greatest ever was raysed in this Province, notwithstanding of our being greatly wasted and impoverished by the present war." [27]

The attack on Durham in 1694, New Hampshire's worst blow in either of the first two colonial wars, necessitated measures by the province government for the relief of war victims. William Graves, who had been wounded in the raid, prayed for "succour and reliefe" to help him support himself and pay his "Chirurgeon." The response to Graves's petition has disappeared from the records, but Usher and the Council previously had authorized a collection for the "supply of the poor people of Oyster River." [28]

2

The hardships that the people of Maine and certain parts of New Hampshire confronted at the opening of the eighteenth century, then, compared closely with those that the men of the fishing settlements had faced nearly a century before. The main end of these people, like that of the first fishermen, was to make a living. It is surprising to find that amid real or threatened death and destruction, privation, and hardship, they found the time and the will for as many of the normal concerns of human life in organized society as they did. The records disclose a mode of life in these communities that reflected a definite desire, at least on the part of the magistrates, for decent social conduct, but one which at the same time bore the earthy stamp of the social tradition that fishermen had founded on a wilderness coast.

The amount of strong drink consumed in the towns east of the Piscataqua must have been prodigious. The Court of Sessions sitting at York in July, 1690, found it necessary to correct the "severall abuses taken notice of in ordinaryes by excessive Drinking of rum, flipp, etc." by prohibiting tavern owners from selling intoxicants to local residents "Except in Case of great necessity as in Case of sickness." Nor, stated the ruling, "shall an ordinary keeper sell unto any stranger more than one gill for a person at one time." * The prohibition suggests that the court looked upon public houses as existing solely for the use of travelers and visitors.† If this was the case, however, it is difficult to understand how the authorities could have justified the large number of licenses in effect from 1690 to 1710—or how their proprietors all could have stayed in business.

Apparently the order was only a temporary one or one which, if it remained in legal effect, never was enforced. It went beyond the regulations imposed in other colonies, to which those of Maine tended to conform. When Joan Crafts received a license in 1695 to keep what became an important tavern at Kittery Point, the only conditions were that she prohibit gambling, that she allow only members of her own family in the house on the Sabbath, that she deny intoxicants to apprentices, servants, Indians, and Negroes, and that she not "suffer any person or persons to be there after nine of the Clock in the night or otherwise contrary to good order and rule." [29]

It was at Kittery, to which some of the Shoals fishermen had moved after the decline of the islands as a fishing center, where taverns were the most numerous. Perhaps Kittery needed more public accommodations than the other towns in Maine. It was a minor port town which shared Piscataqua Harbor with Portsmouth, and was also

---

* *Province and Court Records of Maine*, III, 293. A gill was a quarter of a pint, or four fluid ounces. By comparison, the modern ounce-and-a-half "shot" appears tame indeed.

† These establishments were called indiscriminately inns, taverns, ordinaries, or houses of public entertainment. The court records use the last term almost invariably. I have not been able to discover in the Maine records any distinction among these various terms in law or usage in this period. Carl Bridenbaugh has found that although no sharp distinction could be made in the larger towns during the colonial period, an "inn," generally speaking, was a public house for the lodging and entertainment of travelers, a "tavern" a public taproom or dram shop, and an "ordinary" a house serving a public meal at a fixed price. "Retailers," who abounded in Maine as well as in the large colonial towns, sold liquor in small quantities but provided no food or lodging. See Carl Bridenbaugh: *Cities in the Wilderness* (New York, 1955), p. 108 *n.*; see also his discussion of seaport taverns, pp. 107–15. In Maine and New Hampshire, as elsewhere, the tavern was important to the official and social life of the colonial community and indispensable to the traveler. Houses of public entertainment not only were sanctioned by the Maine authorities, but were required as part of any town's public facilities. Between 1680 and 1690, grand juries presented Falmouth twice and Scarborough once for failing to keep public houses for the entertainment of strangers. *Province and Court Records of Maine*, III, 134, 267, 284.

the ferrying point on the eastern side of the Piscataqua and a natural stopping place on the only road to Falmouth. Whatever the reasons, Kittery, with between eight and nine hundred men, women, and children, could boast in 1696 of no less than ten licensed "publick houses of entertainment," which is four more than the important seaport of Newport, Rhode Island, had in 1680.[30]

Unlike a few of their urban counterparts to the south, none of the frontier taverns, as far as the records of this period show, took on the character of a bawdy house. Even without organized vice, however, many wild seeds were sown. When the results of such escapades became too obvious to hide, the partners normally married.

The courts were lenient with regard to premarital relations between betrothed persons. Such conduct did, however, violate the law, and when the offense was discovered, both partners were forced to appear in court, even though they had married in the meantime. Cases of simple fornication, most frequently between persons subsequently married, were the most numerous of all offenses punished by the Maine courts between 1692 and 1711. These ran somewhat ahead of Sabbath offenses and profanity, and considerably ahead of violations of the liquor laws. No evidence was ever taken in such cases, and the punishment generally was from five to eleven stripes "on the naked back" or fines ranging from twenty to fifty shillings, plus a five-shilling court fee. In nearly every case, it appears, the newlyweds escaped the humiliation of the lash by paying the fine, not infrequently after it had been reduced "by humble petition" of the defendants.

Members of leading families were not exempt from prosecution for this rather common offense, nor did such prosecution stand in the way of future distinction. On April 2, 1695, Abraham Preble, Jr., of York and Mary Bragdon, whom he had married not quite soon enough— eight months previously—were presented for fornication. They "owned the Fact" and were sentenced to pay fifty shillings and fees or receive five stripes each. They paid the fine. They came from two of the most prominent families in town, and Abraham's uncle sat on the bench of the court that passed judgment. The young man became town clerk of York two years later, a selectman in 1700, a deputy to the General Court twelve times between 1702 and 1719, and a justice of the courts from 1715 until his death in 1724.[31] Nineteen years to the week after the sentencing of Abraham and Mary Preble, a grand jury presented their daughter, Mary (whose early arrival had been the cause of her parents' trouble), for precisely the same offense, and her marriage to Samuel Bray was off to the same inauspicious start.[32]

The courts made much more detailed inquiries and passed more severe judgment in cases of suspected adulterous or promiscuous behavior. Adultery, a capital offense by Massachusetts law, was difficult to prove, however. It may have been because the people of Maine believed the prescribed punishment to be unwarranted that in the few cases of extramarital sexual relations tried in these years, the defendants either were dismissed for want of evidence or convicted for a lesser offense such as fornication or "lewdness." [33]

Relations between the sexes frequently took a boisterous turn, and the uncouth contemporary reports of such matters perhaps tell more about this rough society than the escapades themselves. John Amee was convicted in 1703 at York of "unchristianlike behaviour" and "much rudeness," for which he was publicly admonished and ordered to pay sixteen shillings eight pence in court costs. The depositions in the case, taken down in the handwriting and crude spelling of the senior William Pepperrell, show that John had visited Sarah Tenney, an ancient maid of 23, demanding, "by God," that she fulfill on the spot a coquettish promise made on a previous occasion. Sarah was in no mood to oblige, whereupon the impulsive youth decided to use force. Sarah fought back, while four witnesses looked on. Here is how one of them, a young friend of Sarah's named Elizabeth Tyler, described the action:

> Shee run behind my back and he Puled her oute and Said he would kik and nok you and said Sarah Tinny asked said Mee [Amee] where he would nok her with a hatchet or hamer but he said he would nok her with his Prick and then the said John Amee took away the said Tinys [Tenney's] niting worke from her and then she Flew to his hed and took hold of his hare and the said Mee bed her let goe his hare or elce he would Kick her as and withall threw her downe and him fell a Top of her and all her Close was up about her. . . .

Sarah finally drove off her assailant with a gun and murderous threats, for which she, too, was ordered to receive "Public Admonition" in court "for her Rudeness." The court apparently agreed in part, at least, with James Foy, another witness, who observed laconically that "She had no need to a strived so much For I saw no Hurt don." [34]

The robust spirit that marked John Amee's approaches to his beloved was common, not only in affairs of the heart but also in relationships among neighbors. There were frequent quarrels over possession or use of pieces of pasture, timber, or marsh land, accusations of theft, or matters of less import. The family feud, while perhaps not a characteristic institution of life in northern New England, is not unique to Sicily or Appalachia, as the Maine court records demonstrate.*

There is much evidence to support Francis Parkman's description of the state of society at Wells during the first decade of the eighteenth century, soon after attempts to organize a Puritan church in the community:

> In spite of . . . efforts to maintain public worship, they were far from being a religious community; nor were they a peaceful one. Gossip and scandal ran riot; social jealousies abounded; and under what seemed entire democratic equality, the lazy, drunken, and shiftless envied the industrious and thrifty. Wells was infested, moreover, by several "frightfully turbulent women," as the chronicle styles them, from whose rabid tongues the minister himself did not always escape; and once, in its early days, the town had been indicted for not providing a ducking-stool to correct these breeders of discord.[35]

Shades of the old Isles of Shoals!

3

At the beginning of the eighteenth century, the eastern towns varied immensely in the complexity of their economic organization. At one extreme was the society composed of merchants, professional men, shopkeepers, artisans, husbandmen, sailors, fishermen, and laborers that already flourished at Portsmouth; at the other were the simple fishing colonies and trading posts far to the east, which still carried on in the fashion of the seventeenth century. Most typical were the small but slowly developing coastal towns from Kittery to Falmouth and their somewhat more civilized counterparts in New Hampshire— Exeter, Hampton, Dover, Newcastle, Stratham, and Kingston. According to location, the basic occupations in such communities were fishing, farming, and lumbering. Seldom, however, did a man confine his attention to one of these pursuits alone.

A recent biographer of the Pepperrells suggests that the separation

---

* See, e.g., *Province and Court Records of Maine*, IV, 68–9, where we find the incomplete but entertaining account of a bound-running feud between Nathaniel Raynes and Arthur Beale, and testimony taken with what appears to have been a vicious assault upon John Woodman by Isaac Remich and John Staple, resulting from a former disagreement. Remich and Staple were each fined twenty shillings and assessed five shillings court costs and bound to good behavior. The bonds were released three months later.

of Berwick from Kittery in 1713 probably had an economic as well as an ecclesiastical basis. The residents of the more sparsely populated Berwick, formerly upper Kittery, had larger landholdings and were more concerned with lumbering and farming than those of Kittery Point, who followed maritime pursuits. The difference between the two towns, he points out, was one of emphasis. Many of the shipwrights and mariners of Kittery Point lived on small farms and subsisted partly from the produce of their lands, though their incomes were from the sea. The farmers of Berwick, on the other hand, earned what profit they made from their lands "and frequently sent their surplus sons to sea." [36]

As village life developed, the need for more specialized callings grew with it. Two of the first such services required by every community in the region were those provided by the operators of sawmills and gristmills. The many rivers and streams that made mills possible also made reliable ferrymen a necessity. From the beginning, the farmer of northern New England developed a propensity for turning his hand to nearly every sort of artisanship, from wood-turning to tinsmithing, that was necessary to the maintenance of a small farm. Nevertheless, certain craftsmen such as blacksmiths and tinkers had set up shops in the villages by the eighteenth century. Ships and boats were built at Kittery as well as at Portsmouth, and shipwrights and coopers appear in the Maine records of the period along with an occasional bricklayer, carpenter, merchant, schoolmaster, surgeon, and tailor.[37]

The men who toiled at nearly all of these occupations were in some degree custodians of the practical attitudes, the robust behavior, and the salty language of the West Country men who had crossed to America to catch fish a century before. The fishermen and their successors imparted to the society of northern New England a tendency toward self-sufficiency, a tolerance of hardship, and a cheerful eccentricity. The heritage of the fishermen alone, however, was not sufficient to bring a successful civilization to fruition under hostile conditions, for these men also brought their material motives, their tinges of hedonism, their lack of self-control, and their indifference to most community values. These, too, were a part of the fishermen's tradition and, like the positive part of it, were still influencing the life of northern New England at the beginning of the eighteenth century. That a settled society was established in this barbaric corner of the land during the colonial period is due in large measure to the successes of Puritan imperialism from Massachusetts Bay.

CHAPTER VI

The Conquest Bears Fruit
1660–1732

1

Under the rule of Massachusetts, the settlers beyond the Merrimack came gradually to accept the society of the Bay proper as the model for theirs. There was good reason. The government of Massachusetts, which on the whole was both reasonable and effective, aroused the admiration of most of those whose interests did not definitely conflict with those of the Puritan regime.

This was most obviously the case in Hampton, Dover, and Exeter, where the population either had been largely Puritan in the beginning or had become so. But even in Maine, where religious attitudes most often were indifferent at best, there is evidence that the reaction to the new order was in large measure definitely favorable. When the King's commissioners separated the province from Massachusetts in 1665, twenty-two Casco men professed their attachment to the Puritan colony in a memorial to the King. The first signature was that of the influential George Cleeve, who at first had opposed annexation. The memorial praised the administration of Massachusetts, affirming that "her maxims of policy, prudence and moderation, and her principles of amity and justice, so much the causes of her own eminence, have since our short connexion with her, been the means of our contentment and prosperity, far beyond what we have enjoyed during any former period of the same length." [1] It did not take a sanctified Puritan to appreciate the improvement in security and social stability that the new regime had brought.

A still more fundamental reason for the easterners' acceptance of the Massachusetts social model was the existence at the Bay of some positive standards of community life and the absence of such standards in New Hampshire and Maine. It was natural to fill this void when possible with the ready-made model, just as their conquerors had filled the political void.

With respect to certain of these standards, there was no choice. Though the General Court might allow a more liberal freemanship in the eastern parts than existed in the home province, Massachusetts law required the establishment of town churches and prohibited the unauthorized practice of religion.

The magistrates of the eastern courts were understanding in their enforcement of the requirement for churches. To pay a minister, if one could be found who was ready to sacrifice a lifetime in the wilderness, would have been a severe hardship for a tiny settlement such as those at Falmouth or Wells, where John Wheelwright's church had died out when he moved to Hampton. Moreover, since most of the Maine magistrates almost certainly valued churches for their potential social usefulness rather than for their nature as a communion of saints, there was not the urgency in the matter that one might have found in Boston or in Plymouth.

The authorities in Maine, who were not in the habit of debating doctrinal niceties and undoubtedly would have accepted any ministers they could find, sometimes ordered temporary provisions for "aedification on the Lords day" in towns that lacked churches and ministers. In 1659, the county court ordered all the people of Falmouth to meet "from tyme to tyme" for Bible reading, psalm singing, praying, and reading "the labours of known and orthodox divines." This was to suffice "till the favour of god shall soe fare smyle upon them as to give them better means for their aedification." [2] In 1661, the court directed a similar order to Wells. This time, the magistrates appointed two men by name to "improve there best abilitys" in singing psalms, praying, and "readeing some good orthdox [sic] sermons as may most tend to the aedification of those that heare, and the scantification [sic] of the sabboth as the Laws of god and this Jurisdiction doth require." [3]

The people of Maine got along with such makeshift religious services and short-lived attempts at church organization as they could or were willing to devise until 1673, when the Reverend Shubael Dummer was ordained over the first permanent church in the province at York. [4] In New Hampshire, only Portsmouth was without a church from the beginning of Massachusetts rule. There, Joshua Moodey began to preach regular sermons in 1688, and was later installed as pastor of the church that was organized in 1671.[5]

One might expect to find a comparatively tolerant or indifferent attitude toward religious diversity among the basically reluctant Puritans of the north. Curiously, however, the northern New Englanders in some cases, especially in New Hampshire, pursued their duty to suppress error with great zeal. Three itinerant Quaker women visited New Hampshire in 1662, and found the Massachusetts law against the "cursed sect" being rigorously enforced. Acting under a special commission from the General Court, Captain Richard Waldron had the women seized at Dover and imposed the standard punishment for "vagabond Quakers": whipping at the tail of an ox cart through a succession of towns to the borders of the province. In this case, Waldron ordered ten lashes in each of eleven towns, beginning with Dover and ending with Dedham, Massachusetts. The sentence was carried out in the dead of winter, the women stripped to the waist. Fortunately for them, however, they were freed at Salisbury after having undergone punishment only in Dover and Hampton.[6]

During sporadic visits to the northeastern coast between 1662 and 1692, traveling Quakers made numerous converts from Hampton to Falmouth, despite repeated harsh treatment, especially at the hands of the Puritan authorities in Dover and Hampton. The most eminent convert was Major Nicholas Shapleigh, the leading man at Kittery and a constant opponent of Massachusetts authority in Maine. When the Bay government reasserted its jurisdiction in Maine in 1668, the commissioners found the entire town government of Kittery in the hands of Quakers.[7] The Quaker writers noted their relatively kind reception by the people of Maine, where, in contrast to the rather bloody record of New Hampshire, there seem to have been only two instances in which members of the sect received corporal punishment, both in 1671.[8]

The eastern officials' only encounter with Baptists until after 1750 was at Kittery, where William Screven arrived on the scene from Salisbury, Massachusetts, in 1673. He became connected through marriage with the Cutt and Champernowne families, both of which championed the Gorges interests, and in 1679 joined other Kittery residents in petitioning for direct royal control of Maine on the ground that Massachusetts was suppressing religious freedom. Screven was baptized and licensed to preach by the Baptist church in Boston in

1681, and shortly began to hold Baptist meetings in Kittery. Captain Francis Hooke, the Kittery magistrate, found these activities particularly obnoxious, and began to fine persons who attended Screven's meetings. Despite a fine and an order by the court to leave the province, Screven continued to hold meetings at his house. At his request, a Baptist elder of the Boston church came in 1682 to preside at the gathering of a church at Kittery. Ten men and several women signed the covenant and installed Screven as elder. Under repeated harassment by the courts, the congregation finally disbanded and Screven went in 1695 or 1696 to South Carolina, where he founded the first Baptist church in the southern colonies.[9]

Maine and New Hampshire both remained untouched by the Salem and Boston witchcraft scare of 1692 and 1693; the few scattered cases of investigations of witchcraft in the region recorded before then are neither serious nor significant. It is true that the eccentric Rachel Fuller stirred the suspicions of her Hampton neighbors and a coroner's jury in 1680, and at the same time drew renewed attention to poor old Eunice Cole, who was trying to live out the rest of her life peacefully in Hampton after having spent twelve years in a Boston prison for witchcraft. The episode, however, resulted in the conviction of neither.[10]

In 1693, the New Hampshire General Assembly passed an ecclesiastical act modeled upon the laws of Massachusetts—but with important differences. The statute permitted, but did not require, the freeholders of any town, by vote of a town meeting, to hire a minister of their own choosing. He would then "be accounted the Setled Minister of the Towne," and be paid by an assessment of rates. No qualifications for the minister, such as "able, learned, and orthodox," were prescribed, as in Massachusetts law, and persons "Conscientiously" of a "different perswassion" who "Constantly attend the public worship of God on the Lords day according to their own perswassion" were to be excused from paying the ministerial tax. As a practical matter, the exclusion provision was a dead letter both at that time and when the law was re-enacted in 1714, since there were none but Congregational churches then in the province. The law, nevertheless, was more liberal than its Massachusetts model and demonstrates again the incomplete nature of the Puritan conquest. The same law required every town, "Dover onely Excepted Dureing the War," to provide a town schoolmaster or forfeit £10 per year.[11]

2

Gradually through the closing decades of the seventeenth century, a handful of Harvard-trained ministers left Massachusetts Bay to settle in the eastern parts. By 1700, there were nine of them, only five of whom were at that time ordained as pastors over regularly constituted churches.[12] Except for John Cotton at Hampton and John Pike at Dover, who were serving well-established churches with ancient Puritan roots, not a man in this hardy fraternity was over thirty years old. The youngest was Samuel Moody, who had arrived in York in 1698 at the age of twenty-two.

All of the ministers had been born and raised in the same neighborhood, near the mouth of the Merrimack. Nathaniel Rogers of Portsmouth, John Newmarch of Kittery, and John Wade of South Berwick were from Ipswich, where as boys they had listened to the preaching of Rogers's father, later the president of Harvard. John Clark of Exeter, Samuel Emery of Wells, and Samuel Moody of York had come from Newbury.* John Pike of Dover, about twenty years older than most of these young men, nevertheless fitted the pattern, having come from nearby Salisbury.[13]

The remaining two clergymen had been born in New Hampshire. John Cotton of Hampton was the son of the Reverend Seaborn Cotton and grandson of the famous John Cotton of the first Puritan generation. A Harvard classmate of Cotton Mather, John had filled the vacancy in the Hampton pulpit left by his father's death in 1686.[14] Samuel Moody of the Isles of Shoals, a second cousin of his namesake at York, was the son of the Reverend Joshua Moodey of Portsmouth (the only member of this extensive clan to spell his name with an "e"), revered by Puritan historians for his feud with Governor Cranfield in the 1680's. This Samuel seems to have felt a stronger call to the military life than to the ministry. After briefly filling preaching assignments at Hadley, Massachusetts, the Isles of Shoals, and Newcastle, he led a company of militia on an expedition to Newfoundland and later

---

* *Sibley's Harvard Graduates* (for complete citation, see the *List of Frequent Abbreviations*, p. 363), III, 379–82; IV, 39–41, 52–75, 99–101, 179–81, 356–65. Nearly all these young ministers seem to have led exemplary lives. John Wade, however, who was chaplain and physician to the garrison at Brunswick before he began to preach at Berwick, had been expelled from Harvard for adultery. He was later readmitted, took the M.A. in course, and married the daughter of John Gerrish of Dover. He settled in Berwick in 1699, and was ordained at the gathering of a church in 1702, but died a year later. His successor, Jeremiah Wise, also came from Ipswich.

commanded the fort at Casco Bay. There, he became a leader in the settlement of Falmouth Neck.*

Several of the Maine ministers had begun their careers in the pay of the General Court as chaplains to frontier garrisons during King William's War. Such an appointment determined the lifetime fate of young Samuel Moody, and went far toward planting Massachusetts values in the southwestern corner of Maine. Arriving at his post in York less than a year after taking his first degree, Moody found the town a physical and moral shambles. "When I first came hither," related a young soldier who had been sent from Massachusetts to the York garrison, "there was no settled minister, and very little of so much as the form of religion; but on the contrary an abundance of levity and vanity, although it was soon after the destruction of a great part of the town by the Indians." [15] The stone gaol, built in 1653 to comply with Massachusetts law, the meetinghouse nearby, and five two-story garrison houses spread along the east side of the York River were not burned during the massacre of 1692. Other, smaller dwellings must have been built subsequently to replace some of those that had been destroyed, but the general appearance of the sparse colony still was desolate.

There were fewer than two hundred survivors, divided into two groups. Along the lower reach of the York River stretched the homes of the descendants of the English colonists whom Gorges had sent to America to found his city of Gorgeana. The greatest concentration of these small houses was about two miles upstream, where several

* *Sibley's Harvard Graduates,* III, 406–9. Strictly speaking, there was a tenth minister—and sixth church—in the area which now comprises Maine and New Hampshire. In 1685, after preaching there for six years, the Reverend Thomas Weld was ordained over a church organized the same day at Dunstable. The settlement was located twenty-five miles up the Merrimack Valley from Haverhill, the nearest downriver town, and that part of it which was first settled emerged on the north side of the boundary line when it was later drawn between Massachusetts and New Hampshire. One could also add to the list, though his ministerial status was much less definite than that of any of the others, the name of Dr. John Buss, who preached at regular religious services in addition to serving as physician at the Oyster River settlement in Dover, even though this section had not yet been set apart as a distinct parish and Buss had never been ordained. He arrived at Oyster River in 1682 from Wells, Maine, where he had apparently also preached and served as physician for a time. No church was formally gathered at Oyster River (later the town of Durham) until 1718. Unlike most of the frontier clergy discussed here, Dr. Buss was about sixty years old in 1700. *Sibley's Harvard Graduates,* II, 388–91; Elias Nason: *A History of the Town of Dunstable, Massachusetts* (Boston, 1877), pp. 26–33; Everett S. Stackpole and Lucien Thompson: *History of the Town of Durham, New Hampshire* (Concord, N.H. [1913]), I, 171–4, II, 47; New Hampshire Historical Society *Collections,* V (1837), 135–6.

cottages were clustered about the gaol and meetinghouse about a half-mile east of the riverbank. In a smaller, separate settlement about three miles up the river from this village were the dwellings of several Scottish families whose fathers had fled the British Isles after taking part in the unsuccessful royalist invasion from Scotland in 1648.[16]

The town was reduced to a primitive economic state. The house-holders in the vicinity of the village and in "Scotland," as the upper settlement was called, lived mainly by farming. Most of the predom-inant yeomanry had modest holdings; the property of some seems barely to have been sufficient for survival. John Harmon, whose estate was inventoried in 1695, was a substantial yeoman of better-than-average means. He owned a dwelling house and barn on a ten-acre home lot, about seventy acres of farmland in other divisions, an ox, six cows, eleven head of young cattle, four calves, eleven sheep and six lambs, fourteen swine, a horse and a mare, two guns and a cutlass, a modest amount of furniture, and some farm implements. These in-cluded a few woodsman's tools such as wedges and axes. The whole estate was valued at £296.[17] John and Samuel Twisden, whose joint inventory was taken the same year, possessed property worth some-thing over £27. This included about fifty-five acres of land, but the bulk of the estate consisted of domestic implements such as pewter-ware, glass bottles, pots, and "20 pounds of old feathers." [18] Thomas Curtis, a yeoman, owned forty acres of land worth £40, a house and barn worth £35, a bed and bedding, clothing, three cows, four heifers, a young ox, and miscellaneous utensils, making an estate valued altogether at £106 15s.[19]

The Reverend Mr. Moody found that the major part of his duties as chaplain consisted of preaching to the impoverished inhabitants in the meetinghouse of the only organized church in Maine. The con-gregation had been served for thirty years by Shubael Dummer, a victim of the massacre of 1692. Many church members had been killed or captured, and during the few years that Mr. Dummer's place re-mained unfilled, the survivors had reacted in the usual way to the pressures of war and poverty.

Moody's salary as a provincial chaplain ended with the close of the war in 1699. Though the town in its destitute state could not support him properly, he determined to stay. To his petition for a subsidy, the General Court responded readily with a grant of £12; the town voted a salary of £30 and built him a house twenty-four feet wide and twenty-eight feet long, lengthened still more by the addition of a two-story lean-to. The parsonage, standing next to the meeting-

house and surrounded by a stockade of oak and hemlock logs fitted
with elevated "flankers," or shooting platforms, must have been one
of the first substantial postwar additions to the village. It remained
a center of the religious and social life of the town until it burned
in 1744. While his parishioners were building the parsonage, Moody
returned to Cambridge, where he took the M.A. in 1700. On his return
to York with his wife, a Newbury girl whom he had married in 1698,
the church ordained him as pastor.[20]

For the next forty-seven years, "Father" Moody, as he became
known, ruled as spiritual dictator of his adopted community while he
saw it evolve from a frontier hamlet into a Puritan town, and the
church grow from about twenty members to more than three hundred.[21] His fiery temperament, iron will, and sulfurous theology were
exactly suited to his formidable task of molding his unruly flock into
a sober Puritan congregation. As a pastor of unquestioned soundness
and ability, he won the respect of the General Court, which invited
him to preach the election sermon in 1721, and of his Massachusetts
colleagues, who sent him in 1723 and 1724 as a missionary to Rhode
Island, where he organized the First Congregational Church in Providence. As a successful revivalist in his own community during the
Great Awakening, Moody, a "New Light" but an opponent of separatism, earned the admiration and friendship of both George Whitefield and Jonathan Edwards. As the colorful eccentric who was feared
and loved by two generations of York parishioners whom he coaxed
and at times coerced into moral reform and spiritual regeneration, he
became the subject of a lasting local legend.

Moody's methods were direct and unsophisticated, admirably suited
to the plain folk with whom he dealt. He devoted his pastoral rounds
strictly to business, whether emptying the York taverns before the
Saturday sundown initiated the Puritan Sabbath or planting himself
stubbornly in the home of a parishioner until he heard the flustered
man lead his family in prayer.

Mr. Moody fearlessly rebuked his hearers from the pulpit, sometimes by name. Hearing that one of his few prosperous parishioners
had stored away corn in a time of shortage in the hope of driving
up the price, the minister preached from the text, "He that with-
holdeth corn, the people shall curse him; but blessings shall be upon
the head of him that selleth it." Annoyed that the guilty one appeared
unmoved by his remarks, though they were hitting continually closer
to the mark, Father Moody finally shouted, "Colonel Ingraham, Colonel
Ingraham, you know that I mean you; why don't you hang down

your head?" Of the same colonel's richly dressed wife, Moody announced to his congregation as she strutted into the meetinghouse one Sabbath, "Here she comes, top and top-gallant, rigged most beautifully, and sailing most majestically; but she has a leak that will sink her to hell." [22]

Parson Moody devoted a substantial part of many of his sermons to depicting the delights of heaven and, at much greater length, the agonies of hell. "Suppose thou wert cast Naked into a deep Pit, full of Toads, Serpents, Vipers, and Adders, that would crawl over thy Flesh, and in at thy Mouth," he suggested to a youthful congregation in 1701. He added that this would be "nothing to what thou are like to Endure throughout the Endless Ages of Eternity." [23] In the most famous of his sermons, *The Doleful State of the Damned; Especially such as go to Hell From under the Gospel,* Moody again relied heavily upon vivid imagery: "Now, if we can't bear the Top of a Finger, for a few Minutes, in the flame of a Candle, much less an Hand or Foot in a fiery Oven; what will it be to be swallowed up in a flaming Lake, of the most Terrible, Raging Fire?" *

Ten of Moody's sermons and three other of his works appeared in published form, six of them in multiple editions.[24] Three of the most popular of them reflect Moody's early concern, probably for good reason, with the moral and spiritual state of the children and youth of his parish. *The Vain Youth Summoned to Appear at Christ's Bar,* published for the first of four times in 1707, six years after Moody had delivered it at York in person, was the first publication of any Maine resident.[25] His concern for the young also shows up dramatically in his preface to *Judas the Traitor Hung up in Chains,* which was published once in 1714 and three times again in the 1760's, and, most obviously, in *Mr. Moody's Discourse to Little Children,* a sermon preached in 1721 and published for possibly the seventh time in 1813.

Mr. Moody attempted the conversion of small children out of

---

* *The Doleful State of the Damned* (Boston, 1710), p. 36. Moody, of course, was not the first (or the last) to use this particular figure. In 1650, even before the arrival of Mr. Moody's predecessor in York, Mrs. Jane Bond of that community gave remarkable evidence that she had somehow been influenced by such teaching, though not necessarily from Puritan sources. She testified to a court that while Robert Collins was in the act of raping her, she told him, "put your finger but a littell in the fier and you will not be able to Induer it, but I must suffer eternally: you burne in your lust. . . ." Collins was convicted of "Incontinencie" but not of "the forsement." *Province and Court Records of Maine,* I, 140, 143.

sheer terror. In the *Discourse to Little Children,* published at the height of his career in 1721, he wrote:

> Let me tell you, that if you don't *speedily turn* to the Lord, it will not be long before you will be burning and roaring in *hell.* . . . Can you bear to go to HELL? Your hearts are harder than iron, if you can think of it without trembling. I am persuaded some of you will be gone forever in a few weeks, if you are not converted. Some of you, I'm afraid, are grown *dead ripe in sin* already, and when you come to stand before the *judgment seat* of Christ, I will witness against you, and your Parents will witness against you. And what will you do when you come to be bound *hand and foot,* and flung into the mouth of the burning and bottomless pit? You'll cry out, O I can't go down there! but go you must, and lie there forever.[26]

It is apparent that Moody, using evangelistic language and techniques, was attempting his own version of the "harvest of souls" in York at the same time Solomon Stoddard was preparing the way for his grandson, Jonathan Edwards, in Northampton. It is instructive to notice that both these communities, York and Northampton, lay on the very outskirts of the Massachusetts civilization. The inhabitants of both were susceptible only to the most aggressive, vivid, and direct approaches by their ministers. No New England parson could hope to spread either Christianity or his culture on the frontier by approaching his task in the manner of a Harvard tutor. In such places as these— at least in New England—revivalism was born.

The effects of Mr. Moody's ministrations were not always evident at once, but he preached a powerful and uncompromising Christianity that reached well into the marrow of York society, far beneath the thin veneer of the openly pious. A notoriously profligate "young Man of the Place" suffered mortal internal injuries when he slipped and fell in the street on November 27, 1735. He lingered for a few days "in Distress of Conscience," vomiting blood and "lamenting his misspent Life, and giving most solemn and earnest Warnings to the many that came to visit him, especially young People and his vain Companions, that they would leave their evil Courses, and not put off their Repentance till a Death-Bed, as he had done." The dying youth urged one of his friends in particular to use all the money that he would otherwise spend on liquor to buy "good Books," and read them in the time that he would have spent in taverns. The account of the accident and the young man's extravagant penance found its way into the *New England Weekly Journal,* where it was placed by Parson Moody after the boy asked that the clergy "improve his Example for the Warning of others." The minister, no doubt, was only too happy to observe the belated results of his preaching and to have the opportunity to use the unconventional pulpit that was provided by a widely circulated newspaper. Still, he could not forbear expressing some doubts about the state of the youth's soul: "How God has disposed of the Soul of this poor young Man we cannot judge. . . . Tho' true Repentance is never too late, yet late Repentance is seldom true." [27]

Moody's influence upon the development of York was enormous. The wartime appointment of the young minister to its garrison and the subsequent willingness of the General Court to subsidize his meager livelihood with occasional modest grants were as important factors in civilizing this community as the Bay province's political dominion over Maine.

Soon after Moody had revived the church at York, the town turned its attention for the first time to the need for a public schoolmaster. Following a vote of the townsmen in 1701, the selectmen engaged Nathaniel Freeman to teach reading, writing, and "sifering" to "all persons . . . from five years old and upwards, that shall come." The town promised to build him a house and to pay him a yearly salary of £30. The school hours were from eight to eleven in the morning and from one to five in the afternoon. Similarly, the town voted £100 in the same period to Dr. Alexander Bulman in return for his agreement to settle in York as physician for the rest of his life.[28]

Father Moody was the most successful of the wilderness evangelists, and in York, therefore, the Massachusetts authorities could see the most conspicuous results of their imperial experiment. Once Puritan practices were introduced into the eastern parts, however, other towns began to show the results of the labors of their ministers, though none, perhaps, as dramatically. Churches were organized in Wells in 1701, South Berwick in 1702, Kittery in 1714, Scarborough and Falmouth in 1727, and the second, or "Scotland" parish in York in 1732. Some of these towns may have been encouraged by the example of York, and perhaps influenced by a propaganda scheme which the religious and business communities of Massachusetts devised in their campaign to secure complete dominion over the eastern settlements.

"Certain Gentlemen, Merchants, and others, of *Boston*," as they were styled on the title page, asked Cotton Mather to write a tract to serve as "an offer of the glorious *GOSPEL,* unto the Plantations (too Willingly) destitute of an *Evangelical Ministry."* Entitled *A Letter to Ungospellized Plantations,* the pamphlet was distributed in 1702 at the expense of the Boston group. Even at this early point in Moody's career, the missionary-minded Mather may have been calling upon the experience of York when he disposed of the objection that to hire a minister would be too expensive for a poor frontier town. He called such an objection "trifling," especially in view of the benefits to be anticipated. Experience had shown, he wrote, that towns which had seen to the establishment of a "Sanctuary of God" had been so rewarded "through the powerful and wonderful *Providence* of God," that "They have *not been one penny poorer at the years End, than they were before."* [29]

3

By means of political usurpation and practical defensive measures, and moved by a desire for economic expansion and an honest concern for souls, the Puritans of Massachusetts introduced their religious and social systems into the eastern parts. Under the influence of their laws and churches, much of southern New Hampshire was settled, and the unruly inhabitants of the southern Maine coast were in some measure domesticated. The magistrates and ministers of the Bible Commonwealth fell short of their goal of total conquest, and in some cases engendered lasting antagonisms. Their accomplishments, however, can scarcely be overstated. Before 1650, the eastern lands were inhabited for the most part by a people with resources but little economic organization, bravery but few defenses, and vigor but no direction. To this people, the Puritans brought protection, economic opportunity, a little education, some spiritual comfort, and the possibilities of orderly self-government. It would be difficult to argue that the conquest was not salutary.

CHAPTER VII

The Oligarchy Prospers
1700–1730

1

Nestled in crowded disorder between two millponds that emptied through sluiceways and over waterwheels into the Piscataqua, by 1700 the small gothic-style framed houses of Strawberry Bank formed the bustling nucleus of a thriving seaport town of about a thousand people. The center of population in Portsmouth had shifted over the past several decades to "the Banke" from Great Island, which since 1693 had been set off as the town of Newcastle. Between the few large properties on the riverbank, from which the grandees of Portsmouth society oversaw their docks and warehouses and conducted the affairs of the province, and an irregular stockade connecting the two millponds about a half-mile west of the river, lay the recently subdivided estate that had once belonged to Mason's "great house," now disappeared. Little high-posted two-story houses with sharply pitched gables, narrow brick chimneys, and tiny leaded casement windows were beginning to crowd what only recently had been a thousand-acre field, having already filled up much of the rest of the square mile of land bounded by the river, the millponds, and the sharpened posts of the stockade. In effect, Strawberry Bank was a small peninsula with its backside cut off from the rest of the mainland by a log fence.

The Portsmouth householders had built directly on the few narrow dirt streets. There were no sidewalks, and though there was room for sizeable backyards in most cases, little more than a walkway and perhaps an occasional small vegetable patch could be fitted between the sides of neighboring houses. In the center of the peninsula, however, was preserved twelve acres of open glebe land, part of the fifty acres set aside by the townspeople in 1640 for the support of an Anglican church. During the subsequent forty years of rule by Massachusetts, it had become appropriated for Puritan use. Here, the Reverend Nathaniel Rogers, a young man of thirty who presided over the congregation at the town's only meetinghouse, grew his corn.[1]

In one of the most densely settled parts of the waterfront, less than a quarter of a mile north of the South Mill Pond, a narrow inlet some eight hundred feet long rose and fell with the tide. During the century to come, the commercial activity of the town would center here at Puddle Dock, and eventually wharves would be built along the edges to supplement those that already jutted into the river nearby. From the wharves now owned by the Cutts, the Wibirds, the Penhallows, and the Vaughans sailed the two dozen locally owned ocean vessels, and around them clustered many smaller craft such as fishing shallops and river gundelows.[2]

Those few Portsmouth families which did not live at Strawberry Bank were scattered over a large adjoining area. Some lived at Odiorne's Point, the site of Thomson's colony; others lived nearby at Little Harbor, where Governor Benning Wentworth later satisfied his successive whims by adding rooms and wings to a rambling house.[3] Some were scattered westward, in what later became Greenland and Rye, and others northward, in the present town of Newington. Newcastle, though by this time a separate township, was close enough to the commercial and residential center of Portsmouth to be considered in most respects a part of the same community. The shores of Great Island, separated from the mainland only by a short ferry ride at the narrows, were crowded with modest houses much like the majority of dwellings at the nearby "Banke." [4]

Across the North Mill Pond from Strawberry Bank, Richard Jackson had built about 1664 a version of a fairly standard seventeenth-century English yeoman's house on his twenty-four-acre estate overlooking his shipyard.* The medieval features of the house relate it to sixteenth-century or early seventeenth-century England, either di-

---

* John Howells in *The Architectural Heritage of the Piscataqua* (New York, 1937) says the builder of the house was Richard Jackson's father, John. This is neither accepted by local antiquaries nor seems likely, inasmuch as Savage lists a John Jackson of Portsmouth who died about 1654, a decade before the house is believed to have been built. John left a son Richard, who came to Portsmouth with his father from England and took the oath of fidelity in 1656. See James Savage: *A Genealogical Dictionary of the First Settlers of New England* (Boston, 1860–2), II, 530–1. This house, the oldest known remaining building in Portsmouth, is open to the public.

rectly or by way of Massachusetts. Its steeply pitched roof, its small casement windows arranged in groups of three with leaded diamond-shaped glass panes, its bold lines, its massive oak frame, and its stark interior provided the owner with picturesque if severe living quarters. Colonists in Massachusetts were building houses of a similar style and equal or superior sophistication by the late 1630's. The front of the structure, facing the pond and Piscataqua harbor, has a full two-story elevation, but the rear portion of the steep roof sweeps dramatically down almost to the ground, its angle becoming slightly less abrupt as it approaches the bottom.[5]

One careful student of the architecture of the region has suggested that the existence of a ridge-pole and horizontal framing in the roof of the Jackson house, which was used in England but usually abandoned in favor of rafters in the shingled houses of New England, together with the extremely steep pitch of the roof and the availability of long, tough grass in nearby salt marshes, may indicate that Jackson originally covered his roof with thatch instead of shingles.[6] The suggestion is by no means implausible, and indeed the numerous references in the Maine court records to owning or cutting "thatch" in the marshes of nearby southern Maine lead us to speculate that the thatch-roofed cottage may well have been the dominant architectural feature of the region on both sides of the Piscataqua for a good part of the seventeenth century.[7]

One of the newer houses at the Bank had overlooked Puddle Dock since about 1695. Captain John Sherburne, a mariner then in his late forties, built a narrow, high-posted house which must have been comparable to all but the most pretentious Portsmouth dwellings of the late seventeenth century. Sherburne, who was among the many sons of one of Mason's first crew of settlers, seems, like many of his neighbors, to have moved to Strawberry Bank from Great Island. We can speculate that in his case, an obviously successful maritime career had made it possible to build a house in a growing, fashionable part of the community. There, he had the advantage of being only a few minutes' walk from the wharves, the homes, and the countinghouses of the great merchants, who must have been his employers.

The Sherburne house, which the captain lived to enjoy for only about three years, contained only one large room on each of its two seven-foot-high stories. A gabled dormer window jutted from the south side of the steep-roofed attic—an indication that the builder intended to use the third floor for living quarters. By the time Captain Sherburne moved to Strawberry Bank, the builders of Portsmouth had managed to shed an English tradition of long standing which dictated the use of oak for the frame of a house. The frame of his house was hewn largely from white pine, which is lighter, more easily worked, and just as durable as the traditional material. Undoubtedly, however, the housewrights of the region turned to pine framing only reluctantly because of the much greater availability of pine. The first known all-pine house frame in Portsmouth had been constructed as recently as 1671. Modest as Captain Sherburne's new house was, he did not neglect decorative touches. The corners of the high exposed posts were planed off carefully to form flat chamfers; the great summer beams overhead were furnished with more elaborate quarter round chamfers. The walls were plastered from floor to ceiling, and both the plaster and exposed parts of the frame were covered with whitewash. Up the east gable end of the house ran a massive chimney, with fireplaces on both the first and second floors.

Sometime shortly after 1700, at least by 1703, Captain Sherburne's widow, Mary, and her twenty-year-old son, Joseph, who was soon to begin an active career in town politics, exactly doubled the size of the house by attaching almost a duplicate of the original section, complete with a dormer window to match the first one, on the east side of the chimney.[8]

The seventeenth-century dwellings of the embryo Portsmouth gentry are gone. The grandest of these, the "great house" built as a storehouse and garrison house for Mason's colony by Humphrey Chadbourne in 1631 and occupied eventually by John Cutt, the first president and one of the biggest landholders of the colony, had fallen down in 1685. According to a claim by Robert Tufton Mason in 1679, this "was a very fair and large house of stone and timber, and by him called Mason Hall, encompassed by a ditch and strong palisade."[9] Certainly, none of the leading families lived in anything that could be called "very fair and large" in 1700. The scale and pretentiousness of their riverfront houses probably lay somewhere between the stark but substantial simplicity of the Jackson and Sherburne houses and a combined tavern and dwelling built at Strawberry Bank in 1671.

The builder of the tavern was Thomas Daniell, a wine merchant who had married a niece of John Cutt and was himself prominent in the politics of the province. When the new provincial government was organized in 1679, Daniell was among the councilors named in the royal commission. The building became the residence of Lieutenant Governor Edward Cranfield, and then the home of three generations of Wentworths. It was torn down some two and a half centuries after its erection, but thanks to surviving photographs and records and a preserved room and staircase in the Metropolitan Museum of Art, it has not entirely vanished.

The tavern, two and a half stories high and of unusually large dimensions for the period, was framed entirely of white pine rather than the oak that had been customary. Though the "original lean-to," or "saltbox" style still was popular in the larger New England houses at the time Daniell built his tavern,[10] the Portsmouth builders who erected this building displayed their independence from custom by using a centered ridge-pole, symmetrical gables, and a roof that sloped much less severely than was the fashion in 1671. The floor plan on both stories, however, was asymmetrical in order to provide larger rooms in the front of the house. Two parallel summer beams, instead of the usual one, showed through the plastered ceilings of each of the principal rooms. The floor joists that ran perpendicular to these beams, however, though frequently exposed in seventeenth-century houses, were concealed by the white plaster. This was true even of the attic floor joists in the ceilings of the second-floor rooms. The larger of the two front rooms on the second floor, together with one or more of the first-floor rooms, were for public use.[11] Only a handful of houses such as this tavern, most of them undoubtedly somewhat smaller, broke the essentially undistinguished monotony of the Portsmouth scene in 1700.

2

The royal governor of New Hampshire in that year was the Earl of Bellomont, who also held the governorship of Massachusetts and New York. New Hampshire had welcomed him in 1699 as a replacement for the unpopular Samuel Allen, who not only had continued to press the Masonian claim, but had also suspended several members of the Council. The provincial Council, consisting of Richard Waldron, John Hinkes, Nathaniel Fryer, Peter Coffin, and John Gerrish, and which by the Governor's order was soon again to include the displaced William Vaughan, met monthly with Lieutenant Governor William Partridge at a Portsmouth tavern.[12]

Very likely, the tavern was the one built at Manning and Dock Streets by Thomas Daniell in 1671. The building had been acquired from Lieutenant Governor Cranfield in 1683 by Samuel Wentworth, an innkeeper at Great Island. This astute businessman evidently had discerned that the growing center of Strawberry Bank would be a more profitable location for his hostelry.

Samuel was the eldest son of William Wentworth, an emigrant from Alford in Lincolnshire. William, a kinsman of Anne Hutchinson, and two of his cousins had followed John Wheelwright to Boston and then to Exeter in 1637. He had finally settled at Dover, where he cultivated a large farm and operated a sawmill. He also served as ruling elder of the Puritan church at Dover and, for more than forty years, as a lay preacher at Cocheco, South Berwick, Salmon Falls, and Exeter.[13] Samuel, the tavernkeeper, was active in public affairs and had connections with important people. He was a selectman of Portsmouth, the foreman of a grand jury, and an overseer of the will of Governor Walter Barefoote. He died in 1690, leaving the family business to his eldest son, Samuel Wentworth, Jr., who moved soon afterward to Boston to become one of that town's leading merchants. In 1700, therefore, the tavern must have been operated by his mother, Mary Benning Wentworth, with the help of some of the older of her other six children.

The innkeeper's third son, John, had been a lad of twelve when the family moved to Strawberry Bank. He apparently circulated freely among the men who congregated at the tavern to discuss the affairs of town, province, and commerce. The associations thus formed could hardly have been on a frivolous youthful level, especially after 1690. At that time, with his oldest brother in Boston and his other older brother at sea, John Wentworth, at the age of nineteen, shared with his mother the responsibility for a large fatherless family and the most important public house in the province.

In 1693, John Wentworth married Sarah Hunking* and about that time began a maritime career. From 1706 to 1708, he commanded a masting ship, but in 1709 took his place in the business and political community ashore. From his brother, he bought the family tavern, in which his and Sarah's fourteen children were born. At once, he set the style for Portsmouth's grand era by lining the public rooms with elaborate wainscoting and installing a handsome staircase with spiral balusters of oak.

When the next vacancy occurred in the province Council in 1712, John Wentworth was appointed to fill it. There he joined his father-in-law, Mark Hunking, a former speaker of the House, who had been named to the Council two years previously. A year after his appoint-

---

* The daughter of Mark Hunking, the sea captain whom President John Cutt and the Council had upheld against Randolph in 1680.

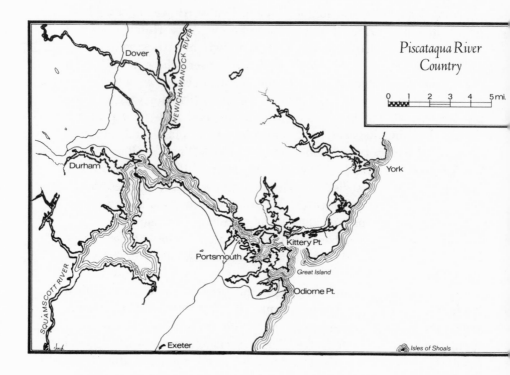

ment, Wentworth's official duties were expanded when he acquired a
seat on the Court of Common Pleas. The names of Hunking and Wentworth, though new at the Council table, were well known to the small,
closely knit business community of New Hampshire. John and his
father-in-law took their places easily, therefore, in the officialdom
of the day.[14]

Thus began the public career of John Wentworth, a good and
capable leader and public servant, who in later years made of the chief
magistracy of New Hampshire a family possession for three generations. Under his inspiration and supervision, the New Hampshire
oligarchy not only gained in wealth and power, but also became welded
together to an extraordinary degree by the ties of kinship. By the
middle of the eighteenth century, there was scarcely a mercantile
family in Portsmouth, including most of the oldest ones, that did
not have some connection by marriage with one of the fourteen Went-

worth children. Appointment of these affluent kinsmen to public posts was taken as a matter of course during the administrations of John as lieutenant governor from 1717 to 1730, and of his oldest son Benning as governor from 1741 to 1767.

3

Between 1700 and 1740, Portsmouth grew from fewer than a thousand to about 4,500 inhabitants, despite the loss during that period of Greenland, Rye, and Newington. Most of this rapid expansion took place during the generation following the Peace of Utrecht, but, unlike most of the towns to the east, Portsmouth had been spared from attack during Queen Anne's War, and her population had at least held its own even in wartime.[15]

The increase in population, because much of it resulted from immigration, reflected the town's growing prosperity, which provided new opportunities for merchants and artisans. The most important cause of economic growth undoubtedly was the settlement of the interior of New Hampshire, which began to take place in a small way after 1713 and more extensively after the grisly woods fight in 1725 in which John Lovewell of Dunstable and a band of his neighbors ended a series of troublesome raids on the border settlements by defeating, at terrible cost, the Pequawket Indians near modern Fryeburg, Maine.[16] A settled hinterland provided farm produce for consumption in the town, flax and forest products for export, and a growing market for English goods imported by Portsmouth merchants.

Throughout the eighteenth century, however, fishing and lumbering remained the principal bases of the Portsmouth economy. In 1747, Daniel Neal found the "produce" of New Hampshire to consist of boards, fish, masts, staves, timber, flax, hemp, and small amounts of tar and turpentine. Neal counted ninety water-driven saws in the province, and asserted that 130 yoke of oxen were constantly at work dragging logs to mills. This resulted in annual exports of more than six million feet of lumber, most of which went to Boston or the West Indies, from what Neal referred to with some exaggeration as "one of the noblest Rivers in *North-America*." [17]

The mechanics of Portsmouth's trade had changed little in a hundred years, except for the inclusion of a cash or credit feature which enabled West Indian or southern European importers to pay for

English manufactures sent directly to New Hampshire. Portsmouth sent boards, staves, shingles, and trash fish to the West Indies in return for sugar, molasses, cotton, wool, rum, and in some cases cash payments or bills of credit which were sent to England to be applied toward English cargoes that were being assembled for Portsmouth. New Hampshire's merchantable fish went to Spain and Portugal in return for some salt and wines, but principally for "remittances" to the English suppliers of cloth, clothing, cordage, metalware, and other manufactured items.[18] The coasting trade to Boston retained its importance, and in 1747, the Piscataqua region was the largest supplier of ships in New England with the exception of Boston. By 1769, the annual production of shipwrights at the Piscataqua totaled sixteen topsail vessels and twenty-nine sloops or schooners.[19]

By early in the eighteenth century, many of the most influential merchants of Portsmouth, including all the members of the Council,[20] had found that some of their best profits lay in owning sawmills and sawing lumber for export. William Partridge, a shipbuilder and lieutenant governor of the province from 1697 to 1703, had been a contractor for masts and ship timbers for the Royal Navy. It was discovered during his term of office, however, that he was also carrying on a lucrative lumber business with Portugal. Lord Bellomont's concern over the obvious fact that much of the Navy's potential mast supply in New England was being sawed up into boards, in part for foreign consumption, was largely responsible for a comprehensive naval stores policy that went into effect in 1705.[21]

Since 1685, a surveyor of pines and timbers had officiated in New England. The function of this official, whose title was later changed to surveyor general, was to supervise the hacking of the crowfoot-like "Broad Arrow" on trees that were to be reserved for the Navy, and then to protect the marked trees from private cutters. The first surveyor, Edward Randolph, had regarded the appointment as only a part-time job to supplement his income as secretary of the Dominion of New England. His successor, Jahleel Brenton, was an absentee official, and Brenton's deputy made a travesty of his office because he was involved in the lumber business himself.[22]

The Massachusetts charter of 1691 had reserved to the Crown all trees twenty-four inches in diameter or more that were not on private property. Until 1705, the provision was virtually a dead letter. In that year, Parliament placed naval stores, including masts, on the enumerated list, set bounties on tar, pitch, rosin, turpentine, hemp, masts, yards, and bowsprits, and appointed Jonathan Bridger the surveyor general.[23]

Modern historians have depicted Bridger, who as an agent for the Navy Board had been trying to enforce the "Broad Arrow" policy in New England since 1696, both as a conscientious, effective public servant and as an egotistical scoundrel.[24] Whatever his personal attributes, Bridger's vigorous campaign against private loggers and millmen quickly aroused universal antagonism throughout the Maine and New Hampshire forests.[25]

The developing oligarchy of New Hampshire had no less reason to oppose Bridger than the upstream woodsmen: first because of their interests in mills; and secondly because to contract for masts with the Navy required a huge and risky capital investment that did not justify the return. Benning Wentworth and his brother Mark Hunking Wentworth were the only New Englanders who ever made a fortune from the mast trade, and that was while Benning served as both governor of New Hampshire and surveyor general in the middle of the century.[26] Nevertheless, to give the appearance of cooperation with the Crown, the New Hampshire Assembly and Council bowed to the urging of Bridger in 1708 by passing an act providing for a fine of £100 for the unauthorized felling of white pines two feet or more in diameter.[27]

The Massachusetts General Court, again at Bridger's request, passed a similar act in 1711 to supplement the charter provision, and in 1721 a Parliamentary act prohibited the unlicensed cutting of *any* white pine tree, regardless of size, not growing within a township. The Act of 1721, the most stringent restriction yet, was essentially the product of Bridger's mind, as was the Act of 1729, which re-enacted the terms of the earlier law and provided better machinery for their enforcement.[28]

Bridger thus was the author of the British woodlands policy for New England, which remained in effect until the Revolution. The widespread hostility in Maine and New Hampshire to both the policy and the surveyor general resulted in constant violations, harsh physical treatment of Bridger's agents, almost innumerable lawsuits over titles to private property, the laying out of "paper townships" to evade the law, particularly in New Hampshire, and a political controversy which as early as the 1720's and 1730's helped widen the gap between the prerogative and the popular parties in Massachusetts.[29] Joseph J. Malone, the most recent writer on the forest policy and its consequences, argues convincingly that the "woodland rebellion" that resulted from Bridger's policies was in fact an early manifestation of the conflicts that eventually brought about American Independence.[30]

In New Hampshire, where the financial and political leadership of the province (with the exception only of the absentee governors in Boston) shared the attitude of the majority toward the proper use of the timberlands, sawed lumber remained a far more important element in the economy than masts. In 1717, the Council, in which the merchant aristocracy of Portsmouth predominated overwhelmingly, concurred with a vote of the Assembly requesting that the Governor complain to the King that Bridger had exceeded his authority by attempting to prevent "all persons in this Province from going into his Majesties woods to cut any sort of timber;—which, for want of a fair representation to his Majestie is very hurtful and ruinous to many of his good subjects." [31]

From 1712 to 1718, a period during which Britain received from her "plantations" 638 "great," 262 "middling," and eighty-eight "small" masts, Portsmouth merchants shipped these wood products to Lisbon and Cadiz alone: 2,176 oak timbers from thirty to thirty-five feet long, 98,925 oak planks, 3,035 oak joists, 43,880 pine planks, 22,-000 pine boards, 93,250 pipe staves, 42,360 hogshead staves, 5,470 oak bolts, 196 standards, twelve knees, 1,511 spars, eight bowsprits, 135 stocks, 1,100 ash rafters, 173 pine timbers (possibly meaning masts), and 152 carriage trucks.[32] An official complaint of 1715 described the situation in the New Hampshire forests as follows:

> . . . there being every winter great number of men and teams chiefly from Exeter sent up into the woods above the bounds and heads of the towns, where they cutt 1500 large pine trees and hall them in loggs into the river called Lampereale [Lamprey], and the great flowing of that river, with which rains bring them down to the rivers mouth; out of which they saw at least 2,000,-000 pine boards, besides oak planks; and as to masts and extraordinary oak timber, there is constantly transported to Spain and Portugal yearly great quantities.[33]

Besides supplying the Spanish and Portuguese shipyards with materials, much to the consternation of the British authorities, the merchants of the Piscataqua continued to send wood products to the West Indies and Boston. Naturally, an increasing volume of timbers and masts was also being used to meet the demands of local shipbuilders.

The political importance of the mast industry, therefore, was out of proportion to its contribution to the economy of the province. The Wentworths, who eventually drew immense profits from this trade as contractors with the Navy and, during Benning Wentworth's governorship, as owners of great tracts of upcountry timberland, were involved in the mast industry as early as 1706. In that year, the first John Wentworth was captain of *Lusitania Galley*, one of the mast ships then active in the Piscataqua trade.[34] During much of the eighteenth century, this remarkable family succeeded in securing both profits and royal favor through its contracts for masts and apparent concern for preserving the King's woods, while at the same time ignoring what had to be ignored in order not to alienate the great bulk of New Hampshiremen whose livelihood depended upon sawing trees into boards and timbers rather than preserving them for Navy masts.

By the middle of the eighteenth century, the traffic in all commodities in and out of Piscataqua harbor compared favorably with that of all but the very largest ports north of Philadelphia. During 1748, 121 vessels cleared for foreign ports from Portsmouth; entries from abroad numbered seventy-three. In addition, about two hundred coasting sloops and schooners carried lumber from the Piscataqua to Boston, Salem, Newport, and other American ports, and about a hundred such vessels entered from those ports with produce and other freight. These figures fell far short of Boston's 430 entries and 540 clearances in foreign trade during the same period, but combined foreign and coasting entries for New York during a similar period two years later exceeded the Portsmouth combined total by only about seventy, and the combined Portsmouth clearances exceeded the New York total by about thirty-five. The Portsmouth foreign trade fell slightly below that of Salem (the port of clearance for the entire North Shore from Marblehead to Newbury), slightly exceeded that of Newport, and doubled that of New London (the port for all of Connecticut). In combined foreign and coastal trade, Portsmouth's entries quadrupled those of Perth Amboy and her clearances totaled nearly eight times those of the New Jersey port.[35]

The prosperity and bustle of the waterfront were reflected in the multiplication of wharves and shipyards and occasional physical refinements that the merchants introduced to facilitate the handling of their ships and merchandise. One of the most striking of these appeared very early in the century. Sometime before 1705, Sampson Sheafe, a merchant who had begun his career in Boston, built a two-story warehouse at Strawberry Bank which extended into the river on a log footing, like a wharf. Gundelows and coasting vessels could dock underneath its projecting second story and load or unload their cargoes overhead. The structure, particularly useful in the rigorous climate of the Piscataqua, was about fifty feet long and stood about twenty-five feet high.[36]

4

In 1716, a relative newcomer to the Portsmouth mercantile clique built one of the finest urban residences in New England. Captain Archibald Macpheadris had come to New Hampshire from Ulster sometime early in the century and, first as a ship's captain and then as the owner of a fleet of at least six vessels, had quickly worked his way up in economic and social standing. In addition to his shipping interests, Macpheadris invested in interior lands and, together with John Wentworth and some of the leading Portsmouth merchants, in an iron works on the Lamprey River.[37] Perhaps with an amorous eye already on Sarah, the fourteen-year-old daughter of John Wentworth, the captain determined to erect a mansion that would be suitable for a bride from such a distinguished family.

Alone of his circle, he built of brick, probably made for the purpose in or near Portsmouth, and introduced to Portsmouth the architectural details of the early Georgian or Queen Anne period. The walls of his house, which were supported by brick underpinning, were fifteen inches thick. The side faced the street, and the central paneled doorway was surrounded by fluted pilasters with Corinthian capitals surmounted by a graceful segmental pediment. Three panes of "bullseye" glass in the upper panels of the massive door took the place of a transom. The handsome doorway was flanked by four windows, two on each side, each surmounted by a low arch in brickwork. Five windows, the middle one centered over the door, were placed evenly along the second floor of the façade, separated from the first floor by courses of brick laid in "Flemish bond." The third floor, used as servants' quarters, was under the eaves and contained five dormer windows on the front side, topped by alternating angular and segmented pediments. The brick wall on the south end was carried up beyond the slope of the roof to form a parapet between two end chimneys. The house was built originally with two parallel gabled roofs in imitation of a style popular in England in the period, but the valley between the peaks (which must have collected a great deal of snow) was soon covered with a low-pitched roof enclosed by a balustrade to form a gambrel roof. An octagonal cupola was added at the same time.

The first-floor rooms were eleven feet high, and the main parlor nearly twenty feet square, unusually spacious for the period. Fireplaces surrounded by Dutch tiles, a "marbleized" treatment of the dining room panels, painted murals on the walls of the hall, and a huge palladian window on the stair landing conveyed the builder's taste for luxury and ostentation. The house, like those of most Portsmouth merchants, overlooked the waterfront in order to give its owner a view of his wharf and ships.*

Captain Macpheadris brought his bride, Sarah Wentworth, to what was by far the best house in town in 1717, the same year that his father-in-law became lieutenant governor of New Hampshire. There were three children, one of whom died in infancy. As might be expected of a Wentworth relative, the captain joined the Governor's Council in 1722, but lived only seven more years. He died in 1729, probably not yet forty years old, leaving the large estate of £6,330, of which the house and gardens were appraised at £2,500. Included in his estate were lands in Londonderry, Chester, Nottingham, Barrington, Bow, Chichester, Barnstead, Gilmantown, Epsom, and Rochester, a small ship and her cargo, two Negro boys and a Negro girl, furniture,

---

* The Macpheadris house, now known as the Macpheadris-Warner house because it was occupied for fifty-four years by Macpheadris's son-in-law, Jonathan Warner, is preserved as a registered National Historic Landmark and is open to the public. In *Architectural Heritage of the Piscataqua*, John M. Howells repeats a tradition of long standing that Macpheadris spent what would have been the phenomenal sum of £6,000 to build his mansion. The appraisers of his estate in 1729, however, valued the house and gardens at only £2,500, leaving the figure of £6,000 open to serious doubt. William G. Wendell has speculated that at some time, the total inventory of £6,330 might have been mistaken for the cost of the house alone. Wendell and others have also questioned Charles W. Brewster's assertion in *Rambles About Portsmouth* (Portsmouth, 1859) that the bricks for the mansion were imported from Holland. The fact that the courses were laid in the fashionable style called "Flemish bond" might have given rise to the notion, but there is no documentation to support it. Neither is there documentary evidence that the bricks were made in New Hampshire, but local antiquaries generally feel that it is more likely that the bricks were made nearby than that they were imported from Europe. Descriptions and pictures of the house and treatments of its history may be found in Hugh T. Morrison: *Early American Architecture* (New York, 1952), pp. 478–80; Howells: *Architectural Heritage of the Piscataqua*, pp. 14–19; Strawbery Banke, Inc.: *Architecture near the Piscataqua* (Portsmouth, 1964), pp. 10–13; Geoffrey P. Moran: "A Survey of the Domestic Architecture of Portsmouth" (unpublished M.A. thesis, University of New Hampshire, 1967), pp. 56–62, 75–7, 86–9; and William G. Wendell: *Jonathan Warner (1726–1814), Merchant and Trader, King's Councillor, Mariner, Jurist* (Newcomen Society pamphlet, New York, 1950), pp. 26–7.

124 ounces of silverplate, a fourth part of the Lamprey iron works, and other lands in Portsmouth.[38]

Not for many years was another house of either the proportions or the refinement of the Macpheadris mansion built in Portsmouth. The captain had, however, shown the way to architectural distinction. It may have been his example that inspired the erection of many fine dwellings of somewhat more modest design during the next twenty years. About 1725, Henry Sherburne, merchant, member of the Council, treasurer and later chief justice of the province, husband of Lieutenant Governor Wentworth's sister Dorothy, and rich cousin of Joseph Sherburne, built a Georgian framed dwelling with hipped roof, an elaborate scroll pediment over the doorway, and wooden quoins at the corners.[39] Daniel Warner, the father of Macpheadris's future son-in-law, built a framed house with a columned portico and balustraded gambrel roof in 1720. In this house, in some respects a smaller, less costly imitation of the Macpheadris mansion, young Warner was born in 1726.[40]

In such surroundings, the members of New Hampshire's ruling class enjoyed their fortunes, dispensed a polite hospitality,[41] governed the province, and carefully planned future family connections. To a degree that seems to have been unparalleled north of Virginia, the gentry of Portsmouth lavished great concern on the preservation and improvement of social status as well as of family wealth and power.

Not all of the successful businessmen of Portsmouth, however, aspired to social grandeur. The majority of the inhabitants remained Congregationalists when Anglican services were introduced in 1732, were democratically inclined, and composed a substantial middle class of artisans and shopkeepers. They controlled the affairs of the town while the merchants controlled those of the province. Captain John Pickering, who by talent and fortune might have worked or married his way into the aristocracy, chose to devote his considerable energies to his lands and mills in York and to his duties as a militia officer rather than to mounting the social ladder. Possessed of an estate of £3,000, he died in 1721, still consciously dedicated to the old ideal of democratic simplicity that the merchant oligarchy had begun to displace.[42]

Portsmouth's shipbuilding industry created a demand for the products of such craftsmen as sailmakers, ropemakers, blockmakers, and blacksmiths as well as shipwrights and carpenters. The expensive tastes of the upper class made it profitable for no less than three silversmiths to dispense their wares in a row of adjoining shops in

Queen Street (now State Street), and John Gaines and his son George were producing fine furniture for which the town became famous. The elder Gaines came to Portsmouth from Ipswich in 1724 with a neighbor, Charles Treadwell, who soon established a flourishing business as hairdresser to the dames of Portsmouth. Treadwell's wife, Mary, sold groceries, dry goods, hardware, and sundries in a shop set up in their house in the middle of the village. She bought produce from country farmers and paid for it in imported goods which she procured from the local merchants.[43]

As in every New England seaport of the early eighteenth century, a small dependent class of servants, slaves, and paupers composed the "meaner sort" of Portsmouth society. The families of the oligarchy each were beginning to keep one or more Negroes for purposes of luxury and prestige, and an indentured apprentice or slave assisted most artisans in their village shops. In 1727, Portsmouth families owned a total of fifty-two black slaves, of whom thirty-five were owned singly. Two families owned as many as four slaves apiece, one family owned three, and three families each owned two.[44] Sometime between 1711 and 1716, the town built a public "alms-house," at which paupers were boarded and put to work by the selectmen.[45]

5

With her commerce, industry, mansions, and public institutions, Portsmouth had by 1730 acquired many of the features of an enviable material civilization. Despite these things, this prosperous port remained nearly as much a cultural wasteland as the coast of Maine.

Although Portsmouth was ostensibly in this period a Puritan town, there is no evidence of the serious grappling with the intellectual and spiritual issues of that difficult faith that one might expect to find in Massachusetts, even during this period when money was replacing salvation as the Yankee's chief purpose. In 1702, the church had only eighty-five members, and sixty of them were women.[46] Not until the years of the Great Awakening did the church attract large numbers, and even then, the upsurge of religious interest was largely a temporary emotional phenomenon.

The upper class patronized the arts of the housewright, the silversmith, the cabinet maker, and the muralist and portrait painter in an attempt to emulate the gracious living of the English aristocracy, with whose ways it was then acquainted chiefly by way of Boston. Its pa-

tronage resulted in some fine examples of architecture and craftsmanship, which were, however, incidental to displaying its own pride of
wealth and social status. Aristocratic entertainment appealed to the
belly rather than to the brain. The upper class gloried in wigs, three-
cornered hats, coaches, and portraits of themselves, but owned few
books. Though the leading men of the town organized a social library
in 1750 and after that date observed the social season with a series of
elaborate balls in the new Assembly Hall, the old moral code was still
highly enough regarded in 1762 to prevent the establishment of a
theater.[47] Not until 1756 did the town acquire a printing press.[48]

The New Hampshire Assembly, like the legislature of Massachusetts, required each town to support a grammar school. Few towns
complied in the early eighteenth century, but Portsmouth hired
Thomas Phipps, a Harvard graduate, as public schoolmaster in 1697.
Phipps stayed until 1701, when the town hired Daniel Greenleaf of
Newbury pursuant to a vote that a schoolmaster be acquired to teach
not only the three R's, but also "the tonges and other learning as may
fit them for the colledg." A schoolhouse was built in 1708, and replaced
by a more adequate one in 1735.[49]

Portsmouth's concern for education was reflected not only in its
care to provide some public schooling for her sons, but also in her early
contributions to Harvard College. When the college made a general
appeal to finance a new building in 1669, the inhabitants of Portsmouth responded with a subscription of £60 and a promise to pay the
same sum annually for seven years. In 1673, by vote of the freeholders,
the town assumed the responsibility for the annual payment.[50] The
number of Portsmouth boys who attended the college, however, was
small. Only two were graduated prior to 1700, three between 1700 and
1712, and four more between 1712 and 1721.[51]

6

In the half-century following the establishment of New Hampshire
as a separate province in 1680, the ruling clique of Portsmouth merchants developed a tightly woven coterie of wealth and political power.
Though their aristocratic airs were perhaps shallow and pretentious,
the Wentworths and their associated clans formed a true ruling class
that controlled both the economy and the government of the province.
Beginning with John Wentworth's remodeling of the old Daniell tavern
and the erection of the Macpheadris mansion, they began to adopt

architectural standards of dignity and luxury, and improved upon a
reputation for hospitality and polite manners for which their province
and town were known at least as early as 1690. In that year, an observer had written that the inhabitants of New Hampshire "live
friendly together, freer in Conversation than most of the Countrey-
men, and given to Hospitality." [52]

But for the firm leadership of its merchant oligarchy, New Hampshire would have remained an economic and social offshoot of Massachusetts Bay, though separated from it politically. Most of the inland
yeomanry and even the Portsmouth middle class shared religious and
social attitudes with Massachusetts more completely than with the
masters of their own province. In the affairs of the province, however,
the will of the aristocratic minority prevailed until the era of the American Revolution.

The Portsmouth gentry, strong and able in the countinghouse and
at the Council table if spiritually indifferent and culturally impoverished, shrewdly and effectively steered their province on a course of
their own choosing. In the face of a great disadvantage of numbers
within New Hampshire and the opposition of the ambitious giant of a
province that surrounded theirs, this was no mean accomplishment.
Given the state of society that prevailed elsewhere in northern New
England, it was also an accomplishment that together with a similar
but smaller and less wealthy group of business and political leaders
in southern Maine, the Portsmouth oligarchy gave to the society of the
Piscataqua a sound economic foundation and contributed a polish to
its way of life.*

---

* See the discussion by Neal W. Allen, Jr., of the "squirearchy" of southern
Maine, headed by the Frost, Hammond, and Pepperrell families, in *Province and
Court Records of Maine,* IV, xliii–xlix. Allen comments upon the interrelationships
of the families who for the most part controlled the magistracy of York County in
the two decades following 1692, and upon the relative wealth that a few of them
enjoyed. Their influence did not last as long as that of the Portsmouth oligarchy,
nor was it at any time a controlling factor in Massachusetts provincial politics.
As a factor in their local dominance, Allen suggests the absence of clerical influence in high places, an observation that one might also apply before 1740 to
Portsmouth.

PART

II

CHAPTER VIII

Expansion
1713–1744

The merchants of the Piscataqua could in many cases trace the beginnings of their prosperity to the economic opportunities that had come with King William's and Queen Anne's Wars. In the years between 1689 and 1713, shipowners such as Archibald Macpheadris of Portsmouth and the senior William Pepperrell of Kittery got rich on privateering and wartime trade, and the Wentworths began their long involvement in the mast industry.[1] At the end of Queen Anne's War in 1713, Portsmouth, untouched by the Indian raids that had devastated much of the coast to the east, was a bustling, unscarred commercial community of a thousand inhabitants or more, and its merchant gentry were on their way up.

In dreadful contrast, most of northern New England was bleeding, scarred, and desolate. Nowhere in the world had the wars of Louis XIV brought greater destruction and suffering than to the savage forest battlegrounds of North America. From New England to the Great Lakes basin to the lower Mississippi, therefore, the colonists of France and England responded thankfully and eagerly to the opportunities for peaceful progress that came with the Peace of Utrecht. There now began a new surge of immigration to the English colonies and a broadening of the zones of settlement in the American territory of both nations. In some cases, this expansion of settlement was more a matter of strategic positioning than merely a peaceful migration. For the Treaty of Utrecht had left unsolved the crucial problem of a boundary between the American dominions of the two colonial powers, and few doubted the inevitability of more fighting some day. For most of the thirty years after 1713, however, the American colonists were free to devote most of their energies to peaceful development.

For northern New England, the business of peace meant rebuilding former coastal settlements that had been wiped out during the wars and venturing short distances inland to settle on new territory. Neither process could have taken place without the constant aid and supervision of the provincial authorities of Massachusetts and New Hampshire, but especially of Massachusetts. In the period between 1713 and the outbreak of King George's War some thirty years later, therefore, the Bay Province refined its imperialistic program north of the Merrimack from the crude adventures of the seventeenth century to what amounted to a full-fledged colonial system. The detail and effectiveness of that system are displayed most dramatically in the process of resettling the abandoned towns. In the new interior settlements, pioneers from Massachusetts and the coastal towns of Maine and New Hampshire developed a different kind of community, the rural country town. For both these reasons, the four or five decades following Utrecht constitute an extremely creative period in the social and political history of the region.

Moreover, land speculators and the far-ranging deputies of Surveyor General Jonathan Bridger and later of Benning Wentworth pushed the search for land and pine well beyond the Kennebec on the coast and far north of any of the interior townships that were actually settled in this period. To the west, Wentworth, in an ultimately unsuccessful attempt to establish New Hampshire jurisdiction in what later became the state of Vermont, granted sixteen townships to speculators before the French and Indian War, making ample provisions in each of them for himself, his political friends, and the Society for the Propagation of the Gospel in addition to the standard thirty-six square miles for the grantees, cheerfully oblivious of the fact that New York had a better claim to the territory. In no case did Wentworth have the slightest assurance that the townships would be settled by the fifty families required by his instructions from the Crown regulating grants of townships. The "New Hampshire Grants" west of the Connecticut, however, assured expeditions of exploration and surveying far into the interior of northwestern New England, if not an expansion of settlement in that direction.[2]

When peace came in 1713, the coast of Maine east of Wells was nearly as desolate as Verrazano had found it two centuries before. A tiny blockhouse of hewn timbers, manned by a garrison of twenty ragged, half-savage provincial soldiers, was all that remained of the once promising Falmouth.[3] To the east, only Father Sebastian Râle's Jesuit mission at Norridgewock on the eastern shore of the Kennebec broke the wilderness between Falmouth Neck and Canada.[4] North Yarmouth, where one of the Lygonian settlements had been dispersed during King Philip's War, established again under Massachusetts supervision in 1680, and abandoned again in 1689, was still deserted. So were all the other English settlements east of Falmouth.

Down the coast from Major Samuel Moody's lonely outpost on Falmouth Neck, the scene was only slightly more encouraging. Scarborough, despite repeated harassments, had been gaining slowly in numbers since the bloody summer of 1703, when eight men, with the help of a two-day rainstorm, had held off a force of five hundred French and Indian attackers from a log garrison house at Black Point.[5] Those few of Saco's former population who remained had retreated into a stone fortress on the Biddeford side of the Saco River.[6]

The real eastern frontier of the English settlements, in any effective sense, was at Wells, the only community in Maine that had learned the lessons of King Philip's War sufficiently to remain intact during the wars of 1689 to 1713.[7] There, nearly thirty fortified dwellings, some enclosed in palisades, stretched along the King's Highway, which ran parallel to the sea and connected the Piscataqua settlements with Falmouth. A meetinghouse and at least two mills completed the rude village setting. It now remained only for the settlers, molded to an extent unduplicated in the eastern parts into a disciplined, effective fighting force, to return to their abandoned fields and resume the growing of grain and the utilization of their rich pasture and meadow lands which had been interrupted by a long period of warfare.

The village of York, only partly recovered to its former state of settlement since the disastrous massacre of 1692, nevertheless boasted several substantial structures, including the meetinghouse, the stone gaol, Parson Moody's new stockaded parsonage, and a few other garrison houses. Here was being enacted the drama, soon to be repeated in other towns, between the old settlers' tendency toward profane carousing and loose morality and the rigorous Puritan code of Mr. Moody, who even now had gained a position of high respect and accomplishment among his brethren in the Massachusetts clergy. The upper and lower settlements of Kittery were sufficiently populated that it was feasible to separate the upper agricultural settlement, thereafter called Berwick, from the fishing and commercial village at Kittery Point in 1713. The following year, Kittery acquired an organized church and a settled minister.

The settlements at Dover, Oyster River, and Dunstable had suffered from the wars, but on the whole the towns of New Hampshire had survived the ordeal more completely than most of the communities to the east. Exeter and Portsmouth had escaped attack altogether, and Hampton had been raided only once with the loss of but one life. That was in 1703 during the first wave of attacks at the start of Queen Anne's War.[8]

The towns of southern New Hampshire and coastal Maine that had remained intact during the wars progressed steadily between 1713 and 1740 in population and in the complexity of their economic and social life. Except in the commercial town of Portsmouth and its economic satellites of Newcastle and Kittery, which shared the same harbor, the surest gauge of a community's advance toward maturity was the extent to which its economy had shifted away from the extractive industries of fishing and lumbering and toward agriculture. Not only did farming give the greatest promise of permanent self-sufficiency for most communities, but the slow shift to a basically agricultural economy produced social changes that were viewed by the sober-minded as vast improvements. Farming demanded a regimen of hard work and constant attention to crops and animals, it fostered an attachment to property and thus to the community in which one owned his land and paid his taxes, it encouraged a close family life and the spawning of many children, it required the development of varied skills of handicraft and elementary business ability, and it served as a natural nursery of the Puritan virtues because in most cases it was undeniably the thrifty, the sober, and the diligent who stood the best chance of prospering.

The transition was slow, and in some towns waited until later in the century. Exeter, for example, relied principally on the lumber industry until the 1760's because the timber supply in the forests surrounding Great Bay was more plentiful and lasted longer than that on the immediate coast in places such as Hampton, Kittery, and York. When the shift did occur there, according to a contributor to the Massachusetts Historical Society *Collections* in 1795, "the alteration produced in the face of this tract of country" that accompanied the failure of lumbering was both spectacular and salutary. Lumbering, wrote Dr. Samuel Tenny, was one of the worst of all "employments" because "it serves to keep those engaged in it in a perpetual state of poverty; while, at the same time, it commonly ruins their morals, and induces a premature old age." Before the "alteration," he wrote, "the taverns in Exeter (of which it always had a sufficient number) were every night thronged with people from this and the neighbouring towns, who seldom all retired sober." Now that the townsmen stayed home and spent all their energies on their farms, "our public houses are . . . orderly, quiet habitations, only for the purpose of accommodating travelers and people, whom business at the courts of law, or at the publick offices, bring into town." [9]

While Exeter was still predominantly a lumbering town and Portsmouth a commercial seaport in the years between the wars, the villagers of Hampton, as they had from the beginning, were harvesting the rich hay in their great salt marshes and were producing good wheat, other grains, flax, and many sheep and hogs. The people of Dover had already abandoned their waterfront homes on Dover Point for Cocheco, located, as Daniel Neal, the historian of New England, phrased it, "a little higher up into the Country," which was favored with good soil.[10] The transition to agriculture began during these years at York, though much of the town provided poor farmland,[11] and the new farming town of Berwick, separated from Kittery in the year of Utrecht, began to grow until by 1765 its population slightly exceeded that of its parent commercial and fishing town.[12]

The gradual shift from fishing and lumbering to farming in the older towns of the region was accompanied by a greater diversity of occupations. The older activities were by no means abandoned, but they tended increasingly to be directed from central locations such as Portsmouth, and, as time went on, the revived port of Falmouth, Maine. Before 1700, the New Englanders had discovered that the banks off Sable Island, Nova Scotia, and Newfoundland provided richer fishing grounds than the nearby waters of Cape Cod, Cape Ann, and coastal Maine. Colonies such as Richmond Island and the Isles of Shoals, therefore, had lost their earlier importance, and except for the few private fishermen who dwelt in the Kennebec region and eastward, the fishing industry tended to concentrate in the large ports. These could support the owners of vessels and fleets that were equipped for long voyages. Now that the British owned Nova Scotia, the New Englanders no longer had to carry on the private wars with French fishermen in the extreme northeastern waters that had contributed to the tensions between the colonists of the two nations at the close of the seventeenth century.[13] The fishing industry, therefore, prospered anew, but it was increasingly an industry conducted and directed from afar by men with capital. There remained little room in it for the little men who had once predominated in the coastal villages. Those few who continued to fish privately in the more southern waters were discouraged by a new scarcity of fish in the 1720's. The *New-England Courant* reported on April 9, 1722, that "there is no catching fish at Winter-Harbour without baiting the Hook with a *Gudgeon*; and it happens to be so all along the Eastern Shore as far as the English Settlements. 'Tis thought by many that the Price of Fish will be very high by reason that Bait is so very scarce." In the Kennebec region, a company of fishmongers in London tried to sponsor a sturgeon fishery in the years following Utrecht, but it failed because of mismanagement and was abandoned after 1725.[14]

The change in the character of the fishing industry led very soon to trouble between employers and employees, especially in Portsmouth, where fishermen gathered to ship aboard vessels that sailed from there to the fishing grounds. The fishermen, who in the seventeenth century had not been accustomed to the discipline involved in relatively large ships and long voyages, sometimes proved ungovernable at sea. Masters and owners, for their part, were not always careful to stow enough food and gear for their men. A New Hampshire law of 1718, passed in response to complaints from ship owners, required every crewman to obey orders during the term for which he had shipped, and required owners to provision and equip their vessels properly. Fines were fixed for violations on either side.[15]

A similar change was taking place in the lumber industry. Years of indiscriminate cutting had led to depletion of the timber supply near the coast in New Hampshire and southern Maine. It was reported as early as 1727, perhaps prematurely, that the center of the mast business had moved from Portsmouth to Falmouth.[16] Like fishing, therefore, this industry was becoming increasingly an enterprise run from afar by merchants in the principal ports. The interior towns that were established in this period passed through a stage, as the coastal towns had done, during which lumber served as a staple for the partial support of families and communities located near the supply, but the old villages were losing their character as fishing stations and logging camps.

Even the smaller coastal towns, however, retained their interest in the sea. Coasting sloops sailed to Boston and farther with their cargoes of wheat, barley, meat, and firewood from these hamlets as well as from Portsmouth and Falmouth. That the ownership and navigation of one of these humble craft entitled any crude easterner who had trouble spelling and knew no better than to "eat Pease with a Wooden Spoon, cut Pork on a Shingle, and pick Bones with his Teeth" to the dignified title of "captain" provoked one supercilious Bostonian of the 1720's to contribute a sarcastic letter on the subject to the local press.[17]

As the towns developed in population and prosperity, they demanded the services of a greater variety of specialized occupations than had been the case in an earlier day. There was room in even the more primitive communities for a few artisans, storekeepers, innkeepers, ferrymen, a minister, and a schoolmaster. Most of them supplemented their incomes by farming or at least raised enough food for their own use. At Portsmouth and Kittery, and later at Falmouth, shipbuilding gave employment to craftsmen of many kinds.

Along with this modest growth and increase in complexity that peace brought to the towns beyond the Merrimack, there came new problems. Though the grim struggle against starvation, exposure, and French and Indian enemies had ended for the time being, neither prosperity nor even bare survival could be taken for granted. Beyond the immediate vicinity of Portsmouth, the settlements of the region stood on the frontier of civilization. Even during a period of formal peace, one ventured into the wilderness beyond the palisades and fortified houses of the villages armed and only at his peril. One could never be certain when nearby Indians, especially those in Maine, might resume their sporadic raids on the settlements or lurk in wait for hunters or villagers working in their outlying fields or searching for a strayed animal. The only certainty was a permanent and deeply felt hostility between the two races, nurtured since the time of King Philip's War by treachery and savagery on both sides, which could not be ended by a peace treaty.

The woods also held wolves and wildcats, against which the settlers waged continuous warfare. Both Massachusetts and New Hampshire law provided for bounties on wolves, but troublesome beasts continued to prowl near the settlements, and kill cattle and sheep even late in the eighteenth century.[18] The reviving towns of Falmouth and North Yarmouth supplemented the four-pound province bounty in 1738 by offering to pay an additional six pounds for each grown wolf killed.[19] Falmouth similarly encouraged the killing of wildcats. In 1735, Jeremy Hodgdon presented the carcass of a cat to the selectmen, who certified with due solemnity that "the Constbel cut of the Ears in the presence of us Seleck men for falmouth." [20] Though destructive animals were feared primarily for their damage to crops and livestock, a black bear killed an eight-year-old boy in one of the new frontier settlements of New Hampshire in 1731.[21]

Roving livestock, though apparently tolerated until after the Peace of Utrecht, now became both a nuisance and a hazard to crops in towns of every size. Swine, which northern New England farmers had been turning loose to feed ever since the days of Trelawney's colony in the 1630's, were particularly hard on farmlands because of their rooting habits. We learn something of the primitive state of agriculture in the easternmost parts of Maine and of the comparatively advanced state of development in the older towns from the Massachusetts acts in 1720, 1726, and 1731 that prevented pigs from running at large. The towns east of Wells, but not those in the more southerly parts of Maine, were excepted.[22] In New Hampshire, unconfined swine were required to wear large yokes during the growing season to keep them from going through fences, and rings in their noses throughout the year to prevent rooting.[23] The town pound, for the confinement of any animal found feeding on land without the owner's permission, had been required by Massachusetts law since the seventeenth century, and was required by New Hampshire law after 1718, the year the New Hampshire Assembly also passed an act for the "taking up" of stray animals.[24] In 1743, it provided for the equitable financing of fences between adjoining fields.[25]

The years of peace in the eastern parts were also characterized by some increase in crime and accidents, though perhaps no more than could be expected among a population of similar size anywhere. It is certain that never in the colonial period, not even in the most populous towns, did the problem of thefts and violent crime approach unmanageable proportions.

Four major concerns transcended all the day-to-day problems that faced northern New Englanders during the period of development between the Peace of Utrecht and the outbreak of King George's War in 1744. Each of them touched the older settled areas and the frontier alike. One was a political conflict between Massachusetts and New Hampshire over the old perplexing question, finally settled in 1740, of the boundary between the provinces. The second was a brief renewal of warfare with two groups of Abnaki Indians, the Norridgewocks on the lower Kennebec and the Pequawkets on the upper Saco. The third great concern of the period was over another enemy that was just as dangerous: contagious disease, especially the deadly epidemic of "throat distemper," or diphtheria, that swept over northern New England in the 1730's and early 1740's. The fourth was the stirring of religious enthusiasm whose beginning can be dated rather precisely at 1727 and which culminated in 1740 with the coming of George Whitefield to the eastern parts. The region's exposure to the great English revivalist began the four or five peak years of its own version of the American Great Awakening of the eighteenth century.

These four great concerns—political, military, biological, and religious—acted variously as barriers and stimuli, and occasionally
gave a special regional flavoring to the continued development of the
older settlements and the parallel process of new expansion that
characterized the years between the wars.

Effective expansion began with the resettlement of some of the
former townships on the deserted Maine coast, a process which deserves—and will shortly get—special treatment of its own. But we
should have a false notion of the period if we thought of it only in terms
of the drudgery and frustration and sweat that characterized the hard
work of building and rebuilding actual settlements. These were years
of hard work indeed, but they were also years of excitement and adventure. In a very real sense, the age of American discovery was far
from over. There is time enough to ponder the severe hardships of
serious pioneering. Before the drudgery, in every case, there came the
vision of possibility to which the hard work was a response.

In 1720, some of the gentlemen proprietors of the Lincolnshire
Company of Boston, which had acquired an old claim to territory on
the Muscongus and St. George's Rivers not far south of Penobscot
Bay, went on an expedition to their unsettled holdings. They took
along some mill equipment and picked up several workmen at Portsmouth and Black Point, intending to set up a mill and begin to prepare a settlement. Most important, the company thought a personal
visit would be the surest way of convincing the Indian sagamores then
in the vicinity to confirm the old deed, made by a chieftain long since
dead. In this, the company eventually failed, resulting in a frustration
of its immediate hopes for developing the land for sale to settlers but
not in stopping Elisha Cooke, head of the company and the contrary-
minded leader of the popular party in Massachusetts during Jonathan
Belcher's regime, from setting up sawmills in the area and making
thousands of feet of boards out of the King's mast pines.[26]

Thomas Fayerweather, one of the proprietors, kept a log of the expedition. His enthusiastic assessment of the possibilities of this empty
territory is not far removed in spirit from the discoverer's-eye-views
of Champlain and Captain John Smith more than a century before. On
Monday, May 2, Fayerweather and his companions explored the Muscongus River by whaleboat and

> landed at ramin point being the Easternmost point of land upon
> the river of which we took possession and mark'd a tree or two in
> behalfe of the Lincolnshire Compa. the shore of which we found

well Stor'd with Spruce—etc. and the soile very promising well
water'd and a levell Champion Country and abounding with safe
Harbours or Coves for Vessells being deep water . . . the land
very promising for cultivation; in short as fine a Country as one
can desire to settle upon; in severall places where we found the
Indians had formerly settled upon we mett with English grass
pretty rivulets of fresh water and indeed nothing wanting to
make the Country delightfull, but Husbandry and an agreeable
people to Inhabit it.[27]

The vision of the Lincolnshire proprietors was shared by dozens of
advance parties which explored the eastern coast and the northern
wilderness for the next fifty years. Their optimistic, sometimes almost
lyrical hopes for the future of this empty land was as much a part of
the spirit of the eighteenth century as the grim practicality with which
the actual pioneers undertook the toil of founding settlements.

CHAPTER IX

Resettlement:
The Massachusetts
Colonial System
1713–1750

1

Besides having profound physical, economic, social, and political consequences in Maine and New Hampshire, the devastation of northern
New England between 1689 and 1713 affected the development of
Massachusetts as an imperial power. In New Hampshire, the expansion of settlement between the wars took place partly in response to the
race between the two provinces to establish jurisdiction in disputed
areas pending the final settlement of the boundary question. By 1741,
the ambitions of the Bay Province for cultural and political hegemony
over all the region beyond the Merrimack had undergone a severe set-
back. Not only had New Hampshire been overwhelmingly the victor
in the settlement of the boundary dispute, but Massachusetts had
lost her single remaining link with the government of New Hampshire with the appointment of a separate royal governor for the
smaller province. In Maine, however, Massachusetts imperialism
developed significantly. In its careful supervision of the resettlement
of the abandoned coastal towns, the Bay government achieved what
amounted to a mature "colonial system."

Peace had scarcely been declared in 1713 when the old proprietors
of those abandoned communities or their heirs mounted another assault on the wilderness. Upon the temporary removal of the Indian
danger, roving cutters, sensing the chance for quick profits, descended
upon the unoccupied timberlands. The refugee proprietors, learning of

these activities, reacted with understandable jealousy and uneasiness. Clearly, their old claims would be forfeited and then forgotten if they did not take steps to restore them.

The proprietors' interest in restoring law and orderly settlement to the eastern townships hardly exceeded that of the Massachusetts government. A speedy resettlement of the eastern parts would help solve Boston's problem of refugees, and resettlement was necessary if Maine was to continue its traditional (and very effective) function as a frontier buffer between Canada and eastern Massachusetts. The Bay Province also stood to gain from the proper exploitation of Maine's rich resources by men who were, in a sense, subjects of Massachusetts. The same settlers would provide a market for coastal traders from Boston, as their predecessors had done through most of the seventeenth century. Whether or not the Massachusetts authorities were inspired by Britain's old colonial system which they had resisted for so long, the parallel between the aims of the Lords of Trade and the aims of Massachusetts with respect to her eastern dominion is a striking one.

In 1713, the General Court revived the old "Committee of Eastern Claims and Settlements," which had been established after King William's War and functioned briefly between 1700 and the outbreak of Queen Anne's War in 1702. The committee was now enlarged from seven to nine members and empowered to examine all claims to the abandoned lands and confirm those it found valid. At the same time, the Court designated five towns for resettlement: Saco, Scarborough, Falmouth, North Yarmouth, and Arrowsick, one of the old settlements, later named Georgetown, in the patent acquired from the Plymouth Colony by the Kennebec Purchasers in 1661. The legislators required that the abandoned towns be replanted by groups of twenty to thirty families. Each family was to live on a small home lot of three or four acres, and each settlement was to take the form of an easily defensible cluster of houses located near the seacoast. The Committee of Claims and Settlements was to enforce this policy by granting permission for the settlement of a township only when it had approved the plans of the proprietors.[1]

The following year, settlers began to arrive in the towns from Saco to Falmouth to take up their old claims. By 1716, twenty families were living on Falmouth Neck and building a meetinghouse with the help of a subsidy of £20 from the General Court. By 1717, Saco had developed to the extent that it was able to hire a full-time minister, also with the help of a provincial subsidy. Scarborough by now boasted not one settlement, but two—one at Black Point and the other at Blue Point.[2]

In 1715, on the recommendation of the Committee of Eastern Claims, the Court accepted the proposals of the recent purchasers of the old Pejepscot patent for the settlement of two more townships, Brunswick and Topsham. The authorization specified that the proprietors and inhabitants were to be "subject to such regulations of this Court, as has been made for their Settling in a defensible manner." Both new communities were freed from province taxes for five years, and received the Court's promise of "encouragement" of the ministry. The proprietors, in return, were expected to grant the usual tracts of land for the use of church, school, and clergy.[3]

The same year, the Court relaxed the statutory time limit for pursuing former claims on frontier lands, inasmuch as "the Setling of the Eastern Parts and Frontiers will be of great benefit to this Province" and that settlement "will be very much retarded and hindred unless Persons can be Secured in their Purchases and Possessions." [4]

Thus the Massachusetts government worked out a comprehensive policy for resettlement during the few years that followed the Peace of Utrecht. The first settlers who repopulated Falmouth, Saco, and Scarborough, however, apparently either were ignorant of or disregarded the plan for close supervision of the process. Not until 1717, for example, did the proprietors of Falmouth petition for permission to settle, although some of them had been there for three years. In their petition, the Falmouth proprietors rehearsed briefly the history of the settlement, which they described as "being very well and beyond most places Accomodated for husbandry, Navigation Fishery and the Lumber trade," expressed concern over the "Great Strip and wast" of their timber by "ill minded Persons," and promised to design their settlement in a compact, defensible manner.

The General Court granted the petition in June, 1717, and directed the proprietors to apply to the Committee of Eastern Claims for advice in laying out the settlement.[5] Not until thirteen months later did the committee visit Falmouth to help the proprietors decide such matters as the location of streets and meetinghouse. It might not have acted even that promptly had it not been for prodding from the Falmouth proprietors, who in the spring of 1718 became alarmed over a movement to settle neighboring North Yarmouth and feared encroachment on their boundaries.[6]

The resettlement of Falmouth and the townships to the west proceeded smoothly when compared with the halting and complicated progress of North Yarmouth from deserted hamlet to full-fledged town.* The process took seventeen years. Partly because of the complications involved, all richly documented in available manuscripts, the resettlement of North Yarmouth provides an especially illuminating display of the mature Massachusetts colonial system in full operation.†

2

The succession of events that had alarmed the Falmouth proprietors began with a petition in May, 1717, from some of the former proprietors of North Yarmouth. It asked the Governor and General Court for permission to "Settle a Towne" on the old site and for the appointment of a committee "to Sett out and butt and bound the Same unto us." Like the proprietors of Falmouth, the North Yarmouth men were concerned about the loss of their timber. The petition called attention to "peoples Unreasonable Strip and Waste of Wood and timber which they unjustly make on our lands there, By such as have no Interest therein," and asked for some sort of prohibition of the practice.[7]

A few of the old proprietors appeared in North Yarmouth between 1715 and 1718 and chose a committee to lay out and assign lots without authorization from the provincial government. According to the com-

---

* In this and subsequent chapters, I shall try whenever practical to preserve the distinction between "town" and "township" that was observed by those concerned in the granting and settlement of tracts of land and in the establishment and governing of municipal corporations in eighteenth-century New England. Since the "town" was then and remains, with some modification in its form and importance, the fundamental unit of political organization in New England, the distinction is a useful one. A "township" was a tract of land, usually understood as a piece of property initially owned in common by a body of proprietors who held their title from the province and whose use and division of the common land were governed by law. A "town" was a municipal corporation or body politic. A "township" could and usually did exist before the incorporation of a "town"—that is, before a municipal government was established to exercise jurisdiction within the borders of the township and before the inhabitants of the township were granted the powers of a body politic. After the incorporation of town government, the distinction between terms in referring to the geographical area over which the town government had jurisdiction became somewhat hazy. In common usage, the "township," understood as a tract of land, usually became, after the establishment of the town government and the division of all or most of the common lands, a "town."

† The colonial town of North Yarmouth, so named to distinguish it from Yarmouth on Cape Cod, embraced the modern Maine towns of Yarmouth, North Yarmouth, Cumberland, Pownall, Freeport, and Harpswell.

plaint of the Falmouth men, this committee included members whose title to a share in the township was at least doubtful.[8] The first job of these proprietors was to rebuild a sawmill, which demonstrates that it was primarily the profit-making possibilities of timber that had drawn not only thieves, but also the presumed owners of the land. This settlement, however, was carried on neither according to the regulations of the General Court nor in pursuance of the petition of 1717. It aroused objections, not only from neighboring Falmouth, but also among the North Yarmouth proprietors who had not returned. The extralegal nature of the settlement became particularly apparent when, on their own authority, the few settlers chose town officers, including "selectmen," who in turn assigned grants of land.[9]

In the summer of 1722, in response to a petition from both resident and nonresident proprietors of the township and upon the recommendation of the Committee of Eastern Claims, the General Court appointed a special five-man absentee committee for North Yarmouth. This committee, operating from faraway Boston, supervised in minute detail all phases of the community's development during the next twelve years.

The appointment of such a committee, which in this case included four of the nonresident proprietors, apparently was based upon ancient local precedent as well as upon Massachusetts usage. The Committee of Eastern Claims discovered that President Danforth had granted the township in 1684 to a committee of four as trustees for all the inhabitants. It recommended, therefore, "that five Suitable Persons be appointed and Constituted Trustees in the Room and Stedd" of the original trustees. The new committee was "to Carry on and perfect the Settlement of that Township According to Such Rules and Methods as was then [viz., at the time of the original settlement] Proposed having Special Regard to the Original Proprietors and Settlers."[10]

To this committee, usually referred to in correspondence as "the Committee for the Resettlement of North Yarmouth," the Court named five of the most prominent men of the province. All of them were interested in eastern lands, including specifically those of North Yarmouth. William Tailor was a former lieutenant governor. Elisha Cooke, the former leader of the popular faction in the assembly and now a councilor, was a large investor in eastern lands whose opposition to the mast agents had made a political issue of the royal timber policies. John Smith, a Boston merchant, was a brother of the Reverend Thomas Smith of Falmouth. William Dudley, a member with Cooke of the governor's council, was the son of Joseph Dudley, the former governor, and John Powell, a Boston merchant, was a brother-in-law of Lieutenant Governor Dummer. All but Cooke owned land in North Yarmouth, and Cooke probably shared the special interest in the township of his fellow committeemen, since the name of his son Middlecott appears on the list of proprietors, though his does not.[11] Though all of its members had investments in the township, the committee acted in theory not as a body of proprietors, but as an administrative arm of the General Court.

The same summer that the Court appointed the committee, about twenty-five families arrived in North Yarmouth to settle. The men divided themselves immediately into three "garrisons," and among the several houses they built that summer were three fortified structures of hewn timbers, stored with extra food and ammunition and capable of housing forty or fifty men in an emergency. The smaller houses were grouped around the three garrison houses, resulting in three protected clusters of buildings, each of which was from two to three miles removed from the other two. The three little settlements each formed a corner of a roughly equilateral triangle. One was at Parker's Point, where Royal's River empties into Casco Bay on the east side of the township. Another was at Peter Weare's mill at the falls on Royal's River. The third was on the west side of Broad Cove, a two-mile-wide harbor to the west of Parker's Point and the river mouth.[12]

The settlers thus laid out the town and organized themselves for defense, but without greatly sacrificing the economic purposes that had brought them there. The three-cornered arrangement permitted convenient exploitation of the falls, the use of a landing and loading place at the mouth of the river, and sufficient dispersal of the population to allow owners and workmen easy access to various parts of the woodlands.

This promising settlement was soon disrupted by Indians. The local leaders sent away the women and children and some of the men after raids at Brunswick, Arrowsick, and Merrymeeting Bay late in 1722. These were the most serious of a growing number of harassments encouraged by the French, partly because the Jesuit missionaries were growing uneasy about English expansion up the Maine coast, and perhaps partly because of recent personal altercations between the Massachusetts authorities and Father Sebastian Râle, the vigorous director of the mission to the Norridgewocks at Castine. The Bay government declared war on the "eastern Indians," and during the three-year conflict that followed, there was a destructive raid upon

North Yarmouth that left the settlement nearly in the same condition it had been prior to 1722.*

The General Court's committee for North Yarmouth, inactive during the war, began after 1725 to hold meetings in Boston to receive the claims of former proprietors, admit new residents, arrange for surveying the town boundaries, lay out lots, and assign lots by drawing.[13] On April 22, 1727, the committee voted to send Captain Jeremiah Moulton and Benjamin Flagg to North Yarmouth to complete the "platting" of the whole township, a task which was reported accomplished on December 19 of that year.[14] In the meantime, the committee had made a rare trip to the township to settle the boundaries with the selectmen of Falmouth.[15]

During the spring and summer of 1727, the committee examined many claims to North Yarmouth lands. When it judged a claim to be valid, it confirmed the claimant as a proprietor of the common and undivided lands and added his name to the list of persons whose names would be matched by drawing to the one hundred ten-acre home lots and, as time went on, to lots in subsequent divisions.

This process was accompanied by much of the private arrangement and circuitous pleading that was a standard part of the proceedings of most New England proprieties in the seventeenth and eighteenth centuries. On May 4, 1727, Hugh Blanning, one of the proprietors, asked the clerk of the committee in writing "to Draw for my Lot and if the Lot that falls to me Shuld not be nigh the waters Side I Desier the faver that you will Change my Lot for wone that iss joneing to the water and if them that you Change with Shuld aske any thing to Boot I Desier you will agree with them on the Easiest terms you

---

*William H. Rowe: *Ancient North Yarmouth and Yarmouth, Maine* (Yarmouth, 1937), pp. 60–2; William Douglass: *A Summary, Historical and Political* . . . (London, 1760), I, 559–61; "North Yarmouth Maine Papers" (Mss., Maine Historical Society [hereafter cited as N. Yar. Mss.]), I, 34. See Francis Parkman: *Half-Century of Conflict* (Boston, 1902), I, Chap. X, for the story of Father Râle, which ends with his death at the hands of a New England force that devastated the Norridgewock village in 1724, and *New-England Courant*, March 12–August 13, 1722, *passim*, for contemporary accounts of the events leading to this war, which is most commonly referred to in the older histories as "Dummer's War" after Lieutenant Governor William Dummer of Massachusetts Bay. Dummer acted as governor of Massachusetts and Lieutenant Governor John Wentworth acted as governor of New Hampshire between the end of 1722, when Samuel Shute, governor of both provinces, returned to England after a bitter political controversy with the Massachusetts General Court, and the arrival of Governor William Burnett in 1728. See, e.g., Thomas Hutchinson: *The History of the Colony and Province of Massachusetts-Bay*, ed. Lawrence Shaw Mayo (Cambridge, Mass., 1936), II, 208–19, 246–7, 252.

Can." [16] The committee by no means discouraged such arrangements. It appears to have had two equally important concerns at this stage. One was to assure that justice was done to claimholders; the other was to assure that the township would be settled by persons of whom it approved. The committee permitted exchanges and sales of land, so long as neither aim was hindered. During 1727, the committee granted permission to many landowners to sell their lots, in each case listing the prospective buyer by name.[17]

Benjamin Larraby of Falmouth tried to secure land in North Yarmouth by sending to the committee a deed of land he said his father had bought from the Indians. Both his reasoning and his syntax were tortuous:

> I would request this to you that you would plese to Consider my Case In Refrence to my Brother's Land that is laid out and by that meanes I am and shall be very much wronged In that affaire and therefore I do pray your Honours to Considder me and to let me have some Land some whare that I may have Justice done mee and I would Intreet you to as I have formerly searved my Countrey and Have fought sundrey Battles In this Partes of the Countrey and my friends have Ben Killed In the spot.

His real reason for asking for land is discovered in the postscript: "I hope your Honours will Consider me other wise I have no place to Settle my Son." [18] The committee, either confused or unimpressed, rejected the claim.[19]

By May, the committee was ready to fix the rules of settlement. Every person admitted to the propriety was, within two years after June 1 of that year, to "Erect and well finish" a house suitable for a family and clear and fence in at least five acres of his ten-acre home lot, three acres of which was to be cultivated. In order to make the accomplishment of this goal as certain as possible, each of the "undertakers" was required actually to move or send a "good able body'd Man" to North Yarmouth by November 25. The owner or his proxy was to "reside their till the Expiration of the aforesaid term, and the Several Conditions respectively be performed which will facilitate the Resettlement with great Safety to the Undertakers," or forfeit his title.[20]

The committee soon found the requirement to be too stringent—a discovery that time and again was to vex proprietors and official bodies who were similarly trying to stimulate settlement of the interior townships during the following fifty years. While maintaining in theory throughout its life the same method of assuring actual settlement, the committee repeatedly relaxed the time limit. The first time was only ten months later, when it restated the policy, this time giving landowners until May 18, 1728, to "Repair to North Yarmouth in Person"; extensions to October 18 were possible for "Satisfactory reasons." At the same time, the committee prohibited sale of lots or shares in them until the owner had performed the settlement conditions, unless with the committee's consent.[21]

Throughout these proceedings, it had been understood that the ten-acre home lot was to be, as in the standard Massachusetts town, only a small part of each proprietor's eventual holdings. But as another means of encouraging the development of home lots and actual residence by the proprietors, the committee made the fulfillment of the various conditions of settlement a prerequisite for a share in the "after divisions."[22] A share in the large tracts of unsettled land was important to every proprietor for reasons beyond the more purely agricultural ones that prevailed to the south. By far the most valuable parts of the town were its extensive timberlands. In their exploitation, a North Yarmouth man had his best hope for a decent, and even, in some cases, very comfortable living. As long as a share in the woodlands was delayed, however, a resident proprietor had to rely on what meager foodstuffs and building materials he could extract from his tiny saltwater farm on the shore of Broad Cove, Royal's River, or Casco Bay.

Meanwhile, timber pirates persisted in their illicit work. Gangs of men, coming in sloops from Boston, cut and made off with many of the best trees. Some proprietors' tenants, having no stake in the continued wealth of the still-undivided lands, were prone to do the same.[23] Even some of the proprietors, to the great disturbance of their fellows, were invading the common lands for private profit.[24] Clearly, an early division of the timberlands would benefit the community and all but the more unscrupulous of the proprietors. The delay in such a division was one of the residents' earliest grievances against the Boston committee. There was another that was more serious.

In the summer of 1728, twelve men were settled on the one hundred home lots. Of these, only seven were owners; the other five were tenants of proprietors who remained away from the scene.[25] This was a poor defense force. The treaty of peace signed with the persistently hostile Abnakis in Boston in 1725 and ratified at Casco Bay in 1726 had done little to remove the constant uneasiness about nearby Indians. For defensive purposes, the residents urgently needed fellow townsmen, permanent neighbors. A larger population also would discourage timber piracy and contribute to the growth of a community to which the lonely men now living in the town could bring their absent wives and families.

Colonial relationships have always bred suspicions. In this case, the North Yarmouth men suspected that the superintending committee was not doing everything it might for the benefit of the colony and those who lived there. From the vantage point of the wilderness, it looked very much as though the nonresident proprietors were influencing policy, to the exclusion of those on the scene.

The resident population apparently almost tripled during the last few months of 1728, for on January 10, 1728/9, thirty-four "proprietors and settlers" put their signatures or marks on the most strongly worded petition yet addressed to the committee for resettlement.

This eloquent plea for more positive action to promote settlement expressed impatience with "the many acts that you have passed concerning the more speedy setling of the town of north yarmouth and the many promises and encouragements we have had from time to time concarning the same." Despite these, the residents complained, "the greatest part of the lots remain unsettled and nobody apeers in there be halfe which thing tends very much to the dis coragement of such settlers as are upon the spot and is great encouragement to the Indians in case they are designd for mischief and will certainly prove the utter ruin and over throw of the settlement without a speedy remedy."

The petition urged the committee to "tak som methods for the speedy effecting of the same so that we may no longer be put off with som promises and nothing more: but that the town may be soon settled in aregular and defensible manner," warning that they would apply directly to the General Court if their demands were not met. In the same document, the residents asked for the speedy trial of a large claim that was holding up the second division of lots, for "sume of those that are here have well neer fullfilled thare articles and want a second division and we want to set up a grist mill and a saw mill forth with in that claim." [26]

The following August, ten residents complained of promiscuous timbercutting, even by fellow residents and proprietors. Talking to the culprits had had no effect, the complainants wrote, because "they say . . . it is not in the committys power nor no Court to putt A stoop to it." Part of the complaint reflected the growing hostility between resident and nonresident proprietors: "their be some that Bring Down several hands with them to work on the comons . . . to make A purse on it which we Do not suppose ever desine to settel hear." The petitioners asked for "A stoop to such Doings and that as soon as may be." [27]

The residents by now, perhaps, had more cause than before to suspect the committee of being insufficiently attentive to their interests. In July, the committee had rejected flatly a respectfully worded petition signed by twenty resident proprietors. The petition had asked for the repeal of an order regarding provision of land for a road along the shore and substitution of a plan that the residents thought more practical.[28]

The Boston committee did nothing more imaginative toward answering the several grievances that year than issue notification that proprietors who did not fulfill the terms of their grant by May 10, 1730, would forfeit their lots.[29]

3

The administrators in Boston, however, deserve credit for some insight into the colonial problem. In May, 1727, during the first flurry of surveying and rule-making, this board of directors had appointed a five-man *resident* subcommittee to "manage the Prudentialls" of the township.* This step indicates a recognition that absentee directors could not properly handle the details of such matters as further land divisions, laying out roads, and adjusting claims to assure equitable distributions of lands that varied greatly in quality and had been surveyed in haste. Moreover, whether or not the Boston committee understood the importance of its decision, it had incorporated into the government of a dependent political unit such devices as delegation of authority, a kind of divided sovereignty (the essence of federalism), and a measure of home rule. Still more important for the people of North Yarmouth, this was the first step toward bringing along the redeveloping community toward the status of a full-fledged town.

Though the Boston committee continued to receive petitions and handle questions of policy, it now had representatives to supervise details at the scene, as when the subcommittee, in response to orders from the Boston directors, laid out roads in 1730, providing the town-

---

* Rowe: *North Yarmouth*, p. 69. That the committee was careful to keep its subcommittee composed only of residents is evident from its replacement on December 10, 1729, of two members who had moved from the township; N. Yar. Mss., I, 93.

ship with plans for seven different roads and four landing places.[30] It could also seek advice from the subcommittee when a decision of policy required the benefit of someone's knowledge of local conditions. The first exercise of the subcommittee's advisory function now on record occurred on June 26, 1728, when it advised against granting Felt Stream to Moses and George Felt, a father and son who wanted to build a gristmill and sawmill on the brook.[31] Beyond advising the Boston committee and carrying out specific directives, the subcommittee occasionally initiated action and procedures that it thought necessary and then sought confirmation from the supervisory committee —much as certain legislation by colonial legislatures was submitted to London for confirmation by the King in Council. The local committee's range of concern included all the public affairs of an eighteenth-century New England town, though of course the relatively primitive economic and social state of the township at this stage resulted in somewhat different emphases from those in the more mature communities. If one were to try to fit these two agencies into the ordinary scheme of New England town government, the best way might be to view the resident subcommittee as the selectmen and the supervising committee in Boston as the town meeting.

It was not long, therefore, before the subcommittee became involved in matters fiscal and ecclesiastical. Religion was not the principal concern of the North Yarmouth proprietors and settlers. The resettlement of the township was, on the contrary, a movement that was frankly commercial and military. But Massachusetts law required a church and school in every town, and there is no evidence that any resident or proprietor ever doubted that North Yarmouth would comply.

As early as February, 1728/9, Jonathan Watson of Medford, later a resident proprietor of North Yarmouth, agreed with the committee in Boston to frame a meetinghouse and finish all the building except the galleries for £205, "the Committee finding all the materialls." [32] By November, 1729, the subcommittee was collecting ministerial taxes —its members, apparently, acting as tax collectors.* At the same time, Ammi Ruhamah Cutter began to preach at North Yarmouth; whether at the invitation of the committee in Boston or of the resident subcommittee is not clear. Ten months later, he agreed to settle there, and two months after that, the townspeople organized a church, over which Cutter was ordained.

---

* In that month, Francis Wyman paid Samuel Seabury, one of the subcommittee, three pounds as the rate on his ten-acre home lot. N. Yar. Mss., I, 92.

The subcommittee worked out the terms of settlement with Cutter, and gave to Captain James Parker, one of its members, written instructions to take with him on a trip to Boston sometime during 1730. The note directed Parker to ask the committee in Boston "whether they have confermd what we have don in order to the Settelment and Salary of mr. Cuttor." Parker was also instructed to discover whether the Boston committee had designated a tax collector, whether it would allow the spending of more money on the meetinghouse as voted by the townspeople, and whether it would approve of "alowances" the subcommittee had granted to owners of lots through which public roads were to be run.[33]

It is apparent, then, that although the resident subcommittee's powers and responsibility for proposing and initiating action extended into every realm of municipal affairs, it could do little without confirmation from Boston. Relations between the resident and nonresident committees were becoming strained at this point. One can admire the wisdom of the Boston committee's appointment of resident representatives and at the same time recognize that as the community's affairs became more complex, the administrative process became more cumbersome—too much so, in fact, for efficient operation. Captain Parker's instructions thus closed with an expression of that exasperation which has always been felt by those whose governors (or employers) are separated from them by distance, experience, or administrative machinery: "But and if they have not don any thing on thos afayrs nor doe not forth with doe them, than that you apply yourself to the Great and Generall Court for releefe in Said afayrs."[34]

The troubles between the resident and absentee directors reflected the differences in interest between the proprietors who lived in and those who lived away from North Yarmouth, and they had only just begun. They culminated in the subcommittee's resignation in March, 1730/1, shortly after John Powell, one of the Boston committee's own number, arrived in the township.

Among the issues which divided the Boston supervisors and the subcommittee were the continued granting of extensions for the completion of residence requirements, the choice of a surveyor for further land divisions (the Boston committee picked John Jones, a nonresident; the subcommittee refused to pay him because it felt a surveyor could be procured locally for less money), the division of the salt marsh meadows, and certain land concessions that the Boston committee ordered made in favor of John Powell. What seems to have been the climactic factor in the subcommittee's resignation was expressed this way in its letter to Boston: "You likewise Impose on us the Advice of Mr. Powell in all Affairs which we as a Committee Cannot Comply with." [35]

Why had the Boston committee not been more indulgent of the men who were at once the leaders of the community and the superintending committee's delegates on the scene? The answer is simple: politics. The North Yarmouth subcommittee constituted only one of several pressures on the Boston men, in whose hands, after all, rested the disposition of considerable property.

Of all the counterpressures, the nonresident proprietors, of whom the committee itself was constituted, provided the most effective. Nine of these proprietors, including Powell and John Smith of the resettlement committee, petitioned the Governor and General Court in 1731 to intercede in the resettlement of the township and require an accounting from the resident subcommittee. The nonresident proprietors, like the subcommittee, were impatient of delays in the division of the common lands. Each wanted his share, and worried lest the residents' desire for status as a town would put nonproprietors in a voting position before the lands were divided among the proprietors.

The nine proprietors based their plea upon their financial contributions to the resettlement and upon the payment of their shares of the meetinghouse assessment and the ministerial and road taxes. They expressed to Belcher and the legislature their fears of "unfaire and Imprudent Management and proceedings" by the resident proprietors, some of whom, they complained, had not yet met the conditions of their grants. Nor, they added, had the inhabitants finished building the meetinghouse or paid Mr. Cutter all his salary and settlement fee.

The petitioners also complained that the resident proprietors "often meet and allow those that are not Proprietors nor Qualified to Vote among them," and that they had at times "neglected and Refused to obey the Votes and Directions of the Committee and Proprietors." For all these reasons, the petitioners argued, "the Nonresident Proprietors cannott with any Reason expect justice will be done to them in the Division of the Common Land or in the Settlement of the Accounts nor in any of the other Articles aforementioned if they Should be Sett off to act as a Town Which we hear they are apetitioning for." The absentee proprietors' fears that the residents of the township, property owners and tenants alike, were developing a firmer bond of common interest than that which united the resident and nonresident proprietors had considerable basis in fact. In this frontier community, as in others where circumstances were similar, a man's fundamental consciousness was not as an owner or nonowner of property, but as a pioneer who was sharing with his neighbors the hardships and dangers of a peculiar way of life. The absentee owners were beginning to recognize this fact, although they undoubtedly failed to understand the reasons for it, and it disturbed them profoundly.

Like the scrupulous stockholders they were, the petitioners followed their businessmen's instincts, which told them that the proper solution to this political problem lay in the ledger sheet. They asked, first, that the Massachusetts government confirm the boundaries of the town if necessary, and order the immediate division of the common lands among all the proprietors. They then demanded "That the Sub Committee at North Yarmouth appointed for building the Meeting House etc. and also the Several Collectors appointed for Receiving the Taxes may all of them be Compelled to give in fair and just accounts to Such Persons as Your Excellency and this honbl. Court shall please to appoint to receive and Settle the Same."

It is interesting that these proprietors apparently viewed the resident subcommittee as a body with only very specific delegated duties, of which the building of the meetinghouse was the most important— no doubt because it involved the greatest expenditure of money. The petition acknowledged that the ultimate goal ought to be full town status, but insisted that the redress of the nonresident proprietors' grievances be a condition of such a move.[36] The General Court, with Governor Belcher's concurrence, responded to the petition by demanding an "Account of their proceedings" from the committee for resettlement.[37]

Influence from still another direction came from the Reverend Mr. Cutter, who more than once appealed to the resettlement committee in desperation because local difficulties in collecting taxes had held up the payment of his salary. In March 1730/1, four months after his ordination in North Yarmouth, Cutter complained to the supervising committee that he had as yet received "Little or Nothing" of the payments due him for his duties before his ordination, and that the first hundred pounds of his settlement fee and his first four months' salary were overdue.

Cutter's letter, though written from a somewhat different viewpoint from that of his fellow residents, reflected some of the same wistful hinting at the extreme difficulty of life in a wilderness settlement, which, all those who were there felt, could be known only by men on the spot. He asked for steps toward levying the proper taxes "so I may have wherewithal for my present Subsistence, and to proceed in My Buildings and Improvements, which in a new Place, as you are sensible, is very difficult and chargeable." [38] On the following August 16, Cutter, again referring to the difficulties of life "in this new Country," reported that he still had not been paid, and that no taxes had yet been collected, "Notwithstanding you were so careful, last March, as to vote my Salary for the Current year, and appoint Collectors." [39] From the frontier, again, where the real business of settlement was taking place, we find a suspicion of bureaucratic ineffectiveness on the part of absentee directors.

On October 9 of that year, the proprietors, apparently acting on an order from the supervising committee, appointed Andrew Ring a collector "to gather the Ministers Sallary and Settlement." [40] Nevertheless, Cutter's financial difficulties continued. On March 9, 1732/3, the minister wrote to Boston in his precise, disciplined hand, threatening point-blank to leave the town "for want of a Subsistence" unless "some good Method can be Speedily taken, to procure my Mony." For the first time, he suggested how the committee might help him out of his difficulty. The collectors, he wrote, complained that their warrants contained no provision for penalizing delinquent taxpayers except those who could actually be "sought out." There was, therefore, no means of enforcing collections from the many (and influential) absentee owners. Cutter proposed "subjecting the Lands to the Payment of the Taxes"—that is, providing for forfeiture of lands on which taxes were delinquent. "But," he added tactfully, "I rest it with the Honorable Committee." Cutter complained in the same letter that although his ministerial lot was to have been cleared and fenced by the previous November, "there is not as yet One Stroke struck towards it." [41] He placed his problem before the committee again the following December, this time also expressing discouragement at the slow rate of the township's development. [42]

Cutter remained as pastor until his dismissal by the church in 1735, despite continued financial troubles. After leaving his pulpit, Cutter, already a dominant figure in community affairs in spite of his parishoners' "uneasiness" over his "rank Arminianism," settled on the lot provided for the permanent use of the first minister and lived as the town's chief and most powerful citizen until the end of his days. [43] Throughout the period when it controlled the affairs of the township, the resettlement committee found in Cutter a persistent and articulate spokesman, both for himself and for his fellow residents.

The minister's troubles were related to those of the various tax collectors. The exasperated tones of Andrew Ring's letters became almost as familiar to the Boston committee as the poignant pleas of Ammi Ruhamah Cutter. His theme was the necessity of having power to sell delinquent tax lands "according to the Province Law, in such Cases provided; or be instructed in some other effective Method of Coming at the Mony." Failing that, Ring told the committee in December, 1732, he wished to "be set free from the Troublesome Imployment of being Collector for North Yarmouth." The committee's answer, while not exactly satisfactory, kept Ring on the thankless job for another year. It merely promised to seek further instructions from the General Court, enjoining Ring, "in the mean time Do all you can." [44] Ring wrote to the committee again three months later, slyly suggesting that his first letter might "By . . . accident have miscarried," and repeated his request and his threat.[45] Finally, on December 4, 1733, he sent to the committee, at Cutter's suggestion, a list of the ten lots for which he had been unable to collect any taxes. To the customary closing flourish of the eighteenth century, he added a Yankee bite:

> And now Gentlemen, I hope you will take These Lots, into your
> own Hands and Discharge Your Humble Servant
>   Andrew Ring.[46]

With that abrupt resignation, the committee's troubles with Andrew Ring were over. His and Cutter's influence, however, no doubt were responsible for the committee's securing authority from the General Court to attach the lands of lax taxpayers only a few weeks too late to forestall Ring's resignation. The Court ordered the collection of all the £215 10s. then due Mr. Cutter, authorizing the collectors to attach goods, chattels, and bodies, and, for lack of all those, to proceed against the delinquent lots.

The committee sent a warrant commanding such action to Rowland Houghton as "Collector of part of the Taxes and fines imposed on the Proprietors of North Yarmouth," using for the first time a printed form with the appropriate particulars entered in the blank spaces. It addressed similar warrants to John Smith, its clerk, to Samuel Seabury, Stephen Larraby, and Phineas Jones, all members of the former subcommittee, and to Edward King. Houghton took his oath as collector on April 18, 1734, and North Yarmouth, though still a closely supervised colony of the General Court, became armed with the necessary coercive apparatus for collecting taxes.[47]

Houghton's name had first been mentioned in connection with tax-collecting duties in June, 1732, when one of the collectors chosen from among the nonresident proprietors petitioned the General Court for more authority and at the same time asked for the appointment of Houghton as an assistant.[48] The legislature answered on July 3, 1732, with an order giving the collectors of North Yarmouth the same authority in their township "as any of the Collectors within any of the Towns of this Province are impowred by Law unto." [49]

This order, curiously, had been either ignored or interpreted with extreme conservatism throughout the exchange between Ring and the committee, all of which was subsequent to its passage. Since November 3, 1731, town and precinct collectors had been empowered specifically to seize lands of delinquent nonresident proprietors and sell them for taxes.[50] It seems not unlikely, in fact, that the complaints from North Yarmouth may have had some influence on the passage of this legislation. The legislature's order of July, 1732, seems to have been intended to provide the collectors of North Yarmouth—technically, neither a town nor a precinct at that point, accounting for the necessity of the special order—with the same authority.

Why, then, was Andrew Ring complaining as much as a year and a half later that he had no means of enforcing collections from absentee proprietors? Except for a rare special delegation to Boston, the town's only source of official news was the supervising committee. Certainly the committee, being composed of some of the leading citizens of the province, including at least two members of the House of Representatives that had passed the order of 1732, knew of the developments in Boston. One can hardly escape the conclusion, therefore, that because of pressures from absentee proprietors, the committee deliberately withheld some of these developments for a time from the settlers at North Yarmouth. Possibly, because of differences or dissatisfaction with the troublesome Ring, the necessary communications were held back until the committee had, in effect, forced his resignation. There is no record of new action on this matter by the General Court during the session that was in progress when the warrants were sent to the collectors in February, 1733/4.

A pressure group of all resident proprietors and tenants countered to a small degree the influence of the absentee proprietors. The supervising committee received frequent letters from the residents in general, or from small groups of them, both before and after the period during which the subcommittee was active. From 1727 to the spring of 1731, however, the residents apparently regarded the subcommittee as their spokesman and were quiet as a group.

The distinction between the public activities of the resident proprietors and those of the whole number of residents is, at best, vague. Occasional meetings of "proprietors and settlers" began at least as early as 1728. In 1729, there was a meeting of the "proprietors residing in North Yarmouth" and another of the "Proprietors of North Yarmouth." [51] It is not clear whether this last included absentee as well as resident proprietors. Finally, beginning in 1731, there were meetings of increasing frequency simply of "inhabitants." The records of these meetings are sometimes ambiguous as to precisely which group took the action; one concludes, therefore, that the distinction between "proprietors" and "inhabitants" meant little to those whose lives were most immediately affected by decisions respecting the development of the township.

"At a meeting of the inhabitants of north yarmouth," begins the record of a session on March 24, 1731, ". . . the town or proprietors mad choice of [two chainmen] . . . to assist Mr. John Jones in the present survaye." The next paragraph begins, "the Inhabitants allso voted," and the following one, "it was allso voted." [52]

It was the inhabitants' consciousness of their shared difficulties as settlers in a wilderness community, not economic distinctions, which shaped their relationship with their absentee supervisors and the absentee proprietors. If, to secure a more impressive number of signatures on petitions or simply because of a feeling of common cause, neighbors who were tenants instead of owners were sometimes invited to attend official or quasi-official meetings, it would not be surprising. The fairly frequent meetings of "residents" or "inhabitants" undoubtedly were ostensibly meetings of resident proprietors. But the resident proprietors were more closely allied in interest with their neighbors than with proprietors in Boston or other places. Therefore, as the alarmed absentee proprietors pointed out in their petition of 1731, they sometimes refused to exclude the other members of the community from participation in their decisions.

4

John Powell, though welcomed with considerable suspicion by many of his new neighbors, brought new life to North Yarmouth. At the age of sixty-one, he left a comfortable city home and the direction of a successful mercantile operation to settle on his extensive holdings in the primitive township whose resettlement he had been helping to supervise. Life in the tiny wilderness community seemed so unpromising to his wife, the sister of Lieutenant Governor William Dummer, that she refused to move with him. On one of his several lots on the shore of Broad Cove, Powell erected the handsomest house in town. He built a sawmill on Felt's Brook, and, at a cost of more than £1,500, experimented unsuccessfully with linen manufacturing.[53]

After his arrival, probably early in 1731, the residents continued to bombard the Boston committee with complaints similar to those of the former subcommittee. Beginning in that year, however, the meetings of "inhabitants" began to deal with a greater variety of public concerns, suggesting the presence of a new and experienced, imaginative, and influential mind at work in local affairs. In March, 1731, the inhabitants voted to "revive" a three-year-old provision for encouragement of a gristmill on Royal's River and submitted their action to Boston for confirmation.[54] The following June, the same body of voters made a fifty-acre grant to a war widow, altered previous arrangements concerning a school lot, voted to lay out some new roads, and voted for a new division of 103 fifty-acre lots.[55] In March, 1732, the Boston committee not only confirmed this division, but more than doubled it.[56] One must attribute this sudden change in affairs, at least in part, to the presence of Powell. The committee had sent him to settle there, apparently, to help resolve the differences between the residents and the committee.[57] The influence of this new resident with the committee and the nonresident proprietors must have been a factor in the new unanimity of purpose that is discernible, for example, in the division of the back lands.

The final accomplishment came in the spring of 1733. In February, the Boston committee submitted a detailed report of its activities to the General Court and recommended that the committee now be dismissed. It proposed that North Yarmouth be granted all the powers and privileges of a town, and that the proprietors now manage the common and undivided lands.[58] On April 6, the Court authorized Samuel Seabury as a justice of the peace to call a town meeting for the election of officers, and directed the delivery of a province law book to North Yarmouth.[59]

The town elected officers at the first town meeting on May 14, 1733, and held another meeting, at which it ordered the selectmen to complete the partially finished meetinghouse, on January 8, 1734.[60] The

records of the General Court indicate that the committee was attempting to finish its business with the Court between February and April,
1734.[61] On April 18, 1735, the General Court received and answered
a petition from the selectmen concerning taxation.[62] This is the first
indication on record that town officers were carrying out their proper
function without reference to the Boston committee. As late as 1738,
however, the committee was instructed to report to the Court regarding some alleged mistakes during its active period.[63] The Court was
careful to keep the supervisory committee on duty until the town government and the propriety, which was formally organized in July, 1734,
were functioning smoothly and all questions about resettlement were
answered. There is, in fact, no record of the committee's ever having
been dismissed.

5

By 1740, North Yarmouth had a fully functioning town government
and a seat (not always filled) in the General Court. It had also
achieved a measure of economic and social maturity.

The proprietors conducted the final division of the lands in 1738
when it gave to each of their number a share in the many small islands
that lay within the town boundaries. In addition, each of the approximately one hundred owners had, besides his home lot, a hundred-
acre lot in the southwest part of the town, a lot of 120 acres near
Royal's River, two lots of a hundred acres each in the northeast part
of the town, and four acres of salt marsh or some equivalent.[64] Most
of these divisions were in valuable timberland. Settlers all along the
coast had found salt marshes to be rich sources of hay and material
for thatching, good grazing lands, and a fine place to hunt for water-
fowl.

The town boasted several gristmills and sawmills, a convenient
wharf for shipping boards, clapboards, and staves, an inn, and a meetinghouse.* Town documents during the 1730's refer to yeomen, housewrights, blacksmiths, millwrights, husbandmen, staymakers, joiners, a
physician (Mr. Cutter after he left the ministry), and gentlemen.
Among the titles in use in the town during this period were "Mr.,"

---

* The inn was owned by David Seabury. Public sales of tax-delinquent lands
were advertised to be held there in the *New-England Weekly Journal,* June 6, 13,
and 20, 1738, and September 15, 1741, and in the *Boston Gazette,* September 7,
1741.

"Captain," "Colonel," and "Esquire." In 1740, the town was raising a tax to pay the salary, not only of its minister, but also of a schoolmaster.[65]

The meetinghouse received the last touches, a steeple and stairs, in 1737.[66] The previous year, the proprietors had considered the provision of special seats in the building for Indians and Negroes, and in 1739 they "seated" the meetinghouse by drawing.[67] When the church was organized in 1730, nine men, including the pastor, signed the covenant. This was a long but fairly standard confession of faith and promise to fulfill the duties both of a church estate and "a godly and a sober and a righteous Life." *

By November 17, 1736, when the church ordained a new minister, Nicholas Loring, the full communicants numbered twenty men and twenty-four women. The congregation also included a number of halfway members who had "owned the covenant" and could have their children baptized but lacked the full status that would have entitled them to receive Communion. Up to 1735, Cutter had baptized fifty-six, including at least two adults. Under Loring's pastorate, which lasted until 1762, the church acquired 149 new members, most of them with "the Priviledge of Setting down at the Table of the Lord." The church exercised the same disciplinary functions that all other churches of the Massachusetts Standing Order performed under the Cambridge Platform. In 1749 and 1750, the church voted several acts of excommunication or suspension for drunkenness, "false speaking," suspicion of theft, and failure to respond to "measures for repentance." [68]

Thus North Yarmouth recovered from the Indian wars. The process was a tortuous one, and it engendered resentments. These very resentments, however, were instrumental in the early development of a

---

* The covenant, which appears in the Records of the First Parish Church of North Yarmouth (Mss., Maine Historical Society), I, is, despite its length, either noncommittal or ambiguous on every peculiar point of traditional Calvinist doctrine, although it contains nothing with which a Massachusetts Puritan of the seventeenth century would have disagreed. Its relative theological vagueness undoubtedly should be interpreted neither as a concession to the Arminian tendencies of Mr. Cutter, the pastor, nor to that dilution or mutation of the religious standards of early Massachusetts in the eastern parts that we have noticed in other connections. It was probably rather a reflection of the standardization and stylized expression of the faith that had crept into the New England churches along with the "free and catholick spirit" of the period. The North Yarmouth covenant is very similar to, and in some of its phrasing identical with the church covenant signed in Scarborough two years earlier. See Records of the First Congregational Church in Scarborough (Ms. copy, Maine Historical Society), pp. 3–5.

camaraderie and a spirit of community solidarity among all the town's residents, whether or not they were owners of property. There is also evidence in the correspondence from North Yarmouth to Boston of a kind of frontier consciousness which expressed itself in the compulsion to relate, or refer to at every opportunity, the hardships of wilderness life. A part of this same consciousness was a suspicion of the men back home—a feeling of being at the mercy of persons who were not only in better surroundings, but also in places of influence and power. The facts justified these resentments and suspicions to a large extent.

But the biggest fact of all is that the General Court, acting through a relatively simple but workable colonial apparatus, nursed a deserted frontier hamlet along the difficult road to a place among equals in the sisterhood of Massachusetts towns. It is doubtful that the few settlers who in the beginning looked upon North Yarmouth as a home rather than an investment could have achieved anything comparable by their own devices alone.

CHAPTER X

Moses Pearson and
Old Falmouth
1727–1764

1

The weary parson frowned and wrote in his diary, "Annual town meeting. The caballing party carried all before them, and got all the officers of their party." [1] It was March 26, 1728. The little town of Falmouth, Maine, whose four hundred residents had become accustomed only recently to the wig, black coat, and ministerial bands that the Reverend Thomas Smith had brought with him from his native Boston, was feeling the pangs of growth. [2]

After peace had returned to the eastern parts in 1713, two sorts of families had begun to settle on Falmouth Neck, the site of old Fort Loyal and of a few scattered houses long since deserted. Some of the settlers, who actually claimed title to the entire peninsula, had lived there prior to 1690 or derived their claims from former inhabitants. They called themselves the "old proprietors." They were swiftly outnumbered by discharged soldiers who had served under Major Samuel Moody at Fort Loyal and perhaps others who had followed the lead of Moody and Benjamin Larrabee, his second in command, and settled on the neck when the garrison was disbanded. These were the "new proprietors," who based their claims upon an act of 1718 by which the General Court had incorporated the town.* The act of incorporation provided that at least fifty additional families be admitted to the

---

* The town as incorporated in 1718 embraced modern Portland, South Portland, Cape Elizabeth, Westbrook, and Falmouth. Falmouth Neck and its immediate surroundings were separated from the rest of the town in 1786 and named Portland.

town and settled "in the most compact and defensible manner that the land will allow of." [3]

The new settlers had taken control of municipal affairs from the beginning of the resettlement. Over the protests of the old proprietors, they had begun at once to admit new inhabitants in order to satisfy the statutory requirement and to perfect their claims, which rested on unsure ground indeed. By 1727, the new proprietors had been strong enough to push through the town meeting a provision authorizing the sale of public lands to all comers who would agree to settle. This enactment had infuriated the old proprietors, especially the nonresidents among them, and no doubt was wholly illegal. The minority stood helplessly by, however, while no less than 138 persons brought their families from Boston, the North Shore, New Hampshire, and southern Maine to settle on Falmouth Neck. Under the town meeting's act of 1727, any person could have a lot and a share in the common land and be admitted as an inhabitant upon his promise to settle and his payment of £10 to the town treasury.[4]

The controversy between "old" and "new" proprietors flamed hotly for the next five years. Mr. Smith, as an assignee of one of the original claimants, favored the "old" side. As the entry in his diary indicates, he shared the indignation of his party over what he felt to be an illegal and unwarranted usurpation of authority and property by the newcomers. As a result of the act of 1727, however, the town gained badly needed inhabitants and money for the empty treasury. The two parties settled their differences in 1732 by agreeing to a compromise under which a new propriety, including both sets of proprietors, took control of the common land from the town government and began to distribute land under an arrangement that treated all the proprietors equally. On the day of the agreement, Mr. Smith wrote, "This was the happiest meeting Falmouth ever had. Thanks to God." [5]

Land hunger and postwar wanderlust drove New Englanders northeastward during the 1720's.* In the case of Falmouth, there were attractions beyond the fundamental one of land: masts and commerce. The *New-England Weekly Journal* observed on May 8, 1727:

> We have an Account that the Mast-Business, which has for some
> time been so much the Benefit of the Nei'bour Province of New-

---

* The speculative fever, of course, was also instrumental in the expansion of the New England settlements in this period, as is noted in Chapter XI. Speculation as a motive for expansion, however, applies principally to investors and to the grantees who became absentee proprietors rather than to the new settlers themselves.

Hampshire, is removed farther Eastward, where it has been carried on the last Winter with such Success as could hardly have been expected, considering the very little seasonable Weather for it. Capt. Farles in one of the Mastships now lies in Casco-Bay, who we hear is not a little pleas'd with the peculiar Commodiousness of that Fine Harbour to carry on the said Business: And as this must very much tend to Encourage the Settlements of those Parts of the Country, especially the flourishing Bay, that will be the Centre of it, so, there is no reason to fear but that our Government will in their Wisdom look upon it very much their Interest to protect and encourage it.

Ralph Gulston, contractor with the Royal Navy for New England masts, explained to his superiors in 1728 that "by reason of the great Waste of late Years made of white Pine Trees, in the Province of Newhampshire . . . I found it impracticable now to get them there, which obliged me to Send a Number of Men, Cattle and Materials, further along the Coast to the Eastward to a place called Casco Bay." [6]

Falmouth now equaled and eventually replaced Portsmouth as a shipping point for Navy masts. Colonel Thomas Westbrook, who was appointed a royal mast agent after service as commander-in-chief of the eastern forces during the Indian hostilities which ended in 1727, moved from his native Portsmouth to Falmouth. The town admitted him as an inhabitant upon his payment of the £10 fee on August 17, 1727. Besides serving the Crown in his official capacity, he soon started a sawmill at Saccarappa Falls on the Presumpscot, built two paper-mills, the first in New England, and became actively and, it proved, disastrously involved with General Samuel Waldo in speculation in lands to the east. [7]

Scores of other ambitious men, some of substantial wealth, joined the migration to Falmouth Neck in 1727 and 1728. [8] Fifteen years earlier, Falmouth had been little more than a charred, nearly deserted army post. It had been organized as a town for less than a decade. As recently as 1725, when Mr. Smith had first arrived at Casco Bay two years before his ordination, he had found only fifty-six poor families, including "some that were soldiers, who had found wives on the place, and were mean animals." [9] Now Falmouth was fast becoming a major Massachusetts seaport.

2

Onto the exciting, turbulent scene of 1727 and 1728 came dozens of the future commercial and political leaders of the Neck. Most of them were more typical of the society that was beginning to develop there than Colonel Westbrook, a product of aristocratic Portsmouth who gave to his modest dwelling on the outskirts of Falmouth the pretentious name of "Harrow House." [10] Among them was Moses Pearson, a "joiner" from Newbury whose grandfather, a Congregational deacon, had emigrated to Ipswich in the 1640's. Falmouth had begun its integration with the society and culture of Massachusetts with the coming of Mr. Smith, who on March 8, 1727, had become the first minister to be ordained east of Wells. The process was completed during the next two years, when families of such stock as Pearson's swiftly outnumbered the few Anglicans, sympathizers with the old Gorges regime, and plain heathens who remained.

Pearson was about thirty years old when he moved his wife and his four daughters from Newbury to Falmouth.* A man of solid means, he was not one of the 138 men who bought an interest from the town for £10 each. Instead, he purchased a special grant of two hundred acres. In 1730, he added to his holding by buying a large parcel of land owned by Daniell Ingersoll, the current holder of one of the oldest claims on the Neck.[11] Pearson thus bought his way into both the "old" and the "new" proprietors. Perhaps it was because of his unique position in the prime local controversy of the day that he was drawn so rapidly into public affairs.

Even before his purchase of the Ingersoll claim made Pearson an "old" proprietor, the new settlers had recognized him as a leader of their group. In January, 1730, the town chose him one of a committee of four "to hear the proposals of the ancient settlers." He was designated clerk of the new proprietors, whom a justice of the peace had authorized to meet as a propriety in 1730, and he continued to serve as clerk of the joint propriety after the "union" of 1732.[12] The records make it plain that Pearson, already one of the largest landowners in town, was instrumental, perhaps more than any other individual, in bringing about peace between the two warring proprieties. His stature in the town assured, he became town clerk, selectman, and town treasurer during his first few years in Falmouth. He represented the town in the General Court in 1737, 1740, and 1749. In 1745, he raised a company of soldiers which he led to Louisbourg, and retained his title of "Captain" for the rest of his days.[13]

---

* Two more daughters were born to the Pearsons after they moved to Falmouth. All six girls lived to marry, and all except one of them bore Moses Pearson grandchildren. Henry Cole Quinby: *New England Family History*, II (New York, 1908–9), 165.

Pearson must have had little time to practice his old trade of wood-working during his career in Falmouth, which lasted until his death in 1778. Indeed, he had progressed so far beyond the station of artisan that in 1749, he was accorded in a legal document the title of "gentle-man." [14] He devoted his energies to his land dealings, to commerce, and to public affairs. When the Royal authorities decided about 1730 to appoint a naval officer to collect customs in the port of Fal-mouth, the post went to Pearson.[15] During much of his life, he was a justice of the peace, and when the new county of Cumberland was set off from York County in 1760, Pearson became its first sheriff.[16]

Sometime between 1752 and 1764, Pearson built a large wharf which projected from the shore opposite his waterfront house, and the evidence, though sparse, demonstrates unmistakably that Pearson had mercantile interests in Falmouth still earlier.* Among his other ac-tivities, he was a licensed innkeeper.[17] His reputation as a dedicated public servant and noted landholder could have been responsible for the invitation from William Pepperrell to raise a company for the expedi-tion to Cape Breton in 1745.[18] It was a different kind of reputation, however, that moved the general to appoint Pearson agent for the entire regiment during the division of the spoils of conquest. Pearson attended to that duty, and to the thousand administrative details re-lating to the equipping and provisioning of his own company, with the precision of an experienced accountant and skilled businessman.[19] This sort of careful attention to administrative and financial matters, upon which Pearson built his personal success, must also have been responsible for his frequent appointment as clerk of the Falmouth proprietors, the town, the First Parish, the proprietors of Gorhamtown, and, after the war, the proprietors of a township named in his honor (Pearsontown, later Standish) which was granted to a group of Maine veterans of the expedition.

---

* On a map of Falmouth in 1775, reproduced in William Willis: *The History of Portland* (Portland, Me., 1831), II, between pp. 156 and 157, and in *Journals of the Reverend Thomas Smith and the Reverend Samuel Deane . . .*, ed. William Willis (Portland, 1849), between pp. 338 and 339, one of the several larger docks on the waterfront is labeled with Pearson's name. The same wharf appears on a "Chart of Portland Harbor" engraved in 1764 by J. F. W. DesBarres, a copy of which is located among the Willis papers in the Maine Historical Society. Of the harbor in 1752, Willis wrote, "There were no wharves extending into the harbor: short piers furnished all the facilities required; large ships were loaded in the stream." (*Smith and Deane Journals*, p. 138 *n.*) This would indicate, if Willis was correct, that all the major pre-Revolutionary wharves, including Pear-son's—nearly all of which were destroyed in the British raid of October 18, 1775— were built between 1752 and 1764.

Moses Pearson, though not entirely overlooked by the local chroniclers, has suffered by comparison with their extensive treatments of Samuel Moody, the Reverend Mr. Smith, Colonel Westbrook, and a few others. His comparative obscurity in the published histories of Falmouth and Portland, while understandable because of the lack of comprehensive documentary remains, by no means reflects his stature in the community during the half-century he lived on the Neck. One might select other men with whom to illustrate the life of Falmouth during the first three decades or so of that period. Pearson, however, demonstrates better than most of his local contemporaries that combination of native business acumen, opportunism, civic consciousness, and scrupulous attention to detail that helped the Massachusetts Yankee to tame the eastern parts. Pearson arrived in Falmouth at the moment that town life was becoming economically and politically stable. He not only shared in its fortunes during the ensuing fifty years of maturation, but contributed significantly to them.

A Massachusetts Congregationalist by birth, upbringing, and more-or-less serious conviction, Pearson reminds us of the importance of his kind in the development of all of the Maine and many of the New Hampshire towns after 1713. He also reminds us of the importance of the wars in the history of Falmouth and the eastern parts, because his reputation and fortunes were affected profoundly by an episode of warfare. Let this introduction to Moses Pearson, therefore, serve also as an introduction to old Falmouth, because the biography of one is in a large sense the history of the other.

3

The Falmouth into which Pearson brought his family in 1728 bore little physical resemblance to prosperous Portsmouth, with which the Casco Bay settlement was just now beginning to compete as an eastern port, or with Pearson's native Newbury, which in ninety-three years of existence had acquired more than 180 houses and families.[20] No Archibald Macpheadris had acquired a fortune in commerce and added a graceful brick dwelling to the village scene. No Benning Wentworth had established a rambling country seat on the outskirts. The only public building was a plain framed meetinghouse, thirty-six by twenty-eight feet, not yet entirely finished inside.[21]

In 1726, the town probably contained something more than sixty dwelling houses, the majority of them on the Neck.[22] By the time

Pearson arrived two years later, some of the 138 men who had bought a town right in 1727 and 1728 must have been building houses. The scene, though a busy one, was far from elaborate. Simple framed houses, one story high and usually unpainted, were the rule.[23] On the islands in Casco Bay and on the shore surrounding the Neck stood a number of fortified log houses, a reminder of the war years. One of these, at Purpooduck (now South Portland), had been built as a combination fort and meetinghouse. Here Mr. Smith preached to the people on the south side of the Fore River every third Sunday.[24] The best house in town was the minister's, but though authorized by the town in 1727, this two-story house, forty by twenty feet, was still four years away from completion.[25]

Thanks to the foresight of the first town fathers and the requirements of convenient apportioning of lots, streets had been laid out on the Neck, which by then was serving as the center of a far-flung township, much as Strawberry Bank was the center of Portsmouth. The Neck ran out from the mainland from southwest to northeast, curving northward as it approached the end. The northern end of the peninsula, a rise of ground called Munjoy's Hill, nearly enclosed a small round bay known as Back Cove between the Neck and the mainland. The principal streets were King Street, which cut about halfway through the peninsula, southeast to northwest, just to the west of Munjoy's Hill, and three roughly parallel streets that ran from King Street to the southwest. These were Fore Street, which followed the waterfront, the back street or Queen Street, laid out lengthwise through the Neck about a hundred rods from the waterfront and an equal distance from Back Cove, and Middle Street, about halfway between "the fore" and "the back" streets. Toward its western end, Middle Street turned fairly abruptly to the northwest to form an intersection with Back Street. An extension of Back Street running west from this intersection, which soon became the site of a hay market, was named Main Street.* Nearly all the other streets that were opened during the eighteenth century ran approximately parallel with King Street, connecting Fore with Middle or Middle with Back Street.

Clustered about the foot of King Street was the commercial center

---

* Everyday usage overruled an official attempt to bestow a proper name upon "the back street," and it was therefore generally known as Back Street rather than Queen Street. This street and its western extension now comprise Congress Street, the principal business thoroughfare in the modern city of Portland. See Willis: *Portland*, II, 19 *n.* King Street is now India Street.

of the town. Here was the most congested part of the village, its public wharf and narrow streets noisy with the bustle of stevedores and sailors. Here the local fishermen brought their daily catches to be sold fresh to the townsfolk or to be salted and dried nearby to provide cargoes for the West Indies. Here lumbermen and merchants assembled other cargoes of boards, staves, oars, shingles, clapboards, and timbers. The fragrance of freshly cut pine and cedar mingled with the pungent aromas of fresh fish, tar, and the sea slime on piles and ships' hulls, the clean tang of salt air, and the heavy smell of the mud flats which wafted over the Neck from Back Cove and Fore River at low tide.

A few yards east of the town dock lay the ruins of old Fort Loyal, whose stockade and timbers had been burned by the Indians when they had overrun the Casco settlement in 1690.[26] Nearby stood the temporary home of Mr. Smith and the residence of Major Moody, who died at the end of 1729, worth £2,447. Since Moody's house included four bedrooms in addition to a garret, it must have stood two stories high—one of the very few of such grand proportions in town.[27]

From the town pier, one of two or three such small structures on the waterfront, sailed a ferryboat to Cape Elizabeth, the most convenient access to the main road to Portsmouth and Boston, and a growing number of schooners and sloops with lumber and fish for coastal ports or the West Indies.[28] On April 9, 1726, Mr. Smith had counted twenty-six vessels in the harbor, and in September, 1727, about thirty "for several days," numbers which he thought sufficiently extraordinary to note in his diary.[29] By 1752, the vessels *owned* at Falmouth Neck totaled but fifteen sloops and seven schooners, the largest of which was of eighty tons burden. Not until the following year did a Falmouth man, Jeremiah Pote, add the first topsail vessel, a hundred-ton brig, to the local fleet.*

Even as early as Pearson's arrival, Falmouth men had made a modest start at shipbuilding. Near the pier at the foot of King Street and in a small cove just to the east stood ways and perhaps the skeleton hull of one or two little vessels. Thomas Smith, whose house then overlooked the harbor, wrote on August 9, 1726, "A sloop built before my door was launched to-day." Earlier the same year, and again in

---

* Willis: *Portland*, II, 110. These figures do not include shipping owned at Cape Elizabeth, which was then a part of Falmouth. In 1745, five schooners and five sloops were owned at the Cape. Until the Revolution, the commerce of Cape Elizabeth rivaled that at Falmouth Neck. Willis: *Portland*, II, 111.

1728, he noted the arrival of Thomas Reddin of Gloucester, who "came down here with a considerable quantity of goods in order to build a sloop here." [30]

The southwestern half of the Neck, which is less than a mile across and about two and three-quarters miles long, was a wooded swamp. The land between Back Street and Back Cove was being divided into long three-acre lots, each with 130 to 150 feet frontage on the street. Probably none of these had been cleared when Pearson moved to town, except a portion of one. This was an oversized four-acre lot owned by John Wass, who had built a house on the north side of Back Street in 1720.[31] The new parsonage, then under construction, was also being built on the same side of that street.[32] Another decade or two elapsed, however, before the area north of Back Street showed substantial development. Munjoy's Hill, which remained undivided and undeveloped because of claims dating far back into the seventeenth century, was cleared for a pasture in 1741, and a stone wall was built to separate the pasture from the village. At least as early as 1744, some of the citizens were pasturing their livestock in this newly cleared field.[33]

4

The economy of Moses Pearson's new hometown rested almost wholly upon commerce. The townsmen neglected farming, for which the Neck was scarcely suitable in any case, because of their obsession with trade. The export of lumber, shipbuilding, and related activities, of course, constituted an entirely appropriate basis for the economy of a seaport on a forested coast. But the repeated failure of the Falmouth population to raise even nearly enough food for its own subsistence often resulted in serious shortages.[34]

The most spectacular exports, but probably not the most lucrative except for a very few individuals, were masts and spars for the Royal Navy. By 1727, the cutters and purveyors of Maine timber had learned that their product in its raw state brought greater profits than sawed lumber.[35] Although the prices of masts dropped steadily between 1690 and 1740, they remained extremely attractive, especially when bolstered by the standard £1 per ton bounty and special wartime bonuses.[36] In 1730, the Navy Board would pay £120 for a thirty-six-inch New England mast a hundred feet long, just under £60 for a thirty-inch mast ninety feet long, about £30 for a twenty-four-inch mast, and about £15 for a twenty-inch spar. In 1740, the price of the largest masts dropped to about £115, but by 1750 it had soared to £190

and in 1756 reached a peak of £218. In addition to these basic prices
and the bounty, New England mast contracts provided for an extra 10
per cent in case of war, and the bonus sometimes rose to as high as 25
per cent for delivery of the larger masts during wartime.[37] Several mast
ships sailed from Falmouth and Portsmouth each year, carrying "45 to
50 good masts per voyage." [38] For the handful of suppliers at these
eastern ports, therefore, masting was indeed big business!

In 1733, Colonel Westbrook, the mast agent for Maine, built "Harrow House" near the head of Fore River, about three miles west of
the village center. Westbrook had lived for a time in Scarborough before returning to Portsmouth after the eastern campaign of 1722–25.
There, he had collected masts on his private account and probably
hauled them along a short road to Long Creek, which empties into the
Fore near the site he now chose for his residence. Back in Portsmouth,
as a principal taxpayer and war hero, he had secured the appointment
as mast agent. At the same time, he seems to have recommended that
his part of the business, at least, be transferred to Casco Bay.[39] By
1743, the colonel's seventy-acre farm contained, besides his house,
"sundry out houses and garrisons round the same, and three small
cottages." [40] This fortified establishment stood on the south side of a
small stream that runs into the Fore river near its head. To the stream
and the village that gradually formed about his small estate, Westbrook gave the name of Stroudwater.

Two miles downriver on the Neck side, the British government
maintained a "mast house," where the masts were hewn to sixteen sides
and given proper taper, probably under Westbrook's personal supervision.[41] The trees for which Westbrook had contracted were floated
down the Stroudwater River or brought to the head of the Fore on
sleds drawn by as many as twenty-six oxen over a straight masting
road laid out for the purpose from the lower falls of the Presumpscot.[42]
At the head of the Fore, the trees were "twitched" into the water under
the eyes of the agent, whose primitive manor house overlooked this
collecting place. The government mast ships, despite their four- to six-
hundred-ton capacity, usually were able to go far enough up the river
to take on their awkward cargoes directly from this processing plant.
There, the hewn trees were loaded through the specially made stern
ports of these great vessels.*

* William Goold: *Portland in the Past* (Portland, 1882), p. 202; Willis: *Portland*, II, 108–9; William Douglass: *A Summary, Historical and Political . . .*
(London, 1760), II, 53. When a mast ship was launched in Boston in 1732, the
press reported that it was thought to be "the largest Ship that has been built in
this Province"; *New-England Weekly Journal*, October 30, 1732.

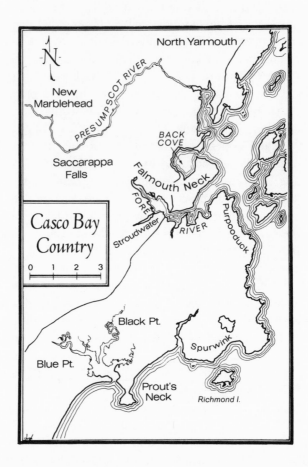

Few of the Falmouth townspeople shared directly in either the immense profits or the great risks of the mast trade. On the other hand, the mast ships and Westbrook and his successor, George Tate, exerted a considerable impact upon the economic and social life of the small town. Westbrook and Tate bought their masts from woodcutters in Falmouth, Scarborough, New Marblehead, and one or two other nearby towns. These men had permits from the surveyor general to enter the royal preserves, which at that time included all land not laid off in townships, and to cut the pines that were marked with the King's broad arrow.[43]

One of Westbrook's principal suppliers was his nephew, Nathaniel Knight, who in 1735 bought a hundred acres of land at Stroudwater Falls, not far from Westbrook's house, and built a two-story house and sawmill.* Here, he not only operated what became the best farm in the vicinity, but set up a lucrative enterprise as contractor to his uncle. His activities included "hunting masts" and working in the woods himself, hiring choppers and ox teams, procuring and feeding "mastwrights" to hew the logs at the mast house, clearing mast roads, hiring soldiers to guard mast parties during the war of 1744–48, and providing supplies for the colonel's farm. Even before moving to Stroudwater, Knight worked for his uncle, and either built or helped to build "Harrow House." [44] For the hardest kind of work, "hunting masts, fitting them, and clearing of roads," in which Knight spent forty-seven weeks for Westbrook in 1738, the colonel paid his nephew a pound a day. Solomon Bragdon, a sawyer on the upper part of the Stroudwater River who apparently entered the business after Westbrook's death in 1744, paid him at the same rate for "hunting, fitting, clearing and halling masts" for seventy-two and a half days. For more routine work around Westbrook's farm and the mast house, Knight charged about half as much. [45]

Between the death of the colonel and the arrival about 1750 of George Tate, the London merchant who succeeded him as agent, [46] Knight supplied Bragdon, Captain Joshua Bangs, and Colonel Jedediah Preble with masts. In the case of Bangs and Preble, he charged for the trees themselves at the rate of a pound per inch of diameter rather than for his time. Apparently, in hopes of making a greater profit, he began to take upon himself all the responsibilities and risks of getting the trees to the delivery point. He followed the same arrangement with Tate, to whom he sold sixty large spars in May, 1757, for £250. He supplied masts to Tate until 1769, but in much smaller quantities than he had to Westbrook. In 1754, Knight contracted with Samuel and Francis Waldo of Falmouth, sons of the general, to deliver fifteen mainmasts, eight foremasts, ten main yards, and ten bowsprits at Stroudwater Landing. The price for the specified "handsome straight and sound sticks" was fixed in advance: two shillings four pence per inch of diameter after Knight had hewed the larger masts "into Sixteen Squares" and the smaller sticks "into Eight Squares as is customary." [47]

* Both Nathaniel and his father, Nathan (who was married to Westbrook's sister), had been born in Scarborough and lived in the Dunstan section of that town, where Westbrook had sojourned briefly before moving to Falmouth. Leonard B. Chapman, "The Mast Industry of Old Falmouth," Maine Historical Society *Collections,* 2nd Ser., VII (1896), 392–3.

While only a few men such as Nathaniel Knight made a regular business of supplying the mast agents, Falmouth felt the effects of the industry in many other ways. There were wages to be earned by woodchoppers, owners and drivers of oxen, "mastwrights," and stevedores. During their three-month layovers in Falmouth harbor, the ships had to take on provisions from this port town, and their necessary repairs and refitting employed many of the more than twenty different kinds of craftsmen required in the shipbuilding industry of the eighteenth century.* Judging by an entry in the Reverend Mr. Smith's diary, it is at least possible that in 1737, the shipbuilders of Falmouth even built a mast ship. "They attempted to launch the mast ship," Smith recorded on October 14, "but she stuck." †

Besides stimulating the economy of Falmouth, the twenty-five-man crews of the visiting mast ships enlivened the social life of this isolated village.[48] It came to be commonplace to see one, two, or even three of these important vessels riding at anchor in the harbor for many weeks at a time. Their officers were well known to the leading citizens and while in port, added dash and glitter to the affairs of Falmouth society. The seamen enjoyed frequent liberty, and indulged pretty much the same appetites as sailors ashore in any age. On January 29, 1733, "Some of the ship's men were put into the stocks by order of Justice Wheeler." [49] Samuel Williams, "of Bristol in Great Britain, Mariner," encountered in November, 1760, at least one Falmouth local who could more than hold his own in a waterfront brawl. Williams swore out a complaint against James Welch, charging him with assault with a two-and-one-half-inch rope, "so that your Complainants Life was dispaired of." [50]

Relationships between the people of Falmouth and visiting ships' crews were usually more cordial. On April 18, 1747, Mr. Smith, who like many a New England clergyman served as the town surgeon as well as the minister, "was present at the taking off the hand of one

---

* See Carl Bridenbaugh: *The Colonial Craftsman* (New York, 1950), pp. 92–5. Captain Farles, whose arrival in Casco Bay the *New-England Weekly Journal* noted early in May, 1727, sailed on August 15. (*Smith and Deane Journals*, p. 52.) Other entries in Smith's journal indicate that this was not an unusual length of stay.

† *Smith and Deane Journals*, p. 87. Willis took this as positive evidence that the ship had been built at Falmouth (*Portland*, II, 107 *n.*) but furnishes no substantiation, nor have I found any further reference to the construction of a mast ship at Falmouth. Conceivably, such an attempted "launching" could as well have taken place after a ship had undergone repairs in drydock as after she had actually been built on the ways.

Doubleday by the Doctor of the mast ship." [51] When General Wolfe's army took Quebec in September, 1759, three mast ships lay in Falmouth harbor. Their captains and crews helped the populace conduct a proper celebration. On September 26, thirteen days after the British victory and nine days after the news had arrived in town, the three captains "made a great barbaque on Hog Island, for a general frolic." More detailed and authentic accounts filtered gradually to the Neck during the next few weeks. On October 15 and 16, the garrison at the fort fired cannon salutes, and at night, Simeon Mayo, who owned one of the larger houses in town, placed candles in all his windows in accordance with the common practice of celebrating great events by "illumination." On October 17, the three captains fired their guns and "illuminated" their vessels, and on November 1, Mr. Smith "dined with Capt. Granger, and spent P.M. on board Darling, with Capt. Hagget." [52]

Because the mast ships provided a popular means of passage to and from England among New England's "better sort," both Falmouth and Portsmouth frequently received visitors from Boston before the departure of a mast fleet.[53] During the wars of 1744–48 and 1756–63, a man-of-war arrived in the harbor a few days before each sailing to escort the returning mast ships. This safety measure, added to the relative comfort and prestige of a voyage in one of these large vessels, made passage in them still more attractive. The convoys included ships from both the northeastern ports, and frequently assembled in Casco Bay.

The men of Falmouth thoroughly enjoyed their company and the excitement of these wartime adventures. On October 26, 1756, a mast ship bearing "several Gentlemen Passangers," Captain Granger commanding, stood out from Piscataqua harbor to join Captain Tenny's ship and a naval escort at Falmouth.[54] Thomas Smith wrote four days later, "The town is full of company. In the harbor are Rouse [the captain of the escort], Tenny, Granger, the Deal ships and a scow from Boston." The assignment of the escort was changed, possibly because of losses suffered by Captain Rouse during his voyage from Halifax. Rouse returned to Halifax, and on November 12, the warship *Centurian* arrived from the northern naval base; soon afterward, the convoy sailed.[55] When another man-of-war reported for convoy duty at Falmouth in 1761, her captain invited Mr. Smith, Moses Pearson, Stephen Longfellow, Alexander Ross, and Enoch Freeman on board and entertained them all afternoon. The escort, a warship of forty guns, formed part of a convoy of seven vessels, including three mast ships, that sailed on August 31.[56]

The indirect effects of the mast industry upon Falmouth included the establishment of various other enterprises by the agent. The bold and energetic Westbrook set up sawmills and gristmills on the Presumpscot, the Stroudwater, and the tiny Piscataquis. Because of their novelty, his two papermills attracted more attention. Only the one near Harrow House on the Stroudwater River ever went into full operation. The colonel's water wheels must have turned the newly invented "Hollander" mill, a rotating cylinder mounted with knives for beating and slashing rags to pulp. His other attempt to establish such a mill was at Ammoncongin Falls on the Presumpscot, several miles inland from Stroudwater in the modern city of Westbrook.[57] Besides the straight masting road over the three miles from Saccarappa Falls, west of Ammoncongin, to Stroudwater, Westbrook built another roadway connecting his establishment at Stroudwater with the Neck. On at least two occasions, Mr. Smith rode over this road, once with a large group of neighbors in 1733 and once with his father in 1734, just to see the colonel's "great dam" and the site of the new papermill.[58]

Westbrook was not the only Falmouth man to enter the business of sawing lumber or grinding corn. He had at least seven partners, including Moses Pearson, in the sawmill on the Piscataquis, which was built in 1732, and was in partnership with Samuel Waldo and others when they built the papermill at Ammoncongin.[59] The export of lumber products was a principal basis of the town's economy. Moreover, the demand for building materials among the growing local populace was in itself considerable. By 1752, there were ten sawmills within the bounds of the First Parish alone.[60]

Because of the great possibilities for profit in lumbering, the sawmills multiplied more rapidly than the gristmills. Until the first grinding mill was built in 1727 at Cape Elizabeth, the families of Falmouth sent their corn to Biddeford.[61] Even as late as February, 1748, Joseph Conant's gristmill at Saccarappa was the only one between Saco and North Yarmouth.[62] After about 1750, a windmill on the south side of Back Street supplemented the town's one or two water-driven gristmills.[63]

The primary imports to Falmouth were foodstuffs, especially corn, from the colonies to the south. Falmouth's neglect of agriculture and heavy reliance upon imported food resulted in frequent scarcity, high prices, and occasionally the danger of real famine. Mr. Smith noted serious shortages of food in 1732, 1737, 1741, 1748, and 1753, and the Boston press reported in 1737 that some at "the Eastward" had actually died of starvation. Moreover, the report said, "Many Cattle have died for want of Provender, and the few left alive are so weak, that they are unfit for any Labour." * [64]

The merchants of Falmouth dealt in the usual variety of imported merchandise, which they received in exchange for shipments of lumber and fish, or for rum and molasses, which Falmouth ships took on in exchange for native products at the West Indies. The port of Casco Bay shared with the ports of the Piscataqua the task of meeting the huge demand in the Caribbean islands for building materials, barrels and hogsheads, and "trash" fish for feeding the masses of slaves who labored on the sugar plantations.† The merchants also experimented with whatever other enterprises appealed to them as offering sound possibilities for investment. Thus Westbrook, Pearson, and Enoch Freeman all had interests in lands. Freeman, one of the few men in Falmouth in the middle of the century who had a college degree, made an extensive business of carrying loads of firewood and lumber in his two gundelows, one of which plied up and down the Presumpscot. The other, he kept at Back Cove. Besides shipping on order, Freeman sometimes rented out his craft at ten shillings a day. He sold all kinds of goods, but the bulk of his business was in Maine lumber and imported meat and produce.[65]

Cash was scarce in Falmouth during the eighteenth century, as it was throughout the colonies. By 1750, when the province used its reimbursement of £183,649 sterling for the Louisbourg campaign to redeem its bills of credit, Massachusetts currency had so depreciated that £11 of whatever "tenor" was worth only £1 sterling.[66] Enoch Freeman probably had more hard money on hand than most Falmouth businessmen when on August 18, 1758, he opened a shot bag in his desk and counted £850 10s 4d, mostly in Spanish dollars, in addition to £45 3s 5d, which he was keeping in a drawer for change.[67]

---

* This dependence upon the Middle Colonies for food was common to the entire coast of Maine throughout the eighteenth century. See discussion by Percy W. Bidwell and John I. Falconer in *History of Agriculture in the Northern United States, 1620–1860* (Carnegie Institution of Washington Publications No. 358, Washington, D.C., 1925), pp. 143–4.

† In a period of about eight weeks in 1731, the island of Barbados alone imported 788,000 boards, planks, and joists, 1,370,000 shingles, 382,000 staves and barrel heads, 180,600 barrel hoops, seventy-five barrels of pitch, tar, and turpentine, and 640 hogsheads and six barrels of fish plus about 20,000 pounds of bulk fish. *New-England Weekly Journal*, April 12, 1731.

More typical was a nameless storekeeper whose account book shows that many of his customers paid their bills in merchandise, "sundries," potatoes, bullets, rum, molasses, wine, shoes, tea, bottles, paper, fish, cloth, candles, boards, shingles, firewood, clothing, labor, or, in one case, "By Shaveing." Though this shopkeeper apparently sold mostly barrels and hogsheads of "West Indian merchandise," Moses Pearson settled an account with him on May 6, 1754, by remitting a gallon of rum valued at four shillings.[68] One catches an illuminating glimpse of the state of the coastal trade from this anonymous business-man's notation that Samuel Parkman of Boston became indebted in the spring of 1754 for 5,000 boards valued at £6 and a year later for a £16 order of unspecified content, and finally paid the bill with two boxes of glass worth £6 and 120 bushels of corn worth £16.[69]

5

The people of Falmouth, most of whom had begun their lives in Massachusetts proper, were conscious of social distinctions in approximately the same degree as the people of any Massachusetts town of comparable size and economic interests. They looked to the "better sort" to serve as selectmen, to render justice in the various minor courts, and to represent them in the General Court in Boston. This upper class, while politically powerful and relatively prosperous, acquired none of the great wealth and developed little of the aristocratic demeanor of the first families of New Hampshire. The divisions of Falmouth society were principally the divisions of economic standing, and the "better sort" simply were moderately successful businessmen. None of them, not even Westbrook (who died insolvent), was able to live the life of a gentleman without attending to the daily press of business. Their main occupational distinction was that in their work, they seldom got their hands dirty.

Perhaps fifteen families, including those of Moses Pearson, Thomas Smith, Thomas Westbrook, the sons of Samuel Waldo, Enoch Freeman, Phineas Jones and his son-in-law Richard Codman, Stephen Longfellow, William Tyng, and a few others, composed the Falmouth gentry. Their cocked hats, wigs, and scarlet cloaks, which they wore over drab coats and breeches, provided symbols of their social standing. Until George Tate came to town in the 1750's, their houses were distinguished neither by great size nor by especially noteworthy architecture. They rode in two-wheel chaises, and although their surroundings lacked the opulence of those of a Portsmouth gentleman, they generally were served by one or two slaves.[70]

Thomas Smith might have been the exception to the rule that the upper class was composed only of successful businessmen. His collegiate education and professional station by themselves undoubtedly would have assured him a place in the gentry, as in most Massachusetts towns, even had he lacked the economic substance of his social peers. In possessions and style of life, however, the minister traveled in the best circles. Even as early as 1742, he owned a handsome estate, principally in lands, which made him the economic equal of all but the very wealthiest of his fellow townsmen. His holdings amounted to eighty-five acres of his own, his "mansion house, barn, etc.," as he described them, shares in eight farms and estates in Falmouth and elsewhere, his library, a chaise, and, by Falmouth standards, a fairly large herd of livestock.[71] In 1744, this consisted of four cows, a heifer, three horses, and ten sheep.[72]

Major Samuel Moody, designated "Esq." when his estate was inventoried after his death in 1729, was the principal local political leader of his day as well as one of the wealthiest men in town. His town rights in Falmouth, fifty acres each on the Casco River and Munjoy Neck, some land in North Yarmouth, and a mill stream and mill privileges (but not a mill) on a branch of the Presumpscot accounted for more than a quarter of his £2,447 estate. He lived comfortably in a large house, served by a Negro man and woman and a mulatto girl, and surrounded by such refinements as pewterware, six high-backed leather chairs, a number of other chairs, an oval table of cedar and another of maple, a couch, pictures, a map of Boston, a looking glass, and military paraphernalia. Moody's livestock consisted of five cows, a bull, a heifer, a calf, four oxen, two steers, ten sheep, two sows and a hog, a horse, and a mare. He owned a variety of agricultural implements and a gundelow.[73]

Phineas (or "Phinehas") Jones, whose name figures prominently in the resettlement of North Yarmouth as a resident proprietor and the principal surveyor of town boundaries, lots, and highways, moved to Falmouth Neck in the early 1730's at the age of twenty-four or twenty-five. He and his father, both of Worcester, Massachusetts, had speculated extensively in the eastern titles of old settlers, and moved to Maine to establish their claims. During his brief stay in Falmouth, which was cut short by an early death in 1743, Jones acquired much real estate on the Neck and extensive mercantile interests, served as a selectman and a representative to the legislature, continued his surveying work, and let out large amounts of money at interest. Most of his large estate of £8,782 was in bonds and notes of credit. He seems to have been a creditor of nearly everyone in Falmouth and many persons in the surrounding towns. When he died, he owned his homestead, which consisted of a house, barn, and small wharf on two acres of land, an interest in other lands, a great deal of furniture, a Negro man named Cambridge, an interest in a sloop and a schooner, three horses, a cow, three hogs, clothing worth over £132, 725 gallons of molasses, 107 gallons of rum, and 176 gallons of brandy.[74]

George Tate, the new mast agent, added the first touch of architectural dignity to Falmouth's housing. He erected a three-story framed house at Stroudwater overlooking the mast landing on Fore River. Tate used the gambrel roof, which was then popular elsewhere in New England. Either at the time of its construction or somewhat later, however, the lower slope of the roof on the front side was partially cut away to allow a narrow vertical surface containing three windows to be set into the roof. This unusual treatment, which gives the effect of dormer windows, is known locally as an indented gambrel roof. The center door was surmounted by a fan window, and the whole was enclosed by primitive doric pilasters and a simple angular pediment.

The interior of the Tate house was rich in wainscoting, and the drawing room contained a beautifully carved recessed china closet with a scallop-shell motif. The wooden floor of the entrance hall was painted in a black and off-white diamond pattern, in the manner of many of the best New England homes of the day. The staircase which led from this hall to the family's bedrooms on the second floor was relatively narrow, making square turns as it wound upward. The third-floor rooms seem to have been reserved for servants.

On the whole, the interior treatment of the Tate house was more successful than the exterior. The attempt to introduce fashionable architectural details resulted in what was all too obviously a compromise with the best taste and workmanship of the day, and the third-story windows were so placed as to destroy the symmetry which was preserved in the lower two stories. One might question, moreover, the aptness of placing in a rural setting a structure clearly designed as a townhouse. The house does demonstrate, however, not only the relative wealth of its builder, but also a self-conscious effort on the part of this newly arrived Londoner to show his Falmouth contemporaries how he thought a gentleman ought to live.

Next to the gentry in social dignity was the usual numerous class of shopkeepers, artisans, farmers, fishermen, and seamen. Such men varied greatly among themselves in means and occupation, but in common with the country yeoman class, lacked both the clearly superior economic and social standing of the "better sort" and any kind of dependent status.

The term "yeoman," in fact, was sometimes used as a social designation even for village dwellers on the Neck. William Rouse, a dealer in hats, was referred to as "yeoman" in the inventory of his estate, which was taken in 1737. The estate totaled something over £96, of which seventy-six felt hats accounted for nearly half. In addition, Goodman Rouse owned clothing, a Bible and some small books, an old ladle, a hundred needles and a supply of thread, a small iron, some "old leather stuff," six pounds of flax, a gun, eight yards of blanketing, a pickaxe, a supply of potatoes, a cow, a calf, seven shoats, and two hens. His wardrobe consisted of a "great coat" worth £2, two old hats, a few silver buttons, a "frocke," an old jacket, a pair of breeches, three shirts, a few pairs of stockings, and a pair of shoes.[75] The estate of Edmond Bowman, a shopkeeper who died in 1736, amounted to about the same value as Rouse's, though it varied in details.[76] Daniel Godfrey, a housewright who left an estate valued at £437 in 1753, was considerably more prosperous.[77] A fisherman named John Mariner owned enough land, livestock, agricultural implements, and standing timber to place him in the upper yeomanry. His estate, which was inventoried in 1748, came to £2,430.[78]

Slaves, indentured servants, and a few habitual or handicapped paupers made up the lower class. Of the town's 2,700 inhabitants in 1753, twenty-one were slaves.[79] These were owned by the leading men, many of whom kept one or two slaves to do household and farming chores and to provide their homes and families with the luxury and prestige of servants. In 1737, Moses Pearson paid Thomas Chute, the tailor who founded New Marblehead, six shillings to make a jacket for his Indian boy and seven shillings to make a coat and a pair of leather breeches for his Negro boy.[80] Twenty-two years later, Pearson bought a Negro man named "Scippio" from James Noyes, a yeoman of Newbury, for eight pounds.[81] Mr. Smith owned a Negro named Romeo, whom he spent much time trying to cure of rheumatism, and whom he finally enlisted as a Revolutionary soldier, granting him his freedom in return for half of his pay.[82] The parson's son, Thomas, a storekeeper in Falmouth, owned a Negro man and woman.[83] Slaveholders were not limited exclusively to the first families, for in 1744,

Robert and Mary Dabney, a couple of the "middling sort," expressed their "good will and affection" toward their "Negro man Sarvant called Prince" by giving him his liberty and £50 in lands.[84]

The English system of apprenticeship was in common use in Falmouth, as in other parts of the colonies. William Bayley was bound for five years in 1724 to Joseph Quinby, a joiner, who agreed to teach him the trade and the three R's, and give him a suit of clothes at the end of his term.[85] Benjamin Titcomb, Moses Pearson's son-in-law, and his wife engaged Priscilla Burrell for a six-year term in 1759 under the usual conditions. Titcomb was a blacksmith, but Priscilla, naturally, was to work as a household servant.[86]

Falmouth was not a rich community, but it seems to have had fewer problems with individual poverty than the larger towns of Massachusetts. Occasionally, however, it was necessary to use public funds for the relief of some unfortunate. On November 24, 1735, the selectmen ordered Moses Pearson as town treasurer to pay £1 19*s* "out of the Money belonging to the poor of the Town" to Mrs. Samuell Cobb, "being so much due to her for Nursing and expences on one ———[illeg.] Kelly deceased." [87]

A few Falmouth residents suffered from the inanity of the debtors' prison. The jail stood near the intersection of Back and Middle Streets, and, particularly after it was adopted for county use upon the separation of Cumberland County in 1760, it housed an occasional pauper as well as criminals. In his capacity as sheriff of the new county, Pearson was frequently obliged to meet the complaint of a creditor by locking up a debtor for an indefinite period. He dealt with at least four such cases in 1763 alone, in each of which the creditor expressed regret that the execution of his complaint required incarceration but firmly stated his intention to collect his debt or have his man in "gaol." [88] Similarly, Thomas Griftin, a Falmouth lad who fathered Mary Day's bastard in 1762, was jailed, however illogically, until he could reimburse the town for the child's support.[89]

6

There were times, as we have seen, when the people of Falmouth were starved for food. During the occasional periods of shortage, the sight of the smallest coasting sloop entering the harbor could set off a minor celebration among the townsfolk because it meant the arrival of enough meat and grain to sustain them for a short while longer.

For one commodity, however, the citizens' hunger never ceased: news of the outside world. The isolation of this coastal community and the relative sparsity of its population acted as a constant stimulus upon the instincts of human association and natural curiosity. The people of the Neck kept craning their eyes toward the sea as a lover watches for the postman. The craving for information was especially marked, of course, during the Anglo-French wars. Thomas Smith noted the events of the world in his diary on dozens of occasions after the arrival of a mast ship, of a local traveler back from Boston, or of the Boston or Portsmouth newspapers. British military successes were occasions for formal services of thanksgiving, the discharge of cannons and musketry, and "illuminations." Military defeats, earthquakes, epidemics of smallpox or diphtheria, and seasons of drought prompted public fast days.

As the northeasternmost port in New England, Falmouth served almost automatically at times as a clearing point for news and military intelligence. Captains of vessels sailing from the far eastern fishing grounds or from the ports of Nova Scotia made Falmouth their first port of call and made it a point to report important observations to officials who could relay the word to Portsmouth and Boston by post or by special messenger. This announcement in the *New-England Weekly Journal* of August 22, 1738, illustrates the procedure:

> . . . the Governour has tho't it proper (for the Information and Caution of the Fishermen that go far Eastward) that the following Affidavit be put into the publick Prints.
>
> *William King* Captain of the Ship Derobernia, and *John Snow* of Falmouth, . . . Testify . . . That on Friday the Eighteenth Day of *August* . . . , they were present with Col. *William Pepperrell,* Esq; at the House of Mr. *Moses Pierson,* in *Falmouth,* when . . . Col. *Pepperrell* sent for one Captain *Matthews,* [who said] That in his Passage from *Canso* to *Piscataqua* he put into *La Have* Harbour about twenty five Leagues to the Eastward of *Cape Sables,* and about Two a Clock in the Morning he was awakened by the barking of his Dogs, . . . and when he was upon his Deck he saw six or eight Canoes coming towards his Vessel; whereupon he ordered his Men to repair to their close Quarters, and presently they discovered there was Indians in the Canoes, who fired two Shot at the Vessel, and attempted to wedge up the Ruther [rudder], and the said *Matthews* threw down a Powder Flask among the Indians, and he believed the Indians in that Canoe were all destroyed; and immediately after the Indians

being about sixty in Number, boarded the . . . Vessel, and a
sharp Engagement ensued . . . , which continued about six
Hours, and at length the Indians and some Frenchmen, as . . .
Matthew believed, quitted the Vessel, and left upon her Deck
nineteen or twenty dead Indians. . . . soon after he met with
two English Schooners, and informed the Men of what had happen'd, and desired them to inform the Fishermen of their Danger.

Such moments of excitement, however, were rare. The only institutions in the town that relieved an essentially monotonous life of
business and occasional preparations for defense were the church and
school. Most Falmouth folk were reasonably dutiful toward religion,
but not overly pious. They seem to have respected Mr. Smith and
enjoyed his company, but most of the leading men did not share his
enthusiasm for George Whitefield and the revivals of the 1740's.[90]
Church attendance was irregular, and particularly slack in severe
weather or when there was reason to fear an attack by Indians.[91]

Between 1727, when Mr. Smith's First Parish Church was gathered,
and 1765, four new religious societies took root in the town: churches
in the Stroudwater, Purpooduck, and New Casco parishes, which
separated primarily for geographic reasons and were served by regular
Congregational ministers ordained according to Massachusetts law,
and an Episcopal church on the Neck. The Church of England men
in Falmouth had nothing in common with the first communicants of
the Anglican church in Portsmouth, who seem to have been moved
essentially by political and social, and perhaps aesthetic considerations.
The Falmouth church originated in a rupture in the First Parish
over enlarging the meetinghouse and installing a steeple and bell,
hiring a ministerial colleague for Mr. Smith, and possibly over re-
taining the old pastor himself. The secession of the minority faction
coincided with the sudden disaffection of the pastor of the New Casco
parish, who unexpectedly declared for the Church of England, accepted
an invitation to serve the new parish, and sailed to England for holy
orders. In 1765 he returned to Falmouth as a missionary, partially in
the pay of the Society for the Propagation of the Gospel.[92]

Like most other frontier towns, Falmouth was slow to honor the
province law requiring a full-time schoolmaster in every town of fifty
families or more. Not until 1729, three years after the population had
reached that point, did the town order the selectmen "to look out for
a school-master to prevent the town's being presented." Action finally
came in 1733, when the town hired Robert Bayley, who had come
from Newbury and been admitted as a proprietor six years previously.[93]

His employment became effective only after Mr. Smith had certified his approval, stating that Bayley was possessed of "a peculiar Talent in Learning to read." [94] From that time on, the town provided public instruction under a succession of schoolmasters, and after 1750, there were two grammar schools taught by male teachers and one dame school for younger children.[95]

The same social impulse that made the thin population of Falmouth thirst for news and to welcome the mast ships to their community promoted also a love for convivial gatherings whenever a suitable occasion arose. When Smith brought his first bride from Dunstable in 1728, he wrote, "we were met . . . at Scarborough, by Mr. Cobb and several of the people, women especially: had a very noble supper prepared for us." [96] Smith noted occasional large dinners and parties, sleigh rides, and fishing and hunting expeditions. The diversions of Falmouth folk, however, were in the main simple and infrequent. Dancing was forbidden by law, and it was not until 1794 that Falmouth residents attended their first play on a local stage.[97]

An important link between Falmouth and the outside world came in 1756 with the founding of *The New-Hampshire Gazette* in Portsmouth and the establishment the following year of weekly post runs from Portsmouth to Falmouth. The first evidence that the paper was serving Falmouth readers is a legal announcement in the issue of November 18, 1757. After that, advertisements and news items from the Maine town appeared frequently. Communication with the area south of Portsmouth, however, remained slow and erratic. It took fifteen days for a letter mailed to Moses Pearson from Marblehead, Massachusetts, on March 24, 1763, to reach its destination.[98]

During the five decades after the resettlement of Falmouth Neck in the early 1720's, the town grew from a frontier village of about 250 to a thriving seaport of 3,770 persons. From the Neck, the population had sprawled out over Purpooduck (South Portland), Cape Elizabeth, Stroudwater, New Casco (modern Falmouth), the two lower falls of the Presumpscot (Westbrook), and the north side of Back Cove. The town thus composed an area of some ninety square miles, of which Falmouth Neck remained the commercial center. On the Neck stood about 140 dwelling houses, four warehouses, several small wharves, two or three shipyards, a jail, a new First Parish meetinghouse on Back Street, and, after 1764, an Anglican church on Middle Street.[99]

The people of Falmouth had experienced a rapid growth in population, commerce, and buildings. They had withstood serious shortages and epidemics and political and religious divisions. They had felt a sense of community importance with the coming of the mast ships, and the excitement and terror of occasional real or imagined close brushes with the enemy during two major colonial wars and one minor one. For all the sophisticating experiences of its people, however, Falmouth, unlike the gay provincial capital of Portsmouth, remained culturally and psychologically a remote, imperfect outpost of Boston.

CHAPTER XI

Into the Back Parts
1719–1750

1

The end of Queen Anne's War in 1713 permitted the revival of the abandoned eastern towns such as North Yarmouth and Falmouth. At the same time, it opened the western and northeastern frontiers of New England to new exploitation and settlement.

A quarter century of warfare had prevented the growing New England population, much of which drew most of its living from the family farm, from expanding into new territory. The New England system of land tenure, adapted to an agricultural society in which a man could easily acquire almost any amount of cheap frontier land if he worked it, provided for the division of an estate among all the heirs. The artificial restraints of war, because they had reduced the opportunity for providing adequately for the new generation of farmers, had put a strain on the system.* Though the maturing society of

---

* Two English observers of the 1760's made similar comments on the New England land system and its effects, both designed for an English audience. *The American Gazetteer. Containing A distinct Account of all the Parts of the New World . . .* , 3 vols. (London, 1762), contains the following description in Volume I under "England, New": "In this country are many gentlemen of considerable landed estates, which they let to farmers, or manage by their stewards, or overseers. But the greater part of the people is composed of an independent and substantial yeomanry, who cultivate their own freeholds. These generally pass to their children by a kind of gavelkind or partition, among them, as is customary in Kent: and this keeps them from being ever able to emerge out of their original happy mediocrity. This manner of inheriting has an additional good effect; it makes the people the more ready to go backward into the uncultivated parts of the country, where land is to be had at an easy rate, and in large portions."

Similarly, Alexander Cluny, in *The American Traveller: or, Observations on the Present State Culture and Commerce of the British Colonies in America, And the*

Boston and some of the other old seacoast towns, including Portsmouth, had openings for growing numbers of young men in trade, the crafts, and the professions, these fields could not begin either to meet the economic and psychological needs or absorb the energies of a largely agricultural population that had doubled since 1690.* Many men from the relatively crowded towns of eastern Massachusetts had seen the possibilities of settling on broad tracts of wilderness land during service in the northeastern garrisons and scouting parties.

Besides preventing any expansion of settlement, the wars had helped create capital among the merchants of Boston and Portsmouth. So far they had invested their growing surpluses only in fishing, trading, and, less frequently, in lumbering. The coming of peace and the opening of the frontier made wilderness lands an obvious outlet for the investments of the businessmen of New England and for the speculative fever that had been sweeping England since the Restoration and had now reached the colonies.[1]

To add to the motives for expansion into the unsettled areas of northern New England, the New Hampshire mast supply near Portsmouth was, by 1700, becoming rapidly exhausted. Before the wars,

---

further Improvements of which they are capable . . . (London, 1769) wrote as follows: "The People of *New England* [meaning, in this case, Massachusetts] owe that Independency of Individuals, in which the very Essence of true Liberty exists, and which is the best Protection of it, to a particular Law of Inheritance, by which the Possessions of the Father are divided equally among all his Children; so that they are kept in that happy Mediocrity, which by obliging them to turn their Thoughts to Industry, in order to avoid Want, exempts them from Temptation to, as well as denies them the Means of gratifying Luxury; and at the same Time, by supplying them with a Foundation for that Industry to work upon, exempts them also from the Necessity of submitting to any Encroachment on their Liberty." Pp. 63–4.

* Dealing with population figures in the American colonies is always hazardous because of the lack of comprehensive or reliable demographic statistics before the United States census of 1790. The standard compilation of contemporary figures, which include many conflicting estimates, is Evarts B. Greene and Virginia B. Harrington: *American Population Before the Federal Census of 1790* (New York, 1932), an indispensable tool for the historian of the period. The figures most relevant to a consideration of the pressures for expansion into northern New England after 1713 would be the combined population of Massachusetts (including Maine) and New Hampshire, since virtually all the expansion in this period, except that involving immigrants from Ulster and a few from Germany, took place from the settled portions of those two provinces. Greene and Harrington provide one estimate for 1688, in which Massachusetts and the old Plymouth colony are credited with 44,000 persons and New Hampshire 6,000, a total of 50,000. The corresponding figures for 1715 are Massachusetts, 96,000, and New Hampshire, 9,650, a total of 105,650. Pp. 3–4.

the choppers had extended their little settlements to the east of Casco Bay, but had retreated during the fighting. When peace came, they pushed the search for masts into Maine once again.[2]

Many towns in the interior of southern New Hampshire—perhaps half of the thirty-four townships granted in unsettled land between the Peace of Utrecht and the settlement of the boundary line in 1741 —owe their origins in some degree to conflicting claims between New Hampshire and Massachusetts. Both provinces granted townships in contested territory to assert their claims to jurisdiction.*

Finally, there was the perennial concern for defense. The Massachusetts legislature in particular valued the line of inland towns it tried to establish primarily for their usefulness as military outposts. When in 1722 the Massachusetts General Court was debating the advisability of making war on the eastern Indians, a correspondent to the *New-England Courant* argued that "it will not be for the Honour of our KING, or the Benefit of this Province, to quit the Eastern Settlements: and, . . . if we should quit them, the Popish Missionaries, who have all along instigated the Indians, will not fail to set them on our *Western Frontiers*." [3] It is perhaps indicative of the renewed consciousness of the Indian danger in that year, that of the thirteen interior townships the government of New Hampshire granted between the Peace of Utrecht and the settlement of the boundary in 1741, five were granted in 1722 alone and a sixth, granted in 1720,

---

* L. K. Mathews: *Expansion of New England* (Boston, 1909), pp. 82–5; William Douglass: *A Summary, Historical and Political* . . . (London, 1760), I, 504–5. The analysis is based upon data contained in *Town Papers of New Hampshire*, XI–XIII. The estimate of half is probably conservative. Massachusetts granted twenty-one of these new townships, New Hampshire thirteen. It is not always possible to ascertain whether jurisdictional competition or pressure from prospective speculators was the principal motive for the grant. But the assertion of jurisdiction appears to have been the major factor at least in the case of the Massachusetts grant of Peterborough and of the so-called "Narragansett" and "Canada" townships, six of which were in what became New Hampshire territory, and in New Hampshire's incorporation of Londonderry and Rochester in 1722 and its granting of Bow in 1727. It was certainly a contributing factor, if not the decisive one, in several others. Hutchinson is less certain of the importance of this motive than Douglass and most of the later historians. He acknowledges that the government of New Hampshire suspected the Massachusetts legislature of making grants for this purpose, and that "this might have weight with some leading men [of Massachusetts], who were acquainted with the controversy." He points out, however, that the General Court made many grants in this period, not only in contested territory, but in other parts of the province as well. Thomas Hutchinson: *The History of the Colony and Province of Massachusetts-Bay*, ed. Lawrence Shaw Mayo (Cambridge, Mass., 1936), II, 251–2.

was incorporated in that year.* The concern for defense is also reflected in the provisions of the grants of this period, which almost invariably required proprietors to lay out their township in a "regular, compact and defensible manner." †

Prompted by various motives and pressures, the governments of New Hampshire and Massachusetts Bay responded to the coming of peace by setting off townships in unsettled land and donating them to groups of proprietors, often on the flimsiest of pretexts; and they overdid it. Even taking into account the unquestioned need for new territory for settlement and widespread postwar wanderlust, the governments granted far more land than was necessary to accommodate those who were actually ready to risk a move to the frontier. The proprietors of practically all the newly granted lands struggled for many decades with the overwhelming problem of securing enough settlers to comply with the law and achieve a self-supporting community. Time and again, one of the provincial governments extended the original time limit for meeting the conditions of a grant. The proprietors resorted to a variety of devices to attract settlers, ranging from loosening the restrictions on the location of dwellings to outright subsidies. Instead of capitalizing on their holdings, proprietors often invested heavily in surveys, fortifications, and public works such as roads and bridges without any compensating gain, at least for many years.

While some of the new townships became settled almost immediately, more of them lay vacant from six to as many as thirty years. In the case of Bakerstown, one of the townships granted by Massachusetts in 1737, no settlers appeared until 1750, nine years after the provincial boundary had been drawn to the south, and not until 1768 did the New Hampshire government incorporate the inhabitants as the town of Salisbury. Peterborough, also granted by Massachusetts in 1737, was settled in 1749 and incorporated in 1760. The proprietors of Chichester, which the New Hampshire government granted along with

---

* Inland townships granted by New Hampshire in 1722 were Londonderry, Barrington, Nottingham, Rochester, and Allenstown. Londonderry and Rochester were incorporated the same year, as was Chester, which had been granted as the township of Cheshire in 1720.

† This particular phraseology is from the Massachusetts act granting the township later called Warner, N.H., to a group of proprietors in 1735. Moses Long: "Historical Sketches of the Town of Warner, N.H.," New Hampshire Historical Society *Collections*, III (1832), 182. A similar provision can be found in virtually every other grant of a township in the period.

five other townships in 1727, failed to attract any settlers until 1758.[4] The progress in some of the Maine townships was even more dismal.

This widespread granting of townships and their spotty colonization and maturation resulted in a dispersal of frontier settlement that was new in the experience of New England. Except during the abnormal period of the wars, which had broken the chain of settlements that stretched along the northeastern shore to the Kennebec, Puritan ideals and natural prudence had promoted a cautious advance of the frontier line from settled area to the territory adjacent to it. In most cases, the governments had granted lands only for the sake of immediate settlement; in the interests of defense and social control, they had followed rather scrupulously the principle of contiguous townships. Exceptions were rare. New towns had resulted more frequently from the division of a parish than from the settlement of a wholly new township in the wilderness. While eight New Hampshire towns or parishes were created in this manner between 1715 and 1741, on the other hand, thirty-four new townships were granted in the same period in previously unsettled land.* The granting of inland townships in Maine lagged several years behind the marking out of new territory in New Hampshire for settlement. The ten new Maine towns founded between 1713 and 1733 all were seaboard communities, either set off from older towns or granted in vacant coastal land in the Kennebec region. From 1733 to 1750, however, the Massachusetts General Court granted seven townships in the interior of Maine.[5]

Thomas Hutchinson, the historian of Massachusetts Bay, severely criticized this departure from tradition. "The settlement of the province was retarded by it," he wrote, "a trade of land jobbing made many idle persons, imaginary wealth was created, which was attended with some of the mischievous effects of the paper currency, viz. idleness and bad economy, a real expence was occasioned to many persons, besides the purchase of the grantees title, for every township by law was made a propriety, and their frequent meetings, schemes for settlement, and other preparatory business, occasioned many charges. In some few towns, houses were built and some part of the lands

---

* The figures do not include the thirteen New Hampshire towns that resulted from the division of Massachusetts townships by the province boundary line of 1741. Except for South Hampton, which was incorporated by New Hampshire in 1742, none of these towns was incorporated until the late 1740's. Salem awaited incorporation until 1750, Hinsdale until 1753. *Town Papers of New Hampshire,* XI–XIII.

cleared." [6] Granted that Hutchinson's analysis was correct in the light of the conservative social ideals of the Puritan magistracy to which he was heir, there was also a creative side to the new dispersal of settlement. In their response to the great problem of populating the townships and the new experience of relative isolation, the proprietors and settlers of the New Hampshire and Maine interior, along with many of those in western New England in the same period, developed almost involuntarily a new kind of community. The innovative aspects of the peopling of the eighteenth-century frontiers introduced a new regional flavor to northern New England, a blend of traditional New England social values and pragmatic response to new physical and economic circumstances. As a result, most of the interior communities emerged from their "frontier" stage, not as reproductions of the well-ordered, tightly settled Massachusetts towns of the seventeenth century that were intended to serve as models, nor of the coastal villages that had evolved under Massachusetts supervision from the fishing colonies of Maine, but as something different: the country town. This new kind of community, which ripened slowly during the half-century between the Peace of Utrecht and the Peace of Paris, predominated in northern New England during the years of the American Revolution and remained the most characteristic regional phenomenon well into the nineteenth century.

2

The proprietors of the new Maine and New Hampshire townships varied considerably in motives, wealth, and the manner in which they acquired their holdings. Traditionally, the sudden expansion of the frontier in this period has been attributed almost exclusively to speculation in lands. The speculative urge, indeed, was a major factor; but it was not the only one, and it was not always responsible for the more successful attempts at inland settlement. A glance at some representative attempts at new settlement will suggest the variey of proprietary types.

In 1714, eight businessmen and politicians, most of them Bostonians, bought title to the old Pejepscot patent, which the Council for New England had granted to its original proprietors in 1632. This new group of entrepreneurs laid out the towns of Brunswick and Topsham and shipped the settlers and their few poor tools and furniture from Boston without charge. [7] The Sheepscot proprietors, who bought land further eastward, operated in about the same way.* Thus began the kind of outright speculation in real estate that characterized a large part, but not all, of the expansion of New England in the eighteenth century.

In 1718, the Reverend James MacGregor, who had led part of his Presbyterian flock from Ulster to New England, and an associate, Archibald Boyd, petitioned the Massachusetts General Court for a tract of land for twenty-eight families then in Boston and forty others still in Ireland.[8] The Court granted the plea, and a large group of Ulstermen sailed for Casco Bay. Finding their first Maine winter more severe than they cared to endure permanently, in the spring they sailed down the coast to the Merrimack, and explored the river as far as Haverhill. There they heard of a good tract of land called Nutfield about fifteen miles upriver. They went to look at it, liked it, found it unoccupied and so far as they could determine unclaimed, and settled it—despite what they must have known to be the small likelihood of finding any great change in the climate. The Massachusetts legislature refused in June, 1719, to confirm this grant, whereupon the Ulstermen procured from New Hampshire the rights for a town. This infuriated the Massachusetts authorities, and brought to a head the question of jurisdiction in that part of the Merrimack Valley.[9]

Thus new immigration and jurisdictional competition, not speculation, brought about the settling and granting of Londonderry, as the settlers named their town in 1723. Unlike most of their neighboring colonists in this period, the men of Londonderry owned and governed their township from within, and were united by ethnic and cultural bonds as well as by common economic interests. In this respect, Londonderry resembled the Puritan towns of seventeenth-century Massachusetts much more than most of the other townships in the back parts, owned at least partly from outside and settled by straggling families and individuals rather than ready-made communities or congregations. The Scotch-Irish of Londonderry gained rapidly in num-

---

* Other companies that bought up parcels of eastern land in the 1720's included the Lincolnshire and Muscongus Companies, in both of which Elisha Cooke, the leader of the popular side in Massachusetts and great enemy of British timber policies, figured prominently. Thomas Westbrook belonged to the Lincolnshire Company, and in 1720 accompanied Cooke and other members on a voyage to their grant near the Sheepscot River to confirm their title with the local Indians and set up a mill. See *Sibley's Harvard Graduates* (for complete citation, see the *List of Frequent Abbreviations,* p. 363), IV, 349–56, and copy in Maine Historical Society of the Ms. diary of Thomas Fayerweather (Bangor, Me., Public Library) that describes the expedition of the Lincolnshire Company.

bers as the result both of further immigration and natural increase. The community, therefore, spawned a number of similar towns, both in the immediate neighborhood and further inland in New Hampshire and in New York.[10]

German settlers came to the region, on the other hand, because of the speculative activities of the Lincolnshire Company, which had received a grant from the Council for New England in 1730, and particularly of its principal shareholder, Samuel Waldo. Waldo, a Boston merchant and politician, had been rewarded with half the company's holdings between the Penobscot and Muscongus Rivers for his work as agent for the company in England. In 1734, he bought still more shares, bringing his interest in the company to about two-thirds of the entire holdings.

As the dominant figure in the company, which then became known as the Waldo Patentees, Waldo recruited oppressed German families to settle, till the land, and manufacture iron and lime at Broad Bay, beginning about 1740. He called the resulting township Waldoboro. To an extent unique in New England, the Palatines, Württembergers, and German Swiss whom Waldo imported to his town were organized in the feudal manner and regarded their proprietor as liege lord. In this relationship, they enlisted in the regiment that Waldo, as brigadier general under William Pepperrell, led to Louisbourg in 1745.[11]

In 1722, the year the New Hampshire government incorporated Londonderry, it granted or incorporated five other townships, including Rochester and Barrington. Rochester had been granted previously by Massachusetts, but had never had any permanent settlers. Its incorporation by New Hampshire at this point, especially in light of its lack of inhabitants, apparently was aimed, as in the case of Londonderry, at asserting jurisdiction.[12] Barrington went to John Wentworth, George Jaffrey, Archibald Macpheadris, and Robert Nelson of the Portsmouth gentry for the "encouragement and accommodation to carry on and maintain" iron works that these merchant-politicians had built on the Lamprey River. Thus the official promotion of industry became a feature of the scheme for new settlements.[13]

In 1727, amidst a flurry of requests for land grants under a variety of pretexts, some of the surviving veterans of King Philip's War and heirs of the dead revived an old petition for new lands. To recruit troops for the war, the governor of Massachusetts had promised them in 1675 "a gratuity of land, beside their wages" if the Narragansett Indians were beaten. The government had never kept the promise. The General Court, confronted with this latest in a series of demands for frontier land and with an eye on the challenge from New Hampshire over territory, now responded by granting two townships in 1728 and five more in 1734. One of these "Narragansett townships" lay south of any possible claim by New Hampshire and two were in Maine. The other four were in contested territory, soon to fall north of the New Hampshire boundary. The government donated each township, six miles square, to 120 proprietors, presumably qualified either by descent or by having fought the Indians a half-century before. In 1735, it granted the first nine of the "Canada" townships to veterans of the Quebec expedition of 1690, an unsuccessful campaign of King William's War, or their heirs.* These grants were the first and most important of many such concessions to war veterans by the governments of Massachusetts and Connecticut during the colonial period, though the ingenuousness of the motive in these cases is questionable.

Among the seven Narragansett townships were Buxton and Gorhamtown, Maine. These became part of the barrier of interior settlements that the General Court set up in the 1730's to protect the redeveloping coastal towns from attack from the north. The two recent wars had shown that a handful of ill-organized fishermen and farmers in a string of dispersed coastal settlements could not defend themselves. In any case, this mode of American occupation was more French than English. The Court now attempted to consolidate frontier settlement by contiguous townships—still another extension of Massachusetts thought and practice into the eastern parts. Like most of the other manifestations of Puritan imperialism, this one aided the development of civilization in that region; like most of the others, the ideal was only imperfectly realized. There is, indeed, a certain irony in the attempt, because the buffer zone that the Court tried to establish could serve its purpose fully only if completely occupied; what actually resulted was a still greater dispersal of settlement.

In 1727, the General Court had ordered a line of townships laid out between the northern points of Falmouth and Berwick. Look at a map of southwestern Maine and you will see what the authors of the scheme meant when they said the settlement of this area would shorten the eastern frontier by at least forty miles. The new townships filled

* Roy H. Akagi: *Town Proprietors of New England* (Philadelphia, 1924), pp. 190–2. That the desire to reward veterans of these conflicts only served as a rather transparent mask for other motives is apparent from the fact that few of the old soldiers were still alive. Of the 120 grantees of Narragansett No. 3 (later Amherst, N.H.), only nineteen were surviving veterans of King Philip's war. John Farmer: "Historical Sketch of Amherst, N.H.," New Hampshire Historical Society *Collections*, V (1837), 81.

out a triangle of settlements whose longest side stretched northeast-ward along the coast from the Piscataqua to Casco Bay and whose shortest side extended up the eastern side of the Piscataqua River system to the northern edge of Berwick. The barrier, if fully settled, would cut straight through the woods across the northern side of this triangle for about forty miles. In ordering the survey, the General Court declared that the line of townships "would tend to the Security of the Eastern-Frontiers, . . . the Defence of the Inhabitants, His Majesty's Woods fit for Masting the Royal Navy preserved, and Room for many of the Inhabitants of this Province made for their Comfor-table Subsistence." The Court appointed a committee to survey these seven townships and admit to each one "Sixty Families of the Peti-tioners to whom preference may be given, and as near unto the Place and Places they Petition for, and unto others who shall be Obliged by themselves, Sons, Servants, or other good Men, to bring forward Settlements therein, by Building Dwelling Houses, inhabiting them, Breaking up, and Fencing in at least Five Acres of their House or Home-Lots, within the space of Five Years." The Court also made the traditional provisions for church, school, and ministry lands and for picking a site for the meetinghouse. It required each settler to pay the committee five pounds to help pay for the survey and other expenses, and provided that any grantee not meeting the conditions of his grant would forfeit it.[14]

Two of the townships in this barrier went to petitioners from Marblehead and Gloucester, ostensibly to relieve a land hunger that was already developing in those two North Shore communities. Of the two, New Marblehead, later Windham, was the more successful. The records of its origin disclose still another motive for expansion, and the creation of still another sort of town proprietor.

In 1734, Abraham Howard and Joseph Blaney, members of the House from Marblehead, petitioned the General Court in behalf of "a number of the Inhabitants" of that town for a grant of land "in consid-eration of the smallness of their Township and the numbers of their Inhabitants, as also the discouragements they have latterly met with in the Fishery." [15] The Court granted a township six miles square "on the back of Falmouth" to sixty Marblehead men, to be selected by a committee appointed for the purpose, "that are most likely to settle and bring forward a new Plantation, and that most need a Grant of Land." [16] Although the populating of New Marblehead did not proceed at all as the petitioners and General Court envisioned, the proprietors of this new township seem to have wanted primarily to relocate their families and begin life anew under pioneering circumstances rather than make profits.

The granting of Peterborough, New Hampshire, by the Massachusetts General Court in 1738 had the same theoretical basis as the granting of New Marblehead and New Gloucester. In this case, however, the boundary dispute, now coming rapidly to a settlement, precipitated the grant. By this time a jointly appointed boundary commission had become deadlocked and both provinces had appealed for a decision to the Crown. Agents for both sides were working feverishly behind the scenes in London; quite obviously, the New Hampshire interests had the edge. The Massachusetts officials, therefore, wanted to fill up as much of the disputed territory as possible with grants to Massachusetts proprietors before the King made his ruling, which most of the observers were correctly predicting would be in New Hampshire's favor. When a group of men from Concord, Massachusetts, renewed an old appeal for a grant on the ground of land hunger, therefore, the Court quickly complied. Shortly, however, all but two of the sixty grantees sold their shares to four wealthy Massachusetts investors, who turned their purchase into a profitable speculative enterprise.[17]

Perhaps the biggest land transaction of all was the sale in 1746 of the vast Masonian patent in New Hampshire to twelve of the wealthiest and most powerful members of the Portsmouth oligarchy, most of them part of the Wentworth clan. This £1,500 purchase, though perhaps primarily speculatory in nature, was closely connected with internal New Hampshire politics.

No single rule, therefore, can explain the push into the northeastern interior during the first half of the eighteenth century. No all-inclusive generalization can accurately describe the origin of all the towns that were established to accommodate the new breed of Yankee settler who now began the transformation of the wooded foothills of the northeastern frontier into rural countryside.

CHAPTER XII

From Wilderness to Country Town
1720–1760

1

The life of a northern country town ordinarily began in a dark, smoke-filled tavern miles away from the forest where the first handful of settlers would eventually clear enough space to build their tiny log houses. If the grantees lived in Boston, as many did, they organized their propriety over Madeira or rum at a public house such as Luke Vardy's. Grants by the New Hampshire government frequently included members of the Portsmouth gentry among the proprietors. In such cases, the first plans for surveying the new township and assigning lots undoubtedly materialized in one of the wainscoted rooms of John Wentworth's remodeled tavern on Manning Street.

Some of the northern townships, such as New Marblehead, New Gloucester, Peterborough, and most of the "Canada" townships, had been granted to a group of men from a single community. When this happened, the new owners of a frontier tract gathered at a local inn or at the home of one of the most important members of the propriety. In the case of the seven "Narragansett" townships, it was a mass meeting of the 840 grantees on Boston Common in 1733 that gave birth to the seven separate proprieties. Soon after Governor Belcher signed the act granting the last five of these townships in April, 1733, all the grantees assembled on the broad cow pasture in what must have been a scene of extraordinary confusion until each of the successful petitioners for frontier land found his proper place with the "society" of grantees to which he belonged. Each society of 120 persons then selected three representatives, who met together at Luke Vardy's in

October, 1733, to assign each of the seven townships to one of the societies. Within a few months, the separate societies began to meet at places convenient for the majority of members in order to elect clerks and assessors and appoint committees to supervise the important first survey of the township and in some cases to visit the grant to "take a particular view of . . . [its] circumstances." [1]

In the case of Narragansett Number 3, or Souhegan East (later Amherst, New Hampshire), the grantees transacted their first business in Salem Village, the home of twenty-nine of the proprietors. Almost as many lived in the neighboring North Shore community of Lynn, and all but four of the others came from Massachusetts towns nearby. Four of the grantees, however, were Maine men: two from Falmouth and one each from Scarborough and York.[2] The proprietors of Narragansett Number 7, or Gorhamtown in Maine, met during the 1740's and 1750's, while that township was developing very slowly, at the home of Moses Pearson in Falmouth.[3]

Just as the new frontier town proprietors varied widely in their motives for acquiring a grant and in their methods of going about it, so did they vary in occupation and status. The men with important political connections who saw a chance to profit from investing in the necessary expenses of surveying a township and establishing settlers were almost invariably well-to-do merchants or professional men, some self-made and others the beneficiaries of the property and social standing of a previous generation. The grantees of the Narragansett and Canada townships, on the other hand, had little need either for respectability or political influence. The General Court had encouraged applications from anyone who could establish a valid connection with one of those expeditions, and made available a sufficient number of townships to accommodate all the petitioners.[4] In the case of the inland barrier of townships in Maine and the so-called "line of townships" that the Massachusetts government ran between the Merrimack and Connecticut Rivers in 1735, a prospective proprietor needed even fewer qualifications. Generally, the grant of such a township went to 60, 100, or 120 inhabitants of a particular Massachusetts town whose selectmen or representative to the General Court had petitioned for land. The number of available proprietorships usually sufficed to accommodate all who were interested and could pay the £3 or £5 fee that the General Court asked from each shareholder to meet the cost of the survey. If there was an overflow, vacancies could usually be found elsewhere.[5] A legislative committee met in December, 1736, at a tavern in Woburn to dispose of the rights in the last four of the townships between the Merrimack and Connecticut "to such persons as shall appear and give Bond for the fulfillment of the Grant, and pay *Three Pounds* each . . . to defray the charges of the Survey, etc." In short, the governments of Massachusetts and New Hampshire were so lavish with grants of unappropriated land between 1722 and 1741, on virtually any pretext, that almost any man of whatever station who yearned for a share of frontier territory could somehow find one, either free or at a very small cost.

The New Marblehead propriety was probably typical of the owners of a good many of the new frontier townships of the era. Its members were, in the main, a substantial but not especially distinguished group. They included two ministers, two merchants, three "gentlemen" and four "esquires," two sea captains, a militia colonel and a militia captain, six carpenters and joiners, four blacksmiths, two fishermen and eleven "shoremen" who worked in connection with the fishery, two sailmakers, two chairmakers, a glazier, a tailor, a hatmaker, a painter, and several of unnamed occupations.[6] Unlike the proprietors of a few towns such as Peterborough, many of whom already had interests in other frontier lands, knew the operations of the legislature intimately, had speculated in a land bank, and intended to sell out for a profit as soon as they could,[7] most of the New Marblehead proprietors undoubtedly intended originally to move to their new township. But so far as the records show, the proprietors of this tract of forest, which was intended to be turned into a village of farmers, included not a "yeoman," "husbandman," or woodsman. We need not look much further to explain why, in the end, few of the New Marblehead proprietors moved to their holdings in person.

Whether aristocratic merchants from Boston, businessmen, lawyers, and politicians from Concord, or fishermen and artisans from Marblehead, the proprietors of the new frontier townships faced the same jobs. Their first task, after being summoned together by the individual or committee appointed for the purpose by the General Court, was to elect a moderator and clerk and decide how to comply with the conditions which the legislature inevitably placed on every grant. The grant of a township to a propriety always had strings attached to it. The details varied, but the outline was always the same.

Within a specified time, usually from three to seven years, the proprietors had to see to it that a certain number of families were actually living in the township, each in a house of a minimum specified size on a home lot that was cleared, cultivated, and fenced. The legislature ordinarily required a compact and defensible layout for the settlement. Within the same time limit, the proprietors were expected to have built a meetinghouse and hired a "learned and orthodox" minister. Since it was assumed that any New England minister of the day probably would make his first parish his life's work and that his family would become permanent residents of the community, the legislature always required that one share in the township become the permanent personal possession of the first settled minister and his heirs. This provision, of course, was designed to help attract a young clergyman who might otherwise hesitate to forsake the easier and more refined life of the older settlements. A second share was to be designated for the "ministry"—that is, a permanent parsonage for the successive ministers who would follow the first incumbent—and a third for the support of a school. By law, the proprietors had to forfeit the grant if they did not meet the conditions within the time limit. In practice, though many proprieties failed to meet the conditions, few of them actually gave up their townships, either because of extensions of time granted during the troubles of King George's War or simply because of legislative laxity.

After electing officers, the proprietors usually chose a committee to tend to the survey and, in most cases, to go to the township to determine generally the likeliest locations for the home lots, the pastures, the meadow lands, and water power sites and the need for roads and bridges. The next step was to assign each home lot except the three reserved for religious and educational purposes to a proprietor, usually by drawing. Provisions for a sawmill and gristmill and for roads and bridges usually came next, ahead of any discussion of a meetinghouse, minister, or schoolmaster. In almost every case, the proprietors discovered early in their proceedings that few of their number were actually ready to move to the new township, at least in time to meet the time limit set by the General Court. Therefore, the problem of attracting other settlers needed attention. Finally, there was the inevitable question of finances. Surveys, public works, ministers, and subsidies of various kinds for the settlers all cost money, and so the proprietors immediately faced the necessity of taxing themselves.

Discovering the realities of financing a frontier settlement may have come as something of a shock to the hundreds of men of modest means who had seized the opportunity to have a free share in a large tract of northern New England soil. We shall never know how many bright dreams of future prosperity and the good life of a country squire vanished with a succession of impossible proprietary tax bills. Though the proprietors had all the responsibilities of local government until the town was incorporated under province law, there was no legal barrier to a proprietor's selling out.* Thus, although the number of "rights" in the township—the number of original proprietors plus three—always remained constant, the actual number of proprietors often gradually diminished, as one proprietor after another sold his share to one of the few of the original group who decided to stay with the enterprise, and perhaps to settle the township in person. Aside from the pure speculators, therefore, the most successful of the proprietors needed both the money and the tenacity to contribute to the necessary expenses and buy some of the shares of his partners during the first difficult years when the township had only uncertain existence.

2

The first piece of work on a new tract of land was the survey. The boundaries of the township had to be marked off in accordance with the legislature's vague description of the grant. The surveyors also had to locate and mark the first range or tier of lots, following the proprietors' instructions as closely as possible. These sometimes included making allowances in the form of extra land if the quality of a given lot were poor. Either as part of the first survey or soon afterward, the first one or two roads in the township were laid out.

Surveying, under the best conditions, is an exact science; in principle, it could hardly be more simple. You find your starting point, set up your transit, squint across the compass in the prescribed direction, making allowances for the magnetic variation in the area, wave your chainman into the line of sight, and have him tighten up on his end

* I have found only one exception to this rule, and it resulted not from provincial legislation but from an act of the proprietors of Penacook, later Concord, New Hampshire. The proprietors voted at their first meeting in 1725 to prohibit alienation of any lot "without the consent of the Community" on penalty of forfeiture of the lot to the propriety as a whole. Jacob B. Moore, a nineteenth-century historian of Concord, offered on reasonably good evidence and logic the explanation that the proprietors, most of whom settled their grant in person, were anxious to exclude the "Irish" who had recently arrived at Londonderry. Each proprietor of Penacook, like those of most of the northern New England townships granted in this period to persons without qualifications relative to military service, paid the government of Massachusetts £5 to be used for the survey or other public purposes in the township. "Historical Sketch of Concord, in the county of Merrimack, N.H.," New Hampshire Historical Society *Collections*, I (1824), 155–6. See also *Journal of the House of Representatives of Massachusetts* (Boston, 1919–64), XI, 31–2. Examples of shares in New Hampshire townships being offered for sale may be found in *New-England Weekly Journal*, February 3, 1741.

of the chain and mark the spot by driving a stake or blazing the nearest tree. If you are using the standard measuring device of the days before the steel tape measure, which consisted of a string of eight-inch light metal rods connected by links, you have now drawn the first sixty-six feet of your boundary or property line. A surveyor of the eighteenth century probably would not have said it that way; he would have said one chain, or four rods. Do the same thing 1,920 times, walking twenty-four miles in the process, and if you have done it properly, you will have marked off the boundaries of a six-mile-square township. You have made a beginning, but if you are trying to duplicate the job assigned to the surveyors of an eighteenth-century township, you must next locate all the property lines, determine the best course of road beds, measure distances and directions to landmarks, and record it all on a map, or "plat."

Understandably, surveying even the ranges, townships, and sections on the relatively flat, open prairies of the Old Northwest under the Ordinance of 1785 was a laborious, time-consuming, expensive procedure, though there was little but the possibility of human error or chicanery to interfere with its accuracy.

The surveyors of the northern New England townships fifty years earlier faced more complicated problems. Burdened with axes and flintlocks as well as a brass theodolite, wooden tripod, and iron chains, the surveyors had to edge through thickets, climb ledges, skirt ponds, and plod over an endless succession of hills and valleys. Slapping at mosquitoes, they were often forced to tramp through a swamp or wet leaves or wade across a stream until they could feel the water swish within their boots at every step, even after they had reached dry ground again. Their hands and faces were raked with blackberry briars and stung by saplings which whipped back at them after catching on the surveyor's chain or the clothing of a companion.

They took their sightings, not across an open prairie, but through dense woods, sometimes cluttered with undergrowth or piles of brush left by surreptitious woodchoppers. Because they could seldom make an accurate sighting or hold a chain tight and straight across sixty-six feet of wild forest floor, surveyors often substituted the "half chain," which doubled the number of necessary measurements. To compensate for the sagging of the chain, most of them added a chain's length to every thirty chains of measured distance, and to allow for the irregularities in the ground which the chain could not follow, they sometimes added the length of a man's arm for every half chain of measurement. Such procedures, however, were never absolutely standardized. Because of the difficulty of handling the chain in the wilderness, occasional surveyors, who should have known better, substituted a hemp line, which shrank in damp weather. Either from carelessness, ineptness, or plain lack of data, many surveyors failed to take into proper account the local variation of the compass needle from true north. What Jeremy Belknap wrote late in the eighteenth century was doubly true at the time of the first surveys of interior northern New England: "Surveyors are often sworn to go according to their best skill and judgment; this they may do with great sincerity, and yet, for want of better skill, may commit egregious mistakes." [8]

Not every township, fortunately, suffered from the arbitrary patchwork that resulted when the proprietors of Upper Ashuelot (Keene, N.H.) decided in 1737 to add a hundred acres of "upland" to each share. The proprietors drew numbers to determine the order in which they should select the new lots, and each man in his turn told the surveying committee where and in what shape he wanted his lot to be. This ingenious survey produced, in the words of a local historian, "figures which Euclid never imagined, and probably could not measure." [9] Even when surveys were conducted on a more systematic basis, however, errors, ambiguities, and the use of moveable or temporary landmarks often resulted in inequities, property disputes, and heated contention between adjoining towns, in and out of the courts, for years afterward.

Laying out a road required more of the surveyor than simply the ability to follow as best he could an official description of a township boundary. It was usually his responsibility to find a suitable roadbed. If he was experienced at wilderness surveying, he looked for a stand of pitch pine, because those trees grow on dry, fairly level land in sandy or gravelly soil. These were ideal conditions for a country road but not for cultivation, so building a road through such a tract would not be breaking up the best potential farmland. Moreover, a growth of pitch pine was generally more sparse than one of white pine, hemlock, and spruce or of hardwoods, and the undergrowth, because of the soil, consisted only of easily removable vegetation such as ferns and wortle bushes. Wherever possible, the best surveyors took advantage of beaver dams for bridging small streams.

The surveyor and his party first marked the path with an axe by spotting the trees along the way and numbering the mileage on a tree at the end of every measured mile. Axe-men came next, clearing away bushes and felling trees along the route, usually for a width of three rods, or about fifty feet. In wet or marshy land, they used these trees

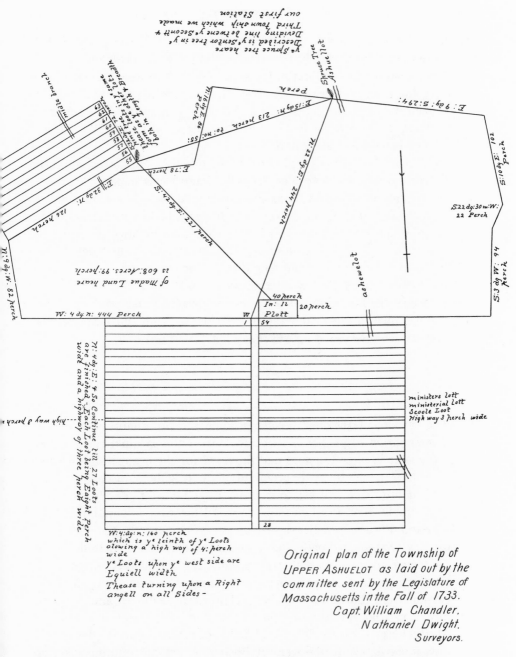

Original plan of the Township of
UPPER ASHUELOT as laid out by the
committee sent by the Legislature of
Massachusetts in the Fall of 1733.
Capt. William Chandler.
Nathaniel Dwight.
Surveyors.

The original survey of Upper Ashuelot (later Keene, New Hampshire), made in 1733.
The home lots are laid out in the conventional Massachusetts manner of the seventeenth
century, with common farmlands available for later division among the owners of the
various "rights." Each of the home lots consists of 8 acres, but the lots are only 132
feet wide, indicating that the proprietors envisaged a compact village. A "perch" is
equal to a rod, or 16.5 feet.

for crude causeways and bridges, which sometimes consisted of little more than a succession of tree trunks laid together across the roadbed. Rocks had to be rolled out of the way, either by brute muscle power or by using poles as levers. A boulder that was too big to move could be broken into smaller pieces with a charge of gunpowder or cracked by building a fire around it and then dousing it with a bucket of cold water when it was well heated.

A road thus cleared was perfectly usable by men, horses, and oxen during most of the year. The deepest winter snows impeded travel, of course, but not as seriously as the spring mud season. A road that ran, of necessity, through loamy rather than gravelly soil was virtually impassable during several weeks in March and early April. It took constant use to keep a road in condition. Shoots sprang up quickly from the roots of felled trees, and only a season or two of disuse was enough to necessitate a whole new clearing operation.[10]

When the township bounds and first property lines were surveyed, however inaccurately, and the first roads laid out and cleared, however crudely, the township was ready for its first settlers.

3

The settlers of the new townships, like the proprietors, made up a diverse group of people. Up to now, one of the cardinal rules of new settlement in New England had provided for the occupation of a new township *en masse* by a group of close neighbors, usually already formed into a church estate and led by a minister. Paradoxically, it was largely Scot Presbyterians from Ulster who followed this New England Puritan practice north of the Merrimack in the eighteenth century. Except in Londonderry and some of her Scotch-Irish daughter towns, the settlers of northern New England in this period came, for the most part, as individuals or as families in a painfully slow procession from the Maine and New Hampshire seaboard and occasionally from Rhode Island or Connecticut, but most frequently from the Massachusetts North Shore and the lower Merrimack Valley or the area immediately to the west of Boston. A few adventurous pioneers left the frontier settlements of the Connecticut Valley of Massachusetts for a still more hazardous part of the same valley to the north, but not until after 1760 was the upper Connecticut Valley populated in large numbers. Emigration to the northern New England frontier between 1720 and 1750 can in most cases be traced to economic motives. Beyond this, generalization is hazardous. In occupation, means, values, attitudes, and abilities, the new pioneers who trickled into the back parts varied greatly.

The settlers of Londonderry, unlike those of most of the new interior townships, came as a group united in religious as well as economic purpose. Because of its special nature, the experience of Londonderry constitutes an exception to the rule that the townships of northern New England filled up only after long and repeated delays. In Londonderry's earliest stage of development, however, its citizens were forced to face the problem of a dangerously sparse population. Only their rapid success in solving the problem was not typical. Like the proprietors of many of the other interior towns, they attacked the problem by resorting to their own ingenuity rather than convention.

The twenty families that settled on the banks of West-Running Brook made up only a small portion of the five shiploads of emigrants from Ulster who had landed in Boston in 1718. Others had remained at Casco Bay and later spread into the interior of Maine, where in some communities they added a sturdy, fiery Scotch-Irish flavor to a stock already composed of a mixture of the old West Country fishing element and descendants of pious East Anglian émigrés to Massachusetts. Others had spent the winter in Boston or on the north shore of Massachusetts Bay. Still others had returned from Casco Bay with what became the nucleus of the Londonderry group but had settled in Haverhill, Dracut, or Andover, Massachusetts, instead of going on to Nutfield.[11] Twenty families, though a better beginning than that made by many of the interior townships a bit later in the century, was not a sufficient basis upon which to found a town or even, under common New England practice, to secure the permanent grant of a township.*

The problem of recruiting new settlers claimed a high priority among the business of the town "committee." On December 25, 1719, the Presbyterian town fathers, paying no more attention to popish holidays than did their Congregational counterparts in Massachusetts, enlisted the whole town in the campaign. In the month following their

---

* Ordinarily, the Massachusetts General Court required at least fifty inhabitants before it would validate, or "confirm," its grant of a township. Although such a condition seems to have been absent from many of the grants by New Hampshire, including the Londonderry charter of 1722, the same principle appears in a royal instruction for the establishment of new townships addressed to Governor Benning Wentworth of New Hampshire in 1761. William Douglass: *A Summary, Historical and Political* . . . (London, 1760), I, 513–14; Colonial Office 5/942, photostat in New Hampshire Historical Society, "Wentworth Ms.," Box 1, Folder 3.

election, the seven committeemen gave to each of the first twenty settlers a sixty-acre lot to offer to any person whom he should like to have
as a fellow townsman. The only restriction was that the prospective
inhabitant and landowner should be willing and able to settle immediately in Nutfield.[12] By this means, and by spreading the news about the
settlement among the Scotch-Irish both in New England and in Ulster,
the townsmen added rapidly to their number during the first year.[13]
By April, 1721, the settlement consisted of 360 persons, including 130
men of arms-bearing age.[14]

In many of the other interior New Hampshire townships from the
1740's through the 1760's, and in all of those of inland Maine, the proprietors struggled almost desperately with their principal problem—
getting settlers. The New Hampshire General Assembly tried to aid
them by passing a general act enabling the proprietors of any town to
assess taxes and take any other measures to promote settlement. The
Assembly also relieved some of the weaker settlements from paying
the provincial rate, and once loaned £100 to the selectmen of Bow.[15]

The proprietors of Narragansett Number 1 in Maine needed inhabitants so badly for their virtually vacant township that in 1736 they
offered £20 to the first ten of their number who would build a house
eighteen feet square and clear four acres of land, provided they did it
within two years.[16] The following year, the propriety doubled the
offer and extended it to the first thirty proprietors who would give a
bond to meet the same terms.[17] In 1742, according to a complaint by
sixty-two residents of neighboring Biddeford and Scarborough, "not
above Ten or a Dozen of the . . . Grantees had begun to build upon
or improve their land." [18]

The proprietors of New Gloucester tried similar tactics. In 1738,
they offered an annual bounty of £10 to any family, whether from
among the proprietors or not, that would settle in their township. They
renewed the offer a year later, voting in addition a gift of £20 to any
proprietor who would settle in person during the coming year. Neither
measure attracted more than a bare trickle of settlers; by 1745, not
more than a dozen families lived in that inland township.[19] The proprietors of Narragansett Number 3 in New Hampshire offered £20 to
any settler who would comply with the conditions of the General Court.
In 1747, seven years after the expiration of the time limit for having
sixty families in the township, the same proprietors were still searching for measures to "oblige sixty families (with those already settled
here) to settle immediately, or procure some to settle here for them." [20]

Troubles such as these were common throughout inland Maine

and New Hampshire, and they were compounded by King George's and the French and Indian Wars. The renewal of full-scale hostilities with the French in 1744 ended a thirty-year period of restless peace between the two European powers just when the infant frontier communities of northern New England most needed peace and stability.

Because the Massachusetts authorities wanted to keep the new townships populated during the wars to protect the frontiers—this, indeed, had been one of the principal motives for setting them up—the government helped out during this period with money and soldiers. Such aid held some of the more vigorous settlements intact; it was not enough to prevent the abandonment of others.

New Marblehead not only managed to survive the war years, but actually gained both in numbers and maturity. Aid from the province helped immensely; so did the energy and leadership of the township's first settler, Thomas Chute. Though perhaps not a typical settler of the back parts in the eighteenth century, Chute illustrates well the qualities and assets that a proprietor needed if he were to turn a grant of frontier land into a positive lifetime asset. Not all the grantees were as happily endowed.

Chute was one of the few original proprietors of New Marblehead actually to move to his land in Maine. He had moved early in life from Byfield, Massachusetts, his birthplace, to Boston, where he worked as a tailor. In 1712, he married. Sometime before 1724, he moved again, this time to Marblehead. There he expanded both his livelihood and his influence by keeping an inn and serving as deputy sheriff while continuing his tailor's trade. As one of the more adventurous and ingenious of the New Marblehead grantees, he took his wife and family to Falmouth a year or two after becoming a proprietor in order to be near the new township while living comfortably and prosperously in the seaport. He set up a tailor's shop and kept an inn in Falmouth while he cleared his lot in New Marblehead about ten miles inland and built a house on it. The Chute family moved to its new home in 1737 or 1738, probably in the spring of 1738.[21] Thomas must have been in his middle or late forties, and by then have accumulated considerable capital in his various callings. As the principal inhabitant of New Marblehead, he further multiplied his activities and undoubtedly his income as well.

By 1743, the tailor had acquired at least eight neighbors, most of whom had come from places other than Marblehead, having bought their rights from some of the original proprietors.[22] A major exception was William Mayberry, the second settler, who, like Chute, had been one of the original grantees. Mayberry, an energetic blacksmith, had come to Marblehead from his native Antrim County in Ulster. Made of the same ambitious fiber as his partner, Mayberry followed Chute to New Marblehead shortly after Chute had settled, taking his wife, his two sons, and his daughter. Among them, the Mayberrys soon became the largest landholders in New Marblehead and adopted a style of living, including liveried servants, that would have seemed outrageously pretentious for one of his craft in an older Massachusetts community.[23]

The settlement of the home lots along the Presumpscot River proceeded steadily through the 1740's and 1750's, but was retarded by the wars of 1744–48 and 1755–60. As early as 1743, warned by indications of uneasiness among the eastern Indians and by news of the Battle of Dettingen, which meant that Britain and France, almost inevitably, would soon be fighting again, the Massachusetts General Court tried to prepare "the Inland Frontiers in this Province" for war. New Marblehead and eight other townships received an appropriation for fortifications. With their £100, the men of the settlement built a two-story blockhouse on the high land that had been designated as the "ministry" lot.[24] During the periods of greatest danger, the entire population lived in the "Province Fort," leaving the stockade only in daylight to work in their fields, and then only under guard. The settlement successfully withstood the five raids that Indians made on the township between 1747 and 1756,[25] but farming came almost to a stop. Recognizing that this and the other barrier towns would be abandoned and so lose their military usefulness if the inhabitants had no means of subsistence, the General Court came to the rescue with a form of subsidy.

In the case of New Marblehead, the legislators simply authorized the assignment of a stated number of residents to the local garrison as members of the province militia drawing full pay and allowances— eighteen men in the summer and nine in winter. For the six years following 1743, the men of Marblehead answered muster when necessary and took their turn at guard duty with the "western men," as they called the Massachusetts soldiers in the garrison. They were not compelled to join in scouting parties, however, and in fact expected the "western" soldiers to stand guard over them while they planted and harvested their corn. When the payroll arrived each month, the residents divided their share evenly among all the families, leaving the official accounting of the matter to "the care of the officer in making up his Muster Roll." [26]

Captain Daniel Hills threatened this happy arrangement when he arrived from Newbury in 1748 to take command of the Falmouth company, to which the "division" at New Marblehead, under Thomas Chute as sergeant, belonged. He erased the distinction between "inhabitants" and "western men," and refused to pay any local man who did not enlist in his company under the same terms as other soldiers. Twenty-two New Marblehead men sent an irate petition to the Governor and General Court, explaining frankly the accustomed arrangement and pleading that so far as they knew, their old practice had been consistent with the intent of the Court. A similar petition from the neighboring township of Gorhamtown, whose soldiers also came under Captain Hills's command, reinforced the complaint from New Marblehead.

Hills replied with a lengthy letter in which he complained that the resident soldiers cost more than they were worth.[27] The Court settled the matter in August, 1749, by ordering all the "pay and Subsistence" due the "Inhabitants-soldiers" of New Marblehead and Gorhamtown to be paid to Moses Pearson in his capacity as a captain of militia. Pearson, in turn, was to distribute the money equally among all who had served.[28] By then, this period of garrison life had nearly ended and the economy of the fortified frontier towns again relied upon lumbering and farming instead of soldiering.

Despite the dangers and inconveniences of war, and even though a half-dozen families deserted the township to live in Falmouth in 1744,[29] New Marblehead actually gained in numbers during King George's War and the uneasy years before the outbreak of the French and Indian War in 1755. Three new houses were built in 1743, three in 1744, one in 1745, one in 1748, two in 1749, six houses and a barn in 1750, six houses and a barn in 1751, five houses in 1752, and a "Duble house" in 1753. Two more houses, including a "Duble" one, went up in 1755, and another in 1756.[30]

4

When the General Court of Massachusetts granted a frontier township in the 1730's, it provided almost invariably as a condition that each grantee build on his "right" a house of at least "Eighteen feet Square and seven feet Stud." The terms presupposed the founding of a settlement modeled upon the commonly accepted village ideal of Massachusetts. This presupposition extended to architecture as well as to density of settlement, form of agriculture, and establishment of religion.[31]

By "house," the legislators meant a structure of timber frame and clapboards of the type long familiar in Massachusetts, Rhode Island, Connecticut, and coastal New Hampshire. They were not concerned that it be of great size, as the words of the condition demonstrate. They probably envisioned a version of the one-story or story-and-a-half house of the type now known as "Cape Cod," early examples of which had been built in southeastern Massachusetts at least by the 1680's.[32] They certainly did not have in mind any departure from the standard framed construction, for not only was any other method of building practically unknown in their part of New England, but without a frame, the term "stud" is meaningless.

In this as in many other ways, however, the settlers found a way of meeting their immediate needs that was more appropriate to conditions of wilderness life as they found them than the legislative ideal. Thomas Chute and his first neighbors along the Presumpscot built their houses of logs. These buildings were not of the classic "log cabin" construction of the later Western frontier. The use of round logs, chinking, and crossed corners was introduced to America by the Swedish colonists who settled on the lower Delaware River in the seventeenth century, and could also have been used by the German colonists at Broad Bay, Maine, in 1742.[33] Neither English nor Scotch-Irish settlers, however, had yet learned this technique, which was indigenous to the forests of northern Europe and Scandinavia. Instead, they adapted to their own use a model that was more immediately available, and which had emerged from their own architectural traditions.

As early as King William's War of 1689–97, some of the scattered settlers on the Maine coast, who were too far from a fort or garrison house for security, borrowed the construction principles that had long been used in these fortifications for their more modest private dwellings. Years before the first attempts to settle the interior of the region, soldiers and settlers had built blockhouses and garrison houses of squared logs laid horizontally one atop the other, their corners formed either by mortising the timbers into corner posts or by joining the timbers together by some form of dovetailing.[34] A wall of oak or even pine timbers could withstand the force of a musket ball and was relatively resistant to fire. Windows were commonly small, and many of these fortified structures were equipped on all four sides with a projecting second story, which unlike the urban frame houses copied from

English medieval models, actually had a defensive purpose. If the building were a garrison "house," intended as a residence as well as a fortification, the timbers were often faced with clapboards for the sake of appearance and protection from the wind and weather.

The blockhouse and garrison house, inventive as they were, actually were extensions of the familiar framed structures at the Bay. Many of the settlers and soldiers in Maine and New Hampshire undoubtedly had worked with "log" (which in New England meant "hewn log") frames in Massachusetts. To erect an entire building of this material, using the same sort of mortising and joints at the corners that English carpenters had long used in constructing the heavy frames of their buildings, was only to carry the familiar procedure a step further.

From the hewn log dwelling houses in the vicinity of Casco Bay, adapted for reasons of defense from larger and more permanent fortifications, both Thomas Chute and the settlers of Londonderry may well have learned the principles of log house construction. Chute lived at Falmouth while building his house in New Marblehead, and a large part of the Scotch-Irish colony passed a winter at Casco Bay before going to Nutfield. In addition, the Londonderry men must have been familiar with the "strong logg house" in Portsmouth that the New Hampshire Assembly ordered built in 1699 for a provincial prison, and perhaps also with Major John Gilman's "Loghouse by the bridg" in Exeter, which was a "publick licensed house for Entertainment" in 1719.*

Chute and his neighbors soon found that one could as well build a house of hewn logs if one of the three sides of each timber were left rounded. Most of the first New Marblehead houses, therefore, were even more rustic in appearance than the small dwellings on the coast

* Hugh Morrison, in his authoritative study of early American architecture, states flatly that on the Maine frontier between 1690 and 1745, "a majority of the ordinary dwelling houses were built with square-hewn logs fitted with loopholes"; pp. 78–9. Morrison apparently relied principally upon the findings of Shurtleff, who in turn based his conclusions partly on deeds and other documents and partly on an undocumented footnote in W. D. Williamson's *History of the State of Maine* (Hallowell, Me., 1832). Williamson's note, on page 77 of Volume II, is as follows: "All [the houses], which were built here [in Berwick], between 1690 and 1745, were of hewed log, sufficient to oppose the force of small arms. There was a block house on the western side of Salmon Fall brook, a mile above Quampeagan, where William Gerrish lived; a mile higher, was Key's garrison;—next were Wentworth's and Goodwin's block houses. The fort on *Pine Hill,* called Hamilton's garrison, was standing in 1750. It was made of poles 20 feet high, and picketed at the upper end." Evidence for the log buildings in Portsmouth and Exeter is in *Provincial Papers of New Hampshire,* III, 88, 760, and 787, quoted in H. R. Shurtleff: *Log Cabin Myth* (Cambridge, Mass., 1939), pp. 82, 178.

that had been adapted from the blockhouses and garrison houses. The settlers saved part of the labor of hewing by flattening only three sides of the log, forming flat surfaces to about adjoining logs and a flat interior wall. According to one historian of Windham, the settlers divided these first one-story log houses into rooms, sometimes by boards, but usually by bedquilts suspended on ropes from the rafters. A loft, reached by a ladder, served as a storage area or a sleeping place for children. A large, rudely constructed stone fireplace and a storage cellar for vegetables were the only other concessions to comfort and convenience. Doors were of rough boards, windows were small and few, and the roofs were of strips of birch bark covered with shingles or clapboards split from pine logs.[35]

Similarly, the Scotch-Irish settlers of Londonderry used the materials readiest at hand and built their first dwellings of hewn logs, covering the sides with bark.[36] When John Morison, one of the first settlers at West-Running Brook in 1719, broke the news to his proud wife that their house would have to be made of logs, like those of their neighbors, he received a disappointed yet hopeful response. "Aweel, aweel, dear Joan," the wife is supposed to have replied affectionately, "an it maun be a log house, do make it a log heegher nor the lave" (higher than the rest).[37] In 1724, the town of Londonderry voted to build a "logg" school house.[38]

The settlers of the northern New England frontier intended their log houses only as temporary dwellings. The men of Londonderry built two garrison houses of stone at West-Running Brook to supplement their private houses,[39] and as soon as it was practical to do so, many of them abandoned the initial compact settlement and developed farms and built frame and clapboard farmhouses on the larger lots. When the Reverend James MacGregor was settled as their first pastor soon after the settlement began, the townspeople built him a framed house two stories high with an added lean-to at the rear.[40]

To a remarkable extent, the first settlers of New Marblehead abandoned their original houses in favor of new ones on adjoining lots. A proprietors' survey of the township in 1759 disclosed that of the forty-nine houses in the township, seventeen were in ruins and three others stood vacant. In many cases, the former occupant of a "rotten down" house was living at the time of the survey in a dwelling erected more recently. Joseph Sterling was living in a house built in 1751 on Lot 7 next to a lot which contained the "Remains of a house" he had built the year before. John Bodge's residence, built in 1752, was next to his "Rotten down" house, which he had erected in 1744. William

Mayberry's original house, which he had occupied in 1740 on Lot 11, was "Rotten down" in 1759; Mayberry was living in a garrison house that he had built on Lot 26 in 1750. Thomas Chute, who had built the first house in the settlement in 1738, was now living instead in a house he had built in 1752 nearly a mile to the south, although his son Curtis was apparently working the old farm. There were seven other similar cases.[41] In Chester, a township slightly north of Londonderry, the first twenty-four settlers from Hampton and Haverhill built houses of hewn logs beginning in 1720, but in 1732 Captain Samuel Ingalls began the trend toward conventional construction by putting up his "great house," framed with hewn white oak and closed in by clapboards.[42]

The construction of hewn-log dwelling houses on the eastern frontier must be counted among the significant departures from New England precedent. This is not so much true of the Scotch-Irish as of the settlers of English stock whose Puritan forebears in Massachusetts had for generations displayed an amazing reticence and even obtuseness about adopting styles and construction methods that differed from those of seventeenth-century England. In this matter, as in others, the practical considerations of defense and economy outweighed tradition, legislation, and habit. The conditions of the frontier encouraged inventiveness, adaptability, and receptiveness to new ideas.

This particular departure, however, seems to have been short-lived. Most likely, the settlers of Londonderry began to build framed and clapboarded houses soon after the erection of the first sawmills in 1719 and 1721. The first sawmill in New Marblehead was finished in 1740 during a lull in the local Indian menace,[43] but at that time only four families lived on the river lots, hardly enough to provide the crew needed for raising a framed house. There was a spurt of building activity beginning about 1750, when many of the original houses were apparently abandoned. We may safely date the general use of frames and clapboards in that town from about this time. By 1750, the town's second sawmill may have been operating at Little Falls.[44] When the means became available, the settlers for the most part abandoned what had been a temporary expedient and resorted to conventional architecture. The assessors' return for 1784 listed sixty "houses" and only fourteen "log houses." [45]

A more enduring departure from precedent came in most communities when the settlers abandoned their temporary hewn log dwellings for permanent ones. For along with their original houses, they abandoned the ideal of the Puritan village. When settlement of the northern New England back country emerged from its pioneering stage, it was generally not as a duplicate of the tightly settled and closely organized communities founded in Massachusetts and southern New Hampshire in the seventeenth century. This was true even in those townships that the Massachusetts government granted to Massachusetts proprietors to be inhabited by Massachusetts settlers, despite one highly respected historian's assertion that "The frontiersmen of New England, like the Plain People of Pennsylvania, continued without much change the social institutions of their fathers." [46] The statement needs qualifying. Though it undoubtedly occurred to few of the first settlers of the back parts to abandon deliberately either the institutions or the values of Puritan New England, the conditions of the time and place influenced the new settlements as much as the intentions of the legislature, the proprietors, or the settlers. One of the most significant departures from precedent, one which permanently influenced the landscape of northern New England and the way of life of its people, was the diffusion of dozens of communities of settlers throughout their townships. In the most characteristic northern country towns, life focused on the family farm rather than on the village, which in most cases was either sharply attenuated or failed to develop at all. Why, and how, did this happen?

CHAPTER XIII

The Country Town
Takes Shape
1725–1760

1

The new wave of northern-bound settlers followed the rivers into the back parts. The inland towns of Dover, Exeter, Durham, and Berwick, all built on the intricate Piscataqua River system, had been settled early in the seventeenth century. Their histories, because they shared a common avenue to the sea, combine naturally with those of Kittery and the towns of coastal New Hampshire. The old Massachusetts town of Dunstable, which by the end of the eighteenth century had furnished parts of no less than ten New Hampshire towns, straddled the Merrimack more than thirty miles from the coast. Yet settlers had moved up the inviting valley to that area at least as early as the 1670's while much land to the south and east still lay vacant.[1] The Reverend Mr. MacGregor's Ulstermen actually discovered their promised land of Londonderry by following the Merrimack until they found an unoccupied tract that pleased them. The paperwork that made it official came later. In the 1730's, settlers from Massachusetts pushed slowly up the Connecticut as far as Northfield; by 1736, they had traversed twenty miles of vacant territory to the Ashuelot River, a tributary of the Connecticut. It is not surprising that New Marblehead and Gorhamtown, which were linked by the Presumpscot with Falmouth and the sea, matured fairly promptly while the neighboring barrier towns of New Boston and New Gloucester, which enjoyed no such advantage, did not.

Rivers and streams, besides providing natural routes to the first new settlements, determined their layout. The first twenty settlers of

Londonderry agreed when they arrived at Nutfield to take up land fronting on West-Running Brook, a stream running into Beaver River, a tributary of the Merrimack. In doing this, they at once decreed a settlement much more dispersed than the ordinary Massachusetts village. Each home lot ran along the riverfront for thirty "perches," or rods, and contained sixty acres.[2] By comparison with Watertown's home lots of eight and fourteen acres, the six-acre lots given to new-comers to Sudbury in 1644, and the ten-acre home lots laid out for the resettlement of North Yarmouth, the tract upon which each Londonderry family was to live was enormous.[3] Even were no lot left vacant, houses would stand, on the average, about five hundred feet apart. The Londonderry men laid out lots on both sides of the brook, which served as a main street. Not until they had put up many houses did they build highways.[4]

The townsmen eventually spilled out over the countryside to live on still larger and more dispersed farms, but here on the "double range"—a kind of middle step between the seventeenth-century New England village and scattered rural settlement—the Ulstermen built their first permanent dwellings. Up the river at Penacook, where Massachusetts Yankees from Haverhill laid out home lots of a more orthodox size and were prevented by legislative enactment from build-ing their houses more than 330 feet apart, the elongated, curving pattern in which they arranged their 103 six-acre lots was nevertheless determined by the course of the Merrimack.[5]

New Marblehead, like Londonderry and Penacook, began as a river settlement. The first act of the fifty-eight unpretentious men of Marblehead who suddenly in 1734 found themselves the owners of a frontier township was to lay out home lots along the Presumpscot.* On April 19, 1735, the legislative committee appointed by the General Court to supervise the settlement and a three-man committee chosen by the grantees visited the new township to survey these first ten-acre lots. The two committees first marked out a road parallel to and about a half-mile east of the stream, then laid off the sixty-three ad-joining home lots in the forest between the road and the river's wooded, precipitous left bank. They also laid out three parallel roads from the main road down to the riverside, running through the tier of home lots. Later the same year, as a part of an elaborate attempt

* Two persons were added to the list before the lots were assigned, making a total of sixty proprietors, as the General Court had provided. Windham Proprie-tors or Grantees Book (Ms., Maine Historical Society), p. 3.

to equalize each proprietor's holdings, the grantees added to each home lot another ten acres on the upper side of the main road.[6]

Unlike the Londonderry resident-proprietors from Ulster, the Marblehead men and the Massachusetts officials who planned New Marblehead wanted a very closely settled village, despite the generous acreage they provided for each home lot. These lots were indeed very deep, but they fronted on the main road and the river for an average of only 165 feet each. Had the settlement of the township taken place as planned, some sixty dwellings would have formed a tight procession of nearly two miles along the riverside, much like the first settlement at Londonderry except that the buildings would have been spaced about a third as far apart.

About twenty miles to the southwest of the Presumpscot River lots, the proprietors of Narragansett Number 1 laid out their prospective village in 1735, the same year that the New Marblehead proprietors were planning their settlement. They followed a strikingly similar pattern. Along the east bank of the Saco River, this group of Narragansett proprietors placed their first lots of twenty acres each. Instead of laying out a road at some distance from the river as the Marblehead men had done, the grantees of the future town of Buxton left a strip four rods wide across the end of each lot at the river's edge "for publick use." [7] While suited to the relatively flat terrain surrounding the lower Saco, this provision for a roadway immediately along the riverside would have been impossible in New Marblehead because of the steep banks of the Presumpscot.

The extent to which rivers and streams dictated the layout of many of the new townships reflects the fundamental importance of these waterways in the life of a northern interior community, especially during its pioneering stage. Rivers and river courses offered the easiest routes into the interior and provided the first highways for communication with the older settlements along the Maine and New Hampshire seacoast, down the Merrimack Valley to Dunstable, Haverhill, and Newbury, or down the Connecticut to Deerfield, Northampton, and Springfield. Many of the broad flatlands or "intervales" along the banks of the Connecticut and Merrimack were naturally clear of trees and thus offered a logical starting point for a settlement and provided the best meadow land in many a riverside township. Rivers and streams turned mills for sawing lumber and grinding flour, and they often provided fish and served as a means of floating logs from the heavily forested back settlements to the coast.

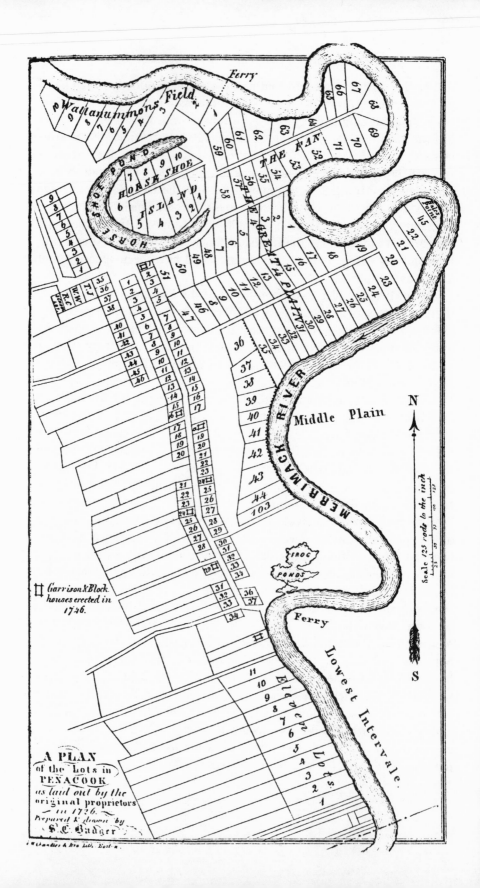

A PLAN of the Lots in PENACOOK as laid out by the original proprietors in 1726. Prepared & drawn by S. C. Badger.

The order in which the proprietors of New Marblehead attacked the various tasks of settlement after the distribution of home lots shows that they assigned priority first to roads, next to a sawmill, then to a cart bridge over the Presumpscot, and finally to a meetinghouse.[8] The voters of Londonderry ordered construction of a sawmill on Beaver River only two months after the first settlers arrived.[9] Most proprieties regarded an operating sawmill as the key to a successful settlement; as one of their first acts, they either held out subsidies and monopolies to lure a private entrepreneur into building one or undertook to do it themselves. Most often, progress was disappointingly slow.

Londonderry, because of its special success in filling the township with settlers, had little trouble getting a sawmill in operation. The town granted the water rights of Beaver River and a piece of adjoining land to a group of four "undertakers," who apparently made good their promise to finish a mill within three months. As part of the agreement, one of the partners also received the privilege of building a gristmill on the river.[10] Within two years, the town's "committee," as the selectmen were first styled, arranged with another group of partners for a second sawmill, fixing in advance the prices to be offered to townspeople.[11]

The proprietors of New Marblehead first discussed and then promptly dismissed the idea of building a mill at one of the six falls on the Presumpscot "at general charge." In August, 1735, the Reverend George Pigot, one of the two Marblehead clergymen in the propriety, offered to build one, but he failed to finish it by the date upon which he and his fellow proprietors had agreed. Finally, the proprietors revoked his privilege.[12] In 1738, soon after they had canceled the long-protracted deal with Mr. Pigot, the proprietors accepted a new proposal from four other partners, also members of the propriety. In return for the right to the waterfall of their choice and ten acres of land, the adventurers promised to start building by August 1, 1738, and be ready to saw logs by November 30.[13] In March, 1739, the proprietors extended the time because a controversy with the Presumpscot Indians had interrupted the building of both the mill and the meetinghouse. Not until the next year, two years after the first settler had moved his family into the township, did New Marblehead have its own sawmill.[14]

The original plan of Penacook (later Rumford and finally Concord, New Hampshire), laid out in 1726. The principal home lots are the small lots at the center, running in a double line along the present main street of Concord. The owner of each "right" also held a corresponding piece of farmland in one or more of the other "ranges." Like Upper Ashuelot, this township was laid out under the authority of Massachusetts Bay.

The proprietors of Narragansett Number 1, in their anxiety to have a mill in their township, issued a blanket authorization to any settler to build one on the Saco in return for the permanent right to the stream.[15] Despite the lack of any of the more-or-less stringent conditions that had been common in New England up to that point, no prospective millbuilder found the prospects sufficiently enticing to take advantage of the offer. In June, 1742, therefore, the Buxton propriety paid Stephen "Myghill" (McGill), one of their number, "and other in Company" £200 to build a mill in behalf of the proprietors.[16] The millwrights went to work that summer and finished the mill early in November. At that time, five houses had been built along the stream and, according to a contemporary witness, there were "several more Scattering a Bought in the township." [17] The proprietors arranged for a second sawmill and a gristmill on Little River in 1752.[18]

Like the Buxton proprietors, the grantees of Warner, New Hampshire, decided to build a mill for the township at their own expense rather than leave this important business to the uncertainties of private enterprise. It was finished in 1740; still unused, it was burned by Indians during King George's War before anyone had moved to town. After the war, the proprietors replaced it, again at their common cost.[19] The proprietors of Upper Ashuelot, on the other hand, simply added a cash subsidy from the propriety's treasury to the usual offer of land and water rights to a prospective private builder.[20]

Even before the falls on and near the Merrimack turned water wheels, they supplied fish. During Londonderry's first days, an Indian visitor took Mr. MacGregor to a hilltop and pointed the way to Amoskeag Falls about ten miles northwestward. That foaming, torrential rapid on the Merrimack, which in the nineteenth century was to power the textile and shoe industries of Manchester, presented too great a challenge to the technology of Mr. MacGregor's day to submit to harnessing. Nevertheless, it provided real wealth. Using hand nets at first, and later fixing seines in the stream below the falls, the Londonderry settlers caught salmon and shad, an important staple in their diet.[21]

At the spring town meeting in 1723, the Londonderry voters, apparently having met some competition at the falls, took the somewhat cryptic action of empowering the selectmen to take any necessary steps for "securing the fishery at Amoskeag." [22] Competition was not the most serious problem arising from the Amoskeag fishery. Alarmed by occasional drownings at the falls, the voters authorized the selectmen in 1731, "in order to the Safety of our towns people at the fishing at ammascegg," to pay three pounds to "Such person or persons as Shall be oblig'd to make two Good Sufficient Cannos and Capable to manage the said Canoos, the Select men obliging the . . . undertakers to Serve the Inhabitants of the town the whole time of fishing before any out towns people, and Shall not Exceed one Shilling per Hundred for all the fish that they shall ferry over from the Island's and the owner of the fish and his atendands is to be ferried backwards and forwards at free Cost." [23]

Long before the falls beside the river lots of New Marblehead became a source of power, the settlers floated masts and timber down the Presumpscot in great quantities. In 1738, the proprietors ordered the four prospective mill owners to take care not to hinder the free passages of logs and rafts* over the falls. In August, 1741, the propriety appointed a committee to consider alterations of the "Great Bridge" above Saccarappa Falls "for the better Securing it from Danger by such Lumber as usually comes Down the River in times of sudden freshets of Water." [24]

The great importance of rivers and streams in shaping the arrangement of the northeastern country town had no real precedent in the planning of previous inland New England towns to the south. In the 1730's, the East Anglian settlers of Watertown, Massachusetts, built their village center about a town common half a mile from the Charles River. The town's highways, for the most part, connected this village center with the inhabitants' holdings in outlying divisions and were oriented with respect to that focal point rather than to the river. [25] When a small body of Watertown men, recent emigrants from the "open field" farming country in the middle of England, went west to the Musketaquid Valley to settle Sudbury, the arrangement of their home lots was similar though their system of holding farmlands was different. [26] In both cases, the low ground next to the rivers served as grazing and meadow lands somewhat remote from the center of settlement. The same was true in the Connecticut River towns of Hartford, Wethersfield, and Windsor. [27]

The settlers of interior Maine and New Hampshire had no well-established overland Indian trail such as the Bay Path to Connecticut.

---

* A "raft" was a collection of logs or timbers bound together for floating downstream or for towing by water, now generally seen only on the larger rivers in timber country. Hence the colloquial expression "a raft of . . . ," meaning a great quantity.

The banks of such small rivers as the Presumpscot, the Saco, and the upper branches of the Piscataqua provided no broad, fertile meadows; the forest grew, in most cases, to the water's edge. The Merrimack was more like the Connecticut and the Charles in this respect, but the settlers of Londonderry and its neighboring offshoot of Bedford needed waterpower before grazing land, so they settled first on the smaller tributaries after using the Merrimack Valley as a transportation route. The greatest reason for the new importance of rivers was the high place of lumbering in the economy of the northern interior towns.

The use of streams as a point of departure for laying out townships contributed to straggling settlement along the banks, which was one step away from the ideal of the single compact town center. The inhabitants of the country towns moved still further away from this New England tradition when they had cut much of the most valuable timber and it had become feasible to cultivate relatively large areas. This further dispersal could not have taken place, of course, had the proprietors not permitted it and the public authorities not either co-operated or looked the other way.

2

The dispersal of Londonderry need not surprise us, even though the Scot tenants of an estate in Ulster had normally lived in a compact village and farmed their lands on the outskirts. The Scotch-Irish of New Hampshire departed from habit when they spread out over the countryside, but so did the Scotch-Irish who emigrated to the frontiers of Pennsylvania, Virginia, and the Carolinas.[28] The village life of Ulster, though traditional, had apparently not been, as in early Massachusetts, practically an article of faith.

One reason for the dispersal, totally unlike the case in most of the northern frontier townships, was the community's success in attracting new settlers. The lots in the Double Range could not accommodate the immigrants who poured into Londonderry during the first few years following 1719, and after sawmills and a summer or two of prosperity had made it possible for some of the original settlers to abandon their log huts on the brook and build more permanent dwellings, they followed the example of the newcomers and raised their framed houses on larger pieces of land. The settlers had soon swarmed far out over the countryside; each one built his house on whatever large farm lot in one of the various "ranges" was assigned to him, or, if he owned more than one, best suited him. The proprietors had laid off the ranges in the best farmlands, regardless of the distance between them. The town historian wrote in 1851 that Londonderry lacked anything like a village within its borders until early in the nineteenth century.[29] One would be hard-put to refute his findings. It is true that the first meetinghouse and first school were both built at the Double Range, indicating that the site of the first settlement was considered the town center.[30] The records do not show, however, that either proprietors or town officials tried deliberately for a single compact village after the first houses were built at what turned out to be a partly temporary settlement at West-Running Brook.

While we lack evidence of any intention to build the town around a nucleated village, we have ample evidence that after the early 1720's, the population was in fact widely dispersed. As early as 1725, for example, the inhabitants discussed the possibility of opening various neighborhood schools.[31] In 1731, the town voted, "for the Better accomodation of the Severall Quarters of this town to have the Benefitt of our Schoole," to build a schoolhouse "in each Quarter in this town, . . . and the Schoole Master to be Remov'd to Each of the said houses and to continue there by Keeping Schoole according to the Equall proportion of Rates that said Quarter of the town pays." Each "quarter" was directed to build and maintain its own schoolhouse.[32]

Another indication is the intense road-building activity that the selectmen undertook between 1723 and 1726. In almost every case, the directions for laying out roads mentioned houses by name. They frequently called for widening the various footpaths that already wound through fields and woodlands connecting farm with farm or farm with meetinghouse. One of the two roads ordered by the selectmen on February 18, 1724/5, for example, was to begin at the common land northwest of a lot that had been granted to Governor Shute and run

> Southerly across the said lott and through Samuel Renkins lott to the line between Thomas Chochran and James Calwok, . . . and Cross William Adams land straight to Patrick Douglas house and to the Lean-too and turning more Easterly across Robert Boys lot to Governour Wentworth's farm and so on the sd farm to the westend of Alexander MacMurphy's second division, and David Coghill's to the brook at the Inlay of the fulling Mill and . . . to Jon Archibald's house and straight to William Gilmores house, and as straight as good ground will alow to Daniel McDuffis new hous and so to James Addams house. . . .[33]

There is further evidence for the broad distribution of the farm-houses of Londonderry in the early division of the township into east and west parishes. The division took place, amidst theological and personal animosities and a fight over the location of the second parish meetinghouse, in 1740. There had been motions in this direction as early as 1733.[34]

Across the Merrimack in Bedford, which in 1737 began to accommodate new Scotch-Irish immigrants and the overflow from Londonderry, the settlement was dispersed from the start. In 1748, the proprietors voted "that one third of the time, Preaching shall be to accommodate the inhabitants at the upper end of the town; one other third part, at the lower end of the town; the last third, about Strawberrie hill;—all in such houses as said committee shall think proper for each part of the inhabitants." [35]

The proprietors of Peterborough, who looked frankly upon their New Hampshire property as a commercial investment, provided from the beginning for the sale of farms rather than village lots. Each of the four largest owners took for himself a 500-acre farm along the Contoocook River, a major tributary of the Merrimack. The speculators then divided about half of the rest of the township into ranges of hundred-acre lots, twenty or thirty of which were owned by each proprietor. Each proprietor divided his hundred-acre lots in half and sold a half of a lot as soon as he found a customer who would live on it, hoping that the tenant would soon be able to buy the fifty acres that went with it. By the outbreak of King George's War in 1744, thirty families had paid about a crown an acre for this land and settled on it. French and Indian attacks drove them out of the township during the war, so the proprietors had to make a new survey in 1749. This time, they laid off a division of fifty-acre lots, which they granted to new residents without charge.[36] These settlers were largely Scotch-Irish from Lunenburg, Massachusetts, twenty miles to the southeast, and from Londonderry, twenty miles to the east. Within thirteen years, about fifty families were scattered broadly about the revived township.[37]

So much for communities settled predominantly by Ulstermen, and for townships planned deliberately as speculative enterprises. Useful as these examples may be as indications of the dispersal of communities in the region during the eighteenth century, their experience hardly constitutes convincing evidence of the mutation of an ideal. For that, we have to turn to communities that were designed initially as at least rough replicas of a Massachusetts town. The problem of securing settlers for the Narragansett and Canada townships and for the "barrier" towns of inland Maine and New Hampshire, exacerbated by the danger of enemy raids on the frontier during King George's and the French and Indian Wars, led eventually to measures for encouraging settlement that abolished the village ideal in inland northern New England. In several cases, as we have noticed already, the decision to let the riverbanks decree the shape of the settlement constituted the first step away from the traditional village layout. Ultimately, however, when the lumbering economy gave way to a farming economy, proprietors allowed the abandonment of even that simple linear "town plan." The gradual, almost unconscious progress of New Marblehead from frontier village to country town illustrates the process well.

During the autumn of 1737 and the early spring of 1738, Thomas Chute and his son Curtis, a youth in his early twenties, repeatedly donned the brown deerskin jackets and breeches that the vigorous tailor made for working clothes, and paddled a canoe up the Presumpscot or led the family mare up the rough clearing that the proprietors called a road to home lot number 12. There they cleared seven acres of land and built their first forest home next to the steep bank of the river. His first neighbors also built near the riverside instead of toward the back of their lots, but as the road became improved, it was recognized increasingly as a more practical route from Falmouth and the best means of communication between neighbors. As this recognition grew, and the settlers of New Marblehead gradually relied more on horses and oxen and less on canoes and bateaux, newcomers to the home lots began to build near the road instead of the river.[38]

When the province fortified the inland frontier in 1743, the New Marblehead men built their blockhouse on the high land intended for the "ministry" on the east side of the main road. The fort, fifty feet square and surrounded by a stockade of twelve-foot posts, stood nearly in the middle of the range of home lots and next to a meetinghouse that had been put up in 1740 to fulfill one of the requirements of settlement. The residents feared that the meetinghouse, which had been made of "Hewn Timber fit for defence," might provide an enemy stronghold if it were ever seized by the French or Indians. They therefore asked the propriety for permission to tear it down and use the materials to enlarge the fort or for other public purposes, promising to build another meetinghouse when the need arose. They then proceeded to wreck the meetinghouse before the proprietors could answer the petition.[39] Thus did the life of the frontier affect Puritan values in the eighteenth century.

For more than a decade, life in New Marblehead centered about the "Province Fort." Here, in times of greatest danger, the entire population lived, leaving the stockade only in daylight to work in their fields, and then only under guard. Here, from 1745 until his death on May 3, 1753, the Reverend John Wight, who had been installed as pastor when a church of seven members was organized in 1743, conducted Sabbath services.[40] Here more than twenty children were born and baptized, at least three couples were married, and ten persons died.[41] Here was headquarters, civil and military, where tensions between resident soldiers on the province payroll and the outlander Captain Hills put more stress on this crowded and abnormal life than the Indians.

The river lots filled up slowly during King George's War and the short period of peace that followed. Then in May, 1755, two months before Braddock's defeat at the Forks of the Ohio, Maine Indians attacked the settlements at New Boston, North Yarmouth, and New Gloucester, all of which were uncomfortably close to New Marblehead. These events put the growing forest hamlet again on alert. By now, the fort could not hold everyone, so the inhabitants fortified five of the stouter log houses with stockades and "flankers." [42] In the only serious local action of the French and Indian War, in May, 1756, the settlers killed the chief of the only nearby Indian band and demoralized his followers. This skirmish, fought more than three years before the reduction of Quebec, marked the permanent end of Indian conflict near the Presumpscot.[43]

As the wars went on and the settlement slowly grew, it became increasingly plain that the proprietors of New Marblehead were fulfilling only one of the two principal purposes of granting such towns as New Marblehead, New Gloucester, and New Boston. By encouraging settlement to the best of their ability, and by giving munitions to the settlers,[44] the proprietors contributed importantly to the defense of the eastern frontier. Thus they were well serving the chief aim of the General Court when it established the interior towns. In addition, however, the legislators thought they were providing new farmlands for straitened Marblehead fishermen "that are most likely to settle and bring forward a new Plantation, and that most need a Grant of Land." The sixty proprietors of New Marblehead, with but three exceptions, seem suddenly to have lost their great need for land. A few, finding money even more attractive, sold off their rights to actual settlers. The rest continued to hold regular meetings of the propriety in Marblehead. They voted whatever investments and divisions of land seemed necessary to meet the terms of their grant, hoped to profit from the timber on the land that was still undivided, and became increasingly alienated in interest and outlook from the men in New Marblehead who cut the trees, tilled the soil, and fought the Indians.

The propriety showed its first real concern about the state of the settlement in January, 1751, when it voted to take an accounting of what each proprietor had spent on the undertaking and at the same time discussed the possibility of departing further from the idea of a compact settlement. The proprietors wrote to Jabez Fox, the representative from Falmouth to the General Court, asking him to inquire around his neighborhood to see "Whether any suitable Number of Persons (likely to Carry on a Settlement) are willing to Settle on some part of . . . [New Marblehead] Provided they have a Grant of forty or fifty acres of Land each, Obliging themselves to settle thereon under proper Conditions." [45] Fox's discoveries are not recorded, nor did the proprietors, apparently, take any action resulting directly from this inquiry. The letter to Fox shows, however, that as early as 1751, the proprietors began to doubt that their town would ever be sufficiently attractive to settlers as long as the village ideal, however modified, was maintained. A decade later, they went very much further.

During the first half of the 1750's, the propriety voted repeatedly to survey "the present State of the Settlement," but not until 1759, and then only at the prodding of the General Court, did a committee of proprietors actually make such an examination. [46] The report of the committee was at once encouraging and alarming.

The committee found that the New Marblehead men had cleared 594 acres and built forty-nine houses, two barns, and the Province Fort in addition to the meetinghouse that had been torn down in 1743. Seventeen of the houses, however, were "rotten down" or otherwise in ruins, and three others stood vacant. [47] The settlers had made a promising start, but had abandoned two-fifths of the dwellings during the war and neglected the rest. Twenty-nine families still lived in the township, not quite half the number originally required to make good the proprietors' grant. The town now had neither minister nor meetinghouse, another condition of the grant, and years of neglect had made parts of the roads impassable. [48]

These findings must have surprised no one, in view of the hazards and difficulties to which all the frontier communities of the region had been exposed during the wars. Less predictable and of far greater significance to the future development of the town was the extent to which some of the settlers had successfully consolidated their holdings in an attempt to transform their "village" residences into relatively extensive farms. This the report of 1759 also disclosed.

After he had cleared seven acres and built his first house on Lot Number 12, Thomas Chute acquired Lots 13 and 14 from their owners in Marblehead and cleared seven acres on each. This gave him a farm consisting of one house on sixty contiguous acres, thirty on each side of the main road. Twenty-one acres of it were cleared for planting and grazing. In 1752, he cleared five acres and built a new house on Lot 42, leaving the original homestead to his son, Curtis, who married in 1754.[49] The committee reported the old house "Rotten down" in 1759.

The Mayberry family illustrates the tendency still more dramatically. William Mayberry moved to New Marblehead in 1737 with his wife, his two sons, John and Thomas, and his daughter, Sea Fair.[50] Instead of settling on his own Lot 57, he cleared and built upon Lot 11, which he acquired from his fellow proprietor Robert Bull, apparently in order to be near Thomas Chute, his only neighbor. In 1750, William moved his family from the original log dwelling and built a garrison house on fifteen acres of cleared land on Lot 26. His son, Richard, born after the family moved to New Marblehead, bought Lot 27 adjoining the new homestead, cleared fifteen acres, and worked the land, though he lived with his father. These two Mayberrys, then, lived together on a forty-acre farm, three-fourths of which consisted of cleared land. The following year, John Mayberry acquired Lot 56 next to his father's original grant, cleared twenty acres, and built a house on each lot. In 1759, he was living in one of the houses; the other was standing and apparently in good condition, but the report listed no occupants. The largest Mayberry farm of all belonged to Thomas, who in 1759 owned Lots 17, 18, 19, and 20, a total of eighty acres, of which fifty were cleared, and a garrison house on Lot 19. An unnamed Mayberry occupied the double house on Lots 2 and 3 jointly with William Maxfield, who also had appropriated the adjoining school lot to his own use.[51] Instead of the twenty acres originally granted to each proprietor in the range of home lots, therefore, the Mayberry clan possessed a total of 180 acres and one of its number was the joint owner of another forty acres, all located within what had been designed as a compact village. Of these holdings, 124 acres had been improved for farming.

One lot removed from Richard Mayberry's holdings was the original small farm upon which John Farrow, the third settler, had built his house. By 1759, Farrow was dead and his house in ruins, but his son occupied the two adjoining lots, and presumably the original one, and lived in a garrison house on one of the two new lots. Of the sixty acres in the three combined lots, thirty-six were cleared.

The most romantic story of the settlement is the tradition that Stephen Manchester, who cleared and built upon the lot next to the Farrow holdings, pursued Farrow's daughter, Grace, into the Maine wilderness from Tiverton, Rhode Island, in quest of her hand. The Farrow family and Manchester had both lived in Tiverton. Farrow acquired Lot 29 from Joseph Gallison, a shoreman of Marblehead, and moved his family to New Marblehead, the story goes, in order to keep Grace away from the impetuous Stephen. Not to be frustrated, the young suitor himself bought a right in New Marblehead, cleared twelve acres, and built a house hard by the residence of his intended father-in-law. He married Grace within a few weeks of his arrival. If the story is as true as it ought to be, the clearing and settling of six of the sixty-three home lots in New Marblehead resulted from this romance.[52] Stephen's father, Gershom, followed his son from Tiverton to New Marblehead in 1752, taking with him his second wife and his ten-year-old son, John, a half-brother to Stephen.[53] In 1759, Gershom was dead, and his house on Lot 15 was "Rotten down," but John was living on the adjoining Lot 16. A total of seventeen acres of the combined lots was cleared.

Ephraim Winship, who in 1730 had brought his family to New Marblehead from Lexington, Massachusetts, owned a house on nine acres of cleared land on Lot 5. His son, Gershom, who was about fourteen years old when the family moved, cleared nine acres and built a barn on Lot 6. Gershom married the daughter of William Mayberry two months after the survey was taken, and shortly built a house on his lot.[54] The next two lots, 7 and 8, were both occupied by Joseph Sterling, who had cleared seventeen acres. John Bodge held Lots 9 and 10, of which twenty acres were improved.

Abraham Anderson, a Marblehead man, owned three adjoining rights which he had bought from three of his former fellow townsmen and cleared forty-four of his sixty acres.[55] John Stevens, Jr., who had come with his father from Newburyport, owned a house on the lot adjoining his father's.[56] In 1759, each had cleared fourteen acres. The Bolton family, of Scotch-Irish origin, came to New Marblehead from Falmouth about 1741.[57] Thomas, the father, first settled on Lot 52, and later on Lot 54. William, his son, built a garrison house on the land between in 1744. Of the sixty acres in the combined Bolton holdings in the home range, forty-one were cleared in 1759. Hugh Crague, another Ulsterman who had found his way to Falmouth, moved to

New Marblehead shortly after his marriage in 1749 and built a house on Lot 51 and a barn on Lot 50.[58]

Since 1740, the owner of each home lot had been assigned a hundred-acre lot in the "second division" to go with it. Some of these were laid out north of the home range, along the river; others were arranged in several tiers east of the home lots.[59] Men like the Mayberrys, the Manchesters, and Abraham Anderson, of course, enjoyed holdings of several hundred acres as the result of the new division because one hundred-acre farm went with each right. There is no evidence that the land in the new division was farmed extensively during the war years. These lands were too far from the fort and the settlers' homes to be worked safely, which perhaps is one reason that many settlers tried to acquire as much land surrounding their own houses as possible. The land in the new division included some of the best in the township, however, and so after 1760, both old and new settlers began to build farms there.

Micah Walker, possibly without realizing it, was the first to depart radically from the established mode of settlement. He owned Lot 49, located between the Stevens's two lots and the two lots occupied by Hugh Crague and was thus prevented from expansion on either side. The committee reported in 1759 that Walker had cleared seven acres on his "home" lot, but was "settled on the hundred acres." The hundred-acre lot assigned to Home Lot 49 was number 23. It was one of the eight in the new division immediately adjacent to the east end of the home lots, and fortuitously placed at the end of one of the three crossroads. Walker no doubt saw little point in allowing two larger farms to close in a home stand which had no chance for expansion when he could establish himself in readily accessible surroundings that were much more spacious.

The report of 1759 opened the eyes of the proprietors to the facts of wilderness life. They saw first that their grant was in danger from their failure to meet the conditions properly. They also saw that Micah Walker had supplied the answer to the future of the township, even though he had gone about his settlement illegally. Beginning with the first settler, Thomas Chute, nearly every New Marblehead family of permanence and substance had demonstrated that the one fundamental attraction of the Maine frontier was the possibility of living upon and cultivating a large tract of one's own land. Only in time of war had these people seen the value of a compact settlement; even then, they had solved the problem of defense by taking temporary refuge in the fort and a few garrison houses. Under these conditions, it

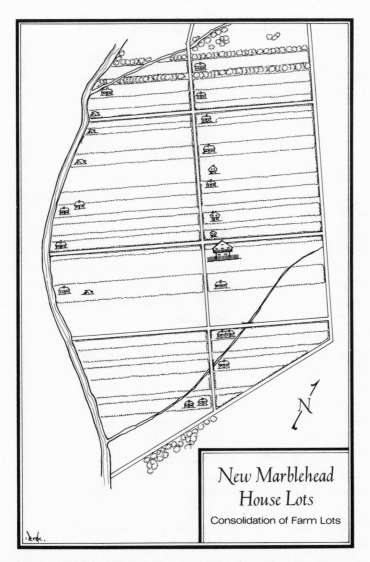

New Marblehead
House Lots
Consolidation of Farm Lots

A schematic representation of the consolidation of New Marblehead home lots, as revealed by the proprietors' survey in 1759. The narrowest lots on the plan above represent the size of each of the original home lots in the southwest corner of the township as laid off in 1735—10 acres on each side of the principal north-south road. By 1759, settlers had built 49 houses and 2 barns, not all of which are shown. Of the 49 houses, however, 17 were in ruins and 3 others vacant. Most of these stood near the Presumpscot River, at left. The inhabited dwellings were for the most part near the road, a half-mile from the river bank. In 13 cases, settlers acquired 1, 2, or 3 adjoining lots from their original owners and thus managed to operate consolidated farms of 40, 60, or 80 acres within what had been planned as a compact village some 3 miles long and about a mile wide. Immediately to the north and east of this range of home lots were 100-acre farm lots, on one of which a settler had illegally built his house by 1759. The survey of 1759 led the proprietors to relax the rules of settlement, which soon led to the complete abandonment of the idea of a compact village. The "province fort" is shown to the right of the main road near the middle of the "village."

mattered little whether their own small houses were 160 feet apart, as originally planned, or two miles apart. In any case, the wars were now over and defense no longer a consideration. It is obvious that the desire for a close community for religious, moral, educational, and social reasons never had been.

Five years earlier, the proprietors of the township of Sebago, a sparsely settled tract of wooded hills on the west side of the lake fifteen miles northwest of the New Marblehead river lots, had learned a similar lesson and acted upon it. At a meeting of the proprietors in Falmouth, they had voted "that such of the proprietors as Desire it shal have liberty to Remove their lotts that are not conveniant for setlement and take other lotts in lew thereof Giving a quit claim deed of there lotts allready deeded to the proprietors again to the use of said proprietors." [60] This meant that prospective settlers were to have free reign in selecting their home sites, and represented the complete abandonment of any sort of town plan.

The proprietors of New Marblehead now petitioned the General Court to permit any prospective settler who owned an original right to build his home in the hundred-acre division rather than on his assigned "home" lot. The petition noted that the original home lots had been made small "to make the settlement compleat and defencable," but that this arrangement had "greatly hurt and discouraged the said settlement." The hundred-acre lots already laid out, the petition went on, "will better suit them, and serve the township in general." At the same time, the propriety prayed for confirmation of the holdings of the twenty-nine settlers, the settlement of a troublesome boundary dispute with Falmouth, and the establishment of a municipal government.[61] On January 20, 1761, the Court granted all of the petition, and gave the settlers a year to complete the terms of their grant and to establish a "district" in place of the existing amorphous "plantation." [62]

A year later, the proprietors voted to clear more roads and build more bridges over the Presumpscot and one of its larger tributaries, Pleasant River, "for accomodating travellers and encouragement of people to settle the hundred-acre lots already laid out." [63] They followed this action, designed to facilitate communication throughout a widespread rural community, with a still more decisive step. On June 3, 1762, they authorized the sale of parcels of the common land, in lots up to a hundred acres, anywhere in the township that was agreeable to twelve prospective purchasers and a proprietors' committee.

Each purchaser was to pay at least one Spanish dollar an acre, come from outside the township, and agree to settle there within a year.[64] Within four months, all twelve lots were sold: nine to Falmouth men, one to a resident of Sudbury, and two to men who had already moved into the township at the time the sales agreement between the twelve purchasers and the proprietors was drawn. The twelve new lots became part of a second division of 140 hundred-acre lots that the propriety laid out in January, 1763.[65]

Even before the addition of these twelve new families, the community had enjoyed an increase in population under the proprietors' new liberal land policy. In September, 1762, the church ordained a minister, the Reverend Thomas Smith's son Peter, who noted in the church record book on that occasion that thirty-nine families then lived in the township.[66] By 1776, the population had increased to 550 white persons, or about ninety families.[67]

The reorganization of the church was the final step in the progression of the community toward maturity. On September 28, 1761, the "inhabitants" had met for the first time as a body politic at the Province Fort. There, following the General Court's order of the previous January, they had organized themselves into a district and elected a moderator, a clerk, assessors, and a collector. They had met again on March 15, 1762, and on June 11, the General Court had incorporated the inhabitants into a town named Windham.[68]

The proprietors of New Amesbury or Warner, New Hampshire, whose township in the defensive barrier between the Merrimack and the Connecticut developed much more slowly than New Marblehead, relaxed the traditional restrictions in much the same way when they reconvened after the French and Indian War to try to reinvigorate their abandoned holding. In 1763, the proprietors voted to abandon their original five-acre house lots in favor of lots of sixty acres each. In addition, they voted to give a forty-acre lot to the first ten persons who would agree to settle immediately, whether or not they were members of the propriety. By this means, they drew to the township its permanent settlers, described by a local historian as "for the most part very poor and illiterate." In 1765, the proprietors voted each of themselves an eighty-acre lot, and in 1766 another sixty-acre lot.

More startling than these profuse divisions of relatively large farm lots was the liberality of the surveying procedure itself. In every case, the proprietor or settler was allowed to select his own site anywhere

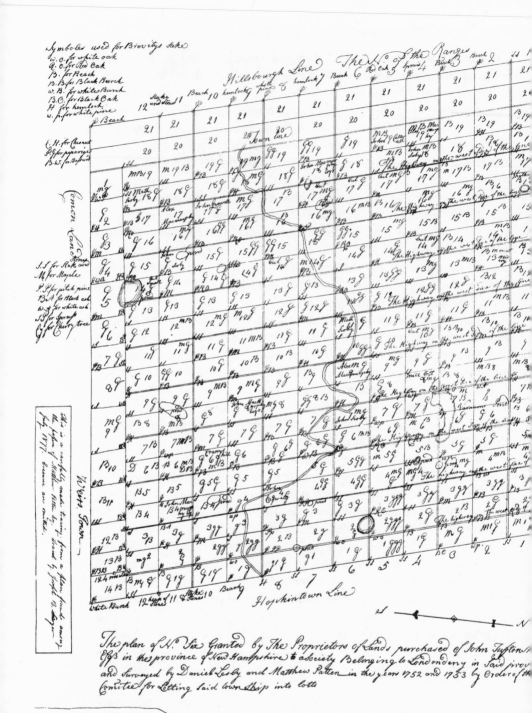

Symboles used for Brevitys sake

w. O. for white oak
R. O. for Red Oak
B. for Beach
B.B. for Black Burch
w. B. for white Burch
B.O. for Black Oak
H for hemlock
w. p. for white pine

C. H. for Chesnut
P. P. for popparige
B. W. for Baswod

Corner Land

S.S for Maple and Stones
M. for Maple
P. P. for pitch pine
B.A. for Black ash
w. A. for white ash
S.S for Sprus
Cf. for Chery tree

Hillsborough Line   The N of the Ranges

Town line

Hopkintown Line

The plan of No. Six Granted by The Proprietors of Lands purchased of John Tufton
Mason in the province of New Hampshire to a society Belonging to Londonderry in said provi
and Surveyed by Daniel Lesly and Matthew Patten in the years 1752 and 1753 by Order of the
Comittee for Letting said town ship into Lotts

Endorsed on the back as follows
"The plan of No. 6 in the line of town with the
Qualifications of the Lotts"
Attest Joseph B Sawyer

Thos D

in the township, and mark off the allotted area in any shape he fancied. If a proprietor was not present to claim his space at the time of a survey, he could exchange a lot that did not satisfy him for one that he surveyed himself in any unoccupied place. In this instance, the experience of New Marblehead was carried a step further, in that landowners were allowed to conduct their own surveys; in the interest of attracting settlers, the proprietors abandoned completely any pretense of a town plan or orderly development.[69]

The nineteenth-century historian of Amherst, New Hampshire, distilled the experience of a host of northern New England communities in his simple, rather imprecise description of the progress of settlement in that town. The first few settlers lived in one vicinity in small houses of logs, but "afterwards took up lots in different parts of the town, leaving their first habitations. Other settlers, from Middleton, in Essex [County, Massachusetts], and the adjacent towns, arrived within a few years, and began settlement in different parts of the town." [70]

To the descendants of the Puritans, as well as those of the fishermen and woodsmen of the Maine and New Hampshire seacoast and the men of Ulster, the vast interior north of the Merrimack offered one fundamental commodity: land. To have a large tract to farm and live upon without restrictions was worth the inconvenience and the suffering that were involved in forsaking the old settled communities for the frontier, even in wartime. As long as proprietors and legislators remained scrupulously faithful to the community ideals of seventeenth-century Massachusetts, they maintained a barrier to the realization of the dream of full enjoyment of a family country estate. Under these conditions, most prospective settlers found the substantial cost and risk of going into the wilderness unacceptable. Upon a realistic appraisal of the situation, proprietors and legislators began, generally in the 1750's, to remove the barriers to spontaneous, as opposed to planned, development. With the barriers down, the embryo villages, most of them already cruelly deformed by stretching, died in birth. In their place, a more healthy infant—communities of dispersed, integrated family farms, located according to the suitability of the land and the desires of the individual settler rather than according to an imposed scheme—grew rapidly to maturity.

Survey of the township of Henniker, New Hampshire, conducted in 1752 and 1753. Notice the absence of any scheme for a village. The plan consists exclusively of large farm lots. One of the surveyors was Matthew Patten, the Bedford diarist.

3

The log hut vanished from the northern frontier with the remnants of the original settlers' hamlets. The inland country towns came of age when the proprietors opened to immediate and permanent settlement the broad farmlands of what had first been designed as the "after divisions." On their new homesteads, the settlers tended to build for permanence, for reasonable comfort, and, whenever possible, for a measure of rural dignity.

Many of the earliest framed houses in the new country towns were little more pretentious than the one- or two-room hovels that the first settlers constructed of hewn logs. Of the twenty-nine occupied houses listed in the New Marblehead report of 1759, five were garrison houses and only two were described as "duble" houses. In the eighteenth century, a "double" house meant a structure with rooms on each side of a central entrance hall. The term could apply to a one-story or story-and-a-half house with two, three, or four rooms as well as to a dwelling of two stories.[71] Very likely, therefore, the great majority of framed houses in the settlement were story-and-a-half buildings with pitched roofs measuring little more than the eighteen feet on each side demanded by the legislature and consisting of one or two rooms, a sleeping loft, and a chimney and fireplace at one end. Such a house could be doubled in size when the need and opportunity arose by raising a section identical to the original one on the other side of the chimney. Equally likely, most of the settlers of Londonderry began to build their framed houses in the early 1720's along the same modest lines, although we are told that a few of the more ambitious farmer-craftsmen built two-story houses similar to Mr. MacGregor's parsonage in the early years.[72]

When Matthew Patten became one of the first settlers of Londonderry's neighboring township of Bedford in 1738, he built a story-and-a-half house similar in style to that of the common end-chimney cottage. It was of a more advanced design, however, in that its more ample dimensions and massive central chimney made possible an arrangement on the ground floor either of four rooms or of a great kitchen on one side of the center hall and staircase and two rooms on the other. The front door, over which Patten placed a single row of windowpanes, was exactly centered in one side of the building, and a group of two windows was centered on each side of the door. The gables of the Patten house, which faced the ends of the building, were symmetrical, unlike some earlier versions of this popular New England style. This treatment allowed more space for sleeping rooms on the second floor.[73]

Houses like Patten's, generally consisting of five or six rooms and finished with unpainted clapboards, probably became the most numerous type of northern New England farmhouse during the fifteen or twenty years before the Revolution. If such a structure seems to the modern reader inadequate to house the large families for which country couples of the period have become famous, he needs only to be reminded that in neither the seventeenth nor the eighteenth century did a New England boy count it a hardship to be packed away in the same bed with one or two of his brothers, nor was it uncommon to find more than one bedstead in a single small bedchamber. The "truckle" or trundle bed for smaller children, which slid under the high bedstead of the parents during the day, was in frequent use, and servants or even the parents of the family often slept in a folding bed, which could be raised on hinges and hidden neatly behind closet doors or a curtain on the kitchen wall. The parents more usually slept in the parlor, one of the two principal main-floor rooms, in the "best bed," proudly displayed in the crowded ceremonial room among the family's other choicest possessions.[74]

One also ought to take into some account a recent demographic study of Bristol, Rhode Island, in 1689, which was then, like all the interior towns of Maine and New Hampshire a half-century later, a new community made up predominantly of relatively young families. The study suggests that the legendary size of the average colonial New England family, at least in communities where most of the women had not lived out their childbearing years, needs some qualification.*

* John Demos: "Families in Colonial Bristol, Rhode Island: An Exercise in Historical Demography," *William and Mary Quarterly,* 3rd Ser., XXV (January 1968), 40–57. Demos estimates the mean age of married women in Bristol in 1689 at 33.6 years; the mean number of children per family was 3.27. He comments as follows: "Families . . . grew slowly. This meant that at any given time only those parents in a certain limited age-range, about thirty-five to fifty, would be likely to show really large numbers of children. [The largest number in Demos's sample is fifteen.] Younger couples would not yet have produced their full complement of children, whereas in the case of elderly parents some or all of the children would have reached maturity and started their own independent lives"; pp. 45–6. The present study makes no attempt at demographic analysis of the interior communities of northern New England, either in their frontier or rural agricultural stages. But the nature of the experience of moving from an established community, combined with what we do know about certain individual cases, informs us more eloquently than statistics that this was a movement of relatively young people, and that the age composition of these communities as a whole between 1740 and 1760 was therefore probably roughly similar to Demos's sample

Some of the settlers, however, began their permanent farmsteads on a grander scale. Two-and-a-half story pitched- or gambrel-roofed houses appeared throughout the countryside, especially after 1760, and soon far outnumbered the seventeenth-century "saltbox" style in which Mr. MacGregor's Londonderry parishioners built his parsonage in the 1720's. In Penacook, which later became Concord, New Hampshire, the Reverend Timothy Walker, the leading citizen as well as the minister of the settlement, erected a handsome clapboarded dwelling house that could have taken its place gracefully among the upperclass dwellings of Portsmouth in the period. Walker built the shell of his house with its gambrel roof and its doric pediments over the centered door and lower-story windows of the broad façade, between 1733 and 1735. He waited until the settlement of the controversy between the proprietors who held their claim from Massachusetts, of which he was a member, and the Bow proprietors of New Hampshire before finishing the interior. Entries in his diary for 1764, two years after the long dispute finally ended, record the installation of a stone chimney, two hearths, and a door stone at the same time that he plastered several rooms and laid a floor of pitch pine boards in his "best room." [75] The same year, Walker's son-in-law, Colonel Benjamin Rolfe, built a house of similar proportions and style, except that it had a pitched roof instead of a gambrel roof.[76]

The settlers of the interior brought with them from Massachusetts that pride in workmanship and emphasis on substantial construction which, when applied to the meetinghouse, was the Congregationalist substitute for liturgy and ecclesiastical art. The inhabitants of Upper Ashuelot (Keene, New Hampshire) proudly reported to the Boston press on June 22, 1737, that "thro' the Divine Goodness of God, [we] have this Day raised a Meeting House, forty Feet long and thirty five Feet wide, and twenty Feet Stud, in the space of five Hours and an half, and not one Man received any hurt; and cheerfully supped on a fat Moose, which was kill'd in Town the Day before." [77] Progress toward closing in the building apparently proceeded more slowly than the enthusiastic report of raising the frame might have promised, but the organization of a church in October, 1738, spurred along the com-

---

of Bristol, which in 1689 consisted of seventy families and had existed as a settled community of the Plymouth Colony for between eight and ten years. If my surmises are correct, the average family during the formative stages of the country towns would have put little strain on the accommodations offered by a farmhouse of five or six rooms. As families and estates grew, wings or "els" of various kinds could be added to an end or, most commonly, at the rear of such a house.

pletion of the building. On December 4, 1738, the proprietors voted "to finish the meeting house, on the outside, workman-like, viz. to cover it with good sawed clapboards, well planed, good window frames well glazed, and handsomely to case the doors; and so far to finish the inside as to lay the lower floor and build the body of the seats, the pulpit, one pew, the table and deacon's seat, all completely workmanlike." [78] Almost four years passed, and the meetinghouse still had no glass windows and no clapboards. The proprietors now voted, in July, 1742, to set the glass in wood rather than lead, and to cover the building with shingles rather than sawed clapboards, "1, because we judge it stronger; and 2, because we can do it at less expense of money." But instead of the "plain" doors originally planned, they voted to install paneled doors, including a "double folding door" at the main entrance, "and that the committee agree with a man to do it well, and decently, as becomes such a house." Not until January, 1744, five and a half years after the raising, did the proprietors pronounce the building finished.[79] They undoubtedly enjoyed the satisfaction, however, of owning a meetinghouse that they considered "decent" and "workmanlike."

The owner of a frame house in the country usually supervised every step of the construction and often did most of the building himself. Captain Phineas Stevens, who commanded the military garrison at Township Number 4 on the Connecticut River, the most advanced northern outpost during King George's War, returned in 1752 from a diplomatic errand to Canada to build a house and settle down in the frontier community that he had defended. It was slightly more than a month, that crisp autumn, between the day Stevens cut the first timber for his house and the raising of the frame.

During the week of September 18, the energetic captain felled trees for timbers and boards, and on September 25, he "Sawed timber clapboards." [80] When Captain John Spafford, under contract with the proprietors, finished the sawmill and turned out the first sawed boards in the settlement in 1744, the significance of the event so elated the nine or ten families of Number 4, whose only homes were log huts, that they spread out the new boards for a dance floor and held a party. Unfortunately for them, they were forced to move almost immediately from their rude dwellings, not into proper framed houses, but into still cruder cabins hastily erected inside a large stockaded fort. Indians burned the gristmill and sawmill during the war, but Captain Spafford rebuilt them and had them in operation again in 1752.[81] A waterpowered vertical saw was available, therefore, to Captain Stevens and the handful of other settlers who began that year to build permanent houses near the east bank of the Connecticut.

On September 28 and 29, he built a road at one end of his house lot, but on October 4 was back at felling trees. Hewing timbers for the frame began the next day. As that work progressed, Stevens hired a crew of "schoars" (scorers), whose job was to limb out the fallen trees, peel off the bark, and roughly flatten the sides.[82] The captain himself apparently did most of the final shaping with the carpenter's broad axe. On Saturday, October 28, while most of the settlement was still busy harvesting corn, Stevens finished hewing his timbers and paid off the last of his crew. It took most of the following week to make the dozens of trips required to drag his timbers by ox team the short distance to his house site. Then on November 7, two friends from outside the settlement arrived to help with the framing. The three men spent four days fitting the heavy timbers together to make sections of the lower part of the house frame, which they began to raise into place on November 11, before they had finished building the frame of the upper story. They worked on the frame on November 13 and 14, and spent the 15th and 16th completing the raising. Two other house frames in the settlement were raised at the same time.[83]

An energetic, capable property owner, therefore, could have the frame of a substantial house standing within a few weeks after he had cut down his first tree. To finish the building completely might take years, as in the case of Mr. Walker's house at Penacook and the Upper Ashuelot meetinghouse. Though most of the heaviest work was over with the raising of the frame, many time-consuming details remained. The frame of a New England house was ordinarily filled with some material such as the "wattle-and-daub" of Elizabethan England, clay, or sun-dried bricks. Uncovered, this combination of heavy wooden frame and clay or masonry filling would have resulted in the characteristically English "half-timbered" construction, which was tried in some parts of the colonies in the seventeenth century. In the wind and rain of New England, however, builders soon found it more than worthwhile to take advantage of the unlimited supply of wood and cover the timbers and filling with shingles or clapboards. Sometimes the filling was omitted. The inside walls were either plastered or covered with boards.[84] Before a family could live in a house, the builder had to put up the massive chimney of stone or fired brick, cover the roof with planking and shingles, board the floors, glaze the windows, hang doors, complete the interior partitions by plastering or wainscoting, and, in the better houses of the period, hire a craftsman to turn out the detailed woodworking that decorated the hall, the staircase, the parlor or drawing room and dining room, and the front doorway.

Physically, therefore, the fully matured eighteenth-century country town of northern New England was a paradox. In its arrangement of lands and buildings, it departed from the example and ideals of an earlier day. It sprawled erratically over a broad, uneven terrain, its farmers tending to favor hilltops for their widely separated homesteads and valleys or "intervales" for meadows and pastures. The arrangement sprang from a gradual adaptation to the opportunities, rather than the necessities, of the frontier by a people who no longer felt bound by Puritan community ideals and who had forgotten the agricultural and land traditions of the Old World. Architecturally, however, the country town, once relieved of the necessity of improvisation, was an imitative rather than an inventive community. As soon as circumstances permitted, it copied first the construction methods of an earlier day and then the tastes and fashions of contemporary Boston and Portsmouth.*

* A striking example of the transfer of a contemporary urban architectural style to the country is the "Ocean Born Mary House," built in Henniker, New Hampshire, about 1767 by Major Robert Wallace. The builder was the oldest son of Mrs. Thomas (Wilson) Wallace, who was born during the voyage from Ulster to Londonderry, New Hampshire, where her three sons spent their boyhood. All three had business connections at Strawberry Bank, and when Robert built his house in a rural setting at Henniker, where his aged mother spent her last days, he apparently deliberately copied the style of some of the better gentlemen's townhouses in Portsmouth. John M. Howells: *Architectural Heritage of the Merrimack* (New York, 1941), pp. 224–5.

CHAPTER XIV

Making Good,
and Three Who Did
1725–1763

1

When a community of inland settlers had cleared enough land to raise a surplus of crops, brought in dairy cattle, built permanent framed houses and barns, and no longer depended either upon lumbering or upon some external subsidy for their living, their pioneering stage had ended. Social and political maturity—the formation of a church, the evolution of certain community habits of visiting, entertainment, and mutual help, the emergence of recognized leaders, and the organization of a town government under charter from the province—ordinarily followed naturally and rapidly after economic maturity. During the period of roughly fifty years between the beginning of permanent settlement in the back parts of Maine and New Hampshire and the beginning of the War for Independence, frontier townships from the Connecticut to the Kennebec gradually became rural agricultural towns.

The transition came quickest in the lower Merrimack Valley and in the inland New Hampshire communities within a day's journey from Portsmouth, most of which were regranted by the Masonian proprietors and chartered by the New Hampshire government after the settlement of the province boundary in 1740. The process took longer in the Connecticut Valley and in Maine, where the settlements were affected more directly by the Indian wars of the 1740's and 1750's. After 1760, a new spurt of settlement into the upper Connecticut Valley, Vermont, northern New Hampshire, and the vast region east of the Kennebec created new frontiers, where new pioneers duplicated the laborious transition to agriculture that had begun in the southern part of the region forty years before. Throughout this period, therefore, somewhere in northern New England one could find every stage of development, from the most primitive hamlet of log huts to the most prosperous community of flourishing family farms.

In a mature country town, the fundamental basis of every man's subsistence and small wealth was the land he owned and upon which he lived. This does not mean that all the yeoman families in such communities farmed and did nothing else. Their homes were not simply a succession of idyllic pastoral settings uninterrupted by signs either of the primitive life of the forest or of an advanced form of industry. Like his counterpart in Massachusetts and Connecticut, the upcountry "farmer" was as much craftsman and tradesman as husbandman. To a greater extent than was true of the men of the older settlements to the south, he was also a hunter and a woodsman.

The importance of manufacturing in rural northern New England was surprisingly great. The first and most vital public improvement in every new township, next to roads, was a water-powered sawmill and gristmill. One was essential for permanent shelter, the other for bread. Beyond that, the ability of many a community to export sawed lumber determined its economic survival so that it could develop to the agricultural stage.

The importance of manufacturing did not stop there. The Scotch-Irish of the Merrimack Valley enriched the life of New England on several scores. Among the innovations they introduced to the region was the professionalization and commercialization of home industry. Spinning and weaving in primitive form had been common enough in yeoman homes throughout New England, but the people of Londonderry actually manufactured for export a product of high quality. Nearly every family had brought from Ireland the hand card, the small foot-powered flax wheel, and the loom with which its members had long produced fine Irish linens. When their lands had been cleared, the settlers devoted much of their acreage to flax. The linen thread and cloth manufactured in Londonderry farmhouses commanded high prices in Boston and other commercial centers, and very early became the principal basis of the town's prosperity. The women did the spinning, but in the earliest years, the men did most of the weaving. To avoid the fraudulent use of the name of Londonderry by linen manufacturers elsewhere, the citizens voted in 1748 to preserve "the credit of our manufactory" by appointing inspectors of local linens and hollands. For a small fee, the inspectors stamped each piece of cloth that passed their approval with a seal containing the name of the town.[1]

Lumbering, including the cutting of masts, spars, logs, and fire-wood, the sawing of boards and timbers, and the "riving" or "cleaving" of clapboards and shingles, was a major feature of the economy of all the northern country towns throughout the eighteenth century. These activities were not confined to professional woodsmen and sawyers, if, indeed, the economic organization of the interior towns was suf-ficiently defined to allow of such specialized trades. The evidence sug-gests, rather, that once an interior settlement had progressed beyond the pioneering stage, or beyond the stage of a lumbering camp such as that on the Saco River at Buxton, most men drew whatever profit they could from their land, their energy, and their talents. They divided their time in varying proportions among lumbering, farming, hunt-ing, trapping, and trading—depending upon the season, their assets, and their abilities.

In such a society, economic success depended less upon one's initial assets, which with the occasional exception of a monied proprietor who moved to the frontier were more-or-less equal in the first stages of most towns, than upon the shrewdness and energy with which one could manipulate his assets and his neighbors. Here, the New England "vir-tues" of frugality, sobriety, and piety were of some use in bettering one's station, but none of them, perhaps, served quite as well as plain Yankee horse-trading.

The manipulation of assets sometimes became downright dishonest rather than simply shrewd. When William Maxfield built his "double" house in New Marblehead with one of the Mayberrys in 1755, he placed it on the boundary between his own home lot and the adjoining one, which had been drawn as the school "right." The structure stood half on one lot and half on the other for years before the town was ready to claim its public property for the support of a schoolmaster. During this period, Maxfield claimed possession by squatter's privilege, not only of the original school lot, but also of the various hundred-acre lots in successive divisions that were drawn to accompany it. Not until 1774, when the town voted to appoint a committee to sue Maxfield off the public lands, did he abandon this plainly illegal claim.[2] Such flagrant behavior in one's private interest was, no doubt, exceptional, but the Maxfield case illustrates both the spirit of opportunism that characterized the frontier settlers and the prevailing laxity of the com-munity in its attitude toward public property.

The settlers of the new country towns added new acreage each year to their small domains of cleared farmland. We have to remind ourselves constantly that the northern New England countryside in the eighteenth century, save for occasional natural meadows, was heavily forested. Farms consisted of tiny pockets of cleared land in the wilderness, threaded together by narrow woods roads. When the Reverend Paul Coffin of Buxton visited the infant settlements of Fryeburg and Brownfield, Maine, in 1768, he was impressed with their location, their people, their houses and large farms, and their prospects for the future, but wrote of one part of Brownfield, "as almost every settler is by himself, we found no large view of cleared interval." [3] Gradually, the clearings grew larger, from eight or ten acres at first to several hundred, and the townships began to "open up" until, finally, one man's cleared meadow or cornfield bordered on his neighbor's.

There were several methods of clearing land. Some settlers copied the ancient Indian practice of girdling, usually in summer. At the same time that he cut the fatal circular incisions around the trunks of the trees, the settler sowed a mixture of English grass and winter rye. He harvested the hay the following summer, and turned the "field," now studded with barren tree trunks, into pastureland, leaving to wind and decay the eventual felling of the dead trees. We cannot know to what extent the settlers of inland Maine and New Hampshire relied upon this wasteful but perhaps frequently necessary method in the eighteenth century, but Belknap asserts that New Hampshiremen were by no means strangers to the practice.[4]

The great need of the settlers for logs, lumber, and firewood and the commercial value of masts and timber suggest that more land probably was cleared by felling trees than by girdling. "The more able sort of husbandmen," wrote Belknap, referring principally to the occupants of the extensive upcountry areas settled after 1760, ". . . choose the method of clearing the land at first, by cutting down all the trees without exception." When a farmer cleared his land by cutting, he usually did it in June and left much of the least valuable wood on the ground until the following spring, when he burned it to complete the clearing. Burning the waste wood, which after a year's time was dead and dry, left a coating of ashes to fertilize and loosen the soil and allowed the planting of Indian corn among the stumps.[5]

The average farmer devoted most of his acreage to English hay, which could be planted with only scant regard to roots, stumps, and boulders because he mowed it with a scythe. The same was true of his fields of grain, which he reaped with a sickle.[6] The sooner the stumps rotted, however, and the sooner he could move the boulders from his fields and garden to their proper place in a rough stone wall, the more easily he could tend to his corn and garden crops. These obstructions interfered with the use of the clumsy wood-and-iron plow, drawn by two or three yoke of oxen, with which the farmer and his son, one of them riding on the beam to make it cut deeper, broke up his land for planting, generally at the rate of an acre or two a day.[7] The farmer had only one other animal-drawn implement, the harrow, such as the one Matthew Patten made for a Bedford neighbor in October, 1760. This was simply a frame of heavy timbers, square if intended for use on thoroughly cleared land and triangular in shape if it was to be used among stumps or other obstacles. The square harrow was fitted with sixteen or twenty-five "tushes," or teeth; the triangular, or "bifurcate" harrow had fewer. The teeth were sometimes only long sharpened wooden pegs, but they did their job of pulverizing the soil or covering seeds more effectively if they were made of iron, and still more so if the iron teeth were steeled at the tips.[8]

The inland settlers of English stock, such as the majority of those who occupied New Marblehead, planted only the modest variety of vegetables and grains then common in the rest of New England: much Indian corn and some oats, rye, and barley but little or no wheat; root vegetables such as carrots, beets, and turnips; vine crops such as pumpkins, squashes, and melons; and peas, beans, and cabbages. In their household garden patches, most families also raised enough flax to supply themselves with cloth for sheets, pillowcases, tablecloths, napkins, linsey-woolsey blankets, bonnets and collars for dress-up occasions, light-weight jackets, and scratchy underwear.[9]

The Scotch-Irish settlers, besides introducing large-scale flax culture and linen manufacturing,[10] brought the potato to New England. Curiously, this staple of the modern North American diet, raised and consumed in huge quantities in the New England back country in the nineteenth and twentieth centuries, grew first in South America but made its way to New England by way of Europe and Ireland.[11] The potato, admirably suited to the thin, rocky soil of northern New England and easily planted among the stumps and roots of land that was only partially cleared, was practically unknown in the region before the settlement of Londonderry. One family in Andover planted some seed donated by one of the Londonderry settlers and tried, without success, to cook and eat the balls formed by the blossoms. Not until the family plowed the garden the following spring did it learn, quite by accident, the facts of potato culture.[12] By the time the farmers of New Marblehead had begun to grow extensive crops, they knew enough about potatoes at least to eat the right part of the plant. At no time before the War for Independence, however, did these men change their diet sufficiently to raise potatoes as a major crop. One New Marblehead settler found after harvesting five bushels of them one fall that he had seriously overproduced. His family of seven could eat only one bushel during the ensuing winter, and there was no market for the surplus.[13]

Potatoes provided not only food for men and animals, but also the makings of a whiskey which the Londonderry yeomen found, in the absence of the Irish counterpart, quite adequate. It was not long, however, before this locally distilled product was replaced in the Londonderry diet by New England rum, the regional beverage.[14]

The back country yeoman supplemented his rum supply, which had to be ferried or carted inland from a seaport, with an equally potent drink of his own manufacture. This, of course, was apple cider, a term which, before the temperance movement of the nineteenth century, applied only to the fermented product.* Cider-making was a major home industry on the farms of northern New England. During its first autumn of publication in 1756, *The New-Hampshire Gazette* featured as one of its most prominent articles a piece on brewing cider, from *Gentleman's Magazine*. The reader who had discovered the article and submitted it to the *Gazette* thought it important enough to be circulated throughout the province, "As many Persons are at this Season employ'd in making and storing of CYDER, and as improving that Liquor might be very serviceable, and tend to lessen the Consumption of Foreign Productions." [15]

Cider in its ideal state had a "high" reddish color, was clear and free from acid, oil, and "rope," and fizzed pleasantly but not explosively when the jug was uncorked. Perhaps it was because much New England cider was badly made that the Boston printing house of Green & Russell found it expedient in 1762 to republish a pamphlet by an English wine cooper entitled *The Cyder-Maker's Instructor*. According to this expert, most cider-makers supposed wrongly that their job had ended, except for bottling the fermented liquor, when they had filled a hogshead with fresh juice and left it exposed to the air to ferment naturally. The author instructed his readers to add yeast to the hogshead, stop the ferment by artificial means after fourteen or fifteen days, keep it bunged up in a cask for at least a year, "rack" it finally into bottles, and store them in sawdust to preserve the color. He included instructions for remedying acid, oil, rope, and "bad flavour," and

* And which, according to the *Oxford English Dictionary*, still should be.

for improving the color by the use of burned white sugar. "Many people," he cautioned, "spoil a great deal of good cyder by boiling and mixing molasses with it, to give it a colour; which not only gives it a bad red colour, but makes it muddy, as well as bad tasted." [16]

Possibly many northern New Englanders were guilty of the errors enumerated by the author of the *Instructor,* but we are led by occasional comments to believe that even the rudest of yeomen appreciated the few amenities his rigorous life afforded and respected all forms of craftsmanship, including the cider-maker's art. We may at least hope, therefore, that either with or without benefit of reprints of English magazine articles and instruction books, the northern farmer matched his great quantity of cider production (The Reverend Timothy Walker of Penacook made twenty-five barrels in the fall of 1764) with appropriate quality.[17]

The New Hampshire farmer had learned the ancient Indian art of tapping the sugar maple and making syrup and sugar from the sap or, as Matthew Patten called it, the "juce." [18] One big maple-studded farm in Brownfield, Maine, near the New Hampshire border, was called the "West-India Plantation" because of the quantity of sugar and "molasses" (maple syrup) produced from the trees, and the owner even talked jocularly of trying to distill rum from the syrup.[19] Apparently this experiment never materialized, but the maple did provide a fine homegrown supplement to West Indian molasses and a substitute for ground sugar, which country farmers rarely purchased.

Chief Justice Paul Dudley of Massachusetts, a fellow and frequent correspondent of the Royal Society of London, thus described the "sugaring" process to its members in 1720: The farmer chiseled a square cavity, or "box," large enough to hold about a pint of sap, into the side of a tree about a foot above the ground. The sap drained from the "box" through a small reed or channeled cedar stick into a bowl or small cask at the foot of the tree.[20] Belknap described the common tap in 1792 as a V-shaped gash, an inch and a half or two inches deep and six to eight inches long on each side. Such incisions killed the tree within two or three years, but in the early years this concerned no one because the trees in the upland sugar areas seemed inexhaustible. It must have been shortly before Belknap wrote his history that the operators of "sugar works" discovered that they could collect as much sap through a small round hole as by great incisions, and that such a hole could be stopped with a whittled wooden plug at the end of the season. This method preserved the life of the tree for many years.

Belknap described the collection vessels as wooden troughs, about a yard long.[21]

The tapping took place in February or March, after the sap had begun to run but while nighttime temperatures still dropped below freezing. The workmen poured the sap into a large pot or kettle, usually installed over a huge outdoor fireplace in the maple grove, and boiled it down to syrup. A second boiling yielded sugar which, if boiled sufficiently slowly and hung in bags to drain, emerged in granulated rather than the more usual candied form and could be used in the same way as ground loaf sugar from the West Indies.[22]

Not until a community had been established for a year or two did the settlers ordinarily keep livestock. Only in early 1723, four years after settlement, do we begin to find records of farm animals in Londonderry; Thomas Chute's mare may have been the only animal in Marblehead until almost 1740. The first three men who wintered in Upper Ashuelot (Keene, New Hampshire) in 1736–37 kept a few oxen in a snow covered meadow, where they almost starved.[23] During their brief pioneer period, the settlers depended for meat upon imports and upon what the more skillful of their number could kill in the surrounding forest. New Marblehead and Gorhamtown on the Presumpscot and Londonderry, Bedford, Derryfield, and the other settlements near Amoskeag Falls on the Merrimack were fortunately situated because both rivers teemed with salmon during the spring migration to the breeding grounds. In virtually all of the smaller streams, the settlers could catch trout. "It was a time of rejoicing in the little settlement," wrote one historian of New Marblehead, "when spring came and the salmon began to run." [24]

Before the settlements were very old, certainly by 1723 in Londonderry and by 1740 in New Marblehead, cows, oxen, sheep, pigs, and usually a horse or two had become part of every farmer's inventory. Livestock was apparently being introduced into Londonderry early in 1723 at a rate which actually alarmed the townsfolk, for they spent much of the town meeting that spring passing votes on the problem. They elected their first hog reeve, required the yoking of hogs during the growing season, directed the building of a town pound next to the meetinghouse, and set limits on the introduction of cattle. Each person was allowed to bring up to six cows into the town. If a resident already owned cattle, he could bring in up to ten additional cows but only if he also provided his own bull. Just as they were jealous of the good name of Londonderry linen, the citizens apparently determined to protect the quality of Londonderry cattle by refusing to entrust the future of the herd, as in some older towns, to a solitary town bull.[25]

By the time a frontier settlement had become a full-fledged country town, the principal occupation of nearly every householder was farming. An occasional miller, blacksmith, or storekeeper might depend largely upon his specialty, but such persons were rare. A good many yeomen, however, supplemented their general farming with a specialized trade or skill. Thus although most farmers could perhaps do crude ironworking and shoe their own horses and oxen in an emergency, it was more satisfactory to take the work to the man on the neighboring farm who had a good forge and long experience in smithing. Another neighbor might find himself called upon with increasing frequency to do wood-turning or chair-caning, and another cobbling. Some of the settlers, such as Thomas Chute and William Mayberry, the tailor and the blacksmith of New Marblehead, came to their new homes already equipped with a trade. Samuel Lane, the fourth in a line of tanners and shoemakers that had begun with his great-grandfather in Boston, moved in 1741 from his native Hampton to the new town of Stratham, New Hampshire, after learning the tanner's trade from his father. There, after building his house, he dug tan pits, built a shop and bark house, and eventually added a bark mill and a barn to his establishment. Although he lived principally on his tanning and leather-working, Lane also owned considerable livestock, surveyed new township and property lines, invested in frontier lands, and, in 1763, "made 53 Barrels of Syder." [26]

The versatility of the Yankee farmer, north or south of the Merrimack, has probably been overrated by his admirers and descendants. It is true enough, as the awe-struck Robert R. Livingston of New York commented during his retirement from public life early in the nineteenth century, that the New England farmer could "mend his plough, erect his walls, thrash his corn, handle his axe, his hoe, his sithe, his saw, break a colt, or drive a team, with equal address." His varied accomplishments, however, were thrust upon him as a matter of necessity. There was little market for most farm produce, and the New England soil and climate was not suitable for raising a salable staple. If he could have devoted his whole farm to a cash crop such as tobacco, cultivated it with Negro slaves, and used the proceeds to buy goods and services, as the most truly versatile member of Livingston's generation did at Monticello, he surely would have done so. Versatility, meaning in this case the ability to subsist by doing most of the necessary jobs and producing most of the necessary goods for oneself, had much in common with the Puritan (but hardly Christian) virtues of frugality and worldly diligence. There was no choice.[27]

It remains true, however, that the broader a man's abilities, the greater the imagination and skill with which he cleared a field, practiced a trade, or struck a bargain, the more likely he was to gain more than ordinary dignity in a society which, despite its "frontier" origins, needed leaders and retained some devotion to a decent measure of useful social distinction. Thomas Chute, Matthew Patten, and the Goffes of Londonderry, Derryfield, and Bedford all illustrate the leading class of country yeomen.

2

The elder John Goffe, the son of a Boston cobbler, had won local fame as a woodsman and professional hunter before he joined the Scotch-Irish colony in Londonderry. Soon after Mr. MacGregor's band of Ulstermen reached Boston in 1718, the young hunter began to act as their land agent. It was partly his knowledge of the upper parts of the Merrimack Valley, called the "Chestnut Country," that led the settlers finally to Nutfield. From the beginning, John Goffe, despite his English Puritan descent, was active in town affairs. As business agent and frontier guide, he was welcomed into the propriety and elected proprietors' clerk. With the organization of the town government in 1722, he became the first town clerk. Because of his services to the new community, he received a special grant of one hundred acres and a mill stream in addition to the share that went to every proprietor.[28]

After moving his family to Londonderry, "Hunter John" saw to it that his son also became a proprietor in his own right. John Junior, a young man of twenty-one when the family moved in 1722, returned that fall to Roxbury to marry. He brought his bride back to Londonderry, where he started a farm of his own and began to take an active part in town affairs along with his father. In 1725 he commenced a long military career by joining John Lovewell's expedition from Dunstable against the Pequawkets in the upper Saco Valley. He was one of the few survivors of the fierce fight at what is now Lovell's Pond in Fryeburg, Maine, which led to the Treaty of Casco in 1726, ending "Dummer's War." Within a few years after his return, the young man began to serve in a succession of town offices: constable, surveyor of highways, member of the committee to run the town lines, and member of the committee to lay out the fourth division of land. The elder John, meanwhile, represented Londonderry in the New Hampshire General Assembly in 1729 and in 1734 became town moderator.[29]

During these years, young John and his two close friends and brothers-in-law, Edward Linkfield and Benjamin Kidder, acquired land just outside the northwestern corner of the town boundary, where Cohas Brook enters the Merrimack. There, in 1734, the three men began to develop a family seat. In the first year, John cleared four acres of land, planted crops among the stumps, and built a house on the north side of the brook near a waterfall. His brothers-in-law helped him build a sawmill and gristmill at the falls and a bridge over the brook.

Aside from its importance to the little settlement that soon grew up at Cohas, this bridge served the settlers who now moved in a slowly but steadily increasing stream up the Merrimack Valley to points further inland. Though the only inhabited settlements among upstream townships in the 1730's were Rumford and Canterbury, the northern interior, particularly along the Merrimack, was beginning to attract settlers. Lovewell had removed the greatest obstacle to the expansion of northern New England by his campaign of 1725, which had initiated a period of peace that lasted nearly two decades. John Goffe recognized the importance of the pioneers' route up the Merrimack and established his enterprises where he could take advantage of the passing traffic.

Besides farming, lumbering, milling, and maintaining a bridge over Cohas Brook, Goffe ferried travelers across the Merrimack by boat and canoe, and as his father had done before him, spent as much time as he could afford roaming the forest for miles around in search of venison.[30] In the course of his wanderings, Goffe kept an eye out for promising land for development and settlement, and especially for potential sources of water power.

The land that young John thought the most promising was not far away. In 1737, two of his neighbors at Cohas, Robert and James Walker, moved across the Merrimack into one of the Narragansett townships, Narragansett Number 5 or Souhegan East (later Bedford). The following year, Matthew Patten and his brother Samuel, also acquaintances of Goffe, cleared a field near the river in the same township and built a garrison house. At about this time, John invited his father, who had long since exchanged his sobriquet of "Hunter John" for the dignified title of "Squire," to live at his farm at Cohas Brook and the younger man moved to the west side of the river. Though the son was not an original grantee of Narragansett 5, his growing affluence and business instincts had enabled him to buy up the rights of four of the proprietors. By 1738, therefore, he was the largest landowner in the township and was still adding to his holdings. Near the west bank of the Merrimack, where the waters of Bowman's Brook tumbled toward the river, Goffe developed a second farm, erected a house, dammed the brook, and built a gristmill.[31]

When war came again in 1744, John marched at the head of a company of militia doing scouting duty in defense of the northern frontier. He returned in 1748 to find his father, who had for ten years managed his Cohas property happily and profitably, nearing the end of an active life. In the summer of that year, the Squire, recording his residence as "a place called Chohass in No Town but in the province of Newhampshire," drew up a will. He left some of his Londonderry lands to two of his grandsons, forty shillings each to his three grand-daughters, a cow and a note for £54 to his daughter May, and "to my wellbeloved Son John Goffe my Mare being a gray Mare whome I likewise constitute make and ordain my Sole Executor of this my Last Will and Testament." The rest of the estate was to be divided be-tween John and the two sons of Mary. The old man, content both in his ignorance of grammatical niceties and in his assurance that he had provided the basis for a distinguished and prosperous line of New Hampshire Goffes, died on August 9.[32]

His son then moved back to his former holdings at Cohas, leaving his own son, John, in charge of his interests in Bedford.[33] In so doing, he plunged into the affairs of another town government, for the settlers at Cohas Brook and some of the surrounding points were now seeking incorporation as a town. Under John Goffe's leadership, the town was chartered in 1751 as Derryfield.[34] Before new wartime duties inter-fered with his ever-expanding business and political life, Goffe became the principal grantee of yet another township on the Merrimack. In 1748, the Masonian proprietors granted shares in the new township to forty-six persons besides themselves, many of them from Bedford, and when the province incorporated the town in 1761, the governor and council recognized Goffe's position of leadership by naming it Goffs-town.[35]

Military affairs took up much of Goffe's attention between 1755 and 1761. He led a company of Bedford, Derryfield, and Londonderry men in the Lake George expedition of 1755, rose steadily in rank and responsibility, and headed the New Hampshire regiment that cut a road from Number 4 (Charlestown) on the Connecticut River to Crown Point in 1760. On their arrival at Crown Point, some of Goffe's men were put to work on fortifications and others were assigned to

Rogers's Rangers during the final hostilities around Lake Champlain and the conquest of Montreal.[36] Although Colonel Goffe saw little action against the enemy during the French and Indian War, his services were important, he achieved a high reputation for leadership, he attracted the attention of Governor Benning Wentworth, and he emerged from the war as the highest-ranking military officer in the province.[37]

During respites from his various campaigns, usually during the winter, Colonel Goffe looked after his business and political affairs and recruited troops for successive expeditions. After the war, he retained command of one of the ten militia regiments in the province, but became increasingly absorbed in civilian pursuits.

In 1762, at the age of sixty-one, he was elected to the provincial legislature as the representative of Bedford and Amherst, though his official residence was in Derryfield, which was too small to be entitled to a representative. From then until 1777, he missed serving only one year as provincial legislator and state representative.[38] Besides having obvious abilities, he knew well how to handle the voters. On May 16, 1771, Matthew Patten "with Divers of this towns people went to Amherst and . . . in conjunction with them chose Col: Goffe for our Representative. . . . Col: Goffe treated bountyfuly." [39]

If Colonel Goffe was not quite typical of the first rank of upcountry yeomen, it was only because his father and he had been more skillful, more forceful, and more fortunate than most. In origin, in essential attitudes and abilities, and in activities—hunting, fishing, woodsmanship, farming, milling, soldiering, trading in lands, and persistent involvement in the affairs of town and church—the Goffes are almost archetypes of the leading citizens of the northern New England country towns.

Their wealth, which was modest enough by urban standards, their political attainments, their titles of "Esquire" and "Colonel," and even the final accolade of having a town named after them were the kinds of distinction to which any number of their contemporaries could reasonably aspire. Few of them equaled the Goffes in possessions, dignity, achievement, or, for that matter, longevity.* It was a rare community

---

* Colonel Goffe lived to age eighty. His son, Major John Goffe, had ten children, one of whom drowned as a young woman, one of whom was killed in the War for Independence, and one of whom disappeared during the war. Of the remaining seven, five lived past eighty (one to ninety-three), and a sixth to seventy-nine. *History of Bedford* . . . comp. Peter P. Woodbury, Thomas Savage, and William Patten (Boston, 1851), pp. 306–7.

in eighteenth-century New Hampshire or Maine, however, that could not count among its inhabitants at least one or two conspicuous men who had realized abundantly the considerable economic, social, and political possibilities that were present in the life of the upcountry yeomanry.

Such a man was Colonel Goffe's friend and sometime neighbor, Matthew Patten of Bedford. Patten's was a world of grain, flax, and haycocks; of oxen, sheep, and cows; of home remedies and homemade coffins; of summonses, town records, minute personal accounts, and Presbyterian sermons. The bounds of this world stretched surprisingly far from his farmhouse on a cleared hilltop a mile and a quarter west of the Merrimack. His personal and public affairs took him throughout the towns of Bedford, Goffstown, Londonderry, Derryfield, New Boston, and Litchfield, occasionally downriver to Dunstable, Haverhill, or Newbury, not infrequently to the seat of provincial government at Portsmouth, and now and then on a marketing trip to Boston.

Money was scarce in eighteenth-century New Hampshire, and the farmers and tradesmen of Bedford, as everywhere, carried on their business with one another largely by barter. Patten always accounted for these transactions, however, in money—a matter that was complicated immensely by the fact that several kinds of currency circulated as legal tender. There were "lawful money" or British currency, Spanish dollars and pistareens, Portuguese Johannas and moidores, and a variety of provincial paper issues. These issues, whether New Hampshire "Old Tenor" of 1709, New Hampshire "New Tenor" of 1741, Massachusetts Old or New Tenor, or paper from other colonies, had all depreciated, some more than others. Matthew Patten kept exact accounts of all his transactions, which, because of the bartering system and scarcity of a circulating medium, usually were left with some balance still due one of the parties.

One Saturday in May, 1761, the prevailing monetary system complicated Patten's affairs more than usual, though he did little more that day than buy some fish, pay back a loan, and collect his fee as appraiser of an estate. "I went to Namaskeig," the diary entry states, "and got 3 shad 2 Thomas Karr gave me and 1 I bot of Zekiel Stevens and gave him 4s/ for it and Mrs. Hall sent my wife a peice of Salmon and I paid Capt. John Stark one johanna [about five Spanish dollars] one Crown Sterling and one shilling and one six pence Sterling with one Dollar was due to me out off his fathers estate and 1½ Dollar was due me on account of prising his fathers Estate amounted to 12

Dollars lacking 6 copers being the intrest due lacking 6 copers for one year of what money I borrowed from him January 8, 1760." [40]

As usual, Patten spent the Sabbath in meeting, but on Monday he was back again at his complex transactions: "I went to Mr. Lutweikeys and got a pair of wool Kards coast ½ a Dollar and ½ £ of Tea and paid a Dollar and I owe 6 Copers of the Tea I borrowed the Dollar from my brother Samuell and Abagail Chamberlain came home along with me to spin at our house and I paid George Pearson 4-6-0 and a pair of pumps he had of me a 7-10-0 paid him for the fortnight he workt with me this Spring all but 4s/ old Tenor." Perhaps it was because he felt the need to withdraw briefly to simpler things that on Tuesday, he simply borrowed his brother Samuel's "oldest oxen" and spent the day carting dung. [41]

Patten raised corn, wheat, rye, barley, flax, beans, potatoes, pumpkins, cabbages, "pease," cattle, swine, and sheep. Farming was only the beginning of his varied economic life. In 1754 and 1755, Patten seems to have carried on an active business as a broker in furs. Although he was a successful deer hunter, he spent more time having his steel traps repaired, lending or selling traps to others, and buying pelts from his neighbors than setting his own traps to catch fur-bearing animals. The sable he "catched" on November 30, 1754, seems to have been his last of the season, but between then and the following April 15, he bought or traded for the skins of twenty-nine sables, or pine martens, five raccoons, twelve foxes, three "musquash" (musk-rats), six mink, a "black cat" (probably the valuable fisher, a larger relative of the marten), and a wildcat. On April 15, Patten set out on a southern trading mission with his store of pelts. He sold most of them in Newbury on the 16th for "71 £ in dollars," went to Boston the next day with six raccoon skins, which he sold for seven pounds ten shillings, and arrived home in the evening of April 22. [42]

Perhaps still flushed with his financial successes of the preceding days, Patten bought another sable skin the morning after his return, but his fur purchases fell off markedly thereafter. He made another brief attempt at doing his own trapping in the spring of 1756, but succeeded only in catching the severed feet of two unfortunate beavers. [43] The next time he drove his horse and cart to Boston, in February, 1756, his principal cargo was tub butter, produced not only on his own, but also on surrounding farms. On his return trip, he brought back 152 pounds of beef, for which he had paid a shilling and two pence per pound. [44]

Toward the end of May each year, Patten and what must have been

most of the male community on both sides of the Merrimack repaired
to Amoskeag Falls to set up their seines for the annual catch of salmon
and shad. This was serious business, as strictly accountable as all the
other dealings among neighbors. Most Bedford, Londonderry, and
Derryfield men fished in companies, or partnerships. Each group
claimed a fishing place from which its members hauled their collec-
tively owned seine, and the partners divided the season's catch. Smaller
fish, principally alewives, were taken with scoop nets during their
annual run to the breeding grounds upriver, and eels were caught in
"pots" of wicker-work, generally set in the falls. The seines, which
were stretched across the current and hauled in from rocks on the
side, frequently trapped hundreds of fish, and were regulated by
province law so as to leave a clear passage at one point in the channel.
In 1762, one group of seine owners took 2,500 shad at a single haul
of their net, and at about the same time, another group trapped 1,500
shad at once.[45]

That year, Patten joined "a Company that had Made a place to set
fish on above the Pulpitt," and worked with the other members to chisel
out a fishing place in the ledge with drill, gunpowder, and stone hammer.[46] By July, the partnership was operating actively and profitably.
On the two days surrounding the Sabbath meetings of July 18, Patten
spent most of his time at the fishery, but on both days he combined his
fishing with at least one vital concern of husbandry. On Saturday, the
17th, wrote Patten, "Pattersons and I got 4 salmon at their brook 2 by
setting and 2 at Cold brook by drawing they weighed 66 £ I got 21 £
and our Cherry cow took Bull." Patten heard two sermons the following day, and on Monday, repeated the fruitful procedures of Saturday.
This time, the catch amounted to eleven salmon weighing a total of
134 pounds; the bull, refreshed by his Sabbath rest, serviced Patten's
black cow.[47]

Although fishing demanded the same serious attention that Patten
devoted to the rest of his affairs, the crowded scene along the rocky
shores of the falls during the glistening days of early June must have
aroused festive emotions. Indeed, the Merrimack Valley community
was fortunate in its fishery not only because it provided food, but because it gave as well an annual release from contact with the perpetual
dirt and dung of an ordinary inland farmer's existence. That Patten
found pleasure in his labors at the falls is apparent from one of the
very few entries in his journal that contain any hint of purely recrea-
tional activity. On June 12, 1758, soon after the fishing season had
begun, he "went a frolicking to Namaskeag with my wife." Patten gives

no indication of the nature of this frivolous interlude, but "Namaskeag" was where Patten had taken 120 shad in two days of fishing for business on July 9 and 10.[48] The next such romantic respite was in October, 1760, when "my wife and I went a Chesnuting but made a poor hand of it." [49]

Patten did a great deal of woodworking such as making window sashes, gunstocks, oars, and an occasional coffin for his neighbors, always in return for suitable compensation in goods, services, or currency. He spent an entire July day in 1762 in "Guming wheting and Setting Bushnells old cross Cutt saw." [50] He went to James Kennedy or James Houston for most of his blacksmith work; and Archibald MacCollum and James MacMurphy, working either separately or as a partnership, sometimes came to the Patten house to make shoes from Patten's own leather. His brother Samuel frequently came to the house to repair shoes. Matthew's relations with his brother, to whom he normally referred in his journal as "Samuel Patten," were conducted on the same basis of strict accounting as those with everyone else. Country clothing was mostly homespun and homewoven, but the Pattens frequently hired girls and young women of the neighborhood to come to the house to help spin flax and wool, and Patten sometimes took a supply of woolen yarn to another house to have it woven. Matthew's best clothes were tailor-made. These were expensive, but he had few of them and they lasted a long time. On March 18, 1758, Patten paid a "Mr. Harris" £10 to "turn" his "great and Straight Body Coat," a process which undoubtedly nearly doubled the life of the garment. In July, 1760, he went to Londonderry to pick up from James Milltimbers "a full coat a Jacoat and 2 pair Britches," all of which cost £38 old tenor.[51]

In one sense, perhaps, the "frontier," which in the Merrimack Valley quickly became rural countryside, fostered a kind of individualism and self-reliance. Here, however, it was the individualism of the entrepreneur rather than the isolation and utter self-reliance of the wilderness pioneer. The yeomanry of Bedford, in fact, were an extremely cooperative lot. One neighbor or another was constantly helping Matthew Patten mow his hay, reap his rye, "thrash" his grain, swingle his flax, or slaughter a sheep, hog, or ox. Fieldwork was not entirely restricted to men in this part of the country, but women, though strong and competent, ordinarily violated the customary division of farm labor only when it was necessary to "help out" in an emergency. After Thomas Mathis had spent six days reaping rye for Patten in August, 1764, and had been interrupted early on the seventh day by rain, Mathis's wife came with him the following day to help finish the job.[52] Patten occasionally took his turn on other farms, but because he was better able than most of his neighbors to pay for such services in money, and because he possessed other merchantable skills such as woodworking, surveying, and writing, he was more apt to hire help for his own farming chores than to work in this way for other men.

The prevailing attitude toward lending and borrowing seems not to have been as strict as that toward the exchange of goods and services. Patten continually borrowed and lent oxen and horses for plowing, hauling logs, and other such work, and seldom noted that any compensation had been made. Though he sometimes borrowed the services of a neighbor's bull or stallion, he never recorded the payment of stud fees. He occasionally borrowed a small quantity of sugar, and often borrowed rum and returned a like quantity, or part of it, a day or two later. When he borrowed rum, it was usually for the sustenance of a crew of men who were helping him with the reaping or haying or to celebrate such occasions as the birth of the annual baby.

Like the Goffes, Patten bought, sold, and traded lands in Bedford and elsewhere. Many of his neighbors, apparently, did likewise until, by the middle or late 1750's, the original allocation of lands had been changed beyond recognition. The readiness of the northern New England yeoman of means to invest in lands is explained in part by Samuel Lane of Stratham, who noted in 1748 that the rise in the price of all goods and the depreciation of currency "makes me Desirous of Laying my Money out in Land." [53]

As one of the first and most successful settlers of Bedford and perhaps one of the most literate,* Patten naturally was chosen frequently for public office. He was town clerk from 1752 to 1772, and a selectman in 1765 and from 1767 to 1772.[54] From 1751 until his death in 1795, he was a justice of the peace, and after Independence, served two terms as a state representative and one on the governor's council.[55] He was active in the Presbyterian church at Bedford from

---

* His neighbors frequently called upon Patten to write letters and draw wills, deeds, and sales agreements, and he owned at least a rudimentary library. On June 22, 1766, Patten noted in his diary that Jonathan Edwards's essay *Freedom of the Will* had been taken from his bookcase without his knowledge and replaced by John Edwards's *Some New Discoveries of the Uncertainty, Deficiency and Corruption of Human Knowledge and Learning.* (*The Diary of Matthew Patten of Bedford, N.H.* [Concord, N.H., 1903], p. 171.) Two years earlier, Patten had borrowed a copy of what he (or the transcriber of his diary) called "the independent Quig." (P. 134.)

its organization in 1757, and served several times as an elder. His affairs were complicated, however, by a bitter and protracted feud with the minister, the Reverend John Houston, whom the church finally dismissed as a Tory in 1775. Despite the animosity between Patten and his pastor, Patten rarely missed a sermon or a "sacrament," and once devoted an unusually long entry in his diary to an implied criticism of Mr. Houston for failing to preach on a day of thanksgiving proclaimed by the province after the peace of 1763.[56]

Patten's duties as justice of the peace, mainly issuing writs and adjudicating minor disputes, provided some income. For performing a marriage in 1763, the second of his career, he received £6 in depreciated Old Tenor currency.[57] Such marriages were unusual in Scotch-Irish communities, where the ceremony usually was performed by the minister during a day of general celebration.

Like Matthew Patten of Bedford, Thomas Chute, the pioneer settler of New Marblehead, enjoyed the status of an acknowledged community leader from the beginning. His local civic eminence, like that of Patten and the Goffes, sprang directly from his arrangement of his economic affairs, which not only were profitable but constantly touched the lives of everybody in the township.

Some of Chute's first public duties were necessarily military. During the 1740's, he headed the New Marblehead "division" of the Falmouth militia company. Later, after the unpleasant interlude of Captain Hills's regime, Chute received a captain's commission and command of his own company, which performed scouting duty during the 1750's. On September 21, 1750, it fell to Captain Chute, as the chief military man in town, to report the capture of young Seth Webb and request aid from the provincial authorities during the ensuing sporadic struggle with nearby Indians.[58]

The church as well as the militia claimed Chute's talents from the time a church was gathered in New Marblehead under the Reverend John Wight in December, 1743. Chute was one of the seven original male members. The prospective members determined before formally organizing that each of them should contribute an amount toward the purchase of the elements of the Communion, and that one member should care for the money and prepare the Sacrament at the appointed times. Thomas Chute, who had been transferred from the Falmouth to the New Marblehead church because of "a paucity of members" at the latter settlement, was given that sacred duty. A few weeks later, he became the first deacon of the new church.[59]

Chute had a facility for adapting his abilities rapidly to his situation, and it was natural that the local militia company and church should entrust their most important affairs to a man of proven practicality and varied accomplishment. Even before leaving old Marblehead, Chute had supplemented his tailor's income in a number of ways. His accounts during those years contain many entries for the serving of writs, laying out of town roads, and other services. He had also sold a variety of commodities, the principal one being, of all things, lemons![60] During the one or two years Chute had spent at Falmouth Neck, he had found new customers for his coats, jackets, and "britches," and had discovered the profits to be made at home in dispensing food, drink, and hospitality to the public.[61] After he had attended to clearing a field and building a house in New Marblehead, Chute had expanded his enterprises still further. He set up a store in his rude dwelling, reestablished his tailoring business, and hired out himself, his son, his mare, and his oxen for various tasks in the woods or on neighboring farms.

About the time Chute moved to New Marblehead, he was doing some tailoring work for Moses Pearson—making a jacket for Pearson's "Indian boy" and a coat and a pair of leather breeches for Pearson's Negro.[62] Beginning at least as early as 1741, Chute began to operate a store in his home. Because many of his neighbors had not yet put their farms in condition to grow the varied produce that Chute could now furnish, they came to him for such necessities and luxuries as turnips, peas, potatoes, beets, squashes, strawberries, small amounts of butter, lamb, beef, and on at least one occasion, a pig for roasting. In addition, Chute sold a little rum and tobacco, crockery, household and farm utensils, and even wigs.[63]

Chute's business, like all the other normal affairs of the community, was interrupted to a large extent by the enforced garrison life of the township between 1745 and 1756. He did manage, however, to keep a garden throughout all or most of this period and sold meat and vegetables, did some tailoring, went four times in 1749 to the General Court to present petitions for the inhabitants, and worked on the roads and helped build two bridges for the proprietors.[64]

After the emergency, when the inhabitants of New Marblehead returned to their farms and in many cases built larger and more permanent houses, Chute became an active innkeeper at his new house. In the 1760's, Moses Pearson made frequent use of Chute's hospitality, perhaps during visits to neighboring Gorhamtown, of which Pearson was a leading proprietor. Chute's account with Pearson shows numerous entries for rum, flip, and "todey," and oats for his horse. He charged five shillings to keep the horse overnight, two shillings for a gill of rum, and six shillings for a mug of toddy. For some reason, the account mentions no charge for bed and board, although Pearson must have stayed at Chute's house on these occasions.[65]

At the same time Chute expanded his affairs to include the tavern business, he added to his store of merchandise. Beginning in the late 1750's, he sold great quantities of hay, presumably harvested on his own extensive meadows. Most of it supplied the prodigious appetites of at least twenty oxen owned by Nathaniel Knight and his sons. The Knights operated the sawmill established about 1744 by Nathaniel's father at Little Falls, a mile and a half up the Presumpscot from the northern end of the original home lots.[66] For five summers in the 1760's, Chute pastured cows, oxen, and other livestock for "Joshuay" Crockett in return for work around the farm, and once sold Crockett a puppy. With a tanner, he bartered chickens, eggs, veal, and tan-bark.[67]

The Chute enterprises were very much a family affair. Mrs. Chute handled the sale of milk and kept the dairy accounts, conducted a dame school for local children before the town appointed a school-master in 1765, and transacted business for the inhabitants whenever she visited her old home in Massachusetts.[68] Chute's daughter Abigail spun and knitted for the townsfolk, and performed household chores when a neighbor's wife was sick or lying in.[69] In 1742, Thomas's son Curtis added £10 to the family treasury with his earnings for moving a family from Saccarappa to New Marblehead. The Chutes frequently performed this service and others, such as clearing land, for new settlers. The moving generally was done with the help of the family "mayre," and as Thomas and Curtis acquired a stable of oxen, apparently six, they put them to work hauling masts and hay. In 1744, both father and son hired themselves out to work on the province fort. As Curtis matured, he become more of a partner with his father and less a hired hand.[70]

Chute seems to have received more currency for his goods and services than Matthew Patten ever did, and inflation was not so marked in Massachusetts as in New Hampshire. Nevertheless, barter-ing figured significantly in Chute's dealings. Samuel Webb, the first schoolmaster, settled his account with Chute, which consisted prin-cipally of tailoring and cutting wood, primarily by teaching the chil-dren of Chute and his friends. It appears that Webb carried on a private tutoring service even before he was appointed the town school-master, perhaps teaching older children whom Mrs. Chute had prepared for advanced instruction. On one occasion, Webb spent half a day cutting logs for Chute in exchange for some service.[71] Caleb Grafton, who lived in one of New Marblehead's four garrison houses and cut mast trees, paid Chute, principally by woodworking, for the frequent use of his oxen, labor, and some tailoring. During 1749 and 1750, Grafton made him an ox yoke, a pair of fetters, and a bobsled, and once spent three days at his house making him a long "slead" (probably for hauling cordwood) and putting bottoms on five chairs. Grafton also "sold" to Chute, in exchange for services, a milk pail and two rakes, and let Chute use his own oxen.[72] Ephraim Winship, a cordwainer, made and repaired shoes for Chute, as he must have done for most of his other neighbors, in return for beef, vegetables, liquor, and Mrs. Chute's tuition services.[73]

Already hardened to the burdens of public office by his experiences with church and militia and his frequent role as official spokesman for the inhabitants before the proprietors and General Court, Thomas Chute acquired still more responsibilities with the organization of the town government of Windham in 1762. His neighbors, few of whom had not been involved in Chute's complex business affairs, chose him the first clerk of the new town. He served in that office for four years, and then was elected selectman for two terms.

Though it does not appear in the records, it is easy to suppose that it was by his own choice that Chute was not elected to further office when his second term as selectman expired in 1767. He was by now well over seventy, his wife had died the year the town was incorporated, much of his affairs were now in the hands of Curtis, and he probably was already contemplating his resignation as a deacon of the church. The church gave its approval for this last step in 1770, the year before his death.

3

The settlers of the northern New England interior defined success in economic terms. In so doing, they departed from the theory, though not really the practice, of the Massachusetts society from which the majority of them had come. It was the most prosperous, not necessarily the most righteous or the most holy, who were likely to find themselves town selectmen, deacons of the church, and representatives in the colonial assemblies. There is little evidence in this region of any conscious rationalizing of this situation, of any attempt to relate mundane achievement to divine favor. Though some version of an unarticulated ethic undoubtedly lurked below the consciousness of the hard-working farmers who looked to the most successful salesmen, bargainers, and speculators for leadership in matters political and ecclesiastical, it did not seem necessary to them to construct a theological basis for their choices.

The northern New England yeoman was only a step removed from the frontier, where his principal concern had been survival. Survival, unless infused to an extraordinary degree with the sense of divine mission and divine presence that men of another age had brought to Plymouth and Massachusetts Bay, is an economic matter, not a theological one. Men such as Goffe, Patten, and Chute had carried survival a step further; they had prospered. Their prosperity reflected such readily understood assets as energy, resourcefulness, versatility, wit, and a way with people. The townsmen reasoned that they could only benefit by putting their public institutions in such obviously capable hands. For they were all practical men.

CHAPTER XV

The Life of the Country Town
1725–1763

1

In winter, the country farmer rose hours before sunrise, hurriedly put on a flannel shirt, a pair of breeches of wool or deerskin, long flannel stockings, and a pair of sturdy shoes of thick leather. He stoked the fire in the huge kitchen fireplace. He donned his fur hat and his woolen "fly coat," which reached about halfway down his thighs, tied a knitted muffler around his neck, and poked a long splinter of pitch pine into the fire from which he lit the candle in his tin lantern.

Then, holding his feeble light in front of him, he plunged through the kitchen door into the darkness. The brisk walk from the backdoor privy through the snowdrifts and the icy predawn air had jolted him fully awake by the time he reached the relative comfort of the barn, warmed by the bodyheat of cattle and horses and the little heaps of steaming dung that had accumulated since the evening chores. By now, the stillness of the night had been broken by the sleepy lowing of cows impatient for the relief of their distended udders, the hunger call of oxen, the restless male thrashing of the bull in his stall, the stamping of horses, the gossip of the hens, and the arrogant cry of the cock. The air hung heavy with rank animal smells and the dry aroma of hay stored in the lofts overhead.

By the time he and his sons, and his black slave, if he had one, or his indentured servant from northern Ireland, had finished shoveling the night's debris through a window onto the dusky mountain of good rich fertilizer in the barnyard, forked fresh hay into the mangers, scattered grain for the hens, gathered eggs, and milked the herd, the farmer's wife and daughters, dressed in ankle-length flannel gowns, had heated an iron pot of bean porridge over the open kitchen fire. This the family ate with wooden spoons from wooden trenchers, accompanied perhaps by a pewter mug of hot chocolate sweetened with molasses and a chunk of toasted brown bread or a roasted apple, while dawn broke over the next hill to the east and the men planned the work of the day.

The routine varied with the season, but only in detail. In summer, the farmer and his sons put on short jackets of broadcloth or linen over their cotton or linen shirts and sometimes, in place of breeches, a pair of very wide trousers reaching to somewhere between the knees and the ankles. The young men of the family, including the servants, might go without shoes or stockings in the summer. The women wore short-sleeved wraparound dresses of calimanco or poplin instead of the flannel pullover gown of the colder months. They, too, often walked barefoot about their household duties.

Instead of feeding hay and grain to the livestock, the farmer's boy or young servant drove the cattle to pasture after the milking, but the dewy early mornings of summer, before the sun had risen high enough to begin to roast and baste a man, made the job pleasant enough. The return climb from the intervale to the farmhouse simply put a sharper edge on his appetite. Breakfast in the warm months usually featured milk instead of porridge, and as an occasional substitute, a basin of cider with bits of toasted bread floating in it, eaten with a piece of cheese.*

---

* Information on food and dress is drawn primarily from an anonymous article entitled "Manners and Customs of Olden Time" in New Hampshire Historical Society *Collections,* V (1837), 225–8. The author purports to describe from memory "the customs and manner of living, of the people, sixty-five, seventy, and seventy-five years ago," which would be approximately the decade of the 1760's. We can only surmise from the medium in which the article is published that the author is speaking of life in New Hampshire. His consciousness of the special nature of the rural setting that he describes lends some validity to the central argument of the chapters of this study that deal with the rural interior and to the choice of the term "country town" to describe the most characteristic communities of that part of the region: "As to what took place in sea-port towns, and places which had a dense population, I can give no account; but in the town where I was brought up, (which I suppose was not materially different from the general state of other country towns) I will attempt to describe"; p. 225.

For variations on the everyday dress of the country yeoman, we can turn to the frequent advertisements for runaway farm servants. Here are two:

From Dover, a Negro, 1729:

"Had on a gray homespun jacket with a striped linen jacket underneath, a good Holland shirt, a pair of striped cotton and woolen breeches, yarn

The day's work depended upon the season, the weather, the variety of the farmer's undertakings, and his labor force. The winter months, when ox-drawn sleds could be used to advantage, were good for cutting trees for masts, lumber, and firewood. The farmer also frequently chose the relatively inactive period of winter to "thrash" the barley, oats, and rye that had been harvested in the fall. Many farmers cocked most of their hay in the meadow when it was dry instead of storing it all in the barn immediately, and during the winter drew it on ox or hand sleds to the barn as it was needed. Maple "sugaring" took place in February and March. Shearing the sheep, spreading manure, plowing, and planting followed, and then the successive operations of cultivating corn and garden crops, performed with the hoe and the ox-drawn harrow. The hay harvest began in July, and the reaping of grain and the picking and storage of other crops continued through the late summer into early fall. October and November were considered the proper time for "breaking up" new ground to be planted in the spring. Most farmers hunted deer from about the time of the first snowfall through January, and some of them set traps for muskrat, beaver, mink, raccoon, and foxes. In fall and winter, the farmer butchered his hogs (which, like the potatoes of the day, were small by modern standards) and occasionally a sheep, a steer, or a recalcitrant cow.† Throughout the year, the farmer had to maintain and add to

---

stockings, and round toed leather heeled shoes." (*New-England Weekly Journal*, November 10, 1729.)

From Newington, "two Irish Men Servants," 1740:

One "had on . . . a reddish colour'd Homespun Coat, with large round Brass Buttons, Duroy Jacket of a dark Colour, dark colour'd Homespun Breeches, a pale Wigg, and a Beaver Hat half worn." The other "had on dark colour'd Jacket and Breeches, a Felt Hat, and dark Hair, if he has not cut it." (*New-England Weekly Journal*, July 8, 1740.)

For one reference to "candle wood," see Diaries of the Reverend Timothy Walker, New Hampshire Historical Society *Collections*, IX (1889), 139 and *n.*

† According to the author of "Manners and Customs," a New Hampshire farmer of the 1760's ordinarily killed from three to five swine whose meat weighed from 100 to 160 pounds each: "it was an extraordinary hog that would weigh nine score [180 pounds]"; New Hampshire Historical Society *Collections*, V, 227. On February 11, 1772, Matthew Patten "butchered our 2 pigs one weighed 120 and the other weighed 150"; *The Diary of Matthew Patten of Bedford, N.H.* (Concord, N.H., 1903), p. 277. By the middle of the nineteenth century, the average weight of hogs received on the Chicago market was 228 pounds; P. W. Bidwell and J. I. Falconer: *History of Agriculture in the Northern United States, 1620–1866* (New York, 1941), p. 441. As for potatoes, the author of "Manners and Customs," in confirmation of other sources already cited, reports, "Potatoes were then a scarce article, three bushels being considered as a very large crop; and I was a considerable large lad before I ever saw a potatoe as large as a hen's egg"; New Hampshire His-

his buildings and fences, attend to the care and breeding of his live-stock, and practice for his neighbors the particular craft or skill for which they had singled him out.

Labor ceased at noon long enough for dinner, the main meal of the day. Again, the meal began with porridge. Next came a course of Indian pudding made of corn meal, by far the most abundant grain in the region. The main course was meat, either pork or beef, which more often than not was boiled with turnips and possibly a few small potatoes in the ubiquitous black iron pot. From November through January, the usual diet might be varied occasionally by venison. Roast beef, goose, or turkey was reserved for Sundays after the afternoon service, the only day of the week when dinner could be put off long enough to allow for the necessary cooking time.[1]

The strict sabbatarian principles of Puritanism, both of the New England Congregational and Scots Presbyterian variety, wielded a sufficiently pervasive influence even among only mildly religious coun-try dwellers that it occurred to few of them to seriously violate the Lord's day. We do read in Captain Phineas Stevens's journal that one of his Charlestown neighbors "had an ox killed by the fall of a tree" on a Sunday in October, 1752, but that was during the very autumn that most of the settlement was struggling hard to have their permanent houses closed in before winter, and it was about six weeks before the beginning of regular preaching in the new town. On November 12, Stevens recorded, "Our people begin to assemble together for the worship of God." [2]

The establishment of churches in the back country, though not always of major importance to the settlers themselves, preoccupied the proprietors of the new towns, who were anxious to demonstrate to the legislature their worthiness of having a grant and to perfect their legal title to it. In 1741, when the township of Amherst, New Hamp-shire, contained only fourteen families, the proprietors hired a minister, having voted previously to give the inhabitants £20 "toward their having the word of God preached among them for the ensuing six months." Later, they voted to give the settlers fifty shillings for every Sabbath that they arranged for preaching in the township.[3] The ab-sentee proprietors of Warner, impatient with the spiritual as well as the material progress of their township, voted in November, 1770, to

---

torical Society *Collections*, V, 225. For references to drawing hay from the meadow in winter and early spring, see e.g., *Diary of Matthew Patten*, pp. 106–7, 120, 164, 236, and Moses Long: "Historical Sketches of the Town of Warner N.H.," New Hampshire Historical Society *Collections*, III (1832), 190.

help the inhabitants support a minister by contributing a specified amount on each right for six successive years provided that the towns-folk settle "a learned orthodox minister in town, on or before Dec. 1772." When the residents finally negotiated a settlement with the Reverend William Kelley* and gathered a church under him early in 1772, one of the numerous practical atheists in the region remarked magnanimously, "Rather than they should fail for members, I will take hold and join the Church myself." [4] The sacrifice of this public-spirited heathen undoubtedly greatly exceeded that paid in 1729 by the heirs of Daniel Emery of Newbury, who besides endowing his own West Parish, provided in his will for gifts of £20 to the first church to be gathered in each of two New Hampshire townships in which he owned an interest, Chester and Nottingham, "for the use of the Communion Table, etc." [5] The Reverend Paul Coffin, who began preaching to the thirty families of Narragansett Number 1 in 1761, received his entire salary from the absentee proprietors. The proprietors continued to pay him until 1774, when the town took over the responsibility two years after its incorporation as Buxton.[6]

Despite such encouragement, the establishment of churches in the back country lagged far behind the expectations of the township proprietors and the public authorities of both provinces. The Great Awakening stimulated religious interest in some interior communities, and in a few cases resulted in the formation of Separate churches. This occurred, however, only when a regular Congregational society already existed. Most commonly, the revival fervor either came to a Maine or New Hampshire rural community only temporarily through the visitation of an itinerant New Light minister or bypassed it completely because the township was only very sparsely settled and still in its rudest pioneering stage until after the revival movement had passed its peak in the mid-1740's. Towns in which churches were founded after the most intense period of revivalism, therefore, show little direct influence of either the excitement or the theological controversies of the Great Awakening.†

---

* Mr. Kelley, like so many other ministers who settled in Maine and New Hampshire during the eighteenth century, came from Newbury, Massachusetts.

† The residual effects of the movement, however, affected the religious life of a good many towns established between about 1770 and 1800, largely outside the scope of this study, in that settlers of those communities commonly founded Baptist rather than Congregational churches. In doing so, they demonstrated their preference for the strain of religious populism that had sprung from the Separatism of the 1740's. See tables in C. C. Goen: *Revivalism and Separatism in New England, 1740–1800* (New Haven, 1962), pp. 310–11, 319–21, 325–6.

The New Hampshire Convention of Ministers voted in 1752 to volunteer as individuals to preach from time to time in Nottingham and Epsom, where the people had "been Some time Destitute of the preaching of the Gospel among them," and tried to take steps in 1754 and 1755 aimed at correcting "the General Remarkable Decay of Religion in our Congregations." [7] In 1770, the convention considered an appeal to the Anglican Governor John Wentworth for funds to provide Congregationalist preaching to "the Inhabitants of the back Settlements in this Province who are destitute of the Privilege of the Gospel Ministry." "Upon Enquiry and Consideration," the ministers eventually decided against approaching the governor, but the un-churched state of the interior remained one of the New Hampshire clergy's principal concerns. [8]

Even in those country towns in which Congregational or Presby-terian churches had been established fairly quickly, the quality of religious life suffered from the worldly demands of rural living and the general absence of anything resembling the scholarly life that had nurtured New England Puritanism. The best young prospects for the ministry were understandably reluctant, after finishing the stimulating experience of Harvard, to commit the rest of their lives to struggling with the elements while ministering to a small group of unlettered woodsmen and farmers. Charles Coffin, who graduated in the same Harvard class with his brother Paul, the minister of Buxton, wrote soon after the Maine backwoods ordination in 1763, "I pitied brother Paul—whose education and social qualities fitted him to enjoy, if not to adorn, the most cultivated and polished society; that he should have his lot cast in that then forbidding field of labor, for I know that he would have given all that he then had or ever expected of this world's goods to have avoided it; but the settlers and proprietors were unanimous that he should remain and the path of duty appeared plain, which, however rugged, he never refused to enter, for brother Paul was a conscientious man." [9]

Business opportunity rather than conscience brought some min-isters to the northeastern frontier. The Reverend Joseph Baxter, who combined speculation in lands and iron works with his preaching, served in 1717 and 1718 as minister to the settlers in the Kennebec region and attempted to compete with Father Râle of Castine as a part-time Protestant missionary to the Indians. His appointment by Governor Samuel Shute came as a direct result of his interest in lands in the region. He would have stayed longer except that his parishioners in Medfield, Massachusetts, wanted him back. [10]

The Reverend Timothy Walker, perhaps the ablest and most influential of the back country clergy, accepted the pulpit offered on very good terms by the proprietors of Penacook while he was keeping a grammar school and reading theology in Andover in 1730. Of all the new townships of New England Puritan origin, this one, later called Rumford and finally Concord, offered a far better promise than most of actually transplanting New England values and institutions to the northern wilderness. The proprietors themselves settled in their township, accompanied by a minister already chosen, in the classic manner of the seventeenth century. A combination fort and meetinghouse was built and much of the land cleared and planted before the settlers began to arrive permanently in 1727. The Reverend Enoch Coffin of Newbury, who acted as a temporary chaplain to the proprietors before they hired Mr. Walker, even accompanied the surveying committee that visited the township for the first time in 1726 and held morning and afternoon services at the campsite on Sunday. The proprietors' choice of Mr. Walker proved to be a sound one, for he was a sincere and learned preacher, if somewhat liberal for the tastes of most of his parishioners. He possessed the necessary personal force to provide political and moral leadership and to fight successfully for the preservation of the grant when it was challenged by a conflicting one by the New Hampshire government after the settlement of the boundary.

Mr. Walker's life, however, if we can judge it by the entries in his diary, was necessarily more that of a farmer than of the usual Harvard-educated minister.* With the help of three Negro slaves, he cultivated a 300-acre farm. As the resident intellectual, he was looked

* One might compare the daily life of Mr. Walker with that of a contemporary, the Reverend Ebenezer Parkman, first minister of Westboro, Massachusetts. Westboro was on the western frontier of eighteenth-century New England, not far from Worcester. During the first decade or so of his pastorate, which began in 1724, Mr. Parkman shows himself in his diary to be much more preoccupied with his ministerial duties and his private spiritual life than Mr. Walker's diary entries ever indicate. After about the age of thirty and especially after about forty, Mr. Parkman's daily routine and his private thoughts seem more balanced and somewhat more given to worldly affairs, including those of his own farm. Never, however, unlike the case of Mr. Walker, does one ever lose sight in Mr. Parkman's diary of the primacy in his life and thoughts of the serious obligations he feels as a man of God and pastor to his flock. See *Sibley's Harvard Graduates* (for complete citation, see the *List of Frequent Abbreviations*, p. 363), VI, 511–27, and esp. Francis G. Walett, ed.: "The Diary of Ebenezer Parkman," American Antiquarian Society *Proceedings*, LXXI (1961), 93–227, 362–448; LXXII (1962), 32–233, 330–481; LXXIII (1963), 46–120, 386–464; LXXIV (1964), 37–203; LXXV (1965), 47–199; LXXVI (1966), 71–201.

to not only to carry the proprietors' fight for survival to the King in Council but also to provide an example to the community in such matters as building a house and farm buildings (including a one hundred-by-forty-foot barn), the scientific cultivation of crops, and animal husbandry. Along with more conventional crops, he even experimented with tobacco. His diary informs us that his days were filled with the details of farming and business, and with an extraordinary amount of social visiting. One wonders where he found the time even to prepare his two thirty-minute Sunday sermons and one weekly lecture. Certainly he was far from the tradition of John Cotton, the progenitor of New England Puritan preachers, who believed a scholar should give twelve hours a day to his studies![11]

In communities where a church was organized, or where a neighboring minister came occasionally to preach, a farm family began the Sabbath day in much the same way that it began the other days of the week. The men put on their working clothes and did the barn chores while the women prepared breakfast. Because there would be little or nothing more to eat until late in the afternoon, the morning meal was more elaborate than usual. Pancakes with maple syrup or molasses, doughnuts, brown toast, and apple, mince, or pumpkin pie formed a typical Sunday breakfast menu. The family washed down this hearty meal with milk, hot chocolate, or, as it became introduced widely to the back parts after about 1740, tea.[12]

The head of the family then put on his one suit of tailor-made small clothes and the great coat that he would own practically all his life. The boys and servants dressed in their best homespuns, and the women in their only calico gowns, usually with ruffles on the short sleeves, elbow-length gloves held in place with strings of braided horsehair, small white aprons, caps, and leather shoes with pointed toes and heels an inch and a half high.[13] The trip to the meetinghouse was either on foot, even if it were as much as five or six miles from the farm, or on horseback, the man riding in the saddle, and the woman, possibly cradling a baby in her arms, on a pillion behind.[14]

The morning and afternoon services, whether Congregational or Presbyterian, copied the simplicity and austerity of Puritan worship of the seventeenth century except that by now the controversy over singing by note had ended in favor of the "new way" of rendering psalms. Both the country deacon and the congregation were thus spared the agony of "lining out" the hymns and followed as best they could the notes in a "singing book." [15] If Mr. Walker of Penacook was at all representative of the north country preacher, the sermons of the time and place were immensely abbreviated from those of an earlier day in more devout (and more patient) communities. The church provided one of the few regular opportunities for isolated farm families to socialize, and we must expect that they took full advantage of the occasion during the break between the morning and afternoon services.

The family, frequently accompanied by dinner guests, returned home in the afternoon to the major meal of the day, and then to the evening chores. Unlike the case on weekdays, which ended about sundown with a supper of broth or porridge, the late afternoon dinner was the last Sabbath meal.

Besides Sabbath and town meetings, the principal occasions that brought the townsfolk together were events of importance in the life of the family: weddings, funerals, and house- and barn-raisings.

The Scotch-Irish showed their more sober countrymen of English origin how a neighbor ought to be escorted into the blessed estates of matrimony and death. A proper Londonderry wedding was accompanied by a festive mixture of shooting, drinking, and kissing, all performed according to fixed tradition.[16] A Scotch-Irish funeral included a wake every night between death and interment. There was some praying and scripture reading early in the evening, but the proceedings were enlivened by rum and often became as hilarious as the wake of the fabled Patty Murphy, who was not a Presbyterian. At the funeral service just prior to burial, the mourners handed round the bottle before the opening prayer and after the final one. Then the large assembly followed the coffin on foot to the grave and returned in a group to the late home of the departed loved one to be comforted again by a glass or two, and usually by a large meal.[17]

When a man died without survivors, the town assured a proper burial. Matthew Patten was a selectman of Bedford when a Captain Bushnell died in 1759. After procuring "a shirt and Sheet and cap" and examining the captain's house to assess his possessions, Patten and the other selectmen set the time for the funeral, then "spoke to John Bell Junior to make the Coffin and got a Quart of Rum from James Walker for the watchers." The next day, "I attended to bury Capt Bushnell with the rest of the selectmen we got 5 Quarts of Rum more from James Walker." In addition, the selectmen inventoried the captain's clothes and sold his crops. Patten characteristically accounted for the source of the boards and the "½ a hundred of nails" used in the coffin.[18]

When the rural folk gathered for a community work project such as a corn husking or the raising of a house, barn, or meetinghouse, they rarely missed the chance to turn it into a party, for country life was lonely. For raisings, the goodwives customarily cooked huge quantities of plain farm food for the workmen, and gossiped while they enjoyed the peculiar feminine companionship that comes from bustling in a group about another woman's kitchen. The men slaked their thirst from time to time with New England rum provided by the owner of the new building—the town, parish, or proprietors in the case of a meetinghouse. As a consequence, raisings were usually jovial affairs, but occasionally they ended tragically. When the townspeople of Bedford gathered on the afternoon of May 15, 1775, to raise James Little's barn, a beam slipped and fell to the ground, carrying John Patterson to his death.[19] Such accidents occurred with some frequency. Husking and quilting "bees," which especially attracted the young and unattached, carried no risk except to the heart and possibly the virtue, and left more time and energy for pure revelry than the strenuous and dangerous communal activity of putting up the hardwood timber frame of a large building. Occasionally, if he found a suitable excuse, a farmer might summon his neighbors together even when he needed no work done. Such an event was the housewarming that Matthew Patten's brother held in 1762.[20]

At social gatherings, the younger blades frequently organized impromptu boxing and wrestling matches, foot races, and jumping contests, which no doubt served their intended purpose of impressing the girls of the neighborhood.[21] Since a maid of fifteen or sixteen was considered marriageable in some of the back settlements,[22] participation by the males in contests of strength and agility was not an inappropriate form of courtship. The tribal rites continued into the evening with the dances, songs, and games of English or Scottish folk tradition. The repertories of both soon became mixed together and enriched by distinctly American accretions such as a step tune entitled "Cape Breton." These were only slightly less boisterous than the rough masculine games of the afternoon and early evening. Country dances began either with couples lined up in two facing rows or as a quadrille or "square," and proceeded according to fixed formula to the tune of a fiddle. Frequently the whole assembly accompanied itself by vigorously singing the words of a traditional song. The popular jig, either by itself or as an embellishment at the end of a prescribed figure, provided greater opportunity for the display of individual virtuosity, which the farming community counted among the important social achievements of a young man or girl. The following words were sung to a jig tune called "High, Betty Martin," familiar in the Yankee settlements of eighteenth-century New Hampshire, though the step that went with it approximated a Scottish highland fling:

> *High, Betty Martin,*
> *Tip toe, tip toe;*
> *High, Betty Martin,*
> *Tip toe fine.*
> *Never found a man*
> *To suit her fancy,*
> *Never found a man*
> *To suit her mind.**

An ordination in the back country, with its visiting clergy from the older settlements, huge community banquet, plenty of rum, cider, and punch, and sometimes a "ball," provided a rare and sumptuous entertainment as well as a significant religious festival to break the monotony of farm life. A young adventurer from Warner joined most of the neighboring countryside at an ordination in nearby Hopkinton in the early 1770's and found himself distracted during the prayer, the sermon, the charge, the imposition of hands, the right hand of fellowship, and the rest of the old New England ceremonial by a nubile young beauty who was sitting a few pews away. He jumped from his seat as soon as the newly created clergyman had spoken his first benediction, shoved his way through the crowd until he reached the creature he had been admiring and threw his arms around her, shouting, "Now I have got ye, you jade, I have, I have." Tradition says the uncouth tactics of the impetuous youth resulted in an early marriage.[23]

---

* The author of "Manners and Customs" reports as follows: "Dancing was considered a qualification of the first importance, especially step tunes, such as Old Father George, Cape Breton, High Betty Martin, and the Rolling Hornpipe. At their balls, dancing was their principal exercise, also, singing songs, and a number of pawn plays, such as breaking and setting the pope's neck, find the button, &c." (New Hampshire Historical Society *Collections*, V, 227.) The words and music of "High, Betty Martin" are found on p. 85 of Eloise Hubbard Linscott: *Folk Songs of Old New England* (New York, 1939). Mrs. Linscott says of this particular song, "The tune and words are traditional and were fitted for a sort of jig that finished off a quadrille. . . . He [Cassius Radford, an old-time fiddler of Pembroke, New Hampshire] remembers this tune and jig as one that was indulged in by those who felt the need of cutting an extra flourish and was executed with steps similar to the Highland Fling." See also Mrs. Linscott's diagrams of dance formations, p. 67, and *Oxford English Dictionary*, s.v. "Country dance."

In the Merrimack Valley and in other river communities such as New Marblehead, the country folk regarded fishing nearly as much a diversion as a source of necessary food. The falls at Amoskeag not only provided nourishment and amusement for the people of Londonderry, Derryfield, Bedford, and Goffstown, but attracted visitors from all over the province, including some of the Portsmouth merchants. During the fishing season of 1739, the Reverend Joseph Seccombe, formerly a missionary to the Maine Indians and finally minister at Kingston, New Hampshire, preached from the riverbank to a large crowd that included the aristocratic Theodore Atkinson. His sermon, entitled *Business and Diversion inoffensive to God,* was based upon the text, "Simon Peter saith unto them, I go a Fishing." *

Londonderry's semiannual fair, authorized by the town charter and held on the common near the First Parish meetinghouse, was a unique institution. There, the householders of Londonderry and the surrounding towns displayed, bought, and exchanged linens and other domestic manufactures, vegetables, and livestock. Eventually, merchants from seaports as distant as Boston came to show their wares. At the autumn fair of 1758, Edward Flint even auctioned off a 152-acre farm in Hamstead, complete with house, barn, and orchard.[24] Matthew Patten bought an ox at the fair in November, 1761, but lost his bridle, stirrups, and some starch to a thief.[25] By 1798, the fair had so degenerated that the town passed strict regulations aimed at curbing "the misconduct and disorderly behaviour of most of the people which frequent the Fair, as now holden." [26]

The first country stores in the northern New England interior were just such enterprises as Thomas Chute conducted from his home in New Marblehead. The Pinkerton brothers of Londonderry took up merchandising as a specialty and, because they offered a unique and badly needed service, became almost unbelievably rich. The older brother, John, started his retailing career by going from one Londonderry door to another with a variety of small foreign and domestic man-

---

* Joseph Seccombe: *Business and Diversion inoffensive to God. A Discourse utter'd at Ammauskeeg Falls in the Fishing Season. 1739.* (Boston, 1743). For years, bibliophiles regarded this pamphlet as the earliest book printed in America on any form of sport. In 1927, however, Lawrence C. Wroth reported that Dr. Seccombe's sermon had taken its place "among the other Ichabods of books from which for one reason or another 'the glory is departed.' " The occasion was the discovery and acquisition by the John Carter Brown Library of Edward Blackwell's *A Complete System of Fencing,* printed at Williamsburg in 1734; John Carter Brown Library: *Report to the Corporation of Brown University* (Providence, 1927), pp. 17–18.

ufactured items, which he exchanged for linen cloth and thread. He peddled these Londonderry products, which were already becoming famous, throughout New England. With his profits, he opened a store in a room of his house about 1750. The younger brother, James, started a second store in his house. The brothers not only sold merchandise, but also became the principal source of loans for the townsmen, always on the soundest possible basis of interest and security. They generally required a borrower to furnish at least two endorsers. With $30,000 of his large estate, John enriched the churches of Londonderry and, in 1814, endowed an academy. James added to the endowment when he died several years after his brother.[27]

The presence of occasional stores and tailors had little effect upon the dress of the ordinary upcountry yeoman and his family. Woolen homespuns colored with bark dye were the rule for all ages, except that the man of the house might wear a pair of leather breeches and have a suit of small clothes of finished cloth for Sundays and funerals. Cotton was rare and costly. A farm woman was fortunate if she could count one calico dress in her wardrobe, for use on special occasions.[28]

There were exceptions to the homely simplicity that predominated in the back parts. William Mayberry, the blacksmith who followed Thomas Chute from old to New Marblehead and set up his forge under a tree in his frontyard,[29] tried to match his large land holdings with appropriate symbols of his position. He kept at least one black slave, whom he dressed in livery, and provided himself and his sons with the best of Chute's handiwork. Among the items in his expense account with the tailor were several jackets for the family, including one of mohair and silk for himself, cotton stockings, coats and trousers, mohair and silk breeches, a blue jacket and red breeches for the slave, and red breeches for two other men, perhaps servants.[30]

Settlers in the New Hampshire townships of the eighteenth century had few peacetime connections with Indians during either the pioneering or agricultural stage. The Penacooks, the Amoskeags, and the Squawkheags were driven out of their villages in the Merrimack and Connecticut valleys by a great punitive Mohawk raid in the 1660's, leaving the lower part of New Hampshire almost empty of native Americans several decades before white men began to settle the interior. Most of the survivors of the Mohawk war had fled northward to mingle either with the tribes on the upper Connecticut or with the St. Francis Indians of Canada. Except for occasional wide-ranging hunting expeditions in the hunting grounds of their ancestors, the Indians came down from the north only to fight in the Anglo-French wars and the intermittent skirmishes between times. There was no occasion, therefore, for any but hostile relationships between the frontier settlers and the Indians.[31]

In at least one case, the territory occupied by an interior township was originally bought from Indians by a white man, but the purchase was of no ultimate importance. In 1717, Colonel Stephen Dudley of Exeter bought from an Indian and his squaw a tract of unsettled land in what had once been part of John Wheelwright's original Exeter purchase. The Province of New Hampshire confirmed the purchase by appointing Dudley *"Colonel* and *Town Major* of *Freetown* . . . , which land you have obtained by deed from Capt. Peter Penniwit and Abigail his Squaw." In 1720, this tract became part of the grant of Cheshire, later called Chester, and in 1764, the area of Dudley's half-century-old purchase was separated from the larger township and incorporated as the town of Raymond. Apparently the purpose of Dudley's purchase and provincial confirmation had been nothing more than the erection of one of the numerous temporary "paper" townships that were established early in the eighteenth century to evade the timber laws. The "purchase"—if, indeed, it was one in the ordinary sense; the deed has never been found—had no bearing at all on the ultimate granting or settlement of the territory.[32]

In Maine, relations with the Indians were more direct and more significant than was ever the case in eighteenth-century New Hampshire. Not only were there important purchases of territory in the region of the Kennebec, but it was in Maine that provincial officials met several times for peace conferences with the "eastern Indians." After the peace treaty at Casco Bay in 1726, the Massachusetts government set up a system of Indian trade under provincial auspices. At a cost of £4,000, the province built, stocked, and manned "truckhouses" at St. George's near Penobscot Bay, at Richmond on the Kennebec, and on the Saco River near Union Falls, some twenty miles upstream from where the stream empties into the Atlantic at Saco and Biddeford. These long, low, smoky buildings (the Saco River truckhouse was fifty-five by twenty-seven feet, and nine feet high at the eaves) were stocked with muskets, steel traps, axes and hatchets, blankets, clothing, food, and rum. Here the Indians of Maine, who often got drunk for the occasion, brought their furs to trade with the province-appointed "truckmasters," each of whom carried out his duties with the help of an official interpreter.[33]

Official encouragement and regularization of the Indian trade failed to alleviate occasional tensions between white settlers in the Maine back country and nearby natives. Until 1756, the pioneers of New Marblehead lived more-or-less constantly with an apprehensive eye on a small band of Indians that camped on the shores of the upper Presumpscot River near the outlet of Sebago Lake, only a few miles from the loose riverbank settlement of whites. In 1739, a delegation of these Indians journeyed to Boston to try to settle their grievances over the New Marblehead community with Governor Jonathan Belcher and his Council. Most seriously, the settlers had blocked the passage of salmon up the river, even though Colonel Westbrook, the Falmouth mast agent, had promised the Indians two years previously that a passage would be left in the dam for this purpose so that the Presumpscot Indians could make their customary spring catch. Moreover, "It was agreed that the Bounds of the Settlement made by the English should be known and . . . the English are encroaching upon our Lands which we never knew or understood was Lawfully purchased and we move that the English may not be allowed to settle any further as yet and that the Government would put a stop to the settlement on those Lands at present, and . . . the English Improvements caused the Hunting to be very difficult so that we cannot get our trade as usual, and we should be glad to have a trade on Pesumscot River."

The governor and council ordered a passage for fish to be opened in all Presumpscot dams and promised to look into the question of land titles, while acknowledging that Indian deeds to the territory surrounding Falmouth thought to have been executed early in the seventeenth century had probably been burned during wartime. As for the requested "trade on Pesumscot River," the government urged that the twenty-five families of Presumpscot Indians use the Saco truckhouse, where the father of the Reverend Thomas Smith of Falmouth was truckmaster, and warned that the province law forbidding the sale of rum to Indians by private persons must be upheld.[34] Until the final defeat and dispersal of these Indians during the French and Indian War, the settlers of New Marblehead confined themselves to the lower part of the township and could never discount the potential hostility of this small group of resentful natives.

Individual Indians occasionally became well known to the backwoods settlers and commanded considerable respect, even during periods when they were actually fighting the English. Captain John Lovewell and many of the men he commanded in the fight at Pequawket in 1725 knew their foes, especially the sachem Paugus, personally because of former peaceful contacts, and the enemies actually exchanged greetings and taunts with each other during the battle.[35] The

New-England Weekly Journal's account of the death of one Maine chieftain in 1727, the year after the end of Dummer's War, combines a sense of genuine awe—and perhaps gullibility—with the chivalry of eighteenth-century Europe:

> We . . . hear from the Eastward, that some days ago Died there Old *Escamburt,* who was formerly the Principal Sagamore of the (now dispersed) Tribe of the Saco or Pigwacket Indians; who has the most signaliz'd himself in the Wars, and made no small Figure in the Conferences that have been had with them. This same Superiour Officer was naturally of distinguish'd Courage and Resolution, capable of the most daring Attempts. He *Hercules*-like had a famous Clubb, which he always carried with him, and on which he had made Ninety-Eight Knotches, being the Number of English-men that he had Kill'd with his own hands.
>
> Upon some Occasion he went home to France, where he had peculiar marks of Respect shewn him, by the French King, by whom he had the Honour of Knighthood conferred upon him. . . . His whole Life has been a Life of War; full of Action, and never more restless and uneasy than when their was Peace. . . .[36]

Never before the peace of 1763 was the typical northeastern rural community as isolated from the world outside as one might expect. The southern Merrimack Valley remained a link with the river towns of Haverhill and Newbury, and thus with Boston. Farmer-tradesmen of Londonderry and Bedford such as Matthew Patten used this route extensively, and quickly found their way overland to Portsmouth. The sprinkling of settlers in the Connecticut Valley during this period used the river as a constant link with Deerfield, the origin of the proprietors of Charlestown and the principal source of that community's supplies until it became self-sustaining after the wars.[37] The settlers of New Marblehead enjoyed easy access to Falmouth, and some of them, like Thomas Chute, carried on considerable business at that seaport.

Beginning in 1757, a weekly post-rider service connected Portsmouth with Falmouth and the towns in between. The following year, a monthly post began between Portsmouth and Albany during the summer. The route included stops at Exeter, Greenland, Dover, Hampton Falls, Kingston, Chester, Londonderry, Amesbury, and York.[38] The summertime run to Albany, like the year-round Falmouth post, seems to have been initiated largely through the efforts of Daniel Fowle, the enterprising publisher of *The New-Hampshire Gazette,* which included frequent "intelligence" and advertising from all over the New Hampshire hinterland.

By late in the 1750's, the Merrimack Valley route and the roads into the interior from Portsmouth had become spotted with taverns. Scarcely a New Hampshire town by then was without one or more public houses in which a traveler to the expanding upcountry settlements could secure a bed, food, drink, and accommodations for his horse. In Londonderry, where at one time or another between 1725 and 1758 no less than sixteen persons had been licensed to keep a tavern or sell bottled liquors, the inhabitants prevailed upon the General Assembly to limit the number of taverns to three and retailers to two.[39] The Maine coastal road from Kittery to Falmouth had been well supplied with taverns since early in the century, but Thomas Chute's informal establishment on the Presumpscot was probably one of the very few in the Maine interior.

Business connections with the seaports of Falmouth and Portsmouth, the beginnings of regular postal service, the widespread circulation of a provincial newspaper, and taverns provided the inland settlers with news and helped to provoke the exchange of ideas and opinions. Connections with the northern seaports, of course, lacked the stimulation that similar connections with Boston, New York, or Philadelphia would have provided. Portsmouth, indeed, was a social capital but it was also a provincial capital; the adjective is appropriate in all its senses. Falmouth suffered from isolation despite its growing trade and the visits of the mast ships. The point is not that the rural communities of the eastern parts were integrated into the economic, cultural, and intellectual life of the colonies at large, but that they enjoyed a ready intercourse with the coastal towns of their own limited region.

2

During the four decades between 1720 and 1760, a varied group of settlers established a foothold inside the string of coastal towns between the Merrimack and the Kennebec. Between the end of the last French war and the beginning of the American War for Independence, new frontiers opened up still further inland as the pioneers of diverse interests and backgrounds who had settled the first interior townships brought to maturity a new kind of American community. A similar process was taking place at the same time in western Massachusetts, but the one movement was carried out with little reference to the other.

The interior town of northern New England as it developed in this period differed in several important respects from the typical seventeenth-century community of eastern Massachusetts or the lower Connecticut Valley. The motives for settling this area were complex and in most cases entirely secular. They included defense, land hunger, the speculative urge, intercolonial politics, and plain restlessness. The kind of settler also varied. In the Merrimack Valley, a homogeneous ethnic and religious community, similar in many ways to the Puritan groups that had settled Massachusetts and Connecticut in the seventeenth century, quickly and successfully adapted its peculiar economic practices and social traditions to the American environment. To other parts of southern New Hampshire came settlers of English ancestry from Massachusetts to establish towns and churches roughly along the old New England lines. The frequent contact between these and the Scotch-Irish communities modified the habits and attitudes of both. The towns of interior Maine were in nearly every case settled by an invigorating mixture of Massachusetts Puritans of East Anglian ancestry, former Maine and New Hampshire coast dwellers whose forebears had come from Cornwall and Devonshire, and Scotch-Irish.

In their methods of building, in the manner in which they laid out their settlements, and in the frequently involved and ingenious manner in which they made their livings, the settlers of the eastern frontier disregarded both official policy and Puritan precedent when they found a more practical means of adjusting to the wilderness. The towns which thus emerged from the pioneering, or "frontier" stage were in most cases composed of widely scattered farms on which versatile yeomen raised their cattle, corn, and families and contributed to the life of the community by engaging in specialized trades or businesses.

Though the inhabitants of the rural towns abandoned the Puritan village (and cared little for the fine points of New England theology), they did not abandon altogether the community cohesiveness that the village concept had been designed to foster. The rural people found that they depended upon one another for help in harvesting their crops and erecting their buildings, for special goods and skills that could be exchanged for others, and for a social life to make the gray routine of a country farmer at least endurable. Mark Ferry, the unshaven, unwashed hermit of Upper Ashuelot who had to be rescued from his riverbank cave when the Ashuelot flooded over in 1738, was a rare exception to the rule that the pioneers of the region retained their social instincts for the sake of both survival and sanity. The determination of Ferry's rescuers to save all the cattle of the settlement before they bothered with him reflects the attitude of the community toward one who had chosen to withdraw from it.[40] The people found, too, that every community needs leaders. Though most yeomen neither accorded deference to nor expected it from their neighbors, they looked to the most successful and personally commanding of the townsfolk to take charge of the common affairs.

The life of the country town, though different in many respects from the life of the Puritan village, owed much to Massachusetts. This was most obviously true in Maine, but applies nearly equally in New Hampshire. In both places, townships were granted either by the Bay Province or under pressure from it, and their settlement was subject to conditions conceived originally by Massachusetts magistrates. Thus there were provisions in every township for a church and a school. Most communities lagged for years in establishing either, but the place of both institutions in community life never was questioned. The frontier towns were expected to provide defense. This many of them did, but one can say as well that protection and encouragement from Massachusetts saved many of the frontier towns from extermination, whether by the enemy or by poverty and starvation. Here again, the Bay Province accomplished an incomplete but nevertheless salutary conquest of the eastern parts.

PART

III

CHAPTER XVI

The Great Awakening and the Great Crusade
1727–1745

1

At best, life in the countryside of northern New England was hard, even after the pioneering stage was over. At worst, it was often tragic. Nowhere in inland New Hampshire or Maine could a family on an isolated farmstead feel completely secure from a sudden, vicious assault by an Indian raiding party. This was especially true during New England's three-year conflict with the Abnakis that ended in 1725 and during King George's War in the 1740's, but a state of formal peace removed neither the fear nor the danger.

Sandwiched between the Indian conflicts of the 1720's and those of the 1740's came another, much more disastrous blow to the northern settlements—a chain of epidemics of "throat distemper," actually diphtheria. This deadly disease struck New Hampshire and Maine much harder than the rest of New England, and the inland country townships worst of all.

Shortages of food occasionally plagued the entire region, the seacoast and the interior alike. Not until after the middle of the century could seaports such as Falmouth rely on the farming towns of their own region to help feed them, nor could the pioneering farmers always support even themselves. The worst period of famine, apparently, was in 1737, shortly after the peak of the diphtheria epidemic, when it was reported in Boston that both people and cattle in the region had actually starved to death.[1]

As if severe hardship and death by war, famine, and pestilence were not enough to keep the nerves of an isolated people on end, they were not even entirely immune from the effects of the fourth killer of the apocalyptic vision, the "wild beasts of the earth." Black bears and wolves were a continual enemy of crops, sheep, and cattle, and a bear killed a boy in the New Hampshire back country in 1731.[2]

Not even the most sophisticated minds of the early eighteenth century were prepared to deal without superstition with one of the most fearsome of all natural phenomena, the earthquake. A number of frightening but not greatly destructive tremors jarred the northeastern coast of the continent from time to time throughout much of the seventeenth and eighteenth centuries. When one of the more intense of them struck New England in 1727, it stirred a temporary religious awakening along the northern New England coast. Combined with other events, and with special regional conditions, it served to start the eastern folk on the way toward their own version of the Great Awakening, which reached its peak with the visitation of George Whitefield in 1741. The revivals Whitefield conducted and the many others he inspired provided an emotional catharsis that the easterners sorely needed.

2

Two events of 1727 helped begin an upsurge of piety in northern New England. One was the earthquake; the other an ordination.

The ordination was that of Thomas Smith, who on March 8 became minister of "the first Church that ever was settled to the eastward of Wells," as he phrased it in the record book of the Falmouth church. Three-quarters of the tiny body of Maine clergy took part in the solemnities. Samuel Moody of York "made the first prayer," Jeremiah Wise of South Berwick "prayed and gave the right hand of fellowship," and John Newmarch of Kittery "gave the Charge." For some reason, Samuel Jefferds, who had taken over the pastoral duties in Wells two years previously, was not included. Instead, a "Mr. Rogers" offered the closing prayer. Since Nathaniel Rogers of Portsmouth had died in 1723, this must have been his brother Daniel, a Harvard tutor who in 1742 was ordained at York as a traveling evangelist and later became pastor of a New Light church in Exeter.[3]

Could the participants in the simple ceremony in the rude Falmouth meetinghouse have looked fifteen years into the future, each would have seen himself in a role of some importance in the revivals and the controversies that resulted from them. It was sufficiently important for the moment that Falmouth should have a minister, especially one who was naturally inclined toward preaching extempore when he dared to try it, and was interested always in outpourings of the Spirit. After preaching at a public fast in January, 1733, Mr. Smith confided to his diary:

> A very full meeting. I was as much enlarged, and had the most extraordinary assistances that ever (I think) I found. I was longer much, and prayed with greater freedom, distinctness and propriety, than ever I did on a Fast day; and I here record it to encourage myself to depend and rely upon God, having been enabled to pray for assistance more than usual, being out of order, and much concerned about it.[4]

On September 16, 1734, Mr. Smith was joined in Falmouth by Mr. Jefferds and the Reverend Ammi Ruhamah Cutter of North Yarmouth for a "public fast to pray for the effusion of the Holy Spirit on the youth." [5]

The earthquake struck during the night of October 29. Though the damage was restricted for the most part to stone walls and chimney tops, the earthquake was sufficiently fearsome to turn many minds, with the help of some judicious preaching, to thoughts of judgment and eternity.

In Portsmouth, where the reaction to the earthquake appears to have been extraordinary, the Reverend Jabez Fitch proclaimed from the pulpit of the North meetinghouse that the "gracious design of GOD in the Earthquake" had been unquestionably "to reclaim us from our Sins." He called upon all "that are in a State of Sin" to "bitterly bewail all their Sins, and especially the Sin of *Unbelief,* in not accepting CHRIST upon the Terms of the Gospel, which is the most heinous of all Sins." The peroration of Mr. Fitch's sermon, which was published in Boston in 1728, sounded like a trumpet call to repentance and regeneration:

> And shall not *the Terror of the Lord* in the late EARTHQUAKE, and the Terror of his Threatnings against Obstinate, Irreclaimable Sinners, perswade us all, to break off our Sins by timely Repentance? And shall not his Wonderful Mercy in sparing us, and waiting to be gracious to us, induce us to an ingenuous Repentance and Amendment of Life?
>
> GOD of his Infinite Mercy grant, that this may be the happy Effect of his *Awful,* and yet *Merciful* Dispensations toward us.[6]

Portsmouth, where men were noted primarily for "their Politeness in Dress and Behaviour" and "their sumptuous and elegant Living," [7] must have seemed unlikely ground for the sowing of such seed. Nevertheless, people started flocking to the churches. In South Parish alone, forty persons joined the church immediately after the earthquake, and Mr. Emerson, the pastor, preached an anniversary sermon on every October 29 thereafter until his death. The forty converts that the earthquake shook into South Church were nearly a third of the 124 members that Mr. Emerson received during his entire pastorate.[8]

Six years after the event, Mr. Emerson's successor was able to write to Thomas Prince's *Christian History* that "the *great Earthquake* in the Year 1727, that put the whole Country into such a Surprize, was a Means of *awakening* a *great many* here: and as to some, there is Reason to think the Impressions have remain'd." He added, however, that most of the converted ones had slipped back "into their former sleepy and secure State" until the revivals of the 1740's brought them out of it again.[9]

Scarcely had the Portsmouth backsliders settled down to enjoy the "sleepy and secure State" once again before New England children began to succumb in large numbers to the "throat distemper." *

The epidemic began in May, 1735, at Kingston, New Hampshire, where during the next fourteen months it claimed 113 victims, including ninety-six children under ten. The dead included more than one-third of the town's children.[10] By June, it had spread to Kittery, where in the lower parish alone it took 122 lives in the next eleven months. It broke out in Exeter in August, and in Durham in September. The toll in Portsmouth was ninety-nine, most of whom died during the winter.

---

* Edwin S. Gaustad, in *The Great Awakening in New England* (New York, 1957), argues against the epidemic, which began and reached its severest heights in New Hampshire and Maine, as a cause of the revivals (pp. 20–1). His argument is a reaction specifically against the tentative suggestion of Dr. Ernest Caulfield, cited below. On the statistical level, and with regard to direct causation, Gaustad's reasoning is impeccable. But statistics, while useful, fall short of telling the whole story. For example, the intimate journal kept by Nicholas Gilman, the most energetic of the New Hampshire revivalists, leaves the sensitive reader with little doubt of a relationship between the loss of two of his children in the epidemic and the development of his spiritual life. The quality and intensity of that development, in turn, profoundly influenced the rise of fanatical revivalism in his community of Durham. (See below.) Moreover, it is not enough to consider only the immediate causes of the revivals. What is argued here is that the conditions of life in northern New England over the course of several decades made the people psychologically receptive to the revivals when they came. For these reasons, the diphtheria epidemic, at least beyond the Merrimack, is of great importance.

In sheer numbers, the old Puritan town of Hampton suffered the worst of all. It lost 265 victims during the twelve months of the epidemic. In the second parish alone, forty-nine died just during the month of December, and about one-sixth of the inhabitants of the parish fell in a year's time. In percentage of fatalities, however, the smaller outlying towns, except for some that escaped altogether, were hit harder than such established communities as Hampton, Exeter, Dover, and Portsmouth.* Even the sparse population of the Isles of Shoals was thinned by thirty-seven as a result of the epidemic. New Hampshire's total loss between the outbreak of the epidemic in Kingston in May, 1735, and the middle of July, 1736, was an astounding 984 persons, about 800 of whom were children under ten years of age.[11] Between July and the end of 1736, another thirteen died in Hampton alone.[12]

The epidemic was somewhat less severe in Maine, except at Kittery, which was struck even worse than many of the New Hampshire towns. It traveled up the coast toward Falmouth during the summer and early fall of 1735, and on October 31, Mr. Smith's people held a fast day "on account of the sickness which broke out at Kingston, N.H., and which is got as far [as] Cape Porpoise, and carries off a great many children and young persons and alarms the whole country."[13] The sickness probably reached the Neck during the winter or the following spring, and finally spread to North Yarmouth. The toll in Falmouth as of May, 1737, was sixty-six, and in North Yarmouth, seventy-five.[14]

Mr. Smith, ever ready to "improve" an occasion such as this for spiritual ends, conducted an exercise on June 16, 1736, that went far beyond the usual "fast day" observances. "On a day of fasting and prayer," reads the account in the church record book, "the church solemnly renewed their covenants; at which solemnity were present all the Church except three male members, two of which were out of town and the third sick; and a very few women absent." The record makes it plain that this "solemn transaction" had been "agreed upon by the Church upon occasion of the terrible distemper that has been and is still prevailing in the land, which has swept away such multitudes of the children and younger people, and which, since it has come into the houses in this town has become greatly mortal."

* Dr. Ernest Caulfield, in *A True History of the Terrible Epidemic Vulgarly Called the Throat Distemper Which Occurred In His Majesty's New England Colonies Between the Years 1735 and 1740* (New Haven, 1939), finds that the disease was more fatal in the smaller frontier towns than in the more settled communities because of differences in immunity (pp. 103–8).

"The whole of the day as well as this particular transaction," the record goes on, "was attended and carried on with an uncommon solemnity, and was taken notice of by the ministers present and assisting, and others. May it have an happy influence and effect, and prove indeed a day of atonement. Amen." If this remarkable day of atonement is not sufficient evidence of the religious interest that the epidemic excited in Falmouth, the fact that twenty-five persons joined the little church in 1736 ought to be. The society had started nine years before with but ten members, and added an average of about ten per year between then and the Revolution. The largest number to join in any one year was forty-nine, and these were added during the peak of the Whitefield excitement in 1742.[15]

In Portsmouth, Mr. Fitch preached two sermons in which he called for "a true Repentance and Reformation" in the face of the tragedy. These were later published in Boston for distribution by Eleazar Russell, a Portsmouth bookseller, along with the minister's account of the epidemic.[16]

In the *Account,* which was published anonymously, Mr. Fitch took pains to point out that numerous families had suffered multiple losses or had lost their only child. In Hampton's first parish, for example, five families lost three children each, one lost four, one lost five within about a fortnight, and three families lost their only children. In the second parish in that town, he reported, nearly twenty families had lost all of their children and twenty-two families all of their sons. One family in the second parish lost seven children, one of whom was an apprentice boy, two lost six each, two lost five each, six lost four each, and about fourteen lost three each. In Dover, two families each suffered the pain of having to bury four children at one time.[17]

One must bear in mind always that it was a rare family in the eighteenth century whose full complement of sons and daughters survived childhood, and that in such an age, death was accepted with far greater complacency than is comprehensible to the modern mind. Nevertheless, Mr. Fitch obviously was sensitive to the extraordinary anguish of the almost countless parents who had watched one after another of their small children succumb to this deadly infection within a short space of time. Repent, he urged them, and "he who is *the Hope of Israel and the Saviour thereof in time of Trouble;* will shew himself an all-sufficient Saviour." [18]

The epidemic abated after 1736, but it had by no means run its course. It broke out anew at York and Wells in January, 1737, at Falmouth in March, at North Yarmouth in May, and at Scarborough in

September. A year later, five members of one Falmouth family died of the disease within a week, and the scourge was reported "still exceeding bad at Saco." [19] Late in 1741 and early in 1742, after the revivals were well started, the throat distemper claimed the lives of two of the sons of the Reverend Nicholas Gilman, the controversial New Light preacher of Exeter and Durham.[20] The distemper broke out again in 1754 and 1755, when another fifty-one persons died in Hampton.[21] During the five worst years of the epidemic, from 1735 to 1740, the death rate was seventy-five per thousand in New Hampshire and fifty-five per thousand in Maine, as compared with between fifteen and sixteen per thousand in Massachusetts and Connecticut.*

While the coastal towns were staggering under the worst blows of the epidemic, the Scotch-Irish Presbyterians of Londonderry, one of the more remote communities not reached by the sickness, were plunged into a local church controversy. After the death in 1729 of the Reverend James MacGregor, the first pastor, the town went through the elaborate and expensive process of procuring a *bona fide* Presbyterian replacement from Ulster in the person of Thomas Thompson, a recent graduate of Edinburgh. Mr. Thompson was ordained by the presbytery of Tyrone before he left Ireland, and was installed over the Londonderry church in October, 1733. About this time, the growing population began to think about a division of parishes. Opinions were by no means unanimous, however, and at a town meeting on December 1, 1735, an angry debate and attempt to take a standing vote on running a precinct line ended in confusion.[22]

The following year, however, a majority managed to agree that the western part of the town ought to be set off as a separate parish. Even

---

* See again Caulfield: *A True History*, pp. 103–8. As a result of his medical findings, Dr. Caulfield draws a cautious connection between the epidemic and the revivals that followed: "Except in a very few towns, . . . one finds no evidence of any great confusion, and certainly there was not the loss of self-control that people usually exhibit during great epidemics. Perhaps this apparent outward calm did not truly reflect the inward feelings of the people, but there is good reason to believe that it did for with implicit faith in God they did not question the meaning or justice of their misfortunes. That they were submissive and composed may be one reason why historians have overlooked this terrible disaster, although it was a major epidemic in the annals of this country and caused more deaths than any pre-Revolutionary war. But it seems that the emotions were only temporarily suppressed, for immediately following these five years of sickness and death, indeed, so close in time that a causal connection might be expected, there occurred . . . 'The Great Awakening' "; p. 3. Caulfield also makes a connection between epidemics and religion in his paper on epidemics of influenza in the colonies, "The Pursuit of a Pestilence," American Antiquarian Society *Proceedings,* XL (1950), 22–3.

before the division was approved by the town, some of the west end residents built a meetinghouse and chose the late Mr. MacGregor's son David as minister of the new church. In 1739, still lacking the necessary approval for establishing a new parish from the New Hampshire General Assembly, the young Mr. MacGregor was installed over the new church and began to hold services in the West meetinghouse.[23]

Meanwhile, Mr. Thompson had died and been replaced by another Edinburgh man from Ireland, the Reverend William Davidson.[24] Because of discontent with this sober minister and sentimental attachment to Mr. MacGregor, some First Parish families switched their membership to the West Parish church, where their influence was heavy enough to move the site of the new meetinghouse a mile to the east. This caused a storm in the new parish, and some of the west enders who resented the influence of parishioners from across the town decided to go back to the First Parish. To make matters worse, the town now voted to drop its original method of supporting the minister by pew taxes alone and place a tax on polls and estates throughout the township. This meant that Mr. MacGregor's people, still lacking legal incorporation as a parish, were forced to pay taxes to help support Mr. Davidson as well as provide for their own minister.[25]

Resentment ran high on both sides both before and after February 25, 1740, when the General Assembly finally responded to several petitions by incorporating the western part of the town as a legal parish. Its members now became exempt from First Parish taxes and could raise their own taxes within their own bounds. In recognition of the special circumstances that already existed, the Assembly provided that up to forty persons in each parish could go to church and pay taxes in the other one.[26] The acrimony between the two parishes was aggravated in the 1740's when Mr. MacGregor attended revivals in Boston and other places and returned a confirmed New Light. His flock went enthusiastically along with him, much to the disdain of Mr. Davidson and his unawakened parishioners.[27]

At about the time the parishes of Londonderry were quarreling over parish lines, meetinghouses, and taxation, a brief but intense excitement over Presbyterianism broke out in Purpooduck Parish, Falmouth. This parish, composed of modern South Portland and Cape Elizabeth, had been set off in 1733 and a Congregational church organized there the following year. Among its members were a few of the Scotch-Irish immigrants who had wintered at Casco Bay in 1718–19 and had not gone with the majority to the Merrimack Valley. In 1736, they began a movement to put their church under the control of a presbytery. They failed, but the resulting commotion was sufficient to cause the summoning of an ecclesiastical council. In November of the same year, the Reverend William MacClanethan, minister at Georgetown of the only Presbyterian church in Maine, arrived on the scene. He drew off enough adherents to form a separate church in Purpooduck, over which he was formally installed in 1739. By 1742, however, Mr. MacClanethan was back in Georgetown, and there is no further record of a Presbyterian society in Falmouth.[28]

It was to a war-weary, frightened, sickened, saddened people, some of whom had begun to feel the venom of stubborn ecclesiastical quarrels, that George Whitefield brought his message of forgiveness and redemption by faith. Whitefield's first day beyond the Merrimack was disappointing. On Wednesday morning, October 1, 1740, he preached an open-air sermon to "some Thousands" at Hampton, "tho' not with so much Freedom as usual." The wind almost drowned out his voice and only a few were "affected." The afternoon was worse. He preached in Portsmouth "to a polite Auditory, and so very unconcerned, that I began to question whether I had been preaching to rational, or brute Creatures." Samuel Moody had come as far as Hampton to meet the evangelist, and after the exercises at Portsmouth, accompanied him by ferry to York. There, the next day, Whitefield found a congregation well prepared by their parson, to whom the evangelist referred as "a worthy, plain and powerful Minister of JESUS CHRIST, tho' now much impaired by old Age." Moody told Whitefield before his sermon in the parish meetinghouse that he would "preach to a hundred new Creatures this Morning." This, in Whitefield's view, was indeed the case: "I preached both Morning and Evening. The Hearers looked plain and simple; and Tears trickled apace down most of their Cheeks. Indeed we saw the Outgoings of the Lord in his Sanctuary." [29]

On October 3, Whitefield spent his final day of the tour in northern New England, preaching again at Portsmouth and Hampton. He found the people of Portsmouth changed over two nights, and "many, as I heard, who before had industriously spoken Evil of me, were ashamed of themselves." The Reverend William Shurtleff, new minister of South Church, told him, "You have left great numbers under deep Impressions, and I trust in GOD they will not wear off; but that Convictions of some will be kept up and cherished, till they have had their desired Effect." The "several Thousands of People" who gathered to hear him at Hampton that afternoon also seemed profoundly impressed.[30] Mr.

Smith journeyed to York to hear the evangelist and returned on October 4. The next day, a Sunday, he "preached extempore A.M. about Mr. Whitfield." [31] For northern New England, the revival had begun.

3

In Portsmouth and Falmouth, the two principal seaports of the region, the coming of Whitefield aroused great interest in the personality of the evangelist and in the revivals generally. During the three years following 1740, William Shurtleff of Portsmouth's South Church wrote many impressive accounts of reformations of character and concerns for salvation, especially right after Whitefield's first visit.[32] Mr. Browne of Queen's Chapel and Governor Wentworth, on the other hand, complimented each other on the extent to which their own congregation had resisted the "Contagion of Enthusiasm," though even the rector was forced in 1742 to admit the frequency of "Strange Commotions of a Religious nature." Several times thereafter, however, he reported that they had abated.[33] Obviously, since each minister was writing primarily about his own people, the impact of Whitefield and Gilbert Tennent, who also visited Portsmouth,[34] was confined almost wholly to Congregationalists, and therefore generally to the middle and lower classes. The only immediate institutional change in Portsmouth was the strengthening of the Episcopal society by defectors from Congregationalism who favored order, dignity, and social and political respectability over the embarrassing eccentricities* of the new "heart religion." In 1757, however, after the fervor had run its course among most Congregationalists, a New Light faction from both the North and South churches began to hold private meetings with a lay exhorter. In 1761, the same group organized a Separate church under Samuel Drown, a Rhode Islander with Baptist inclinations.[35]

Thomas Smith, the minister of Falmouth, welcomed the revivals because of their potentially beneficial effects upon the religious and moral life of his community. He shared this view with most of his colleagues in northern New England.† The Awakening brought many

---

* For example, Mr. Shurtleff reported *"a general Out-cry"* at a meeting held on Friday, November 27, 1741, and the widespread belief among a crowd that evening "That CHRIST *was coming to Judgment"* when they saw reflections from a chimney fire in several windowpanes. *The Christian History . . . For the Year 1743* (Boston, 1744), pp. 384–5.

† Together with Samuel Moody and Samuel Chandler of the two parishes in York, Mr. Smith attended a convention of ministers in Boston in July, 1743, where they endorsed a statement approving the revivals but opposing lay preaching,

Falmouth people into the church for the first time, and most church members seem to have shared their pastor's enthusiasm for Whitefield and the lesser evangelists. As in Portsmouth, however, the wealthiest and most influential of the townsfolk opposed the tumultuous movement. The difference in opinion brought about no ecclesiastical split on the Neck (although the Great Awakening may have been indirectly responsible for a church schism in Purpooduck in 1756), and the "leading men," as Smith called them, never forsook their New Light pastor even though they disagreed with him on this issue.

Early in 1742, Mr. Smith went to hear Whitefield during his second visit to Portsmouth and returned to become something of an itinerant himself. He preached at Stroudwater, Scarborough, and Gorhamtown, and in the spring of the following year even found "extraordinary acceptance" at Portsmouth. During the same year, he added forty-nine persons to the Falmouth church and the congregation raised his salary.[36]

In the fall of 1744, after the peak of the revival enthusiasm had passed, Mr. Smith put his career on the line by persisting in an invitation to Whitefield to come to Falmouth during his third tour of New England. Moses Pearson tried personally to convince his pastor to abandon the plan for inviting Whitefield to Casco Bay and led a campaign among the merchants to urge the parishioners to put pressure on Smith to drop the idea. The evangelist's visit was delayed by illness, and in the meantime even some of the Maine ministers who had endorsed the revivals were doubting that he should come eastward because of what Smith called the "great and prevailing clamors everywhere against Mr. Whitefield." *

---

departures from Calvinist orthodoxy, and ministers who preached in parishes other than their own without the approval of the local pastor. Later, the other eight of the Maine clergy unanimously concurred in writing. *Journals of the Reverend Thomas Smith and the Reverend Samuel Deane . . . ,* ed. William Willis (Portland, 1849), pp. 104–7 *n.*; *Christian History, 1743,* pp. 157–76.

* *Smith and Deane Journals,* pp. 114–16. The Reverend Raymond B. Wilbur of York, Maine, has recently made a penetrating study of the controversy that raged in America over Whitefield between 1740 and 1745. On the basis of both quantitative and qualitative analysis of the published contemporary literature of the Great Awakening from 1730 to 1750, he concludes that it was above all the introduction of a strangely "charismatic" figure into the New England revivals, not simply the issue of itineracy, or even that of Separatism, that seemed to threaten Christian unity and the New England ecclesiastical establishment. Thus Whitefield transformed a movement which began, in New England, as a revival of religion serving the established churches into one which appeared to threaten the traditional bases of political and ecclesiastical power and occasioned a vehement controversy centering precisely on the personality of the evangelist.

The Falmouth minister stood his ground, however, and finally had the satisfaction of entertaining the illustrious Englishman in his home during the evening of March 22, 1745, and of hearing him preach to "multitudes" from his pulpit the next morning. In all, Whitefield spent about seven days in Maine; Mr. Smith, determined to make the most of what he considered a momentous event, heard him preach twice in his own meetinghouse, twice in North Yarmouth, once in Purpooduck parish, and once in Scarborough. Aware of "a violent opposition to him [Whitefield] among all our leading men except Mr. Frost, and . . . unwearied pains taken to prejudice the people against him," the pastor feared "such a quarrel as would be fatal to me." Fortuitously, however—Smith said because of "the wonderful providence of God"— Whitefield arrived in Falmouth at the very time that Moses Pearson, John Waite, Henry Wheeler, Dr. Samuel Moody, Enoch Freeman, and the other principal opponents of Whitefield were all out of town on business. Not until Waite returned to the Neck on April 2 was the parish "in a buzz about Mr. Whitefield." By then, it was too late to do the minister serious damage.[37]

Apparently nobody on Falmouth Neck reacted quite as strongly to Whitefield's visit as Smith himself, who described himself as "all in a blaze." He tried to tone down his newly inspired preaching in order to avoid controversy, but had trouble restraining himself. "I went to meeting resolving to be calm and moderate," he wrote six weeks after Whitefield's visit to his town, "lest the people should think that it was wildness, and effectation to ape Mr. Whitefield; but God (I see) makes what use of me he pleases, and I am only a machine in his hand." [38]

The differences over Whitefield and revivalism caused temporary fallings-out between Mr. Smith and a handful of his parishioners. These hurt the minister while they lasted, but they were soon resolved. Despite his great attraction to New Light revivalism, Smith was more concerned for harmony in his parish than for the dominance of his point-of-view. In any case, less than two months after Smith recorded his ambivalent comments about his own inspired preaching, the news of the capitulation of Louisbourg arrived in Falmouth. Minister and people alike now were united in a new matter for concern and rejoicing.[39]

4

Whitefield and the wave of revivalism caused moderate and temporary disruptions in the social and religious life of Portsmouth and Falmouth, and reinforced the work that such men as Mr. Moody of York and Mr. Wise of South Berwick had been trying to do in their communities for years. In a few towns further inland, the results were very different.

A Boston missionary of the Society for the Propagation of the Gospel reported home in 1742 that the followers of Whitefield and the "strange Effects" of their doctrines "prevailed chiefly in Country Towns." [40] If by "strange Effects" this correspondent meant violent theological controversies, ecclesiastical splits, lay exhorting, and some of the more grotesque manifestations of revivalism, there was nothing in the experience of New Hampshire, at least, to prove him wrong.

After young Mr. MacGregor had been awakened by Whitefield, the two Presbyterian churches of Londonderry refused to commune with each other, though cooperative celebrations of the Sacrament were a beloved Scot Presbyterian custom of long standing.[41] When two ecclesiastical councils had met and given divergent views, a New Light faction seceded from the Congregational church at Exeter in 1744, and in 1748, installed Daniel Rogers, an ordained roving evangelist, as pastor.[42]

Samuel Lane, the tanner of Stratham, who was a man of scholarly inclinations though he had little education, commented extensively in his carefully kept journal upon the state of religion in the surrounding countryside. His dispassionate analysis of the Separate movement probably paints the picture as vividly as any writer has done since. Writing in 1743, four years before Stratham had a Separate church of her own, Lane commented:

> It may not be improper here to make a Memorandum that there is great Religious Commotions in the country in general. Many People, in some places especially, that a year or two ago seemed greatly concerned for their souls, and to have [made] hopeful beginnings, now seem to run into great extremes on many accounts, especially in exclaiming against Ministers as unconverted; and many will separate themselves from their minister and church and set up separate Meetings and Meeting-Houses, and get preachers of their own way of thinking to preach to them. They refuse to come to the sacrament or to have their children Baptized by those Ministers they call unconverted. These things and many others cause great Disturbance in Towns, in churches, and in Families; Ministers and People, husbands and Wives, Parents and Children divided against each other, judging and condemning one another. These separate people are called by many "New-Lights" and "schemers" and the like. These and such like practices cause

many people to stumble at and be much set against what they some time ago called a good work.[43]

After several years of violent scrapping between factions, the Stratham church suffered a schism in 1747. The trouble began in 1744, when the New Lights invited an itinerant preacher named Dudley Leavitt to share the preaching for a short time with the regular minister. After an "Uproar in the Meeting House" the first time Leavitt appeared, his opponents complained to Governor Wentworth. The sympathetic governor, undoubtedly with some glee, responded with an order to the high sheriff of the province, who on the following Sunday hauled Mr. Leavitt bodily from the pulpit.[44]

Troublesome though it was, the turmoil in Londonderry, Exeter, and Stratham failed by any stretch of the imagination to equal the frenzied effects of revivalism in Durham, an early offshoot of the old Puritan town of Dover. There a fanatical minister whipped up the religious emotions of a people who had suffered far more than their share of the difficulties and tragedies of frontier life and had, in addition, long experience with church quarrels. The result was less an "awakening" than a debauch.

Nicholas Gilman, a son of the most prominent family in Exeter, accepted the Durham pastorate early in 1740 after spending an uncommon amount of time drifting from one temporary teaching or preaching assignment to another. That fall, while commuting from his home in Exeter to preach weekly sermons in Durham, he was among Whitefield's most attentive listeners on the village green at Hampton. "O that there may be a plentifull Ingathering of Souls to Christ in New England," Gilman prayed in his remarkable spiritual diary after hearing the evangelist and talking with him at dinner.[45]

Though Gilman's private spiritual life, as reflected in his diary, underwent an extraordinary development during the two years that he preached in Durham before his ordination there, the external affairs of the parish went on for a time in quite ordinary fashion. The turning point came on Sunday, November 15, 1741, when after preaching at the Sabbath morning service as usual, Gilman held an evening service at which he read a sermon by Jonathan Edwards. The next morning, a nineteen-year-old girl came to his house "under strong convictions," claiming she had been "awakened" for the past five weeks and inquiring of her pastor "the Way of Life." That evening, he visited a man who said he had been "awakened the Last Evening" and was "crying out of his Sins." On Tuesday, thirty or forty parishioners arrived at

Gilman's house on a rumor that he would hold a revival meeting. Gilman obliged, supplementing his own prayers and "Exhortation" with more readings from Edwards. The same scene was repeated Friday evening, and on the following Sabbath, an unusually large congregation stayed in the meetinghouse between services to hear more public readings from Edwards. By the second week in December, daily sermons had become the rule in Durham and Gilman could write, "Numbers Now Awakened Daily. Blessed be the Name of the Lord." *

Right in the midst of this burgeoning revival, Gilman lost two of his five sons, Bartholomew and Nicholas, to the "throat distemper." A third became dangerously ill but recovered. Gilman did not suspend his evangelizing during these trying days, either in Durham or in the nearby towns of Newmarket and Exeter, but the loss of his two sons affected him deeply. He could not hide the tears that lay behind the single pathetic diary entry on the day he buried eight-year-old Nicholas: "The Remains of My Little Son laid in the Silent grave." [46]

Praying that the Lord would "Teach Me to Behave under these Visitations," Gilman found the answer to his grief in sublimation. He plunged into the affairs of the parish with renewed energy, and on the night of January 31 experienced the pinnacle of his career both as evangelist and as spiritual pilgrim. His own words tell it best:

> I had more Joy than Usual thro the Day, but when the Assembly was dismissed at Night, as I saw the people preparing to go out, I was moved to tell 'em if I could See them flocking to Heaven as they were from Meeting it would Make My Heart leap within me; upon hearing that they turned about—I continued My Discourse, and the people drew into the House again and were Attentive. We continued in religious Exercises all night. Had the presence of the Lord with us in a very Wonderfull manner. He was graciously pleased to Reveall Himself to My Soul. . . . I was constrained to cry out with a loud Voice—Glory to God on high—Glory to the Redeemer etc. for some considerable Time. What Shone forth and made the deepest Impression on My Soul, was a Marvellous display of the Manifest Wisdom of God in Mans Redemption by Christ. (2 Cor. 4.6. I am sure I can say exactly

---

* Gilman referred to the Edwards work he read publicly on November 15, 1741, as the "sermon on the danger of the unconverted." In the absence of any published sermons by Edwards of that or a similar title, the reference is somewhat puzzling. However, among the three works of Edwards published in 1741 was his famous Enfield, Connecticut, sermon, *Sinners in the Hands of an Angry God* (Evans 4713), the substance of which certainly coincides with Gilman's description.

with the Apostle in this Verse—and Blessed, for ever Blessed be God for his goodness to Such a poor Self-destroying Sinner.) It Seemeth to Me and the Event will better show, that the Lord did then Anoint me with that Holy Anointing . . . and as it were touched My Lips as with a Coal from his Altar. . . .

We held on thro the Night, Blessing and Praising admiring and Adoring God and the Redeemer. Sometimes praying, then Singing, Exhorting advising and directing, and Rejoycing together in the Lord. It seemed the Shortest and was I think the Sweetest Night, that I have Seen.

During this frenzied night-long vigil, it was reported later, several of the congregation had experienced visions of bright lights and angels. Through the rest of the winter and the following spring, the appearance of visions became the distinctive feature of the revival in Durham. Gilman himself claimed to have experienced, not a literal vision during the January 31 revival, but a very Edwardsian doctrinal one. "At One View," he wrote later, "there Seemd to be a Marvellous display of the Most important truths of the Gospel, I Seemed to Behold in Christ a Body of Divinity, and to have a Glorious Discovery of the Manifold Wisdom of God in Mans Redemption—Such as I can compare to Nothing More fitly than, the Blank paper in the printer's press receiving upon it a Variety of Truths at One and the Same Impression." *

Most of the Durham visions, however, seem to have been simpler pictures and messages, all of which were reported to the minister, who transcribed and interpreted them. Gilman then read his notes in public meetings, usually to the eventual accompaniment of moans, cries, and further trances.[47] By 1746, the Durham revival meetings had taken on still wilder aspects. Samuel Chandler, a friend of the revivals, visited Durham with Mr. Wise of Berwick that summer and reported that Wise's preaching and praying were greeted by four or five of Gilman's flock who "made all manner of mouths, turning out their lips, drawing their mouths awry, as if convulsed, straining the eyeballs, and twisting their bodies in all manner of unseemly postures." Others, he wrote disapprovingly, "were falling down, clapping their hands, groaning, talking . . . and saying aye, that is true, 'tis just so and some were exclaiming and crying out aloud, glory, glory." When Mr.

---

* Nicholas Gilman's Diary (Ms., New Hampshire Historical Society), February 8, 1742. For valuable insights into the sort of Edwardsian "doctrinal" vision that Gilman apparently experienced on the night of January 31, see Jonathan Edwards: *A Divine and Supernatural Light* (Boston, 1734), with which Gilman could easily have been familiar.

Gilman entered the meeting, he was followed by another flock of fanatics, including one Hannah Huckins, who enlivened the proceedings
further by "dancing round the room, singing some dancing-tunes, jiggs,
minuets, and kept the time exactly with her feet." [48]

One of Durham's most prolific vision-seers, Mary Reed, nearly
ended her pastor's career less than a month after his ordination by
coming to the parsonage on the evening of March 26, 1742, having been
"exceeding full of Joy all day." Unfortunately, Gilman's wife and
family still had not moved from Exeter, and Mary elected to stay four
days, spending most of that time in bed. According to Gilman's account, she lay in a trance all the while, imagining her soul in heaven
and not awakening from this long vision until the evening of March
29. For a reason he did not explain, however, she did not leave the
minister's house until the morning of the thirtieth. On April 13, Gilman complained to his diary about "a great and very unreasonable
disturbance made in the Town about her being at My House." These
were extraordinary days for Durham, however. The scandal soon blew
over and on May 9, Mary was admitted to the church.

The talk about Mary Reed may have soon ended, but it was not
so easy to end discussions of visions and frontier exuberance in the
church. Some of the leading men of the community, especially Dr.
Hugh Adams, the town physician and former minister, opposed Gilman
and the antics of his followers vehemently. He still commanded a considerable following in the town, especially among the residents of the
Durham Point area, who tried unsuccessfully to gain status as a legally separate parish with Adams at their head.[49] Outside of Durham,
Gilman naturally was regarded with horror by the few Old Light ministers in the neighborhood such as John Odlin of Exeter.[50] Before long,
moreover, Gilman was making enemies even among New Lights.

Gilman's extraordinary spiritual powers and extreme sectarianism
remained a powerful influence in Durham even after his death in 1748.
After the installation of his much more conservative successor, the
Reverend John Adams, the former partisans of Gilman tried to form a
Separate congregation. The opinions and behavior of some of this faction were too much even for Isaac Backus, the Separate-Baptist leader,
who visited Durham a few times in the 1750's to encourage the
Separate movement. During his first visit in 1751, Backus discovered
at least one man in Durham affected by "many awful wild extreams
about religion." [51]

An informal schism, in fact, split the church even before Gilman's
death. When the Congregational ministers of New Hampshire decided

in 1747 to organize themselves into a permanent "Convention," they singled out the Durham church, alone of all of those in the province, as needing "some tender Notice." A committee of visitors reported to the Convention that fall that Gilman had for practical purposes withdrawn from the ministry while the most extreme fanatics held separate meetings where "there were very disorderly and vile and absurd things practiced (such as profane singing and dancing, damning the Devil, spitting in Persons Faces whom they apprehended not to be of their Society etc.) greatly to the Dishonor of God and Scandal of Religion." Even then, a more sober-minded faction was taking steps to try to rescue the church from anarchy by looking for a replacement for Gilman.[52]

Gilman had stirred up a storm of enthusiasm that finally became too wild for him to lead or control. Weakened physically in his last years by tuberculosis[53] and emotionally exhausted by a severe case of religious fanaticism and its schismatic consequences, in the end he simply abdicated his pastoral responsibilities while his church all but collapsed around him.

There were few men like Nicholas Gilman anywhere in New England, and especially north of the Merrimack, where the clergy tended to be moderate New Lights such as Mr. Shurtleff of Portsmouth, Mr. Smith of Falmouth, Mr. Wise of South Berwick, and John Newmarch of Kittery.

5

Mr. Newmarch's most distinguished parishioner in 1744 was William Pepperrell, an opulent and pious merchant who was about to become a hero. On January 26, 1744/5, by a majority of one, the Massachusetts General Court voted approval of Governor William Shirley's plan to attack and lay siege to the French fortress of Louisbourg on Cape Breton Island. The governor appointed the popular Pepperrell, justice of the peace, president of the Governor's Council, and colonel of all the Massachusetts militia in Maine, to command the land forces in this audacious assault. Pepperrell had never in his life seen action against an armed enemy. Before deciding to accept, he consulted George Whitefield, who was staying at the Pepperrell mansion in Kittery while preparing for his eastern tour to Falmouth and North Yarmouth.

The evangelist was a personal hero of the colonel's, and perhaps the one man Pepperrell respected above all others. Whitefield knew this, and seems also to have had a more realistic view of the proposed expedition than Governor Shirley and William Vaughan, the principal proponent of the venture. Whitefield told him, therefore, "that he did not think the scheme very promising; that the eyes of all would be on him; that if it should not succeed, the widows and orphans of the slain would reproach him; and if it should succeed, many would regard him with envy, and endeavor to eclipse his glory; that he ought therefore to go with 'a single eye,' and then he would find his strength proportioned to his necessity." [54]

On this bit of comfortless encouragement from the great Awakener, and on further prodding from Shirley, Pepperrell consented, convinced, perhaps, that to lead the expedition would be to fulfill a duty to God as well as to King. Henry Sherburne, Portsmouth merchant and commissary of New Hampshire, later asked Whitefield to give his positive endorsement to the campaign and to provide its motto. Whitefield at first hesitated, then consented. The motto: *"Nil desperandum Christo duce."* [55]

With Christ as leader, Parson Moody of York, now sixty-nine, enlisted under Pepperrell as senior chaplain to the crusade—for that, in his eyes, was precisely what the expedition was to be. Within two months after accepting command and commissions as lieutenant general of the militias of Massachusetts, New Hampshire, and Connecticut, Pepperrell had raised the entire force of 4,300 men planned for the expedition.[56] Five hundred of these were from New Hampshire, and of the 3,250 Massachusetts troops, Maine contributed a third. In Wells, sixty-one men enlisted in one day. About fifty enlisted at York, forty-six at Saco, and nearly fifty at Berwick.[57] Pepperrell wrote to Moses Pearson on February 8 suggesting that he supplement his Falmouth recruits with enough men from Newbury to make up a company, but that he would have to "hasten" if he were to get them.[58] Pearson replied on February 25 that although other recruiters had secured some of his Falmouth prospects ahead of him, he expected to have a company of thirty or more.[59]

Besides supplying the commander of the expedition and troops far out of proportion to their population, Maine and New Hampshire could claim as a joint son Pepperrell's third in command, Brigadier General Samuel Waldo. In addition, the commander of the provincial naval squadron, Edward Tyng, was a Falmouth man. Tyng was promoted from captain to commodore and placed in command of thirteen vessels, two of which were provided by Connecticut, one each by New Hampshire and Rhode Island, and the rest by Massachusetts.[60]

Spirits were high, especially in Maine. The excitement over raising the expedition overshadowed even the anticipated coming of Mr. Whitefield to Falmouth, and probably helped save the parish from serious dissension. "All the talk is about the expedition," wrote Mr. Smith on February 22. He noted "a marvellous zeal and concurrence through the whole country with respect to it; such as the like was never seen in this part of the world." Smith joined the other ministers of the province in holding the annual fast on February 28, an earlier date than usual because of the planned campaign.[61] The experiences of recruiting officers in the eastern regions were bearing out the lament of the Reverend Thomas Prince of Boston, who had observed sadly as he saw the "heavenly shower" of the revivals abating that "from fighting the devil," the recently awakened multitudes "must turn to fighting the French." [62]

In fighting the French, however, some of the participants, including especially the senior chaplain, were certain that they were waging war upon the whore of Babylon. A hundred years of religious backsliding in New England had done little to erase the old English horror of Rome. The recent revivals, with their re-emphasis of Calvinist doctrine and introduction of many easterners for the first time to a positive consciousness of their Protestantism, had helped to confirm such feelings. For as long as New England had existed, the French in America had represented a threat to English territory, English commerce, and English religion. Especially for the easterners, French Jesuits, by their influence upon the Indians, had been responsible for the wars that for a half-century had killed loved ones, disrupted settlements, and destroyed property. The bold plan for a large-scale assault upon the principal French stronghold presented a chance to participate in an historic effort to drive both the secular enemy and the anti-Christ from the continent. Mr. Moody carried along to Louisbourg a hatchet with which he proposed to destroy the idolatrous images in the French church, thereby affirming what to his mind was the specifically religious nature of the crusade.*

The Massachusetts troops, including the three regiments from Maine, sailed from Nantasket on March 24 and joined the New Hampshire forces at Canso, Nova Scotia. On April 22, Commodore Sir Peter Warren joined the provincials at Canso with a squadron of three

---

* This tradition, which seems to be well grounded, has been recorded by virtually every writer on either Mr. Moody or the Louisbourg campaign. See, e.g., Jeremy Belknap: *The History of New-Hampshire* (Dover, N.H., 1812), II, 160, and esp. Francis Parkman: *Half-Century of Conflict* (Boston, 1902), II, 80.

ships of the Royal Navy. The combined force embarked for Louisbourg on April 29 and arrived in the harbor the next morning. The
French garrison, inefficient and lazy, abandoned the main battery to the
invaders in a panic. After a vigorous cannonading of forty-six days,
during which the clumsy and inefficient but spirited New England
troops suffered only negligible losses, the French surrendered.[63] Among
the first within the gates of the captured fortress was the energetic
Father Moody, who used his "Sword of the Lord and of Gideon," as
he had christened his hatchet, for its intended purpose. Then he submitted the denuded church to the final indignity by preaching a
Protestant sermon to a congregation of rustic Yankee soldiers. His text
was "Enter into His gates with thanksgiving, and into His courts with
praise." [64] Presumably, if he intended to identify the "gates" and
"courts" with those of the fortress, they had not really been "His"
until the moment of conquest.

The news arrived in Falmouth on July 6. The townsfolk spent the
afternoon at the fort "rejoicing," as Mr. Smith put it, and firing the
cannon five times. They kept the celebration going throughout the next
day, though it was the Sabbath, and "extravagantly blew off a vast
quantity of powder." [65]

Governor Shirley proclaimed July 18 a day of public thanksgiving,
and Thomas Prince preached in Boston from the text: "This is the
Lord's doing! It is marvellous in our eyes!" Every step of the preparations and the assault, the favorable weather, the strength and skill of
the untrained New England soldiers, and all the circumstances surrounding the campaign—many of which seem indeed to have been un-
commonly fortuitous—Prince ascribed to "a particular Providence."
New England ought to rejoice, said Prince, not only for the salvation
of the colonies and for British trade, but also because "a *great Support*
of *Antichristian* Power is taken away, and the *visible Kingdom* of
CHRIST enlarged." When the pious New England army marched into
the fallen city, the minister thought, "the LORD strong and mighty in
Battle" went in with them and "set up his Standard, proclaimed his
Gospel of Peace, the glad Tidings of Salvation, opened the Prisons, re-
deemed his Captives, and began to receive his grateful Incense of pure
Adoration." Prince prayed that the conquest of Louisbourg would be
"the *dawning Earnest* of our DIVINE REDEEMER'S carrying on his
Triumphs thro' the *Northern Regions,* till He extends his Empire from
the *Eastern* to the *Western* Sea, and from the River of *Canada* to the
Ends of *America*." [66]

Few New Englanders would argue either with Mr. Prince's analysis of the victory or with his prayer for a Protestant continent, though the ranks of at least the eastern companies had undoubtedly been filled with farmers' sons who were more adventurous than pious. The minister had failed to mention, however, the great psychological fact of the expedition. This was not that God was on the side of New England, which had always been common knowledge in Boston anyway, but that the men of New England could plan a major military campaign virtually on its own and, with the help of a small British naval force, successfully carry it out. On August 23, General Pepperrell, still at Louisbourg, received word that King George had made him a baronet.[67] The King also promoted Commodore Warren to admiral, and New Englanders almost to a man now suspected that the British were giving him more credit than was due him for his part in the conquest.[68] This suspicion merely increased the New Englanders' acclaim of their own hero.

King George's war continued for the next three years, during which both the eastern frontier of Maine and the western frontiers of New Hampshire and New York suffered frequent Indian attacks, while many New England soldiers in the occupation garrison at Louisbourg died of disease.* By the inconclusive Treaty of Aix-la-Chapelle, the possessions of Britain and France returned to their prewar owners and so, to the great dismay of New England men, pious and otherwise, Louisbourg was given back to the French. The settlement of the Anglo-French struggle for North American empire was again postponed, but the fired-up Yankees who gladly left their farms and fishnets to follow their great native hero to Louisbourg had demonstrated that Britain no longer could dismiss her American provincials either as pious eccentrics or as rustic clowns. This was particularly important to the easterners, who more than anyone else in the colonies, perhaps, needed reassurance on that score.

* See *Smith and Deane Journals*, pp. 121–31, for accounts of the effect of nearby Indian attacks on the population of Falmouth in this period. See also "Solomon Bragdon's Account Book 1745–1762" (Ms., Maine Historical Society) for an account of a typical small expedition by untrained men in search of harassing Indians. This one left Falmouth on April 24, 1746, to scout the shores of Sebago Lake under Solomon Bragdon. Bragdon and his men found nothing but the tracks of "Mogersons."

CHAPTER XVII

Religion, Society, and Politics

1730–1752

1

The Great Awakening contained many lessons. One was that a man's religion often has at least as much to do with a preference of style, a sense of identity with one or another competing political or economic or intellectual group, a response to charismatic leadership, or the accidents of circumstance as with doctrine. This had, of course, always been so. But the stark issue of revivalism, upon which one could not easily equivocate, brought long-smoldering differences to a head, forced divisions in a New England that had fancied itself united in religion, and made obvious what to many had not been obvious before—that culture is a part of religion and religion is a part of culture.

One practical effect of the new religious enthusiasm on the secular life of northern New England was its transferal to the enthusiasm of adventure and warfare which helped make possible the capture of Louisbourg. With much more deliberate intent, the aspiring rulers of New Hampshire found that religion could be a most useful political tool. Changes in the community of Portsmouth that were ostensibly of a religious nature, therefore, become very much a part of the story of how Benning Wentworth took charge of his province. Conversely, the struggle from which this strong governor and his associated ruling class emerged was nearly as much a conflict involving religious and social antagonisms as a contest between competing political factions.

Portsmouth had been Congregational since 1671, when a church was gathered according to the Massachusetts practice and the Reverend Joshua Moodey, the first minister, took possession of a piece of the glebe land and built a house on it. Chances are that by then, few Portsmouth families retained much special devotion to the Church of England, since Mr. Gibson, the only Anglican preacher in Portsmouth during the seventeenth century, had made his enforced departure nearly thirty years before. Whatever popularity Mr. Moodey may have lacked at first, he gained during his feud with Lieutenant Governor Edward Cranfield, a supporter of the royal prerogative and a staunch Church of England man. The culmination of the little battle came in 1684, when Cranfield imprisoned the minister for refusing to administer Communion to him and other royal officials according to the Church rubric. Upon his release, the conditions of which forbade him to preach in New Hampshire, Moodey fled to Boston. He returned, a martyred hero, in 1693, eight years after Cranfield had been removed, and served the church for the remaining four years of his life.[1]

Since then, despite the tepidness of Portsmouth religion and a split in the parish that was occasioned by a row over the location of a new meetinghouse in 1713, Mr. Moodey's successors in both parishes had lived and worked harmoniously with the townspeople and with each other.[2] It seems unlikely, therefore, that the movement by the leading men of Portsmouth for an Episcopal society in the 1730's could have been related importantly to any deep-seated attachment to their ancestral religion.

It appears, rather, that the movement was in large measure a political one, aimed at cultivating favor in London at a time when relations between New Hampshire and Massachusetts were approaching a crisis. In 1731, after a half-century of dispute between the two provinces over boundary lines, the New Hampshire House of Representatives appointed John Rindge, a Portsmouth merchant bound for England on business, to petition the King for a settlement of the matter. Through the efforts of Rindge, Captain John Thomlinson began his career as New Hampshire's extremely able resident agent in London and started his campaign for fixing both the southern and eastern boundaries in the way most favorable to New Hampshire.

For the first families of the province, there was a great deal more at stake than the settlement of a long political quarrel and the enlargement of the province for its own sake. The Portsmouth merchants wanted a separate governor for New Hampshire. There was reason to suspect that Governor Jonathan Belcher, who governed both Massachusetts and New Hampshire, favored the larger province whenever the interests of the two collided. Much of New Hampshire's trade with England was identical with that of Massachusetts, and any advantage of influence that the province could secure with Crown or creditors would benefit the New Hampshire oligarchy. As the province stood, however, it was too small to attract a royal appointee of any consequence. The governor's salary and perquisites amounted to £800, a sum not worthy the attention of any English gentleman of good standing except as a supplement to the more lucrative Massachusetts post. If New Hampshire's boundaries could be expanded, however, the opportunity for land speculation by the governor and his friends would be opened immediately, and the prospect of an increase in population would mean an eventual growth in the ability of the province to support a governor in proper style.[3]

It was no mere coincidence that at about the time Squire Rindge was presenting the New Hampshire petition at Whitehall in 1732, men such as Theodore Atkinson, John and Benning Wentworth, and Henry Sherburne saw to the building of an Anglican chapel on a hill overlooking the harbor among the riverside residences of the Portsmouth merchants. One of the heaviest contributors to this effort, and indeed the guiding genius behind it all, was Captain Thomlinson. Such a step not only would give the Portsmouth merchants an ecclesiastical tie with their English creditors, which their Massachusetts competitors lacked, but would also give the province the appearance of being an Anglican haven in hostile territory. In addition, it might suggest the possibility of having a New England base at the Piscataqua for the missionary activities of the Society for the Propagation of the Gospel (S.P.G.). None of this could hurt the campaign for a separate royal governor. Besides financial support from Thomlinson and some of his acquaintances in London, the builders of the chapel received from Caroline, the consort of George II, a supply of prayer books, furniture, and silver Communion and Christening vessels emblazoned with the royal arms. To identify the new society with this last gift, also no doubt arranged by Thomlinson, the builders gave to their structure the name of "Queen's Chapel." [4]

A few missionaries of the S.P.G. read Common Prayer, preached, and administered the sacraments from time to time in the new chapel during the next two years. Among them was the Reverend Arthur Browne, who in 1728 had been appointed the missionary at Providence. The Portsmouth men liked Mr. Browne, and Mr. Browne saw the opportunity of making more converts and a better living in Portsmouth and Kittery than at his current station in Rhode Island. In 1734, Theodore Atkinson, Christopher Rymer, John Wentworth, Isaac Sumner, and Joseph Pierce addressed a petition to the Venerable Society in which they asked for Mr. Browne's appointment as missionary to Portsmouth. Lieutenant Governor David Dunbar endorsed the request, and Captain Thomlinson, whose cousin was rector of Wickham and later supplied Mr. Browne with a substantial library, used his influence with the S.P.G. The Society authorized the change in 1736, and social and religious life at "the Banke" was never quite the same.[5]

By 1738, Queen's Chapel had fifty-two communicants, and in that year Mr. Browne baptized seventeen infants in six months' time.[6] Three years later, the missionary reported that of the six to seven hundred families in Portsmouth, between fifty and sixty were "of the Church of *England,* and all the rest Independents, there being neither Quaker, Baptist, Heathen, [n]or Infidel, that he knows of, among them." His schedule included public prayers every morning from May to September and a weekly lecture besides his Sunday services. During these years, the size of the congregation remained very stable; Mr. Browne had only one more communicant in 1741 than in 1738.[7]

In 1741, Thomlinson and the Portsmouth merchants secured an advantageous settlement of the boundaries and the appointment of a separate governor for New Hampshire in the person of Benning Wentworth. This was quite to the liking of the priest, who probably understood very well the political reasons for which he had been brought to New Hampshire and expected in return that the new regime would strengthen the Church of England in the province. Mr. Browne sensed, or at least implied that he did, a conspiracy between Governor Jonathan Belcher and the revivalist party of the Great Awakening to oppose the political goals of the New Hampshire oligarchy by means of religion.

He complained that shortly before the appointment of Wentworth, Belcher had tried to "trepan and overset us, pouring in Preachers from all Parts, pestering and pelting us with Sermons and Lectures some times three or four in a Day." [8] Since the Massachusetts governor had once told the rector of King's Chapel, Boston, that he would rather cut off his daughter's legs "than see her go into the Church," and that Churchmen in New England were "only a loose disaffected Company," [9] there may have been some basis for the suspicion. The Portsmouth men were using religion as a tool to help undermine Belcher, after all, and there is no reason to suppose that the Puritan governor would have scrupled to fight back in kind.

Benning Wentworth, on the other hand, Browne told the Venerable Society, exerted a steadying influence on religion in New Hampshire. The minister reported in 1742: "The steddiness and zealous attachment of his Excellency Governor Wentworth to the Church of England, His discountenancing all our modern extravagances, conferring Posts of Honour upon several of my Parish, showing myself all necessary Countenance in the discharge of my Office by Example and otherwise, have check'd in some measure the growth of Enthusiasm which like an Inundation bid fair to overwhelm us." The change in government, wrote Browne, had been both necessary and providential. Governor Wentworth had proved faithful to a promise he had made to the Bishop of London "to protect and take care of the Church," and "nothing (in human probability) but a Revolution in the Civil affairs of our Province at the critical Juncture it happened could have diverted the Storm. The Enemys whole Artillery seem'd levelled against us, Governor Belcher at the head of them." [10] The new governor now joined the S.P.G., and as a member, occasionally wrote the annual report from Piscataqua in Browne's stead. In each of them, he used the opportunity to heap lavish praise upon the missionary, who became a virtual private chaplain to Wentworth as well as a religious and social leader of Portsmouth.

Both of Portsmouth's Congregational churches were hospitable to the "enthusiasm" of the Great Awakening against which the missionary and the governor fought side by side, and so Queen's Chapel became the obvious resort for all opponents of the revivals in Portsmouth. In the three years following Mr. Browne's report of 1741, his congregation more than doubled. He reported in July, 1744, "that the Infatuation, which had so violently seized both Minister and People among the Dissenters, is much abated, and he [Browne] hath a large Congregation, which behave well, and shew an uncommon Regard to the Rubrick of the Church, and 112 of them are regular Communicants." [11]

The introduction of Anglicanism as the fashionable religion in Portsmouth (and the essential one for any man with aspirations in province politics) brought about changes in the Congregational way of doing things. Mr. Browne noticed soon after his arrival that "The Teachers in those Parts, upon the first Introduction of our Church among them, discovering a wonderful Inclination in the People to a Bishop and Church, have artfully dropt the distinguishing Terms of Teachers and Meeting-houses; and appropriated those of Bishops and Churches to themselves. And now their Teachers are all Bishops, their Meeting houses Churches, and he is a high Flyer that undertakes to shew the Difference." [12]

Mr. Browne was not, of course, an unbiased observer. There is other evidence, however, that the rank and file of Portsmouth, few of whom had occasion to abandon their meetinghouses for Queen's Chapel, and even the Congregational clergy entertained an ill-concealed fascination with Anglican practices. When the Reverend William Shurtleff died in 1747, his parishioners, on a distinctly un-Puritan impulse, buried his remains under the Communion table of the South meetinghouse.[13] In 1763, two "wardens" of First (or North) Parish joined the selectmen of the town in petitioning the governor and General Assembly for permission to hold town meetings henceforth in the "State House." Their reasons, while understandable to the Anglican leaders of the province, would have thrown any Puritan of an earlier generation into an iconoclastic tantrum. The wardens and selectmen were concerned, not only about damage to private pews and cushions in the North meetinghouse, the traditional site of town meetings, but also that "many in the Parish" had complained that it was "a very indecent thing to make an house appropriated and consecrated to the worship of God, the scene for public civil affairs, where the warmest Disputes and Contentions often happen; and woul'd be so estimated by serious Persons of any Religion whatsoever." The General Assembly complied with the request after a second petition from the selectmen a year later.[14]

The presence in Portsmouth of Mr. Browne and his small but influential Anglican congregation, therefore, affected the life of the community profoundly, though sometimes subtly. In a variety of ways, the Piscataqua seaport, never a community of diehard New England saints anyway, departed dramatically from the influence of Boston under the rule of Benning Wentworth and the ministry of Arthur Browne.

2

On the morning of Thursday, January 14, 1741/2, Benning Wentworth announced to a combined session of the General Assembly of New Hampshire that he would "in all faithfulness to the Trust comitted to me strictly support the Honorable interest and Prerogative of the Crown." [15] Thirty-two days previously, royal commission in hand, the new governor had arrived in Portsmouth to take charge of an enlarged province now fully independent of Massachusetts. He had been greeted handsomely with receptions and speeches, in one of which someone praised Wentworth for "rescueing New-Hampshire from contempt and dependence." [16]

For much of the population of the province, including most of the Portsmouth merchant class, there was indeed reason to rejoice. New Hampshire now had her own government, headed by a native son. The King had settled the long boundary controversy with Massachusetts to the great advantage of New Hampshire. Jonathan Belcher, the principal enemy of the Wentworth clan, had been replaced as governor of Massachusetts by William Shirley, an ally and friendly adviser of Wentworth's. Now it was Governor Wentworth's duty to set the tone for his administration, which proved to be the longest continuous one (twenty-five years) in the history of the American colonies.[17] He did it by declaring himself staunchly committed to the interests of the Crown, which he identified with the good of the province, and in effect daring enemies of the prerogative, whether within the province or out of it, to defy his ambitious intentions at their peril.

The governor's policy and the program he presented in his first speech to the Assembly may have raised an eyebrow or two, coming as it did from a man who had gained political prominence principally by taking the popular side against the previous royal governor. In 1730, after the death of his father the lieutenant governor, Wentworth had moved the headquarters of his exporting and importing business from Boston to Portsmouth. As the eldest son and chief heir of John Wentworth, Benning now took his place among the Portsmouth gentry, though he did not abandon his frequent voyages to Spain, where he personally conducted the exchange of the Wentworths' New Hampshire lumber for wine and British credit.[18] Belcher had been appointed governor of Massachusetts and New Hampshire in 1730, a few months before John Wentworth's death, and had plunged almost immediately into a bitter feud with the Wentworth family.

As lieutenant governor under Samuel Shute and William Burnet, John Wentworth had led the faction in New Hampshire that sought the complete separation of the province from Massachusetts. By the 1720's, the fear of proprietary claims, which had been a principal factor in the willingness of the men of New Hampshire to accept the protection of Massachusetts in the seventeenth century, had been largely replaced by apprehension over the more aggressive territorial claims of Massachusetts. Governor Shute had justified such fears by granting Massachusetts townships within territory claimed by New Hampshire, but had secured the support of an influential minority in New Hampshire by including members of that group among the grantees. Wentworth had responded by making his family and its associates, along with every member of the Assembly, proprietors of several townships that he had granted in the name of New Hampshire. Thus there arose a Wentworth party, which controlled the Assembly, and a "Massachusetts party," controlled by Shute and dominated in New Hampshire by the Waldron and Sherburne families, which possessed most of the appointive offices in the executive branch.[19]

When Belcher was being considered for the appointment as governor, John Wentworth had sent him a letter wishing him success. Belcher discovered after his appointment, however, that the lieutenant governor had sent a similar letter to the rival candidate. In his anger at the duplicity, the governor refused Wentworth the customary allowance out of his own salary. He also excluded the Wentworth-controlled Portsmouth oligarchy from any patronage, an act which apparently occasioned his first hostile encounter with young Benning. As a result of Benning's "insolence and ill manners" during that meeting, Belcher informed his friends in Portsmouth that "notwithstanding the young gentleman's pertness, you may let him know I will be his master and every body's else in the Province." [20]

Personal animosity now combined with conflicting interests over lands to provoke open hostility between the two parties and reinforce the desire of the popular Wentworth group to secure an advantageous settlement of the boundary lines and a government that it could control. David Dunbar, who succeeded John Wentworth as lieutenant governor, had had a recent falling-out with Belcher. In order to oppose the recently invigorated "Massachusetts party," which Belcher had made his own by dispensing appointments in crucial places, Dunbar determined to have at least some of his own men on the Council. He asked the Board of Trade to name Benning Wentworth, Joshua Pierce, and Theodore Atkinson to the Council, whereupon Belcher submitted affidavits opposing the "contemptible simpleton" Wentworth in particular, seeking to demonstrate "how unreasonable it is that such a rascal shou'd sit at the Council Board with the Governour." [21] Despite Belcher's opposition, the Board appointed Dunbar's choices. By a legal device, Belcher delayed the seating of Wentworth and Atkinson for two years, but during the delay the two men were elected to the House of Representatives. There they assumed the leadership of the opposition and effectively harried Belcher and his party for seven years by advocating an inflated paper currency and blocking appropriations for salaries and defenses when their paper money bills were vetoed. It was the House that commissioned John Rindge, Wentworth's cousin, to act as agent for the province during a business trip to London; it was Rindge who hired John Thomlinson, the London merchant who became principally responsible for the new fortunes of New Hampshire and the Wentworths, as well as of the Church of England in Portsmouth.[22]

A stroke of bad luck in business had put Benning Wentworth in the governor's chair. In 1733, after he had delivered a huge shipment of timber for the Spanish government at Cadiz, relations between Spain and England took a stormy turn and the Spaniards refused to pay. In order to satisfy his creditors in Boston, Wentworth borrowed money in London. Efforts by the British diplomatic service to secure the payment ended late in the 1730's, when it became apparent that war was inevitable. Wentworth became bankrupt, indebted for £11,000, for which he entered a claim against the British government. Thomlinson secured an agreement from Wentworth's creditors not to jail him if he should come to London, and in 1738 summoned the bankrupt to England, where he informed him of a plot among his creditors to assure him of the governorship if the provinces should be separated. This, Thomlinson had convinced the merchants, was their only hope of being paid, and they had secured a promise from the Duke of Newcastle to make Wentworth governor of New Hampshire upon the settlement of the boundary. The British minister to Spain also approached Newcastle with the argument that Wentworth should be reimbursed for his sufferings from Spain. Thomlinson wrote to Atkinson, who had married Benning's widowed sister Hannah, to promote a collection among the Portsmouth gentry of the £300 that the commission would cost. The commission was signed on June 14, 1741. Two years later, Thomlinson arranged to have Wentworth appointed surveyor general at a salary of £800. In return for this new appointment, Wentworth had to pay Dunbar, the incumbent, £2,000 and agree to drop his claim against the government, thereby assuming personal responsibility for his debts.[23] During the next quarter-century, the new surveyor general realized in full the varied possibilities for profit that induced him to invest so substantially.

Thus it was thanks to his creditors, his friends and relatives in Portsmouth, and the agent of the Assembly that Wentworth was addressing the Assembly as governor on that January 14 instead of lying in a debtor's prison. His manner and demands, however, were anything but humble. Belcher and the Wentworths' enemies in Portsmouth had noticed at least ten years previously, to their great irritation, that Benning had acquired from his long trade with high-placed Spaniards the haughty air of a Spanish grandee. Because of his incessant recounting of the dangers of the mountain passes between Granada and Madrid, they had christened him "Don Granada." [24] Neither his aristocratic manners, which were vexing enough, nor his vociferous attachment to his adopted church settled well with the plain men who made up the majority of his former allies in the House of Representatives. Now, abandoning his old "patriotic" position altogether, Wentworth asked for a permanent salary "suitable to maintaine the dignity of my office" and not subject to depreciation, a limit to paper emissions, a provision to complete the running of the new boundary lines, improvement of the fortifications at Fort William and Mary at Newcastle, construction of a new fort near Lake Winnepesaukee, reimbursement of all who had supported the New Hampshire boundary claims, compensation for Thomlinson, and payment of all the province debts.[25] His friends in the Assembly defined a "suitable" salary as £1,500.[26]

The House promised cooperation but balked at fixing a permanent salary, which Wentworth regarded as a crucial point in establishing royal supremacy in his province. In February, he rejected a vote to pay him £1,500 O.T. (£375 sterling) for his salary till the end of 1742 with the comment that "this so nearly concerns the Honour of the Crown, the Prosperity of the Province, and the peace of its inhabitants, that I should stand highly chargeable with want of duty to my Royal master should I give up so tender a point." He did accept, however, an allowance of £500 out of an unused appropriation for an expedition to the West Indies toward his expenses "in coming to the Government." [27]

By March 3, after several more-or-less courteous exchanges between the governor and the House, Wentworth was so annoyed with the Assembly's failure to settle upon a permanent means of raising money for his salary that he scolded both houses in a message that declared, "Be assured on this point . . . that you are contending with the Crown, and not with the Governor, and that your non-complyance with my request as the Kings Representative, will be Esteemed by his Majesty as the highest act of disobedience." [28] The House then voted an outright grant of £250 to the governor and an additional £250 annually if he would consent to a larger emission of paper currency than he had previously approved. Wentworth hesitated until the Assembly voted another £250 salary for the current year and a £100 allowance for house rent. He then accepted the condition, although the bills of credit authorized over the past three months now exceeded by more than £700 the limit set in the King's instructions to Wentworth. The Crown, however, consented to the compromise.[29]

In the first small round of the contest between governor and Assembly, both sides had made concessions, but on balance, it was a clear defeat for Wentworth and the royal prerogative. The lines of conflict were familiar ones in all the colonies: a permanent salary for the governor rather than one fixed annually by the legislature, paper money, appropriations for defense, and above all, the question of whether the King's representative or the popular assembly should win the struggle for political power. Wentworth, who had fought on the "patriotic" side against Belcher, now had suffered his first defeat in the opposite role. He had made it clear to the Assembly, however, that old friendships and alliances counted for little in his determination to uphold the Crown. The fight promised to be a long one, and the new governor no ordinary contestant.

3

The New Hampshire over which stout Benning Wentworth assumed charge in 1741 had not only been greatly increased in area, but had doubled in population since 1730. There were now 20,000 inhabitants in about twenty-five towns, thirteen of which were large enough to send representatives to the General Assembly. Some of the new population, not yet incorporated into New Hampshire towns, had been living in the northern parts of six Massachusetts townships when the new boundary had been drawn to the south of their villages and farms. The twenty-eight townships recently granted by Massachusetts between the Merrimack and the Connecticut, some of which contained a few inhabitants but none of which was an incorporated town, were now also within the province.[30]

The residents of the coast and the Piscataqua River region were enjoying the benefits of a mature village society despite the unsettling effects of political uncertainty and ecclesiastical quarrels. A string of rural townships had transformed the Merrimack Valley into a fruitful agricultural country as far north as Concord. Pioneering Ulstermen or their sons were beginning to push their search for farms to the west of the Merrimack, and a few small settlements, such as the ones at Upper and Lower Ashuelot (Keene and Swansey) and Number Four (Charlestown) had sprung up around frontier garrisons established by Massachusetts in the Connecticut Valley.

During the next nineteen years, under Governor Wentworth, the population doubled again.[31] In the same period, the province incorporated another twenty-two towns, not including the townships Wentworth granted west of the Connecticut in his attempt to establish the jurisdiction of New Hampshire in the present state of Vermont.[32]

During the 1730's and 1740's, the upper class of Portsmouth added importantly to the growing number of gracious houses that distinguished the little seaport. Because it was readily and cheaply accessible, wood remained the usual building material. In scale and style of construction, however, several houses of this period were worthy neighbors of the brick mansion of Archibald Macpheadris.

The houses of the thirties began with a clapboard dwelling built on Court Street between 1730 and 1740 and later acquired by Stephen Chase. While on the whole rather plain and perhaps a little forbidding in appearance, this large house, with its gambrel roof and small dormer windows, pediments and corinthian pilasters at both front and side doorways, and angle quoins at the corners, is an authentic and dignified example of the early Georgian style.[33] In 1732, Captain Samuel Frost built a house of comparable size but of an older style. This, too, had a gambrel roof, but there were no dormers. It retained the massive central chimney of an earlier day at a time when the more stylish builders were using two smaller and more graceful chimneys on the back side of the roof in order to provide larger front rooms, more fireplaces, and a more convenient and more handsome stairway. Though the façade of the sea captain's house was symmetrical, the second-floor windows were smaller than those on the ground floor and looked as though they had been crowded under the eaves. Captain Frost made no attempt to introduce the classical details of the Georgian period.[34] In 1735, Matthew Livermore, a Harvard graduate who had recently progressed from town schoolmaster to attorney general of the province and King's advocate in the Courts of Admiralty, added a stately clapboard residence to the Portsmouth scene.[35] The Livermore house featured the gambrel roof, two chimneys, and a handsome segmental pediment and fluted doric pilasters at the front doorway.[36] Since Livermore was an appointee of Belcher's and an attorney for the governor, his fine house provided tangible evidence that taste and means were not limited to the Wentworth circle, whose contest with the Belcher men was at that time still far from won.*

* In 1731, after having taught school in Portsmouth for seven years while reading law, Livermore was admitted to the New Hampshire bar as the first college-educated lawyer in the province. When Belcher offered to appoint him attorney general in 1733, Livermore held out until he was also given the post of King's Advocate. He was paid by Massachusetts for services rendered during the boundary dispute, despite the fact that he was at the same time attorney general of New Hampshire. Barred from the Portsmouth oligarchy and from important offices after 1741 because of his former connections, Livermore nevertheless was

Several important houses were built about 1740, the most elaborate one by Colonel Nathaniel Meserve, a shipbuilder. Meserve's house overlooked his shipyard on the North Mill Pond. Despite the flat cornice treatment of the doorway, the dormer windows of this house were surmounted by scroll pediments. Its gambrel roof, clapboard construction, and angle quoins on the corners make the Meserve dwelling almost a classic example of early Georgian architecture, much like the Chase house. Successive additions to the west end of the building have transformed the structure into a row house.[37] In 1749, the parishioners of the Reverend Samuel Langdon, pastor of North Church and later president of Harvard, built a simple but handsome parsonage with gambrel roof, segmented pediment, and a pair of imposing gateposts flanking the seven granite steps between the street and the door.[38]

While the life of most of northern New England was devoted almost single-mindedly to the pioneer tasks of rebuilding and new settlement in the aftermath of King William's and Queen Anne's wars, the residents of Portsmouth, in their relative comfort and security, shared with the more populous urban centers to the south some of the larger public concerns of the day. Commerce and provincial politics commanded by far the greatest attention from the rapidly developing oligarchy. But as readers of the Boston press, Portsmouth people also followed with fascination the debate over smallpox inoculation that raged throughout the English-speaking world in the early 1720's, the attempt to provide explanations both natural and supernatural for the troublesome series of minor earthquakes that visited New England from 1727 through the 1730's, and the various paper currency schemes of the few years surrounding 1740. Like colonists in Boston and Philadelphia, they watched eagerly for accounts from the court of their new German-speaking King, from the gentlemanly battlefields on which the gaily dressed armies of the Bourbons and the Hapsburgs were acting out the current phase of the European power struggle, and from "Petersburg" (New England newspapers eschewed the popish "Saint") for the latest glimpse of the fascinating

---

paid in frontier lands for legal services to both Governor Wentworth and the Masonian Proprietors. Eventually, therefore, he became a proprietor of twenty-seven New Hampshire townships. He also served, in his later years, as a member and clerk of the House and as a justice of the peace. Livermore was a Harvard classmate of two prominent Portsmouth men, Colonel William Vaughan and Richard Wibird, who was collector of customs and sheriff in New Hampshire under Belcher, but was later accepted into the ruling class and given a seat on the Council and two judgeships. *Sibley's Harvard Graduates* (for complete citation, see the *List of Frequent Abbreviations*, p. 363), VII, 88–90, 128–36, 139–41.

spectacle of a Russia being yanked precipitously by Peter the Great into the western world of the eighteenth century.[39]

Except when an issue touched their immediate interests, however, the Portsmouth gentry and "middling sort" observed the larger affairs of the day merely as a diversion. At this stage, the town boasted no intellectual or cultural life worth mentioning; even as late as 1756, a correspondent to the newly founded *New-Hampshire Gazette* scolded his countrymen for their indifference to education and exclusive concern for their own "patrimony." [40]

We know that the Boston press was read in Portsmouth and some of the other towns beyond the Merrimack because of the frequent advertisements and correspondence from these communities that appeared in such journals as the *New-England Courant* and the *New-England Weekly Journal* during these years.[41] James Franklin introduced his lively *Courant* to New Hampshire by sending free copies to Portsmouth taverns in 1721, only to have it suppressed by provincial authorities the following year when he ran a series of satirical comments on the province's controversial new law against "Riotous and Tumultuous Meetings." [42]

Although Eleazar Russell was selling books in Portsmouth between 1716 and 1736,* there was no printing press in the town until 1756, and the upper class showed little interest in literature until 1750, when thirty-four of the gentry formed the "Library Society of Portsmouth." [43] Supported by a lively commerce, however, and intrigued and titillated by the social and religious innovations and political power struggles which they were observing at first hand, the men of Portsmouth were prone to congratulate themselves during the early Wentworth years for living in an exciting time and place.

4

Different attitudes toward two fundamental questions lay at the bottom of all the issues that divided Benning Wentworth and his

---

*See Charles Evans, ed.: *American Bibliography* (Chicago, 1903–34), entries 1842, 2784, 2960, 2961, 4014, and 4015, for books printed in Boston especially for distribution by Russell. All of them were of purely local interest: two editions of the laws of New Hampshire, two sermons by the Reverend William Shurtleff, minister of Portsmouth's South Church, and the account by the Reverend Jabez Fitch, minister of the North Church, of the epidemic of "throat distemper" in New Hampshire in the 1730's, and his sermons on the epidemic. This epidemic and the reactions to it are discussed in Chapter XVI.

aristocratic friends from a strong opposition party. The first was whether the province would remain in any sense a "colony" of Massachusetts, either by eventual reunion or by some lesser and more subtle degree of alliance. The question was partly social, partly religious, and partly a matter of personal advantage to be answered depending upon where one felt his best interests lay. Even at this late hour, the renunciation of the cultural and political conquest of the seventeenth century was not a matter of firm consensus.

The other question was that of the constitutional relationship between the governor and the Assembly, though it was practically never debated in such terms and undoubtedly seldom conceived of in this way in New Hampshire or any other colony. Wentworth, like most royal governors, determined to prove his and the province's loyalty to the King by rigidly following his royal instructions. These he regarded as the only legal (he never used the term "constitutional") basis of government in the province, including the existence of the Assembly itself. His opponents in the Assembly, on the other hand, habitually theorized about the prerogatives of the legislature. They based their arguments upon precedent and, occasionally, upon drawing parallels with the English Parliament—but never, in that period, upon theories of popular sovereignty. The "constitutional" struggle—for that is what it really was—was to the contestants merely a fight for power; the side one took in this fight was likely to be determined by the same considerations that fixed his attitude toward the question of Massachusetts.[44]

At the beginning of Wentworth's administration, the principal allies and closest associates of the governor were Theodore Atkinson, his brother-in-law and chief lieutenant; Joshua Pierce, whom Dunbar had nominated with Wentworth and Atkinson to the Council; Mark Hunking Wentworth, the governor's brother and an assemblyman from Portsmouth; George Jaffrey, who had married the governor's sister, the widow of Captain Macpheadris; the Reverend Mr. Browne; and, in London, Captain Thomlinson. Atkinson, Pierce, and Jaffrey were serving on the Council along with three former Belcher men, Henry and Joseph Sherburne and Richard Wibird. Henry Sherburne was an uncle of the governor by marriage, and Wentworth may have considered the Sherburnes reliable supporters at first. But Henry Sherburne, Jr., the son of the councilor, soon was elected to the Assembly and dared challenge the prerogative. The alliance, if there ever was one, between the Wentworths and this prominent rival commercial family promptly ended. On the other hand, Wibird, whose sister was married to Mark Hunking Wentworth, was absorbed rapidly into the Wentworth group.*

Against the powerful Wentworth faction was arrayed a much more diffuse but nevertheless effective opposition. Its leader was Richard Waldron, who as a descendant of the principal settler of Dover (Major Richard Waldron), the first president of New Hampshire (John Cutt), and the Vaughans of Portsmouth, probably could claim a more respectable ancestry than any other man in the province.[45] As provincial secretary, judge of common pleas, councilor, judge of probate, and naval officer under Belcher, Waldron had become the governor's principal weapon against Lieutenant Governors Wentworth and Dunbar and now assumed the leadership of the old Belcher party and remained thoroughly committed to reunion with Massachusetts. Waldron had relied for a living upon political preferment rather than upon commerce, was a staunch member of North Church, lived in the "Plains" section of Portsmouth rather than at the "Banke," and was married to the daughter of Colonel Thomas Westbrook,

---

* Though Henry Sherburne, Jr., and his cousin Benning Wentworth fought in opposite political camps during much of their careers, the governor seems always to have maintained a high respect for the abilities and the patriotism of his kinsman. Sherburne, whose great-grandfather was one of Captain John Mason's original "servants" at the Piscataqua and who also shared with the governor the same Wentworth grandfather, was as much a part of the Portsmouth gentry as the governor himself. He inherited and furthered the fortunes of a flourishing mercantile business, lived in his father's house at the "Banke," and married the daughter of Daniel Warner. Wentworth recognized in his cousin's long and varied public service a truly "loyal opposition," and despised only Sherburne's abandonment of Queen's Chapel for South Church and his attachment to the New Lights during the revivals. Sherburne's fellow members of the large and important class of 1728 at Harvard included an interesting assortment of New Hampshiremen: Samuel Wentworth, Benning's brother, who became a Boston merchant, stayed out of politics, and was assigned a social rank in the class second only to that of the second William Phips; Thomas Wibird, the son of Richard, who was involved with Sherburne in a college scandal involving the beating of freshmen; Joshua Pierce's son Daniel, who married the daughter of John Rindge in 1742, became the second highest taxpayer in Portsmouth, and like his father, held a variety of town and provincial offices; and Joseph Newmarch, son of the Reverend John Newmarch of Kittery. Young Newmarch married the sister of Sir William Pepperell, and in 1751 was appointed a councilor from Newcastle by Governor Wentworth. The third-ranking member of the class was Jonathan Belcher, the son of the Wentworths' foremost political enemy, who became governor of Massachusetts and New Hampshire in 1730. *Sibley's Harvard Graduates*, VIII, 341, 343, 455–7, 460–3, 490–5, 526–7, 530–2. For members of the Council in 1741, see *Provincial Papers of New Hampshire*, V, 87.

whose relationship with the Portsmouth oligarchy is unclear because he moved to Falmouth before the beginning of the Belcher regime.[46] For all these reasons, Waldron had little in common with the commercial aristocracy. Furthermore, his commitment to Belcher, which had ripened into one of the former governor's very few firm personal friendships, was so deep as to be unretractable at the time of Benning Wentworth's appointment, even had the Wentworth group solicited his support. Within a few years, Henry Sherburne, Jr., became Waldron's chief deputy, and after Waldron's death assumed the leadership of the "patriot" forces.

Waldron found most of his support, however, in the old towns of Dover, Hampton, and Exeter, the three communities in the province with authentic Puritan roots in the early seventeenth century, and in a few of the new interior communities near the Merrimack. The large and influential Gilman family of Exeter and Newmarket was to a man fiercely opposed to the Wentworths and carried the burden of the fight against the prerogative in the Assembly in the years immediately following Benning Wentworth's accession. At that time, this important clan of Congregationalist yeomen, headed by Major Peter Gilman of Exeter, furnished three of the twenty members of the House of Representatives.[47] The family included Nicholas Gilman, the eccentric New Light minister in Durham. The diary he kept from 1740 to 1744 deals mainly with his own spiritual development, but it also contains occasional political comments, which are inseparable from his views on religious matters. In the early 1740's, the minister made frequent references to "New England" but few to "New Hampshire" except, on fast days, to refer to observances in "both provinces." His prayers and his travels indicate that he felt a much greater attachment to Boston, the northern Massachusetts towns, and the communities of southern Maine than to Portsmouth, which he visited only rarely. In March, 1740, among observations on community and family happenings, illnesses, and fears of a new war —all religiously "improved"—Gilman wrote, "Portsmouth gentlemen in hope of a new Governour—I hope they will in Mercy be disappointed." In May of the same year, he not only reflected his own religious sentiments, but undoubtedly gave a very mild expression of the political views of his entire family when he commented: "It Seems now on all hands expected that the Line will soon be Settled between Massachusetts and New Hampshire and that this will be a separate Government. May all be in Mercy to this poor divided province." [48]

5

The fundamental goal of the "patriot" party remained unchanged through the first ten years of Wentworth's administration: to get rid of the new governor. The basic strategy was to prevent Wentworth from complying with his royal instructions in order to discredit him with the King. Both sides, therefore, attached great importance to the question of the fixed salary, a matter of high priority in Wentworth's first instructions.

Wentworth's basic counter-strategy, equally uncomplicated, was merely to replace his strongest foes in the Assembly with his friends. When, on two occasions, he attempted to pack the House by calling representatives from towns that had been unrepresented before, the House denied his right to issue election precepts. During the ensuing constitutional crises, the business of the province stood still until one side or the other capitulated. In the first instance, it was Wentworth who gave in, temporarily sacrificing his long-range objective of establishing the prerogative in order to secure enough funds to carry on the war of 1744–8. After the war, however, at the cost of causing a hiatus of all legislation for three years, Wentworth emerged from the second such crisis with an unqualified victory.

Within three or four years after Wentworth became governor, his relations with the yeoman-dominated House of Representatives became rancorous in the extreme. Although Wentworth yielded to the House when necessary for tactical reasons, the haughty manner in which he phrased his demands and the frequent scoldings he administered to the uncooperative representatives quickly brought latent hostilities to the surface. The question of maintaining Fort Dummer, a frontier stronghold that had been established by Massachusetts but which was located north of the new boundary, provoked the first constitutional crisis and a particularly sharp exchange between governor and representatives.

In September, 1744, the King ordered Wentworth to take charge of the fort and keep it in defensible order. Simply because the King had commanded it was reason enough for Wentworth to proceed, but there were also other advantages to be gained in following the order. By taking over the fort, Wentworth could ingratiate himself with his friend, Governor Shirley, who put pressure on New Hampshire to defend it, and enhance his plan for expanding the dominion of the province beyond the Connecticut River. By this time, however, he understood his opponents' strategy and knew well that they would use their majority in the House to block any appropriations for Dummer. To change the balance of power, therefore, Wentworth ordered elections of representatives in five of the new towns and districts that had never before been represented in the General Assembly.[49] When the Assembly convened in January, 1744/5, the House elected Nathaniel Rogers of Portsmouth as speaker, but not before voting to prevent the representatives of the new places from taking part in the choice. The governor approved the speaker in order to avoid a prolonged dispute at a critical time, but warned the representatives that they had been guilty of "invading the Prerogative of the Crown," and that he would take his case to the King.[50]

As Wentworth had foreseen, the assemblymen balked at fortifying Fort Dummer, especially since most of them questioned the value of a fort on the Connecticut far to the west of the towns from which most of them were elected. The upcountry representatives, awakened, evangelical, and anti-French, shared Wentworth's enthusiasm for the New England expedition against Louisbourg in 1745 and, with the governor's encouragement, issued £10,000 in bills of credit to finance the campaign and provide other wartime expenses.[51] Not even the warning that the King might restore the fort and a large tract of adjoining territory to Massachusetts, however, was enough to provoke speedy action on Fort Dummer. Part of the assemblymen's reticence resulted from their being irked, with some justification, because the governor had demanded immediate action on the matter after withholding the King's order from the Assembly for more than a month.[52] Their message to the governor on April 3, 1745, in which they needled him on this point, brought forth the following retort from Wentworth:

> Your Message of this day is not the first instance wherein you have trifled with the prerogative and Royal orders laid before you, treated the King's Governor in terms unworthy to be repeated from the Chair, and in language unbecoming an address to an Inferior.[53]

The House reacted explosively with two replies, one drafted by Rogers, the speaker, and the other by Henry Sherburne, the governor's New Light cousin. Both responses virtually declared open warfare upon the prerogative. Sherburne's reply, full of patriotic rhetoric, was somewhat the bolder of the two:

> Your Excellencys manner of treating this House, the Representatives of a Free People is intirely new unparliamentary and with-

out Precedent of which your Excellency's verbal and written Messages of the 3rd Current are not the first Instances. Your Excellencys Reflections on the House are so Gross and Coarse that should we answer them in equal Terms and Language it might be justly stiled unworthy and unbecoming and till your Excellency pleases to point out particular Instances to support your high charges these Indignities according to your Excellency's own Maxim must Center upon the author and we shall think ourselves and the People we represent highly injured—

We assure your Excellency that all Messages from this House are the genuine sentiments of the House and flatter ourselves that if your Excellency had duly deliberated on the Truths contained in our Messages and the Method of treating free Parliaments the Reflection on this head would have been spared—[54]

Speaking through Sherburne, the "Representatives of a free People" claimed that during previous administrations they had "been strangers to arbitrary power and this makes any thing that looks like an Invasion upon our Rights and Privileges the more irksome and tedious to us." Though Sherburne could complain eloquently about gubernatorial insults, he himself was not above indulging in a turn of phrase well-calculated to stir the governor's rage. While promising that the Assembly would settle the matter of Fort Dummer if given time to consider it thoroughly, Sherburne refused to permit his colleagues to share any of the blame for the delay. "In the mean time," he wrote, "[we] must say that if any Part of the Province should be lost for want [of] a Resolve of this House to go by the Fleet now in Port waiting for a wind the Blame must not lay on this House but must wholly lay where His Majestys Royal Orders in Council lay all the Month of March." [55]

Despite the Assembly's firm resolve to resist dictation by the governor, there was some sentiment in the House for adopting Fort Dummer in order not to rebuke the King and risk an alteration of the new boundary line. Andrew Wiggin of Stratham, a respected former speaker of the House, presented an articulate statement of this view to the House on the same day that the two virulent replies were directed to the governor.[56] Perhaps because of Wiggin's influence and because the governor finally complied with a demand for an attested copy of the King's instruction, the number of members who favored accepting the fort increased in a month's time from two to six. This was still only half the number of opponents, however, and on May 3,

Wentworth dissolved the Assembly and called at once for new elections.[57]

The governor's men went to work in the local hustings throughout the province and succeeded in unseating Meshech Weare of Exeter and Ebenezer Stevens of Kingston, two leaders of the opposition, and managed to delay the seating of Israel Gilman of Exeter, another key opponent. They were most successful in Dover, where they secured the election of three definite supporters. The new Assembly convened on June 5, and on June 15, when Sherburne was absent, Wentworth's supporters introduced the measure for accepting Fort Dummer. The result was a vote of 12–4 in favor and the passage of a resolution to support twenty men at the fort for six months.[58] In winning his first important victory, Wentworth had demonstrated both his obstinacy and his political adroitness, but had created a legacy of bitterness between himself and the popular side which in succeeding years required all his power and skill to surmount.

The year after the resolution of the Fort Dummer affair, the Wentworth oligarchy presented the assemblymen with a new reason for hostility. Twelve of the Portsmouth merchant class bought up the old Mason claim just as the General Assembly reached a long-delayed decision to buy the claim in the name of the province. The purchasers, known thereafter as the Masonian proprietors, included most of the leading merchants except the governor himself. Wentworth's kinsmen and associates, in fact, carried out the deal behind his back, and he was as furious as his opponents in the Assembly. He soon backed down, however, from a move to force the proprietors to surrender their large holding to the Crown.[59] Though the shrewd governor, for once, had had no part in an unpopular power play, the Wentworths and their relatives acquired more than half of the claim.

The purchasers quieted the fears of settlers in townships within the Masonian patent that had been granted by other authority by deeding the lands in those towns to the existing proprietors. They granted other townships in the claims to various groups of petitioners under the usual terms of settlement, often without fees and always without quit-rents, reserving only fifteen rights in each township for themselves, two for their attorneys, one for the ministry, one for the first settled minister, and one for a school. The proprietors' wise administration of the purchase calmed most of the opposition to their claim, even among those who could not ignore the fact that Governor Samuel Allen had bought title to the New Hampshire lands from the heirs of Captain Mason in 1691, and that Allen's title had been recognized in the Massachusetts charter of 1692. Local conflicts over the bounds of the purchase, however, continued until the Revolution because of the difficulty of surveying the curved line sixty miles from the mouth of the Piscataqua that marked the outer edge of the Masonian lands. Such controversies, of course, served to intensify the political alienation of the upcountry yeomanry from the oligarchy of Portsmouth.[60]

Until the end of King George's War, Governor Wentworth skirmished constantly with the Assembly. The assemblymen won their cause time and again when the governor gave in to demands for emissions of paper currency that exceeded the limit fixed by the King and other popular legislation in order to keep the government functioning so that the province could meet the demands of war. The return of peace in 1748 ended Wentworth's urgent need for appropriations. In the more relaxed atmosphere of the postwar years, he determined to win his battle for the prerogative at any cost. At the same time, Richard Waldron, whom Wentworth had removed from the Council and dismissed from his other official jobs in 1742,[61] was at work on a new plan to get Wentworth out of the governor's chair.

Waldron's strategy was two-fold: to find a suitable candidate who was ready to spend the time and the money it would take to seek to replace Wentworth, and then to secure sufficient strength in the Assembly to file an official complaint against the governor. Waldron and his associates—the Sherburnes, Councilor Ellis Huske, and Assemblymen Peter Gilman, James Clarkson, and Thomas Millet—found their man in Colonel Isaac Royall, a wealthy merchant and representative to the Massachusetts General Court from Charlestown. Royall, like Henry Sherburne, Jr., was a close friend of George Whitefield, the evangelist. He was willing to spend £500 for the governorship and was supported by Slingsly Bethell, a wealthy and influential member of Parliament from London. At the same time, Nathaniel Sparhawk (pronounced Sparruck), the son-in-law of Sir William Pepperrell, the hero of Louisbourg, gave Wentworth's opponents what seemed to be yet another trump card by proposing the celebrated baronet for the post. Sir William himself, however, never actively pursued the candidacy, which was apparently taken seriously by few aside from the ambitious Sparhawk, who had his eye on the fruitful office of surveyor general of the woods. Waldron made Belcher privy to the conspiracy to remove Wentworth, but in New Hampshire, kept the plan a secret from all but a few of his most trusted allies.[62]

The popular party hoped to dominate the elections to the House of Representatives in 1748, and wanted particularly to return Waldron to the Assembly, where he could better direct the plan for addressing an official petition to the Crown. Wentworth, though he never gave any sign that he was aware of the conspiracy against him, had his own ideas about the coming elections. On them, he determined to establish the right of the King's representative to issue precepts to towns of his own choosing and to enforce the Royal instructions upon the House. He delayed calling the elections, therefore, until he had received instructions from the Crown. On June 30, the Lords Justices sent the expected instructions to dissolve the present Assembly and order new elections, including specifically the election of assembly-men by the King's writ in the towns and districts whose representatives the House had refused to seat in 1745. "The Right of sending Representatives to the said Assembly," wrote the judges, "was founded originally on the Commissions and Instructions given by the Crown to the respective Governors of the Province of New Hampshire, and His Majesty may therefore lawfully extend the Privilege of sending Representatives to such New Towns as His Majesty shall judge to be worthy thereof." [63]

The elections were held late in 1748. The popular party was successful in electing Waldron from the old Massachusetts town of Hampton rather from his own town of Portsmouth, and seven of Waldron's firm adherents, including Henry Sherburne, Jr., and Peter Gilman. Five of the twenty-five members had been elected in the new towns and districts on the King's writ issued by Wentworth. When the Assembly convened in January, 1748/9, the House elected Waldron speaker after barring the representatives of Chester and South Hampton, the only two of the five new members who appeared on the first day, from taking part in the choice. The governor disapproved of the selection, and the House replied with a long constitutional argument attempting to demonstrate its right to pass upon the qualifications of its own members. A heated exchange of messages took up all the business of the province until April 7, when the House adopted a strong petition to the King listing the assemblymen's grievances against Wentworth. It ended with a plea that the Assembly "may be continued in their ancient usage and custom of having a vote in the Privileging of Places to send representatives to the said Assembly" and that Wentworth "may be removed and a Gentleman of more knowledge in Matters of Government, and a better Disposition to cherish the Duty and affection of your Majestys subjects to your Majesty, may be placed in his room." [64]

The petition was sent by way of John Thorpe, a lawyer of Lincoln's Inn, who replied that the law was on Wentworth's side, and that the petition was more likely to strengthen royal support of the governor than to weaken it. Thus discouraged, Royall removed himself from the candidacy for the governor's chair.[65]

Far from prosecuting an aggressive campaign against the governor, the Waldron party now found itself in the position of a defendant whose very life was in danger. The financial state of the province was precarious, but Wentworth was making a good living and paying off his debts through his activities as surveyor general and by fees from granting interior lands. He was prepared for a "war of attrition," as Leonard W. Labaree has phrased it, and kept provincial business at a standstill for three long years by adjourning the Assembly repeatedly during its refusal to admit the new members and elect a different speaker. The Assembly weakened once in 1750, when it offered to admit the new representatives if the governor would submit the original copy of his royal instructions for the perusal of the House. Wentworth replied that the instructions were addressed to himself only, and that

> I know of no Instructions that the King has commanded to lay before you, more than has been laid before former Assemblys as occasions offered, there are many which I am to communicate to his Majesty's council; because their advice and consent is necessary therein, but I don't find in the whole body of the Royal Instructions, that I am commanded to advise and consult with the Assembly, or lay any Instruction before them for their consideration, but for their complyance only therewith.[66]

The deadlock ended only with the expiration of the Assembly in January, 1752, under the terms of a province law which fixed a limit of three years on the life of any Assembly. After a delay of eight months, Wentworth summoned a new Assembly, which within twenty days had admitted the new representatives, chosen a speaker acceptable to the governor (Meshech Weare), increased the governor's salary, and conducted several other important matters of province business. Not until 1775 did the Assembly again challenge a governor's right to summon representatives. By choosing a time of peace for his decisive battle with the House, Wentworth was spared the necessity of appealing for vital appropriations for defense at whatever cost to the prerogative. It was the Assembly, concerned over the exposed condition of the frontier towns that it represented and the lack of circulating currency, that finally gave in. "Had there been more Benning Wentworths in the provinces," wrote Labaree in his authoritative study of royal government in America, "colonial history might have taken a different course." [67]

6

After Wentworth's unqualified defeat of a popular challenge to his authority, an unusual event in the colonies made all the more extraordinary in the light of the political acuity of the opposition, relations between governor and Assembly took on a markedly different tone. Though Waldron was elected to the Assembly of 1752, he did not take his seat. He resigned the following February, and died in August, leaving what remained of the popular party largely in the hands of Henry Sherburne, Jr. Sherburne balanced his "patriotic" views, which probably never were as extreme as those that Waldron had found convenient to espouse after the removal of Belcher, with a sense of honesty and public responsibility. As a result of service as a delegate to an intercolonial convention on the war in 1746 and to the Albany conference with the Six Nations in 1754, he had acquired a breadth of view that extended beyond provincial politics. He performed valuable service as a member of many legislative committees, and served for three years as clerk of the House and thirteen years as speaker. When he was re-elected speaker in 1762, Governor Wentworth approved the choice but expressed his reluctance, not because of animosity toward his cousin but because of Sherburne's poor health.[68]

After 1752, Wentworth dealt with a chastened Assembly and a leader of the opposition whom he not only respected, but with whom he must also have felt a certain identification. Sherburne, after all, was a close kinsman of the governor's and a member, however errant, of the same Portsmouth gentry. In any case, the warring parties entered an era of at least partial reconciliation, which had progressed so far by 1767, when the aged and gout-ridden governor retired to make room for his nephew, John Wentworth, that the Assembly praised him almost to the point of extravagance. A resolution of the House thanked him "for all the signal services you have done this

Province . . . during the long time you have with such Reputation and Honor fill'd the Chair; for the steady Administration of Justice, the quiet enjoyment of Property, the Civil and Religious Liberties and Priviledges his Majesty's good subjects of this Province have experienced and Possess'd during the Period." [69]

One ought not to suppose, however, that the political conflict that Benning Wentworth fought and won between 1742 and 1752 resulted merely from a vendetta between the Wentworths and the Belcher-Waldron alliance. Personal grievances were of course instrumental in the hostilities, as they have been in political struggles, great and small, throughout history. Nevertheless, the fight for power in New Hampshire was far more than a quarrel between two strong, hostile men. In the hope of achieving his own ends, Waldron championed the cause of plain country yeomen who shared republican prejudices against Wentworth's manners and style of living, a Puritan hostility toward his religion, the desire of any debtor class for an inflated currency, a frontiersman's concern for local protection, and the Yankee suspicion of strong government. Neither Waldron nor any other man created this cluster of attitudes; instead, he attempted to capitalize on attitudes that already existed among the majority of New Hampshiremen. The men who held them were far more representative of New Englanders as a whole, including northern New Englanders, than the plutocrats who dined at Wentworth's banquet table and took Communion from Parson Browne.

Wentworth's victory not only established the royal prerogative in the government of New Hampshire but also demonstrated the dominance of the merchant oligarchy of Portsmouth in all the affairs of the province. After 1753, this powerful group could claim, if so inclined, that it had even furnished the leader of the severely weakened opposition. The oligarchs did more than simply dazzle with courtly pretensions the country folk who came to sit in the legislature. They understood the economy and the politics of the province, the nature of intercolonial rivalries, and the uses of favoritism.* Through their agent, Thomlinson, they possessed a well-oiled machinery for access to Whitehall—an advantage which becomes all the more con-

---

* Jere R. Daniell, in "Politics in New Hampshire under Governor Benning Wentworth, 1741–1767," *William and Mary Quarterly,* 3rd Ser., XXIII (January 1966), correctly emphasizes Wentworth's effective use of political and economic rewards, especially judicial and military appointments and lavish grants of land, in gaining and encouraging political allies in the Assembly and elsewhere. Daniell's article is based in part on his important unpublished dissertation, "New Hampshire Politics and the American Revolution, 1741–1790" (Harvard University, 1964).

spicuous when compared with the fumbling attempts of the Waldron group to secure a royal hearing. Equally important was the fluency with which men experienced from youth in foreign trade could speak and understand the language of diplomats and statesmen.

The oligarchy used all of its urbane advantages, first against Massachusetts and then against the New Hampshire majority, in a relentless campaign for wealth, power, and prestige. The accomplishment of Benning Wentworth and his small group of associates in gaining unquestioned supremacy in the province is proof of their unusual energies and abilities. It was an accomplishment that eclipsed, and in many ways reversed, the Puritan conquest of New Hampshire.

CHAPTER XVIII

Cultural Beginnings
1750–1760

1

The decade of the 1740's had been a tumultuous one for the north-eastern seaboard society centered at New Hampshire's stylish capital on the Piscataqua. The Massachusetts boundary question, the struggle for political power between the Wentworth oligarchy and the upcountry yeomanry, the excitement and disputes of the Great Awakening, and the campaigns of King George's War all had contributed to a sense of more-or-less continual crisis. Now all this was over. Gentry and plain folk alike settled down to enjoy and profit from the temporary calm in provincial and intercolonial affairs that came after 1748. With the achievement of political stability and self-sufficiency in New Hampshire and a new indulgence of sophisticated tastes, there came at last a limited awakening of the mind.

The erection of handsome upper-class residences in Portsmouth that had begun on a significant scale in the 1730's continued through the 1750's and beyond. Now, however, there was a noticeable new elegance. About 1750, Portsmouth builders began to place three stories beneath the eaves of a much flatter roof than had been the custom with the gambrel or hip roofs of most of the early Georgian houses. One of the first examples of this trend was the house built for Jacob Treadwell by his parents at King (now Congress) and Middle Streets. The interior of this house, with its heavily paneled drawing room, square columns and elliptical arch separating the entrance hall from the stair hall, and slender turned balusters, complemented the graceful four-square exterior, which probably contained a greater variety of academic details than any other house yet built in town.[1] The three-story design became increasingly popular in the 1760's and thereafter, but never entirely replaced the use of third-story dormer windows. In 1757, for example, Captain Gregory Purcell bought a tract of land on Broad Street (now State Street) from Nathaniel Peirce and between then and 1759 built a beautiful gambrel-roof house of the older type for his bride, Sarah Wentworth, the governor's niece.*

While the merchant class, a few professional men, and even the more prosperous of the artisans and shopkeepers were erecting a growing number of distinguished residences, the townsmen of Portsmouth also saw to the provision of adequate public buildings and public works. By 1750, the town could boast eight to ten taverns, three churches—the North and South meetinghouses and Queen's Chapel, several bridges, a broken-down gaol, a schoolhouse, a public "pest house" for the care and quarantine of victims of smallpox, an "alms house" for the poor and insane, and even a town clock.† In 1761, the town built a brick watchhouse—a sort of one-man police station ten feet square—on a hill near the North meetinghouse.[2] In 1755, it set up a haymarket in a square at the lower end of Islington Road, complete with scales for weighing loads of hay that were bought and sold

---

* John M. Howells: *Architectural Heritage of the Piscataqua* (New York, 1937), p. 158. This house, which still stands, is commonly known as the John Paul Jones House because the Revolutionary Naval captain boarded there during the building of the sloop-of-war *Ranger* in 1777 and the ship-of-the-line *America* in 1781 and 1782.

† For a list of "taverners," see Kenneth Scott: "Colonial Innkeepers of New Hampshire," *Historical New Hampshire*, XIX (Spring 1964), 41–2. This list does not make it possible to know precisely the number of licenses in effect in any given year, but ten licenses were granted in Portsmouth during the fifteen years prior to 1750, and another one sometime before 1753. The General Assembly made an accounting of taverns in the province in 1758. The report enumerated eight taverns in Portsmouth and eighty-four in New Hampshire as a whole. *Provincial Papers of New Hampshire*, VI, 686. The decrepit state of the "province prison" or "Province Gaol" is evident from the frequent resolves of the General Assembly to inspect and repair the premises and at least one jailbreak that was attributed to its poor condition. See *Provincial Papers of New Hampshire*, V, 224–5, 355, 452, 503, 505, 513, 530, 542. For references to the schoolhouse and "alms house," see Chapter VII above. The "pest house" was authorized by vote of the Assembly on June 18, 1747, upon the outbreak of a minor epidemic of smallpox. If a victim was unable to bear his own expenses in this primitive hospital, his town was to pay the cost. *Provincial Papers of New Hampshire*, V, 512–13. In 1740, the North Parish voted to grant permission to anyone who was so inclined to install a clock at his own expense in the steeple of the meetinghouse "so that the hammer of said clock might strike on the bell." In 1749, Daniel Peirce and several other gentlemen bought a clock by subscription, presented it to the town, and after it was accepted by vote of the town on March 25, had it installed in the steeple of the North meetinghouse. Nathaniel Adams: *Annals of Portsmouth* (Portsmouth, N.H., 1825), pp. 172, 187. For bridges, including one drawbridge, see Adams: *Portsmouth*, pp. 151, 161.

at this central location.[3] It built a new almshouse on the glebe land the same year.[4] In 1757, the General Assembly authorized a lottery to raise money for a bridge from Portsmouth to Newcastle, and in 1759, after trying unsuccessfully for eleven years to keep the old gaol in repair and negotiating for a new one for another four, it replaced the unsatisfactory prison with a new two-story building "of timber hewn square and covered with iron bars, well spiked to the timber, and lined with plank." Attached to it was a house for the jailkeeper.[5]

The business of the province ordinarily was carried on at one of two public houses, the Wentworth tavern on Manning Street or Colonel Packer's tavern on Pleasant Street, both of which had rooms reserved for the Assembly. Less frequently, the House of Representatives met in one of the two Congregational meetinghouses.[6] After 1750, the Council met in a room the governor furnished for the purpose at the old farmhouse at Little Harbor that he had inherited from his mother. From the time Wentworth moved to the house until his death, he constantly remodeled it and added and rearranged rooms. Off the paneled Council chamber, Wentworth installed cardrooms and an alcove in which he placed a billiards table and a circular buffet.[7] To this country seat, Wentworth summoned the councilors for occasions official and unofficial with the words, "Governor Wentworth's compliments, and commands you to come to Little Harbor to drink the King's health." [8] Although the governor's mansion continued to serve for state functions throughout Wentworth's administration, the province at length built a "State House" in the center of Portsmouth, thus providing for the first time an official seat of government. This building, erected by vote of the General Assembly in 1758, was a two-story frame structure eighty feet long and thirty feet wide. The lower floor, later used for Portsmouth town meetings, was unpartitioned. The second story was divided into three rooms—one for the Council, one for the House, and one for the courts.[9]

The shipping trade of Portsmouth during the administration of Benning Wentworth was much the same as it had been earlier in the century except that now an occasional cargo of lumber was being sent to Halifax as well as to the West Indies and ports to the south. Because the forests close to the Piscataqua had been cut extensively, merchants were complaining that lumber "is very dear to them, the Cartage out of the woods to the mills being now a long way." Wood products, nevertheless, remained the principal export, supplemented by bricks, coal, hay, oil, hogs, cheese, fish, and pork. The larger vessels cleared for the West Indies and often returned by way of Spain or England with cargoes usually described as "sundry European goods." [10]

The merchants of Portsmouth apparently had little trouble disposing of their imports once they arrived at the Piscataqua. An astonishing variety of clothstuffs accounted for the bulk of "English, India, and Scotch Goods" imported from London creditors. These were sold either at retail from the merchants' warehouses or at wholesale to the numerous shopkeepers of Portsmouth who supplied the townsfolk and farmers from the interior who journeyed to the "Banke" to exchange their produce for manufactured goods. In November, 1756, Thomas Durant advertised the following merchandise "Reasonable for Cash, or good Pay, by Wholesale or Retail":

> Beaver Coating, Rateen, German serges, scarlet cloth, velvet French Alimode, Camblets, Venetian and Hungarian Stuffs, Tammys, Callimancoes, Garlix, Tandem Hollands, Dowlas, Cotton Hollands, Scarlet and blue Honey Comd Plush, Scarlet Everlasting, Lemonee and Bandanna Handkerchiefs, Cotton Romall ditto, Cotton Gowns, black Silk Mitts, Buff Gloves, black hair Hats, black Bone Lace, Felt Hatts, Bamboo and Ivory Fans, sewing Silk, Buttons and Mohair, Pins, Gauze, Figur'd and Silver'd Ribbands, spotted and flower'd Lawns, Cambricks, Gauze Shades, Wool and Merry Andrew Cards, black Horn Buttons, Jett ditto, choice Bobea Tea, Coffee and Loaf Sugar, Rhode Island Cheese, 6d, 10d, 20d London and Bristol Nails, Powder, Shot, Bar Iron, Flower, Raisons and Currants, Nutmegs, Pepper, Snuff, Scots Threads, Checks, strip'd Hollands, Bed Ticks, Linnen Handkerchiefs, Irish Linnen, Pewter Plates, Basons, Dishes and Spoons.

In addition, Durant offered "London, Sheffield and Bermingham Cutlery and Ironmongery Wares," other hardware, and supplies for tailors and cobblers. In February, 1757, the same merchant advertised Philadelphia iron and German steel, and two months later he had acquired a shipment of pepper, nutmegs, cinnamon, cloves, mace, Philadelphia flour, pork from Connecticut, and "a Parcel of very neat MUSQUETS." [11] When Robert Traill's 120-ton *Peeks* arrived home from Bristol in 1757, her owner not only offered to sell her cargo of grindstones, ship's stores, fishing tackle, dry goods, hats, firearms, farm tools, carpenter's tools, violin strings, and brass trumpets, but put the ship itself on sale. [12] Except for the coastal schooners and sloops that brought in entire cargoes of grain and meat from the Middle and Southern colonies, such as the schooner *Friendship*'s load of "Good Virginia Corn, Wheat and Oats" in June, 1757, nearly all the vessels that arrived at the Piscataqua carried a variety of merchandise similar to that advertised by Durant and Traill.[13]

Many of the merchants' imports were eventually sold in the shops of such Portsmouth storekeepers as Nathaniel Barrell, Mrs. Odiorne, and Stephen Deblois, Jr. None of them appears to have specialized in a particular "line" of merchandise. Their advertisements, instead, offered an indiscriminate mixture of dry goods, hardware, occasional Bibles and books, and home furnishings, but cloths nearly always predominated.[14] The families of the oligarchy, besides providing an excellent market for the fine cloths and clothing found in every Portsmouth general store, stocked their cellars with the best wines that the merchants could import. "People of fortune," wrote James Birket after visiting the town in 1750, "have very good rum and Madeira wine in their homes; indeed the wine most commonly Drunk here is from the Canaries and Western Islands, called 'Vidonia.' " [15] In 1756, Samuel Griffith advertised "Choice Snakeroot and Orange Water, distilled from good Barbados Rum." The following year, Joseph Buss offered for sale in any quantity, not only "West India Rum," but also "Good Fyal Wines." [16]

About the middle of the century, an increasing variety of tradesmen established shops, which also appealed to upper-class tastes. Noah Parker made a business of producing and repairing small arms, swords, and cutlasses "in the neatest Manner," and Samuel Griffith operated a goldsmith's shop.[17] Another shopkeeper made, repaired, and sold pewterware at the "Sign of the Plates." [18] In July and August, 1757, John Harmon, a staymaker from Boston, spent several weeks in Portsmouth. He established himself temporarily at the home of John Knight, Esquire, where, he announced, "all Ladies may be well accommodated in the best and neatest Manner, with quick Dispatch." [19]

2

By mid-century, the Portsmouth gentry and "middling sort" had become well accustomed to their own rather opulent version of the good life. The first real indication that their conception of such a life reached more deeply than the enjoyment of splendid houses, rich furnishings, and fine wines came in 1750, when thirty-four gentlemen raised £936 among them and bought a library of books.

The "Library Society of Portsmouth," as the subscribers called themselves, seems to have been inspired by the Library Company of Philadelphia and perhaps Newport's Redwood Library, which was organized in 1747 and opened in 1750.[20] Unlike its Philadelphia model, however, the Portsmouth library contained a preponderance of theological works, mostly in an Anglican vein. In fact, the Society bought its first eighty volumes from Parson Browne of Queen's Chapel. In a gesture of catholicity, however, the subscribers made the Reverend Samuel Langdon of North Church, once the town schoolmaster, their librarian. In 1755, the Society added another sixty-seven volumes to the collection.[21]

The first subscribers to the Library Society comprised virtually every important member of the oligarchy except the governor. They also included such outsiders as Mr. Langdon and Matthew Livermore, probably the two most scholarly men in town, and Richard Waldron, Wentworth's principal political opponent. Their articles of agreement were an almost painfully transparent admission of embarrassment that they had not yet matched the material side of their society with appropriate intellectual accomplishments. The themes of the agreement were self-improvement and community pride—both to be achieved deliberately on a sound basis of shrewd investment and proper management:

> As the Advancement of Learning and the Increase of all useful Knowledge is of great Importance both to the Civil and Religious Welfare of a People and as all Gentlemen who have any Taste for polite Literature or desire to have any Acquaintance with the various Affairs of Mankind, to know their different Customs and Sentiments, to find out Truth in our Searches after which we should not think any Cost or Pains too much when it has any Close Connexion with our true Happiness or to be informed of whatever is curious and entertaining, cannot but look upon it to be a great Privilege to have always a good Collection of Books at hand out of which they make [sic] take their Choise for their Amusement at Leisure Hours, without the Expence of procuring a Library each Man for his own private Use, forasmuch also as great things are sometimes effected from little Beginnings, and Rhode Island, and Philadelphia and other Places on this Continent have reap'd great Benefit by such public Libraries; it is therefore propos'd to the Gentlemen of This Town, and a Number of Persons whose Names are Subscribed have agreed to join in purchasing a set of Books to the Value of about twelve Pounds for each Man concern'd, as the Beginning of a Library for their common Use as a Society; the Library to be increas'd at the

Cost of the Society from year to year as they shall think proper;
this first Sett of Books to be purchased without Delay; and the
Society to be formed immediately after this Purchase. . . .[22]

Though there is nothing in the records to prove it, it seems likely
that the Society may have been in large measure the brainchild of Mr.
Browne, who must have been acquainted with similar efforts in Newport. Certainly, none benefitted from the founding of the library more
than he. His collection of books, many of them of a polemic nature,
stood a much greater chance of wide readership when transferred to
such a repository than if they had remained in the rectory, and he was
reimbursed for them substantially. He qualified for membership in
the Society by donating Cudworth's *Intellectual System,* which his
associates valued at £18 16s, rather than by paying the subscription
fee of twelve pounds Old Tenor.[23]

Portsmouth's exposure to books and to public and intellectual affairs outside the province gained another substantial boost in 1756,
when Daniel Fowle came to town, set up a print shop, and began pub-
lishing the weekly *New-Hampshire Gazette.* Fowle was a voluntary
exile from Massachusetts who had come to New Hampshire in dis-
gust at his treatment by the authorities in Boston.[24] The men of Portsmouth and the surrounding towns in New Hampshire and southern
Maine had been reading and sending correspondence and advertisements to several Boston newspapers since the 1720's, but now they had
a much more effective organ of information and opinion along with an
extremely energetic resident printer and bookseller. In the first number
of the *Gazette,* which appeared on October 7, Fowle solicited "the
Favour of all Gentlemen who are Friends to Learning, Religion and
Liberty," and invited contributions from "Correspondents of Genius
and generous Sentiments" and the communication of "any good Intelligence, provided they be sent free from Charge."

During the next four years, besides printing his newspaper regularly, Fowle's press produced twenty books and pamphlets, mostly
sermons and other religious tracts, an annual edition of Nathaniel
Ames's almanac, occasional acts of the General Assembly, and a
broadside poem celebrating the conquest of Quebec.[25] Fowle also
became at once the town's principal seller of books. In the third
number of the *Gazette,* he advertised 104 titles, including works by
Watts, Edwards, Locke, Bunyan, William Penn, George Whitefield,
and Addison, in addition to a Book of Common Prayer and a few
books on architecture, anatomy, navigation, and shipbuilding. The

next week, Fowle continued his "catalogue" with seventy-one more titles, including four illustrated volumes of Shakespeare, a two-volume book entitled *The Beauty of Shakespear,* many works by classical authors, and several books on medicine and navigation.[26]

It was undoubtedly the recent establishment of Fowle's *Gazette,* with its appeal to enlightened gentlemen, that inspired an anonymous correspondent to make an eloquent plea for "noble and enlarged Sentiments" in northern New England. Fowle printed the letter in November, 1756. The author complained of "the Prevalance of Ignorance, in a Country where the most superior Advantages are enjoyed for the obtaining Knowledge, where all rational Acquirments are become remarkably cheap and easy." Obviously a man of intelligence, this nameless apostle of the Enlightenment must have known that his dream of combating both a narrow religious outlook and a preoccupation with business by means of "a virtuous and learned Education" was indeed ambitious, even for Wentworth's Portsmouth. The eastern parts were scarcely ready for a cultural flowering, or even, in some of the up-country towns, a grammar school. But as the founders of the Library Society, the provincial school laws, and Fowle himself had demonstrated, he was not alone in his concern. He expressed it well:

> I am certain, that great Numbers of Children, instead of being sent to School, are permitted to trifle at Home, to rove up and down the Streets, in search of mischievous Adventures; or constantly exercised in some hard and laborious Employment. . . . They now enter upon the Stage of Action unfurnish'd with every Science but that of getting Money, and have scarce any other Views, but to increase their Patrimony. These Persons are commonly Strangers to all Generosity, to all noble and enlarged Sentiments; they seldom feel the soft movings of Pity and Compassion, and are utterly regardless of all the Concerns of Mankind, as they stand unconnected with their own private Interest.—We shall generally perceive, these people are endowed with a prodigious Stock of Arrogance and Pride; we shall find them the greatest Extortioners, and the most severe Oppressors of the Poor; and though they refuse to part with any of their Estates, in the Defense of their invaluable Liberties, either sacred or civil; yet they prove without Exception the most liberal Dealers of Damnation, to all who differ with them in their religious Sentiments, or Notions of Government.

The writer went on to deplore the standards of judgment of "People that have no Acquaintance with any thing beyond the narrow

Limits of the Family or Parish where they were born." Indulging in a minor sophism, he contrasted provincial narrowness with "Virtue and Honour," and suggested that parents not only utilize the schools to re-place the former with the latter, but work from their children's infancy to instill generous thoughts and "a Consideration of the gracious and diffusive Manifestations of the bountiful Author of Nature" in their "tender Minds." [27]

Whatever else this letter indicates, including a tendency toward Deism on the part of the writer, it is symptomatic of the same uneasy provincial consciousness that had been reflected by the founders of the Portsmouth Library Society six years before. The people of New Hampshire and Maine were aware not only that they were colonials, which most Americans of this generation found unflattering enough, but also that a large number of their fellows to the south could look upon them with some reason as rustics. Comparative isolation and pre-occupation with their own meager "Patrimony," except during the temporary excitements of the Great Awakening and a few of the cam-paigns against the French, had cut them off from the intellectual cur-rents of the big colonial centers of population. Possibly the Wentworth oligarchy, secure in its local political supremacy, its favored position with the Crown, its fine houses, and its comparative wealth and fashion, was immune from embarrassment. Benning Wentworth's im-perial designs west of the Connecticut and extravagant wooing of the S.P.G., however, suggest that even he, in his own way, was expressing a deeply felt need to save his province from insignificance.* To the correspondent of the *Gazette* and the founders of the Library Society, the best remedies for rusticity were education and the communication of ideas.

Neither New Hampshire nor Maine had cause for pride in its educational record. The school laws for both were identical. They re-quired every town of fifty or more families to support a schoolmaster to teach the three R's, and every town of a hundred families or more to have a "grammar school" to prepare young men for college by instruction in the "learned tongues." In New Hampshire, many towns learned early in the eighteenth century how to evade the law. "It was the interest of ignorant and unprincipled men, to discourage litera-ture," wrote Belknap, "because it would detract from their importance, and expose them to contempt. The people in some places, being thus

---

* Wentworth, besides joining the Venerable Society and frequently corres-ponding with it in behalf of the Reverend Arthur Browne, reserved land in every new township for the S.P.G. and the Church of England.

misled, thought it better to keep their children at work, than provide schools for their instruction." [28] Beginning in 1722, some of the interior towns were excused from the requirement for a grammar school because of the war, but even afterward, the law frequently was ignored.[29] Not until seven years after Falmouth, Maine, had fifty families did it acquire a schoolmaster.[30]

By the 1750's, however, most of the New Hampshire towns and the older communities in Maine had established the schools required by law. What had aroused the writer to the *Gazette* was the failure of parents to send their children to them. The coastal communities from Hampton to Casco Bay contained a growing number of men with Harvard degrees, not all of them in the ministry. Samuel Langdon of Portsmouth's North Church was establishing a pastoral and scholarly reputation that was to make him president of Harvard in 1774, Matthew Livermore was introducing New Hampshire to the learned practice of law, and Daniel Treadwell, a young native of Portsmouth, was attracting sufficient notice from John Winthrop, the renowned Harvard scientist, to be appointed professor of mathematics at King's College, New York, upon his graduation from Harvard in 1754.[31] In January, 1760, the *Boston Weekly Newsletter* published an anonymous letter from Portsmouth which contained a learned discussion of observations of a comet, referring at one point to the *"Newtonian* Philosophy." It shared the columns of that issue with a letter on the same subject from Nathaniel Ames, the celebrated almanac publisher of Dedham.[32]

A modest intellectual awakening, centered at Portsmouth but extending in some degree throughout the region, was indeed coming to pass by the 1750's. Part of its cause seems to have stemmed from a felt need to build regional self-respect by encouraging participation in, or at least the intelligent observation of the intercolonial exchange of opinions and cultural interests that was developing along the entire seaboard. Undoubtedly the region's introduction to George Whitefield and a brief concern with the religious issues of the day during the previous decade was also a factor.[33] So, certainly, was New Hampshire's new consciousness of occupying a place of importance in the Empire. Just as instrumental as any of the other factors was the simple and quite natural fact that as the society near the Piscatqua grew in numbers and affluence, more young men of the region found their way to college. When they returned, as many of them did, they brought with them not only the mental discipline and skills appropriate to the learned professions, but a breadth of view that resulted from new associations and an exposure to the new learning of the Enlightenment.

The New Hampshire clergy began to establish extraprovincial connections in the 1750's for quite another reason. Again, however, the clerical activities of the decade show a new awareness of the world outside New England. At the same time, they demonstrate the seriousness with which the ministers of the province looked upon the Anglican challenge to Congregationalism in Portsmouth and its implications for New Hampshire politics.

In October, 1750, during the deadlock between the governor and the legislature that would end fifteen months later in an unqualified personal victory for Benning Wentworth, the annual New Hampshire Convention of Congregational Ministers voted to open a correspondence with the Protestant Dissenting Deputies in London.[34] This lay body of English Presbyterians, Independents, and Baptists had recently come to the aid of American Congregationalists by supporting the claim of the Reverend Joseph Torrey to a farm in South Kingstown, Rhode Island, that had been designated for an "orthodox minister." Mr. Torrey's claim was being contested by the Reverend James MacSparran, an Anglican missionary of the S.P.G. The case was still pending in the Privy Council (it was decided in Torrey's favor in 1752), but the Dissenting Deputies already had acquired a reputation as cooperative and useful friends of their co-religionists and sympathizers in America and in 1749 had begun their long involvement in the larger fight against the introduction of Anglican bishops to the colonies.[35]

The New Hampshire ministers had no specific issue with which to approach the Deputies, but were uneasy about the threat to the New England ecclesiastical system that was clearly being presented by the Church of England and its missionary society in theirs and nearby provinces. The Reverend John Odlin, minister at Exeter and moderator of the Convention, started the correspondence in behalf of his colleagues. In July, 1751, he wrote to Dr. Benjamin Avery, chairman of the Deputies:

> The Churches of New England in general, particularly those of this Province not having the privileges of a Charter Government stand in need of your assistance and protection. You are sensible we are not wholly out of Danger of Enemies, there may be secret designs against our Constitution and Liberties: which may require the utmost Care and vigilance and call for powerful advocates

among you: We therefore entreat you to have a tender Concern for us to give us timely notice of Every danger which may threaten us and to act for us in any affairs of moment in which your interest may be serviceable.

The letter also acknowledged the Deputies' "endeavors to prevent the sending a Bishop into these American Colonies," and urged them "still to Continue your pious Care to defend us from an Evil greatly dreaded among us." [36] After a gracious reply from Dr. Avery, Mr. Odlin wrote again to London at the request of the Convention.[37] The second letter, dated in June, 1753, after Governor Wentworth had won his battle with the Assembly, thanked the Deputies for their part in the Rhode Island ministry farm controversy and then turned specifically to New Hampshire politics:

> The House of Representatives in the Province have been hitherto of Congregational or Presbyterian Principles, and we hope the other Branches of the Legislature will continue to vindicate us in our Rights. We should be glad if any Rational Methods could be taken to Secure a Succession in the Council of our own Persuasion as it cant be supposed that Members of the Church of England can be so Zealous for our Interests. At present we have a majority there. Tho' we cannot expect it will be so long; But if any apparent difficulty or Danger arises with respect to our Interests, We shall endeavor to give you notice of it and must Intreat Your Assistance. It will be very agreable to hear from you, and to have Correspondence by Letter at least annually, that our Union may be the better continued.[38]

The Dissenting Deputies apparently never had occasion to intervene directly on behalf of the New Hampshire Congregationalists, nor, it seems, did the Convention of Ministers maintain for long its specific fear of Anglican domination of the province. The records of the Convention contain no further correspondence with the Deputies. On a broader stage, however, the colonists as a whole remained very much concerned over the possibility of an American episcopate and the infringement of what the enlightened divines of the day were with increasing frequency calling "religious liberty."

Apparently under the influence of an intercolonial movement for church unity inspired by ministers such as the Reverend Ezra Stiles of Newport, the Convention of Ministers voted in 1763 to confer with the Southern Association "on the great Necessity of maintaining Union amongst ourselves in order to promote the common Interest of Christianity, and guard against all Encroachments on the liberties of the Churches." [39] The movement for "Christian Union" in the 1760's, promoted by Old Light ministers such as those who had formed the New Hampshire Convention in 1747, was characterized by scholarship, urbanity, religious cosmopolitanism, and theological liberalism. Not only the fear of bishops but also a desire to overcome to some extent the divisions of the Great Awakening and provide a religious basis for intercolonial harmony and brotherhood impelled cultivated ministers such as Mr. Stiles to search for and plead for a rational, latitudinarian, and catholic (but congregational) religious style for America.[40] The New Hampshire clergy appropriately named their most learned colleague, Dr. Langdon, the future Harvard president, to head the committee that was to begin the conversations.[41] If any such conference was ever held, there is no report of it in the Convention records during the succeeding years, but the action of 1763 does indicate a desire on the part of the clergy to share in an important intercolonial movement and an awareness, at least, of contemporary trends in American intellectual life.

3

Under the influence of Benning Wentworth and his gentry, Mr. Browne and his church, a lively commerce, political intrigue, a rudimentary cultural awakening, and a new breadth of view on the part of the Congregational clergy of the province, the people of Portsmouth and its immediate surroundings soon began to pride themselves upon an urbanity of outlook. Their pride was perhaps excusable in view of the recent political accomplishments of the oligarchy and the favored position that New Hampshire now held in the Empire. One senses this pride in the following news item in a *Gazette* of 1757, in which the printer shared with his Portsmouth readers a tart observation upon the more rustic inhabitants of a less-favored place:

> We are informed by a Gentleman, that as he came through Wrentham one Day last Week, he saw at least Forty Horses hanging about a Justice's House, and some hundreds of Persons assembled there; and on enquiring the Occasion, was told, there was going to be a Court held, one Man having sued another for a Debt of NINETEEN PENCE,—One may conclude from this, that that curious Assembly valued their Time at a very low Rate.[42]

The people of the Piscataqua, long accustomed to oceanic commerce, had now watched at close hand a sophisticated maneuvering for personal fortunes, imperial favor, and provincial power. They were absorbing the ideas of the Enlightenment from their own weekly newspaper. To their elegant houses and expensive furnishings, they had added a respectable library, and their men of learning were beginning to achieve recognition commensurate with that already accorded their remarkable governor. Slowly but certainly, they were being drawn into the intellectual and cultural life of an intercolonial seaboard society. Was there not, then, in 1757, some reason to feel superior to the "curious Assemblies" of Wrentham and many other places?

CHAPTER XIX

Northern New England in 1760

1

To the amateur soldiers of New England who had gone with Sir William Pepperrell to Louisbourg, the Treaty of Aix-la-Chapelle was a disappointing anticlimax to the highest moment of their lives. By European diplomacy, they lost what they had won by Yankee ingenuity, strenuous work, real bravery, and great luck.

Ten years after the distasteful treaty, in the late summer of 1758, the provincial seaports of British America again rang with cheers and cannon fire, and bonfires leaped high into the night sky. Louisbourg was taken again, emphatically confirming the turning of the tide in the French and Indian War. Though New England preachers again marveled from their pulpits at the glorious effectiveness with which God had once more proclaimed Himself a Protestant, the victory received only grudging approval from some of their parishioners. The second conquest of Louisbourg, after all, was a feat of British regulars, not the plain men of the New England soil and fishing grounds who had shown the way. A few Bostonians, in fact, flatly protested the public celebration.[1]

Then in September, 1759, came the much greater victory at Quebec, followed by louder cheers, brighter bonfires, and longer sermons. By 1760, New France was dead and for all practical purposes the last of the intercolonial wars was over. Britain was assured of dominion over North America, and the colonists of northern New England were freed forever from the peril of Indian raids and French invasion.

As in 1713, an army of land-hungry New Englanders, many of them veterans of Lake George, Ticonderoga, Crown Point, or ranging

parties in the undefined wilderness from Lake Champlain to Nova
Scotia, was poised to rush into vacant territory. This time, the forest
of northern New England beckoned to men from Rhode Island and
Connecticut as well as from Massachusetts, coastal New Hampshire,
and southern Maine. During the next fifteen years, the new wave of
settlement reached up the Connecticut Valley more than halfway between the Massachusetts boundary and the river's source near the
Canadian border, and it spread well into the Maine and New Hampshire
back country and westward into Vermont. With great expansion of
settlement and an impending Revolutionary crisis, northern New
England began a distinctly new period of history.

A century and a half of steadily advancing settlement, especially
the accomplishments of the past forty years, had worked impressive
changes in the physiognomy of the region, despite occasional periods

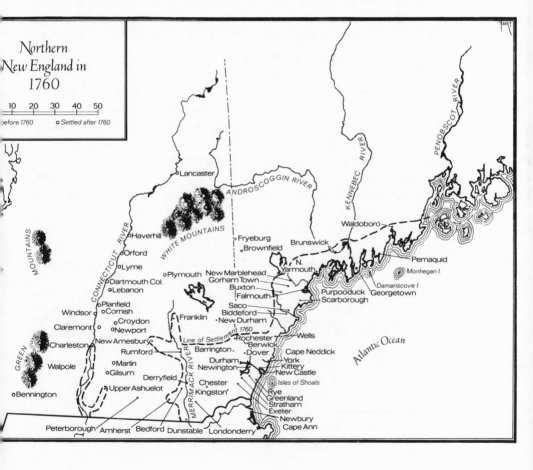

Northern
New England in
1760

10   20   30   40   50

before 1760   o Settled after 1760

of retrenchment. True, a broad expanse of green forest remained the dominant regional feature in 1760. For many miles inland, however, the giant pines were gone and much of the wild game had retreated. Throughout a belt extending some forty or fifty miles in from the seacoast, the woods were cut through with straight masting roads and winding wilderness paths connecting one settler's little house with another. The shores of the Piscataqua and Great Bay were studded with closely settled villages, and similar clusters of substantial dwellings huddled about coves and river mouths at intervals from Kittery to North Yarmouth. The harbors of Portsmouth and Falmouth were bustling centers of commerce and shipbuilding. The banks of such rivers as the Merrimack, the York, the Saco, and the Presumpscot were lined with clearings where crops grew and cattle grazed. On dozens of streams that had once rushed toward the sea without hindrance, timber dams had created placid millponds where great creaking paddled wheels powered the rasping vertical pit saws that sliced timbers into boards and the rotating horizontal millstones that ground Indian corn into flour.

The population beyond the Merrimack had increased ten-fold in the seventy years since the political map of New England had assumed its permanent shape and the first of the intercolonial wars had begun the work of devastation and dispersion in the region. In New Hampshire, where in 1690 not more than 4,000 persons had been settled in four towns, there were in 1760 about 40,000 inhabitants in fifty incorporated towns.[2] The population of Maine had grown from less than 2,000 in 1690 to perhaps not far from 20,000 in 1760, and the number of incorporated towns from eight to fifteen.* The great increase during this significant period of growth and development is all the more remarkable in view of the retrogressive effects of the wars with the French and the Indians, which, if one counts the local Indian war of

---

* The population of Maine was about 2,000 in 1701 and of the three Maine counties of York, Cumberland, and Lincoln in 1765, 21,817 (E. B. Greene and V. D. Harrington: *American Population Before the Federal Census of 1790* [New York, 1932], pp. 4, 21, 22 *n*.). The data on townships was compiled from Ava H. Chadbourne: *Maine Place Names* (Portland, 1955), a convenient source for this purpose because it includes the dates of the granting or settlement and the incorporation of every city and town in the state. One must always be aware that population figures for the American colonies are at best rough estimates, and that contemporary estimates vary greatly. The figures used for both Maine and New Hampshire throughout this book, except in occasional instances in which exact enumerations for individual townships are cited, are no more than approximate indications of the degree of settlement.

the 1720's and occasional isolated skirmishes, occupied not far from half of this span of years. By comparison with the area immediately to the south, however, the population remained small. In 1760, New Hampshire and Maine together contained little more than one-eighth of the inhabitants of New England. Their combined population was about a third the size of Massachusetts proper, less than half that of Connecticut, and about equal to that of Rhode Island.[3]

In contrast to the extremely spotty colonization of the next fifteen years, when pioneers would bypass miles of wilderness and create islands of settlement in favorable intervales far removed from one another, the frontier line in 1760 was at least definable, even though irregular. In the Connecticut Valley, the frontier stood about thirty-five miles north of the Massachusetts line at Captain Phineas Stevens's tiny fortified settlement of Charlestown, which still wore the raw color of freshly cut boards. In the next township to the south on Great Falls, Colonel Benjamin Bellows, who had moved in 1752 from his native Lunenburg, Massachusetts, presided from a hundred-foot-long palisaded fort over the settlement and organization of Walpole, a community composed at that point largely of his own relatives. This unusual town, run by a patriarchal figure who owned or controlled most of the shares in the propriety granted originally by Benning Wentworth, was just on the verge of an extraordinary development. From a fortified family seat in a frontier clearing, Walpole shortly emerged into a center of lively hospitality whose several taverns served as a resting place and supply base for settlers who made their way toward the upper Connecticut or into Vermont during the next several decades. Before the end of the century, it attracted a widely known coterie of resident lawyers and literati known as the "Walpole Wits." *

In the summer of 1760, Charlestown, the battle-scarred old Township Number 4,† was the marshaling point from which eight hundred

---

* I have learned most of what I know about Walpole from Miss Dorothy A. Pettit, one of my graduate students at the University of New Hampshire, who has presented her findings in a seminar paper entitled "Walpole, New Hampshire: The Development of a Frontier Town" (1968).

† The township had received its new name in 1753 when the New Hampshire government confirmed the original grant by Massachusetts and incorporated the proprietors. It was named in honor of Commodore Sir Charles Knowles, who had been so impressed by Phineas Stevens's three-day defense of the fort in 1747 that he had presented Stevens with an expensive sword. Henry H. Saunderson: *History of Charlestown, New Hampshire, The Old No. 4* (Claremont, N.H., 1876), pp. 38, 58.

New Hampshire militiamen under Colonel John Goffe cut a road through the Vermont wilderness toward Crown Point in time to be in on the capture of Montreal.[4] From this outpost, whose couple of hundred inhabitants had as much reason as anyone in America to celebrate the fall of Canada,* the frontier line trended east-north-eastward along the spottily settled forty-mile "line of townships" that the Massachusetts government had laid out between the Connecticut and the Merrimack in 1735. Between this sparse barrier and the Massachusetts boundary some forty miles to the south, however, much land was still vacant—some of it, in fact, still ungranted "province land." Only in the valleys of the Upper and Lower Ashuelot, the Contoocook, the Souhegan, and a few smaller tributaries had settlers strayed more than a half-dozen miles from the banks of the Connecticut on the west or the Merrimack on the east.

In the Merrimack Valley itself, settlements extended as far north as Franklin, slightly less than twenty miles upriver from the flourishing settlement at Rumford where the Reverend Timothy Walker made his jovial round of pastoral calls and farmed his broad acres, and about an equal distance west of the southern part of Lake Winnipesaukee. The frontier line ran roughly eastward about thirty-five miles from Rumford to the Maine border and the beginning of the inland tier of Maine townships at Berwick. Only the tiny settlement at New Durham five miles southeast of the southernmost tip of Lake Winnipesaukee stood beyond a fairly well defined frontier, separated from the area of relatively extensive farmlands to the south by about fifteen miles of woodland.

In Maine, the frontier line ran approximately parallel to the north-eastward-trending coast from Berwick to the Kennebec, about twenty miles from the sea. Again, it was the river valleys—the Piscataqua and Salmon Falls system, the Saco, and the Presumpscot—where most of the farming communities of the interior were concentrated. As in the barrier of frontier townships between the Connecticut and the Merrimack, the line of forward settlement in Maine contained many gaps.

A coastal road now connected all the settlements from the mouth

---

* Charlestown had twenty-six families in 1756. If one uses a factor of 5.5 to 6 per family (the average size of a family in the United States was 5.7 by the federal census of 1790), the population in that year was between 143 and 156. By 1767, when the New Hampshire government took a census of the province, the township contained 334 inhabitants. Undoubtedly the great bulk of the growth took place after 1760 and most of it after 1763. The estimated figure of 200 for 1760, however, does not seem unreasonable, although it is possibly slightly high. See Greene and Harrington: *American Population*, pp. xxiii, 74.

of the Merrimack to the Penobscot region. South of Falmouth, only rare stretches of more than a few miles along it were devoid of farms and houses. Settlements had also developed along roads from this highway down to the shore at Rye and Scarborough. Beyond North Yarmouth, which was solidly settled along the shores of Broad Bay and Royal's River, houses were sparse except in the region of the Kennebec. There, scattered clusters of fishermen's huts stretched along the shores of Merrymeeting Bay, the lower Kennebec, and New Meadows River.*

Beginning about 1750, coinciding with the limited awakening of the mind that is noticeable near the Piscataqua, northern New Englanders had begun to pay increased attention to the need for better communications throughout their developing region. Roads were just as important as schools, libraries, and newspapers if there were to be fuller participation in the life of the colonies at large. In 1749, for example, the 207-mile trip along the coastal road from St. George's Fort on the Kennebec to Boston involved nine ferry crossings, six of them between North Yarmouth and Portsmouth.[5] To eliminate two of them, York County raised money by lottery in 1758 to bridge the Saco River at Biddeford and the Presumpscot River at Falmouth.[6] In 1750, to facilitate communication between the coastal settlements and the newly settled frontier, New Hampshiremen cut a wilderness road paralleling the Cocheco River from Dover about thirty miles into the interior, to the very fringe of settlement in the eastern part of the province.[7]

Portsmouth was at the northern end of the colonial postal service.[8] Mail addressed to other points in Maine or New Hampshire was kept at the Portsmouth post office until it was claimed. In November, 1756, the post office listed fifty-seven letters it was holding for addressees in Portsmouth, Dunstable, Kittery, Exeter, Newcastle, Londonderry, York, Dover, Berwick, and Wells. The weekly post from Portsmouth to Falmouth after 1757 and the summertime monthly post from Portsmouth to Albany after 1758, both arranged by Daniel

---

* One may gain a very good view of the state of settlement in the 1770's by reference to the excellent pilotage charts of the American coast prepared by Joseph F. W. DesBarres for the use of the Royal Navy and bound in *The Atlantic Neptune*, I (1780). The various copies of this publication differ in their arrangements of the charts. I have used the copy in the John Carter Brown Library, charts numbered 95 through 100. An undated view of Portsmouth as seen from the east side of the Piscataqua is numbered 101 in this copy. In using these charts to describe the extent of settlement, it was necessary to make certain allowances for changes between 1760 and 1780.

Fowle, improved mail service in the region considerably, as well as facilitating the distribution of the *New-Hampshire Gazette,* which of course was Fowle's main intention. Still another advance was the weekly stage from Portsmouth to Boston and back that John Stavers began in 1761. Carrying up to three passengers in his two-horse curricle, Stavers left Portsmouth every Monday morning, stopped overnight in Ipswich, and delivered them at Charlestown Ferry on Tuesday at a fare of 13s 6d each. Stavers left Charlestown on Thursday and arrived home at his own sign of the Earl of Halifax each Friday.[9]

Passengers in Stavers's wide two-wheel curricle, with its matched pair of horses hitched abreast, rode in relative luxury compared to most of the travelers on the road from Boston to Portsmouth and Falmouth. Normally, one either simply rode in a saddle or in a two-wheel open "chair," large enough for two persons and pulled by a single horse. It was in such a vehicle that young David Sewall drove the senior tutor at Harvard, Henry Flynt, from Cambridge to Portsmouth in June, 1754. The trip gave Sewall a few days' vacation from his studies and a chance to visit his family in York while his eighty-year-old teacher attended to whatever business had taken him to the Piscataqua. Just outside Portsmouth, the horse stumbled on its way down a small hill in the sandy road. Mr. Flynt flew headlong into the dust, skinning his forehead but sustaining no other damage that was not quickly cured by sharing a few bowls of lemon punch with a solicitous and genial group of young Portsmouth blades at Clark's Tavern in Greenland.[10] Stopping at this or another tavern in Greenland twenty years later, Dr. Alexander Hamilton of Annapolis "had some billingsgate with a sawcy fellow that made free in handling my pistols." Disappointed at finding only "a sett of low, rascally company" in the country tavern, he rode on toward more agreeable society at "the Banke." [11]

Never during the colonial period was traveling in the eastern parts less than an ordeal. As late as 1771, John Adams, who made regular trips to Maine as a circuit judge, described a ride to Falmouth as "the most flat, insipid, spiritless, tasteless journey I ever took." Riding alone through Saco after dark, he found "many sharp, steep hills, many rocks, many deep ruts, and not a footstep of man except in the road; it was vastly disagreeable." [12] Traveling into the interior was still worse. Nearly all the inland roads of the period paralleled rivers or streams, both because the waterway had formed the original route to the road's destination and in order to take advantage of the relatively low, even terrain of a riverbed. Certainly none in 1760 was

much better than the newly cut road that the Rev. Paul Coffin rode
in 1768 from Buxton, Maine, forty miles up the Saco River Valley to
the new settlement at Fryeburg. Mr. Coffin marveled that he and his
two companions had been able to make the journey on horseback in
thirteen and a half hours of traveling time, despite at least one difficult
ford, one "long rocky hill," and a three-mile stretch of "rocky and
muddy travelling" near the end of the trip. "A great deal of the road,"
explained Coffin in accounting for the unexpected ease of the journey,
"was pitch pine land, like a house floor"—that is, hard, dry, and
relatively flat.[13] Despite the still-primitive conditions of travel in the
1760's, northern New Englanders were beginning to make progress
toward linking a formerly isolated people with the rest of colonial
society, even as the region was on the verge of a contrary movement of
greater dispersal.

2

Although northern New England could accurately be called an agricultural region by 1760, one ought not to allow that fact to hide the
diversity of economic and social life. Workmen hired by mill owners
and mast agents still ranged the forests and harvested timber. Fishermen and seamen, carrying on a New World tradition of six generations,
still sailed in large numbers from the ports of the Piscataqua and
Casco Bay. Even the more rudimentary communities had room for a
few artisans, storekeepers, innkeepers, and ferrymen, most of whom
supplemented their incomes by farming or at least raised enough food
for their own use. At Portsmouth, Kittery, and Falmouth, shipbuilding
continued as an important industry which gave employment to craftsmen of many kinds. A merchant class presided over Falmouth as well
as over the society of Portsmouth and the politics of New Hampshire.

During the decades of growth and innovative development that
reach a discernible transitional point about 1760, the people of
northern New England faced a variety of social problems produced
by conditions ranging from frontier to urban. By that time, the northeastern Yankee had certain social and cultural accomplishments to
show for his struggle with the wilderness. A catalogue of his problems
and accomplishments might be one useful approach to trying to understand more about the special nature of his society.

Throughout the century and a half between the first attempts at
setting up permanent fishing bases on the Maine coast and the end of

the wars with the French and Indians, the paramount concern of most northern New Englanders was survival. Not only were many communities involved directly with the dangers of Indian warfare, but poverty and food shortages also plagued many an eastern town. By 1760, the struggle for survival had been won in most of the region, but the fact that few of the inhabitants had at all times been far removed from the danger of violent death or starvation can scarcely be dismissed by anyone who would hope to understand their motives and their attitudes.

A barely separable problem was the protection of their resources. Standing timber, ocean fish, potential water power, and animals valued either for meat or fur made up the principal natural wealth of the region. After the introduction of agriculture, crops and farm animals became equally important.

It was obvious to most New Englanders as well as to the Navy Board that the supply of timber was not inexhaustible. Quite apart from the Broad Arrow, authorities at various levels tried a number of approaches to protect proprietors and towns from being stripped of their most valuable resource. The protection of trees from thieves both within and out of their own ranks was the main reason that the proprietors of North Yarmouth sought a speedy resettlement of their township in 1717. As early as 1698, the Massachusetts General Court had fixed fines for cutting trees on another person's land or on common land. The fines were doubled in 1726, and in 1727, the Court legislated specifically against joint owners who cut trees on the common land without giving notice to the other proprietors. This last act received further refinements in 1737.[14] In 1724, the New Hampshire General Assembly supplemented existing laws against trespassing on common lands by passing an act closely modeled, as so many New Hampshire laws were, after the Massachusetts legislation. In both provinces, the prohibitions extended to removing stones, ore, gravel, clay, and sand as well as timber.[15] The previous year, the town of Londonderry had taken upon itself the responsibility of regulating the cutting of timber on the town common. By Londonderry's "act or By Law," inhabitants had the privilege of cutting lumber or firewood for their own use within the town, with permission from the selectmen. Anyone who cut common timber to sell to outsiders, however, was subject to a fine of twenty shillings for each tree felled. The action was provoked, apparently, by the practice of "maeking staves for a market out of the Town" from trees on the common land "so that the Town is Like to be Greatly Impoverished for want of Good Timber."[16]

Conservation of saltwater fish was not a problem in the offshore waters, especially since the commercial fishery moved late in the seventeenth century from the Gulf of Maine to the larger and more fruitful banks off Nova Scotia and Newfoundland. Upon the settlement of the interior, however, country dwellers soon discovered the value of the migrating salmon, shad, alewives, and eels that ascended the streams to spawn in lakes and ponds many miles from the sea. To protect this important source of food, it became necessary to regulate dams and seines. In 1755, the New Hampshire Assembly forbade placing obstructions in Cohas Brook to block the passage of alewives into Massabesick Pond in Derryfield, and limited the fishermen who flocked to take advantage of the spectacular annual spring herring run to the use of hand nets.[17] In 1764, the Assembly limited fishing in the Merrimack by seines or drag nets to three days a week and outlawed weirs at the outlet of Lake Winnepesaukee.[18]

Even earlier than the protection of fish came under official cognizance, the authorities concerned themselves with the protection of deer. In 1741, the New Hampshire Assembly, alarmed by the slaughter of deer "when they are verry Poor, and big with young," limited the deer season to five months a year, August through December, and required the election in each town of two inspectors to enforce the law. In 1758, the same provisions were reinforced and the fine for killing out of season was fixed at a substantial £15 for the first offense and £30 for a second offense in the same year.[19] In somewhat belated compliance with the law of 1741, the voters of Londonderry elected two men "for Inspecting into the killing of Deer" in 1750.[20] The problem apparently was not recognized until several years later in the more sparsely settled Maine. The town of Windham, formerly New Marblehead, elected its first "Informers of Deer and Moose," later called "Dear Reaves," in 1771.[21] In New Hampshire, the laws (which undoubtedly were enforced with small success) failed to keep the deer herd from diminishing seriously. In the 1790's, wrote Belknap, deer had actually become scarce.[22]

In 1760, the various restrictions enacted early in the century in both provinces to protect crops from roving livestock remained in effect, and varied little from similar provisions in the rest of New England. The century-old practice of allowing cattle to graze in the salt meadows of Hampton, however, eventually created a unique problem. These lush fields had been the principal attraction of the place when the Reverend Stephen Batchelor had led his flock there in 1638. A hundred years of unrestricted grazing resulted in serious erosion. "The shrubs and Beach Grass are destroyed," stated the preamble of a surprisingly enlightened New Hampshire law of 1755, "in Consequence whereof, in Storms and High winds the Sand is driven from off the said Beach upon the meadows and the meadows thereby much Injured and damnifyed." From then on, the marsh was fenced in and reserved for a common hayfield.[23]

Disputes over land among provinces, township proprieties, and individuals—about which enough has already been said—occupied much time and attention, frequently resulted in complicated lawsuits and long family feuds, and sometimes prevented settlement and cultivation. One must therefore count among the major social problems of the period the great number of conflicting claims, complicated as they were by the loss of documents in wartime, the ambiguity of official grants, the vagueness of Indian deeds, the difficulty of surveying, and some plain dishonesty.

The growth of the older towns in size and complexity was accompanied by an inevitable increase of thefts and violent crimes. Not even in the two biggest seaports, however, did the problem ever get out of hand. Executions for capital offenses in the region were remarkable only for their rarity,* but there was a noticeable increase in thievery in the 1750's, especially in Portsmouth. In December, 1756, a thief broke into the shop of Daniel Jackson and took twenty-six yards of cloth. The following spring, the editor of the *New-Hampshire Gazette* warned his readers to look out for "two or three Fellows with offensive Weapons, ranging the Town, suppos'd to be upon no good Design, as they have made some bold Attempts already." This gang may have been responsible for the theft during the previous week of several silver and gold articles from John Nelson's goldsmith's shop.[24] In March, 1759, a New Hampshire court convicted John Carson and his wife, Margaret, of twenty thefts in Portsmouth and Greenland. John's twenty stripes were laid on the same day. Margaret was allowed to escape whipping by paying a fine of £5, but was sentenced to the unusual punishment of being sold as a servant for a term of two years and nine months.[25] About 1754, Portsmouth

---

* The executions on record include the double hanging of Sarah Simpson and Penelope Kenny in Portsmouth in 1739 for the murder of their bastard infants, which were the first executions in New Hampshire, and the hanging in 1755 of Eliphaz Dow of Hampton Falls for killing a neighbor with a hoe during the culminating argument of a long feud. Not until 1772 was a murderer convicted and hanged at Falmouth. Nathaniel Adams: *Annals of Portsmouth* (Portsmouth, N.H., 1825), pp. 172, 194; William Willis: *The History of Portland* (Portland, Me., 1831), II, 220–1.

began lighting the streets, and in 1760, the New Hampshire Assembly responded to the problem of nighttime disorders by authorizing the "Walking Watch" in any town to lock up any person who could not account satisfactorily for being out at night.[26] In Maine, serious crimes were extremely rare, though in 1757 a thief named Clark caused a sensation throughout the region by shooting one man dead and maiming two others with an axe before he was finally captured and taken from Falmouth to the county gaol at York.[27]

Portsmouth and Falmouth seem to have been spared the gross disorders of some of the larger seaports to the south, but no waterfront could ever escape an occasional sailors' brawl. When two fishermen fell to scuffling on board their boat at a Portsmouth wharf one Saturday night in 1756, both combatants fell overboard and one drowned.[28] The most harrowing night of the year for Portsmouth residents came to be November 5, when the "meaner sort" (and others, no doubt) annually tried to surpass in vigor and imaginativeness the previous year's observance of Guy Fawkes Day. When the New Hampshire legislature decided in 1768 to end all celebration of the occasion, on pain of spending two days in gaol, the drafter of the law supplied a colorful and perhaps nostalgic account of the way it had been done in Portsmouth for several decades:

> . . . it Often Happens that many Disorders and Disturbances are Occasioned and Committed by Loose Idle People under a Notion and Pretence of Celebrating and keeping a Memorial of the Deliverance from the Gunpowder Plot on the fifth of November and the Evening following as Servants and boys Tempted to Excessive Drinking and Quarreling—Surrounding Peoples doors with Clamor and rudely Demanding money or Liquor making mock Shows of the Pope and other Exhibitions making bonfires whereby buildings are in Danger in Populous places and Stealing Materials for such fire with many other Irregularities which Disturb the Peace of Such places and tend much to Corrupt the Manners of Youth.[29]

Since the laws of New Hampshire regulating taverns and sales of liquor tended to follow those of Massachusetts, the same basic requirements, all designed to keep the business temperate and well mannered, prevailed in both New Hampshire and Maine. New Hampshire introduced the posting of names of "Drunkards, or common Tiplers" in public houses, for example, in 1719, eight years after the passage of the comprehensive Massachusetts "Act against Intemper-

ance, Immorality and Prophaneness, and for Reformation of Manners," which included that provision among many others.[30] Occasional
New Hampshire laws, however, such as an act of 1721 against "gaming
in public houses," resulted from the discovery of local conditions that
the legislators wanted to correct.[31]

In 1742, the Assembly found that because of the many new towns
and the recent growth in population, the public convenience demanded
the removal of a long-standing statutory limit on the number of taverns.[32] Sixteen years later, however, in response to a petition from
Londonderry, where the inhabitants had once tried to ban all "tipling
houses" by local authority, the legislators imposed a limit on the
number of taverns (three) and liquor retailers (two) that applied to
that town only.[33] The restriction lasted only three years, after which
the selectmen pleaded that their town needed more "licienced houses"
for the use of travelers, and the limit was removed once more.[34] Thus
the growth of population and an increase of traveling in the interior
produced demands that overbalanced Presbyterian fears for "the
Morals of the Young and Inconsiderate Persons."

While most taverns no doubt were as respectable as they were
essential to the traveling public, licenses for inns were susceptible
to abuse by the occasional country-dweller who procured a license
with no thought of accommodating "strangers" and their horses—
which by law was the only justification for such an establishment. In
the little town of Sandown, New Hampshire, Moses Blake, who was
nearly penniless, was licensed to operate a tavern at his poor, run-down
house which lacked, among other things, a barn. His business consisted of buying an occasional jug of rum and selling drinks to his
neighbors—or, as the unsympathetic selectmen put it in 1760, of
keeping "a sort of tipling house for bad husbands like himself." [35]

The youth of the region probably had less to fear in the dangers
of strong drink than in the dangers of contagious disease. Whether in
the seaports or on the frontier, the possibility of serious illness was
always present. By far the worst epidemic was the disastrous wave of
diphtheria that swept over northern New England in the 1730's and
early 1740's. Measles were common throughout the period, and such
local physicians as were available knew no more about fighting that
disease or caring for its young victims than about curing the "throat
distemper." [36] Potentially at least as dangerous as the epidemic of
diphtheria, and certainly greatly feared, was the exposure of the
Portsmouth waterfront to smallpox, which was occasionally brought
in by ships from abroad and from other American ports. In 1749,

the town followed the lead of Boston by buying a small island in the Piscataqua and building a "pest house," where victims of smallpox were isolated and cared for. For several years before that, the select-men had occasionally hired houses in remote places for the same purpose.[37] In 1757, the selectmen tried to squelch rumors of an epidemic by announcing that they had made a thorough investigation and found no "SMALLPOX to be in any House in this Town, but the Pest House, nor any Person that has the Symptoms of it; and that the utmost Care will be taken to find out all suspected Persons, that they may be immediately removed." [38]

By far the most rigid precautions against smallpox were taken during the Boston epidemic of the early 1760's. The road into Portsmouth from the south was fenced off and travelers from Boston barred from proceeding until they, with their baggage, had undergone the ordeal of the smokehouse. All vessels from Boston went through quarantine upon arrival at Piscataqua, and a few Portsmouth residents traveled to Boston to take the controversial inoculation. Perhaps because of wise precautions, and perhaps simply because the northern seaport was not yet sufficiently crowded or dirty to foster the uncontrolled spread of this infection, Portsmouth seems to have escaped all the smallpox epidemics without serious harm.[39] The same was true of the smaller towns, though Samuel Lane of Stratham recorded in 1760 that the disease "was in almost every Town round about more or less." [40]

One urban problem threatened Portsmouth repeatedly, but again, both town and province spared none of their resources or ingenuity in meeting it. The streets of Strawberry Bank were closely lined with wooden buildings and the riverside with wharfs and ships. When a twenty-gun warship burned in the harbor in January, 1744, the towns-folk, awakened to the possibility of disaster, voted to use a gift of £20 toward the purchase of a mobile hand-powered water pumper and began to organize themselves into fire companies. Not until 1756 did a town meeting actually order the selectmen to buy the apparatus, at a cost of not more than £40, but in the meantime, the town had made provisions for sounding a fire alarm and drafting fire-fighters. Drilling of fire-fighting units began in 1756, and in 1758, the provincial legislature, with Portsmouth particularly in mind, worked out procedures to be followed in every town in case of fire.[41] Daniel Fowle thought the legislation sufficiently important to reproduce in rarely used large type on the front page of the *Gazette*.[42] Besides authorizing towns to form fire companies and elect appropriate officials, the act fixed penalties for refusal to comply with impressment by "fire wards" and for looting.

The Portsmouth fire companies soon became fashionable social groups in which members of the merchant class as well as the lower ranks of society enthusiastically participated, each man with his own initialed leather bucket. They met their first severe test on January 26, 1761, when a fire in a barbershop on King Street spread to a nearby tavern. The fire-fighters stopped it in two hours, but only after it had consumed the tavern, a barn, and some outbuildings.[43] It took the General Assembly only a little more than a month to apply some of the lessons of this incident, in which the Portsmouth fire companies had performed well but against handicaps that could not be overcome by a good stream from the pumper and a well-drilled bucket brigade alone.

The provisions for fire-fighting were now supplemented by rigid prevention measures. The new act authorized the fire wards of Portsmouth to inspect all buildings for fire hazards, including improper fireplace foundations, and require owners to correct any dangerous conditions within thirty days. The same act permitted the town to demand that owners demolish "Decay'd" buildings at their own cost, and required each house in Portsmouth to have a ladder high enough to reach the ridge pole and, if two stories high and containing as many as four fireplaces, a leather bucket. The act noted that "all the Buildings in the Town of Portsmouth two or three Excepted are of Wood and are So Compact That if One of them should take Fire in a Windy Season almost all the rest would be in Danger." [44] By 1763, the town had three fire engines, which were used to save buildings only ten feet away from the house of John Wendell, which burned to the ground.*

Fire was as dangerous an enemy to the broad woodlands of the region as to the crowded streets of Portsmouth. Clearing operations in the new settlements were especially hazardous, since great piles of dried brush and useless wood from the past summer's work were commonly burned in the spring. Occasionally, these immense bonfires got out of hand and destroyed hundreds of square miles of forest, along with any buildings or fences that were in the way. A pro-

---

* Adams: *Portsmouth*, p. 207. The *New-Hampshire Gazette* of November 4 and December 2, 1756, reported the destruction of houses in North Hampton and Exeter by fire. While the smaller, more dispersed towns were not faced with the danger of widespread destruction as compact Portsmouth was, they also lacked the advantage of having fire-fighting equipment and a large, organized body of men readily at hand.

longed drought, such as those that caused shortages of hay and grain throughout the region in the summers of 1761 and 1762, could result in critical danger to the wilderness settlements and even to the older towns next to the sea. In the summer of 1761, a forest fire raged steadily for two months in the town of Arundel, Maine, and spread at least as far as Biddeford and Buxton until a mid-August downpour, the first substantial rain since March, brought it within control.[45]

In a region where the great majority of men worked on their own land or in private trades, one is inclined to overlook the problems that arose between employers and employees or between masters and servants. Perhaps the most serious of such problems involved the system of Negro (and Indian) slavery, though the number of slaves was never great. Practically all the slaves in New Hampshire and Maine either were domestic servants or worked beside their masters in the field or shop. Aside from the inhumanity implicit in the idea of chattel slavery itself—which was recognized by few in the eighteenth century except Quakers—most owners seem to have treated their slaves with as much consideration and decency as an essentially barbarous system allowed. Indeed, by the 1760's there had arisen among the 150 or so Negroes of Portsmouth a semi-official society of their own in which the rank of each slave reflected that of his master. With the encouragement of their owners, they formed their own government, headed by a "king" who was elected annually amidst pomp and pleasure, and they dispensed their own justice for minor offenses.[46] Nicholas Gilman recorded in his diary the dying words of a farm slave who affectionately told his master that he had been "as kind as a Father," and that he now ought to trust in the Lord "to take care of you in your old age." [47]

An occasional master, however, breached the commonly accepted standards of humanity. Apparently the worst such case occurred as early as 1695, when Nathaniel Keen of Kittery was charged with murdering his Negro woman, who died after a beating. The court's action undoubtedly reflected the callousness typical of this early day: the charge was subsequently reduced to "cruelty" and Keen was freed after paying a fine of only £5.[48] In 1718, the New Hampshire General Assembly found it necessary to legislate against "Inhumane Severities, which by Evil Masters or Overseers may be used towards their Christian Servants." The law required any servant or slave who was maimed by his master to be set free; murder of one's slave, whether Indian or Negro, was made a capital offense.[49] Slaves and indentured servants occasionally ran away from their masters, as is evident from repeated notices in the Portsmouth and Boston press and in official letters of the period, but it is not possible to know to what extent they were provoked beyond the normal desire for freedom.[50]

There seems to have been no antislavery agitation in northern New England during the colonial period. Though the New Hampshire Assembly banned further introduction of Indian slaves into the province in 1714, it was for fear of rebellion and crime by ungovernable Indians, who never did prove to be satisfactory slaves, rather than for any moral concern.[51] Perhaps the relative sparsity of slaves in the region, the rather democratic manner in which blacks and their masters lived and worked together on farms and in shops, and the comparative mildness of the regimen of domestic servants in the fashionable homes of Portsmouth and Falmouth concealed from virtually everyone the fundamental atrocity involved. In 1760, there probably were not more than five hundred slaves in New Hampshire, or about one to every fifty whites; in Maine, there were still fewer.[52]

Still, one could not escape the harsh realities of the slave market. In 1758, a shipload of "Likely Negro Boys and Girls" arrived at Portsmouth from Gambia and were offered for sale in the advertising columns of Fowle's newspaper.[53] The publisher, in fact, became a sort of broker in slaves, for in most cases, a prospective buyer was asked to "enquire of the Printer" for further information about the numerous slaves advertised for sale in the *Gazette*.[54] Although mothers and small children were usually sold as a unit in Portsmouth, there was no law preventing their separation, and indeed one can find numerous cases on record in which Negro families were broken up much in the way one might dispose of a litter of kittens.*

The problems of eastern society thus varied according to the several stages of community life. At the outer limits of settlement, the pioneers' concern for survival, which up to 1760 had included the problem of defense, precluded occupation with less important matters. These settlers, however, were not long in transforming their six-mile-

* Mrs. Constance Ward of Portsmouth, New Hampshire, has investigated this problem among others associated with the institution of slavery in Portsmouth, and concluded that slave families were always subject to separation and occasionally were in fact broken up. She relied for this conclusion primarily upon advertisements in the *New-Hampshire Gazette,* wills, records of the South Church of Portsmouth, and two secondary sources: Charles W. Brewster: *Rambles About Portsmouth,* 2 vols. (Portsmouth, 1859 and 1869), and Lorenzo Johnston Greene: *The Negro in Colonial New England 1620–1776* (New York, 1942). Mrs. Ward's findings are contained in an essay presented for the Bachelor of Arts degree to the Department of History, University of New Hampshire, entitled "Negro Slavery in Colonial Portsmouth" (1969).

square tract of wilderness into a rural town. In the process, they worried about property bounds and the exhaustion or usurpation of the timber supply. They entered the next stage not as pioneers, but as farmers. In this role, they faced an increasing variety of problems involving the keeping of livestock without trespassing on each other's property, the protection of crops, and the pooling and partial division of labor. Along the coast were closely settled villages, established in an earlier day. There the problems arising from close associations with neighbors were more pressing than in the country or on the frontier and problems involving wild animals, inland fish, and the lack of social institutions such as schools and churches were less so. Finally, the inhabitants of Portsmouth and Falmouth were experiencing in a small way some of the problems of urban life.

By 1760, northern New England had become a region of diversity. It was about to become one of stunning growth.

CHAPTER XX

The Breaking of the Dike

1760–1775

When the fall of Canada made it safe for the cramped inhabitants of the New England settlements to pick up and move if they wanted to, the possibilities for migration were rather strictly channeled. Westward expansion since 1713 had filled up the colony of Connecticut with occupied townships, and recent migrants finally had begun to trickle into the last of the empty lands in western Massachusetts between the Berkshires and the fertile lowlands of the Housatonic and Connecticut Valleys. What little vacant land remained in Massachusetts was being deliberately bypassed because of suspicions, not always well founded, that it was infertile.[1]

The Proclamation of 1763, by erecting a legal barrier to expansion west of the Appalachians, closed off what must have seemed one of the most promising possibilities for new settlement. In the same year, the government of Nova Scotia ended a program of land grants and bounties to new settlers that for the past four or five years had made that British colony an attractive resort for some of the restless and land-hungry in southern New England.[2]

Not a few New Englanders now continued the movement to the south that had been a sporadic factor in American population shifts ever since a group of emigrants from Massachusetts settled Gravesend, Long Island, in 1640.[3] But for most of the prospective pioneers of Connecticut, Rhode Island, Massachusetts, and southeastern New Hampshire, the most obvious place to go was north.

For northern New England, the past century and a half of halting growth and painful transition had been but a prologue to the dynamic expansion of the next fifteen years. During this long formative period, the territory beyond the Merrimack had gradually lost its special character as a region distinct from New England as a whole. If not every town had its school and Congregational meetinghouse, it was only because the economy did not yet permit it. The yeomen of the region, largely of Massachusetts origin, had surpassed all other elements of the population in numbers. If they tended to be more worldly, less speculative, and somewhat less deferential to the clergy and to social rank than their fathers had been, these were tendencies that reflected the time as much as the place. The northeastern country town, great mutation of the original Massachusetts ideal though it was, had undergone a process of dispersal and acquisition of its own permanent characteristics that was not much different from the contemporary experience of the other New England frontiers in western Massachusetts and Connecticut, where, Stephen Hosmer complained in 1720, "It would Grieve ones Soul to see a Numerous and Plentiful Increase of reasonable Creatures Scattered up and down the Wilderness, as Sheep, having no Shepherd." [4] Even the merchants of Portsmouth, hostile as they were toward Massachusetts, had much in common with their contemporaries in Boston, who had long since adopted gentle manners, built fine houses, and in a few cases even joined the Church of England.[5]

Thus it was sometimes in ways that the Puritan conquerors of the seventeenth century had not anticipated that their plan for bringing northern New England within the social, cultural, political, and economic scheme of Massachusetts had been brought to fruition by 1760. By a shift to a largely agricultural economy, which encouraged a stable domestic and community life and promoted an attachment to locality, by a small cultural awakening that was stimulated in part by the introduction of printing to Portsmouth, by the eventual acquisition of schools and meetinghouses in most of the country towns, by improved transportation, and in part by changes in a worldly direction in southern New England, the "second New England" beyond the Merrimack gradually but perceptibly had joined in the life of the first.

Now was the great swarming time. Up the Connecticut Valley trooped pious men and women from Connecticut, solid citizens with Bibles and pinched faces and an eye for town meetings and account books, to settle the New Hampshire townships of Marlow, Claremont, Newport, Plainfield, Gilsum, Lebanon, Campton, and Orford, among others. Some planted themselves instead on a string of townships along the western side of the river where Benning Wentworth busily marked off and granted thousands of acres of territory in a grandiose attempt to enrich himself and his political friends and to establish a somewhat dubious New Hampshire claim to the present state of Vermont. Similar families from Massachusetts made their way along the same route or up the Merrimack Valley to Plymouth in central New Hampshire, Weare in the south central "province land" west of the Merrimack, Cornish, Croydon, and Haverhill on the upper Connecticut, and Lancaster high on the Connecticut only forty miles from the Canadian border.[6]

From the western parts of Connecticut and Massachusetts, rustic pioneers who had already tried one frontier and were ready now to tackle a new one, some of them religious dissidents whose side had come off badly in the local church fight occasioned by the Great Awakening, migrated into some of those townships in Wentworth's "New Hampshire grants" that lay west of the Green Mountains. There they confronted the occupants of conflicting claims from the province of New York. Rhode Island, eastern New Hampshire, and even Scotland contributed to the stream of settlers that swelled the population of Vermont from 120 families in 1763 to about 20,000 people in 1776.[7]

From eastern Massachusetts and New Hampshire, migrants pushed into Maine and up the valleys of the Saco, the Kennebec, and the Penobscot, more than doubling the settled area. The Massachusetts census of 1776 counted 15,546 persons in forty-three settled places in Lincoln County alone, the region of the Penobscot and eastward, which in 1760 had been almost empty of English settlers.[8]

By the beginning of the War for Independence, northern New England had a population of at least 150,000—an increase of about 90,000 in just fifteen years. As might be expected in view of the emigration northward from southern New England, where there was practically no vacant land left in 1760, the rate of growth in Maine, New Hampshire, and Vermont surpassed that in the rest of New England during these fifteen years. Instead of containing one-eighth of the total population of the region, as it had in 1760, the northern tier now was home for slightly more than one-fifth.[9] New Hampshire, in fact, grew faster between 1761 and 1775 than any of the other twelve English colonies that took part in the American Revolution.[10]

Why did New Englanders flock northward in such great numbers after 1760? The full answer must await the detailed study of a host of individual cases. Perhaps it will be found, as seems likely, that the obvious and classic factor of exhaustion of land, both in quality and quantity, drove most of the migrants in search of new territory as soon as the long years of constraint were ended. Scholars have also pointed to other reasons, particularly in the occupation of Vermont. Bennington, for example, Wentworth's first "grant" in contested territory, was settled by a faction of New Lights who migrated after a church schism in Hardwick, Connecticut. Other religious frictions in Massachusetts and Connecticut, including especially the desire of Anglicans and Baptists to escape church taxes, seem to have been a factor in the settlement of other Vermont communities. Disputed land titles in other parts of New England and the great increase in speculation in the unoccupied lands also encouraged migration.[11]

The occupation of the far interior after 1760 had certain characteristics that were different from those of the first movement into the back parts between 1720 and 1750. For one thing, it was a quick, massive onslaught. The earlier movement had been tentative, hesitant, almost reluctant. It was as though now, for the first time, the dike had truly given way and a sea of settlers flooded the intervales almost as far as Canada. For another, this was much more a community movement. Instead of migrating as individuals or families, as the pioneers of the mid-century had done, groups of families from a single or from neighboring Massachusetts or Connecticut towns often moved together to a new township in northern New England.

Most of the first twenty-eight families in Marlow, New Hampshire, for example, were from Lyme, Connecticut, and Newport, New Hampshire was begun by six families from North Killingworth, Connecticut.[12] The profusion of Connecticut place names in that short stretch of the upper Connecticut Valley from Windsor, Vermont, to Lyme, New Hampshire, reflects the origin of settlers as much as proprietors.

Still another difference was the exuberant willingness of the settlers of the new migration to bypass many miles of vacant territory in search of the best lands, even though it meant leaving great gaps between settlements. As one more conservative Vermonter complained, "The newcomers do not fix near their neighbors and go on regularly, but take spots that please them best, though twenty or thirty miles beyond any others."[13] Whereas in 1760 only one New Hampshire township, New Durham, lay beyond the frontier line, there were four such isolated settlements in 1765, three in the Connecticut Valley and one, Plymouth, in the upper Merrimack Valley. This kind of highly selective settlement continued until the early 1770's, leaving the less desirable lands to be filled in by later comers.[14]

[*Plan of Meredith, 1753.*]

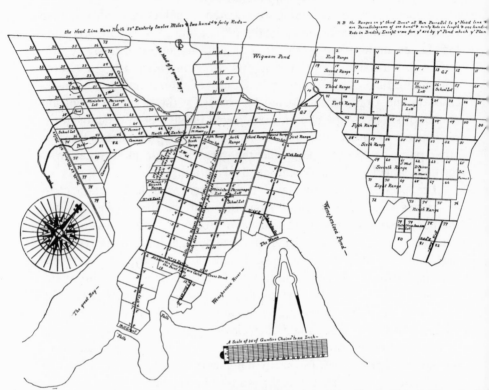

A Plan of a Township Called Palmer's Town lying to yᵉ Westward of Wenepesioca Pond Province of New Hampsʳ and was granted to Samⁿ Palmer E:s:q: & other Petitioners, by tᵉ chers of yᵉ Right of John Tuftan Mason E:s:q: Survey'd A:D: 1750 & 1753.——
by Jonᵃ Longfellow Survᵉ

N : B the Township is laid out into three Divisⁿ the first Divisⁿ Contains one hundᵈ Acres Right & are those Lots Numbr'd with Red from yᵉ out let of Wigam Pond Downward to yᵉ the 2ⁿᵈ Divisⁿ Contains Eighty Acres to each Right & are those Lots Numbr'd with Black Divisⁿ Contains one hundᵈ & twenty Acres to each Right & are those Numbrᵈ with Red on yᵉ of Wigwam Pond. &c. &c——

N : B: the Ranges in yᵉ Second Divisⁿ Run Parrallel to yᵉ Six Mile Line & are 160 Rods in which is yᵉ Length of yᵉ Lots the Lots are Parrallel to yᵉ Head Line of yᵉ first Divisⁿ viz Nᵒ are 80 Rods in Bredth, Some few excepted which appear by yᵉ Plan——

This Plan of the Tract of Land granted to Samˡˡ Palmer Esqᵘʳ and others Decʳ 31ˢᵗ 174 agreable tò yᵉ Vote pass'd May 3ᵈ 1754 for rectification of yᵉ head Line—was accepted and R by the Proprietors at their Meeting held may 3ᵈ 1754——
attest. Geo: Jaffrey Propᵗᵒʳ

The preliminary and final surveys of the township of Meredith on Lake Winnepesaukee, the first conducted in 1750 and 1753 and the second in 1770. The owner of each "right" held a total of 315 acres, divided among substantial lots in each of the 3 divisions. The names of the Masonian proprietors, from whom the grant of the township was procured, appear among the lot owners. A "Gunter's chain" of 100 links was the standard surveyor's measurement, equivalent to 4 rods, or 66 feet.

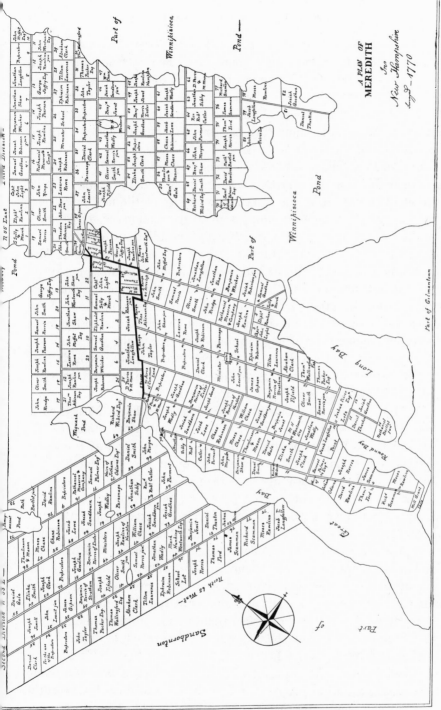

A PLAN OF
MEREDITH
in
New Hampshire
1770

N: B: The first Divisions of Lots contain 100 Acres each and are Numbered with Red Ink, and lay to the
Southward of the Green Line from the head of the Great Bay to the head of Winnipisioca Pond——
The Second Division contains 120 Acres to each Right and are numbered with Green——
The Third Division lays on the North Easterly part of the Town, is Numbered with Red, and contains 95
Acres to each Right

Memorandum The Lots below the Green Range Way from Nº 1 to 14 are called Point Lots

This plan of Meredith drawn by a Scale of thirty five chains to an Inch is agreable to the plan made by a
Committee chosen to lay out and plan the Second and third Divisions of Said Town which plan was accepted
by the Proprietors the first Division being also annexed to the Said Second and third Division in said Plan is
now presented by us as a Comittee of ye Proprietors the Grantees of Said Township, to the Proprietors the
Grantors for their Approbation & acceptance—at Portsmouth ye 12 day of December 1770 & at their meeting
then held   Josiah Sanborn ⎱ Comee
                                                                                         Ebenezer Smith ⎰

As in the earlier migration, the settlers followed the river valleys, which provided both the easiest routes and choicest fields and meadows, often with only a minimum of clearing. From the great valleys—those of the Connecticut, the Merrimack, the Saco, the Kennebec, and the Penobscot—the pioneers branched up tributaries and eventually formed networks of connecting settlements that extended through passes in the hills.

The ideal of village settlement, which had long since broken down in most of the townships settled between 1720 and 1750, was missing even at the outset from the typical community of the new migration. True enough, Benning Wentworth's royal instructions of 1761 which governed the granting of new townships required provisions for a village site in each town.[15] But the 129 townships in New Hampshire and Vermont he parceled out between 1749 and 1764 went mostly to groups of speculators, including in every case himself, who later sold individual lots to settlers and left to chance and the inclinations of the actual inhabitants the form that the community would take. By 1770, the typical layout for a newly granted New Hampshire township was simply a division of the land into about three sections, each divided checkerboard-style into fifty-acre farm lots except for the 500-acre farm reserved in each township for the governor.[16]

In Maine, the abandonment of the village ideal was no less complete. The Reverend Paul Coffin, minister of Buxton, might be expected from his profession and upbringing to have been as jealous of tradition and social order as anyone north of the Merrimack. Yet when he visited the three-year-old settlement at Fryeburg on the upper Saco in 1768, he had nothing but praise for the progress of the community even though it consisted exclusively of large farms in a spot where "Nature has formed . . . the desirable rural retreat which poets describe as the most amiable situation in life." The minister was likewise impressed with neighboring Brownfield, particularly the farm of his host, who had "planted near the center of 200 acres of interval, all his own. . . . His situation is extremely convenient." He found nothing to criticize in the fact that his ride "through most of the inhabitants" in the lower end of Brownfield covered six miles.[17]

The brief, restless years between the collapse of French Canada and the shooting on Lexington Green gave a new face to northern New England: thousands of people on the move, some of them just recently settled in new homes on the frontiers of only yesterday, already acquiring the taste for pioneering that would soon send them or their sons across the Appalachians and into the West; hundreds of new clearings in the wilderness, stretching far to the north toward the St. Lawrence Valley and eastward along the coast toward Nova Scotia; the audacious Ethan Allen, very much on the make, and the Green Mountain Boys, scampering about the hills of Vermont defying New York jurisdiction with gun and torch, and finally going it alone against Ticonderoga; Eleazar Wheelock and his Indian college at Hanover, founded in 1769 with the encouragement of Governor John Wentworth; the flourishing of a frontier literary community at Walpole; Revolutionary resistance at Portsmouth and Falmouth, so infuriating in the Maine seaport that the British Navy felt compelled to punish the town by burning; the end of the Wentworth oligarchy. For 150 years a mere fringe of colonial society, a province of the provinces, the region began about 1760 to take on brimming vigor and self-confidence. Now began a brief golden age, lasting through the Revolutionary era and on into the early nineteenth century. That age deserves its chronicle as much as the origin and transition of northern New England society that has been the subject of this book. One day, with great good fortune, it will have it.

A LIST OF FREQUENT ABBREVIATIONS,

NOTES,

ESSAY ON AUTHORITIES AND SOURCES,

INDEX

A List of Frequent Abbreviations

Bull. Metr. Mus.	*Bulletin of the Metropolitan Museum of Art,* New York
DAB	*Dictionary of American Biography*
DNB	*Dictionary of National Biography*
Doc. Hist. Me.	*Documentary History of Maine*
Mass. Col. Records	Nathaniel B. Shurtleff, ed.: *Records of the Governor and Company of the Massachusetts Bay* (Boston, 1853)
Me. Hist. Soc.	Maine Historical Society, Portland
M.H.S.	Massachusetts Historical Society, Boston
MPCR	*Province and Court Records of Maine*
NEHGR	*The New-England Historical and Genealogical Register*
N.H.H.S.	New Hampshire Historical Society, Concord
N. Yar. Mss.	(See note 7 for Chapter IX.)
PPNH	*Provincial Papers of New Hampshire*
Pub. Col. Soc. of Mass.	*Publications* of the Colonial Society of Massachusetts
Sibley's Harvard Graduates	John Langdon Sibley: *Biographical Sketches of Graduates of Harvard University;* Clifford K. Shipton: *Biographical Sketches of Those Who Attended Harvard College*
SPNH	*State Papers of New Hampshire*
TPNH	*Town Papers of New Hampshire*

Notes

Chapter I · The Forest and the Sea

1. William Douglass: *A Summary, Historical and Political, of the First Planting, Progressive Improvements, and Present State of the British Settlements in North-America* (London, 1760), II, 53; Timothy Dwight: *Travels in New-England and New-York* (London, 1823), I, 12.
2. Jeremy Belknap: *The History of New-Hampshire* (Dover, N.H., 1812), III, 78.
3. John Smith: *The Generall Historie of Virginia, New-England, and the Summer Iles* (London, 1632), p. 214.
4. Charles Herbert Levermore: *Forerunners and Competitors of the Pilgrims and Puritans* (Brooklyn, N.Y., 1912), I, 100–1.
5. George Parker Winship, ed.: *Sailors' Narratives of Voyages along the New England Coast 1524–1624* (Boston, 1905), p. 22.
6. Christopher Levett: *A Voyage into New England Begun in 1623 and ended in 1624* (London, 1628), p. 2.
7. William G. Saltonstall: *Ports of Piscataqua* (Cambridge, Mass., 1941), p. 10.
8. See Smith: *Generall Historie,* p. 205, and map facing p. 203.
9. Levett: *Voyage,* p. 1.
10. James Rosier: *A True Relation of the most prosperous voyage made this present yeere 1605, by Captaine George Waymouth, in the Discovery of the land of Virginia* (London, 1605), p. C4.
11. Smith: *Generall Historie,* p. 216.
12. *New-England Weekly Journal,* August 5, 1734.
13. Benjamin F. da Costa: "Norumbega and its English Explorers" in *Narrative and Critical History of America,* ed. Justin Winsor (Boston and New York, 1884), III, 167–218; Sigmund Diamond: "Norumbega: New Eng-

land Xanadu," *The American Neptune,* XI (April 1951), 95–107.

Chapter II · Our Main End Was to Catch Fish, 1610–1680

1. Charles Knowles Bolton: *The Real Founders of New England* (Boston, 1929), Appendix B, pp. 166–77. Bolton's appendices list the names of settlers and "sojourners" in New England prior to 1628, early New England settlements, original names for localities, and primary sources for each. A similar list, this one of voyages to New England from 1602 to 1630, appears in Charles Herbert Levermore: *Forerunners and Competitors of the Pilgrims and Puritans* (Brooklyn, N.Y., 1913), I, 20–4.
2. Lois K. Mathews: *The Expansion of New England* (New York, 1962), p. 14; James Phinney Baxter, ed.: "Trelawney Papers," *Doc. Hist. Me.,* III (Portland, 1884), 166.
3. Henry S. Burrage: *The Beginnings of Colonial Maine* (Portland, 1914), p. 145.
4. Jeremy Belknap: *The History of New-Hampshire* (Dover, N.H., 1812), I, 13–14.
5. Burrage: *Beginnings,* pp. 166–7; Charles M. Andrews: *The Colonial Period of American History* (New Haven, 1934), I, 334.
6. Belknap: *N.H.,* I, 14.
7. Belknap: *N.H.,* I, 14–16; Nathaniel Adams: *Annals of Portsmouth* (Portsmouth, N.H., 1825), pp. 9–12; William G. Saltonstall: *Ports of Piscataqua* (Cambridge, Mass., 1941), p. 10; Frank W. Hackett, ed.: *1645–1656 Portsmouth Records* (Portsmouth, N.H., 1886), pp. vi–vii.
8. Belknap: *N.H.,* I, 19–21.
9. Adams: *Portsmouth,* pp. 22–4; Belknap: *N.H.,* I, 21.
10. Belknap: *N.H.,* I, 27–9; Burrage: *Beginnings,* pp. 197–8. See also Chap. IV, below.
11. Belknap: *N.H.,* I, 30 and *n.*
12. Burrage: *Beginnings,* pp. 230–3.
13. See Burrage: *Beginnings,* p. 288, which includes a remark by Gorges to this effect quoted from James Phinney Baxter: *Sir Ferdinando Gorges and his Province of Maine* (Boston, 1890), III, 287–91.
14. Burrage: *Beginnings,* pp. 317–21; James Phinney Baxter: *Agamenticus, Bristol, Gorgeana, York* (York, Me., 1904), pp. 38–9.
15. Burrage: *Beginnings,* pp. 199, 211 and *n.,* 212–14.
16. William B. Weeden: *Economic and Social History of New England* (Boston and New York, 1890), I, 137. The characterization of Winter is by the ebullient John Josselyn in *An Account of Two Voyages to New England . . .* (London, 1674), p. 26.

17. See Burrage: *Beginnings,* pp. 209, 210 and *n.,* 297, and R. V. Coleman: *The First Frontier* (New York, 1948), pp. 309–10, for accounts of Winter's troubles with Cleeve and with Richard Tucker, both also from the West Country, who had claimed part of the Trelawney patent in 1630.

18. Baxter: "Trelawney Papers," pp. 30–2, 57. See also Coleman: *First Frontier,* pp. 311–12.

19. Burrage: *Beginnings,* p. 225; Weeden: *Ec. & Soc. Hist. N.E.,* I, 125.

20. Baxter: "Trelawney Papers," p. 55.

21. Baxter: "Trelawney Papers," pp. 52, 92.

22. Baxter: "Trelawney Papers," p. 53 and *n.*

23. Baxter: "Trelawney Papers," *passim.* See pp. 183–90 for an example of one year's accounting by Winter with his workmen.

24. Josselyn: *Account,* p. 11.

25. Baxter: "Trelawney Papers," pp. 147–9.

26. Baxter: "Trelawney Papers," pp. 170, 172, 181; Coleman: *First Frontier,* pp. 310–11.

27. Baxter: "Trelawney Papers," pp. 87 *n.,* 170 *n.*; Coleman: *First Frontier,* pp. 250, 309; *MPCR,* I, 68–9.

28. Coleman: *First Frontier,* pp. 314–15. See also Chap. III, below.

29. Baxter: "Trelawney Papers," p. 171.

30. Baxter: "Trelawney Papers," p. 88 *n.*

31. Baxter: "Trelawney Papers," pp. 163, 165–6.

32. Baxter: "Trelawney Papers," p. 71 and *n.*

33. Robert G. Albion: *Forests and Sea Power* (Cambridge, Mass., 1926), pp. 233–4.

34. Baxter: "Trelawney Papers," p. 23 *n.*

35. John S. Jenness: *The Isles of Shoals* (2nd edn., New York, 1875), pp. 82–3, 121.

36. Byron Fairchild: *Messrs. William Pepperrell: Merchants at Piscataqua* (Ithaca, N.Y., 1954), p. 18; Raymond McFarland: *A History of the New England Fisheries* (New York, 1911), p. 67.

37. Jenness: *Isles of Shoals,* pp. 135–6.

38. Jenness: *Isles of Shoals,* p. 136.

39. Jenness: *Isles of Shoals,* pp. 135–8.

40. Jenness: *Isles of Shoals,* pp. 141–2.

41. *MPCR,* III.

42. "A General History of New England," M.H.S. *Collections,* 2nd Ser., V and VI (1815), 427, 647–8.

43. Cotton Mather: *The Fisher-mans Calling* (Boston, 1712), pp. 43–4.

44. *MPCR,* II, 38 *n.*

45. *MPCR,* II, 115.

46. Jenness: *Isles of Shoals,* pp. 105–6.

47. *MPCR,* III, 25.

48. *MPCR*, III, 47. See also pp. 51 and 72.
49. *MPCR*, III, 118, 197–8.
50. *MPCR*, III, 159.
51. *MPCR*, III, 148.
52. Jenness: *Isles of Shoals*, p. 126.
53. *MPCR*, II, 16–17.
54. *MPCR*, II, 219.
55. Samuel G. Drake: *The History and Antiquities of Boston* (Boston, 1856), p. 430 and *n.*
56. Adams: *Portsmouth*, pp. 50, 56.
57. Jenness: *Isles of Shoals*, p. 145.
58. "A Description and Historical Account of the Isles of Shoals," M.H.S. *Collections* (1801), pp. 254–8.
59. Jenness: *Isles of Shoals*, p. 146.
60. *PPNH*, III, 319, quoted in Jenness: *Isles of Shoals*, p. 147.
61. Josselyn: *Account*, pp. 20–2.
62. Josselyn: *Account*, pp. 23–5.
63. Josselyn: *Account*, p. 26.
64. Josselyn: *Account*, p. 207.
65. Josselyn: *Account*, pp. 207–8.
66. Josselyn: *Account*, p. 208.
67. Josselyn: *Account*, p. 209.
68. Josselyn: *Account*, pp. 210–12.
69. McFarland: *N.E. Fisheries*, pp. 67–8.

Chapter III · The Puritan Conquest, 1638–1658

1. Thomas Hutchinson: *The History of the Colony and Province of Massachusetts-Bay*, ed. Lawrence Shaw Mayo (Cambridge, Mass., 1936), I, 49–52, 59–66; Charles H. Bell: *John Wheelwright. His Writings . . . and a Memoir* (Prince Society Publications, Boston, 1876), pp. 1–30; Charles M. Andrews: *The Colonial Period of American History* (New Haven, 1934–8), I, 476–87.
2. Emery Battis: *Saints and Sectaries* (Chapel Hill, 1962), pp. 155, 157–9, 301–28.
3. John Wentworth: *Wentworth Genealogy* (Boston, 1878), I, 72–99. See Chaps. VII and XVII, below.
4. Battis: *Saints and Sectaries*, p. 261.
5. Bell: *Wheelwright*, pp. 31–42.
6. Everett S. Stackpole: *History of New Hampshire* (New York, 1916), I, 33–5; Hutchinson: *Mass. Bay*, I, 93–5; "Ecclesiastical History," *Collections, Historical and Miscellaneous: and Monthly Literary Journal*, II (August 1823), 234; Battis: *Saints and Sectaries*, pp. 270–1. Battis

suggests, not unreasonably, that Underhill "probably professed mystical and Antinomian beliefs only to mask [his] own flagrant immorality."

7. Frederick Lewis Weis: *The Colonial Clergy and the Colonial Churches of New England* (Lancaster, Mass., 1936), p. 122.

8. Jeremy Belknap: *The History of New-Hampshire* (Dover, N.H., 1812), I, 45; Weis: *Col. Clergy*, p. 122.

9. Belknap: *N.H.*, I, 45–6.

10. Stackpole: *N.H.*, I, 36.

11. Nathaniel B. Shurtleff, ed.: *Records of the Governor and Company of the Massachusetts Bay* (Boston, 1853), I, 236–7.

12. Belknap: *N.H.*, I, 36–7; Shurtleff: *Mass. Col. Records*, I, 167.

13. Hutchinson: *Mass. Bay*, I, 95.

14. Shurtleff: *Mass. Col. Records*, I, 236.

15. Shurtleff: *Mass. Col. Records*, I, 259.

16. Alonzo Lewis: *The History of Lynn, including Nahant* (2nd edn., Boston, 1844), pp. 78–94.

17. John Winthrop: *The History of New England from 1630 to 1649*, ed. James Savage (Boston, 1826), II, 44–5.

18. Lewis: *Lynn*, pp. 94–6; *MPCR*, I, 164, 176.

19. This factor is suggested by John S. Jenness in *The Pascataqua Patents* (Portsmouth, 1878), p. 47, quoted by Frank W. Hackett in his notes to *1645–1656 Portsmouth Records* (Portsmouth, 1886), p. 57.

20. Charles W. Brewster: *Rambles about Portsmouth* (Portsmouth, N.H., 1859), I, 41–2; Robert Hayes Dunn: "A History of the Diocese of New Hampshire 1802–1952," *The New Hampshire Churchman*, V (June 1952), 4.

21. Shurtleff: *Mass. Col. Records*, I, 342.

22. Belknap: *N.H.*, I, 50.

23. Stackpole: *N.H.*, I, 55.

24. Winthrop: *N.E.*, II, 66.

25. Shurtleff: *Mass. Col. Records*, II, 29.

26. Edmund M. Wheelwright: "A Frontier Family," *Pub. Col. Soc. of Mass.*, I (March 1894), 276; Shurtleff: *Mass. Col. Records*, II, 43.

27. Bell: *Wheelwright*, pp. 45–75; Henry S. Burrage: *The Beginnings of Colonial Maine* (Portland, 1914), pp. 309–10.

28. William D. Williamson: *History of the State of Maine* (Hallowell, Me., 1832), I, 325; Burrage: *Beginnings*, pp. 204–7.

29. Williamson: *Me.*, I, 325–7; Burrage: *Beginnings*, pp. 357–8. There is a question whether Wells actually accepted the authority of this government. Charles Thornton Libby in *MPCR*, I, 133 *n.*

30. *MPCR*, I, 136.

31. Charles M. Andrews: *The Colonial Period of American History*, I (New Haven, 1934), 427–8.

32. Shurtleff: *Mass. Col. Records*, II, 285.

33. Burrage: *Beginnings,* pp. 359–61.
34. Williamson: *Me.,* I, 334–40; Burrage: *Beginnings,* pp. 367–8.
35. Williamson: *Me.,* I, 340–5; 351–2; *MPCR,* II, 5–7; *Doc. Hist. Me.,* IV, 71–2; Burrage: *Beginnings,* pp. 381–2.
36. *MPCR,* II, *passim.*

Chapter IV · *From Servants to Oligarchs, 1635–1692*

1. Nathaniel Adams: *Annals of Portsmouth* (Portsmouth, N.H., 1825), pp. 18–19, 23.
2. Jeremy Belknap: *The History of New-Hampshire* (Dover, N.H., 1812), I, 37–8.
3. *PPNH,* I, 45–7.
4. *PPNH,* I, 45–6.
5. *PPNH,* I, 48.
6. For one summary of this episode, see Howard T. Oedel: "Portsmouth, New Hampshire: The Role of the Provincial Capital in the Development of the Colony, 1700–1775" (unpublished dissertation, Boston University, 1960), pp. 17–19.
7. James Savage: *A Genealogical Dictionary of the First Settlers of New England* (Boston, 1860–2), I, 494–5; Charles Edward Banks: *Topographical Dictionary of 2885 English Emigrants to New England* (Baltimore, 1963), p. 56.
8. Savage: *Gen. Dict.,* IV, 368; Belknap: *N.H.,* I, 143.
9. *NEHGR,* IX, 55–6.
10. William G. Saltonstall: *Ports of Piscataqua* (Cambridge, Mass., 1941), pp. 12–14.
11. Robert G. Albion: *Forests and Sea Power* (Cambridge, Mass., 1926), pp. 234–5; Saltonstall: *Ports,* p. 14.
12. Diary of Samuel Sewall, M.H.S. *Collections,* 5th Ser., V, 188–9.
13. Belknap: *N.H.,* I, 152.
14. Customshouse returns showing both coasting and foreign trade in 1692 appear in *PPNH,* II, 77–84.
15. Using papers in the Manuscript Division of the Library of Congress, Saltonstall has found instances of prosecutions for such violations after the enforcement of the acts resumed. *Ports,* p. 16.
16. Thomas Hutchinson: *The History of the Colony and Province of Massachusetts-Bay,* ed. Lawrence Shaw Mayo (Cambridge, Mass., 1936), I, 230.
17. Belknap: *N.H.,* I, 88, 137–40; *PPNH,* I, 381–2; *Calendar of State Papers, Colonial,* X, 47, 352, 1036, 1041.
18. See the royal commission for the President and Council, *PPNH,* I, 373–82.

19. Belknap: *N.H.*, I, 139, 143.
20. Belknap: *N.H.*, I, 147–8, 150.
21. Belknap: *N.H.*, I, 148–9.
22. Cranfield's commission and instructions appear in *PPNH*, I, 433–44.
23. *PPNH*, I, 458–62.
24. Belknap provides a summary of the events of the administrations of Cranfield and Barefoote in *N.H.*, I, 153–61, 178.
25. Belknap: *N.H.*, I, 190–4.

Chapter V · Growing Pains, 1660–1713

1. William D. Williamson: *History of the State of Maine* (Hallowell, Me., 1832), I, 402–4, 412–27; *Doc. Hist. Me.*, IV, 202–4.
2. Williamson: *Me.*, I, 431–9.
3. Williamson: *Me.*, I, 448–52, 554.
4. *MPCR*, III, xi–xvii.
5. Williamson: *Me.*, I, 572–6, 599–600.
6. Samuel Maverick: *A Briefe Discription of New England* (wr. 1660, pub. Boston, 1885), pp. 7–11.
7. James Phinney Baxter, ed.: "Trelawney Papers," *Doc. Hist. Me.*, III, (Portland, 1884), 71 and *n.*, 88 *n.*, 163–6; Robert G. Albion: *Forests and Sea Power* (Cambridge, Mass., 1926), pp. 233–4.
8. William G. Saltonstall: *Ports of Piscataqua* (Cambridge, Mass., 1941), p. 14.
9. Saltonstall: *Ports*, pp. 14, 17.
10. Byron Fairchild: *Messrs. William Pepperrell: Merchants at Piscataqua* (Ithaca, N.Y., 1954), p. 19.
11. Fairchild: *Pepperrell*, p. 22; Williamson: *Me.*, I, 618.
12. John S. C. Abbott: *The History of Maine* (Boston, 1875), pp. 234–5.
13. Edward E. Bourne: "Garrison Houses, York County," Me. Hist. Soc. *Collections*, VIII, iii. See also Chap. VIII, below.
14. William Willis: *The History of Portland* (Portland, Me., 1831), I, 191; Abbott: *Me.*, pp. 245–6.
15. Abbott: *Me.*, p. 251.
16. Williamson: *Me.*, II, 29–32; *Doc. Hist. Me.*, IX, 94.
17. Williamson: *Me.*, II, 32–3; Francis Parkman: *Half-Century of Conflict* (Boston, 1902), I, 36–40.
18. *MPCR*, IV, xxxviii. For a glimpse of wartime life in Hampton in 1692, see James Dickinson: *A Journal of the Life, Travels, and Labour of Love . . . of . . . James Dickinson* (London, 1745), p. 58.
19. Carl Bridenbaugh: *Cities in the Wilderness* (New York, 1964), p. 233.
20. *Journals of the House of Representatives of Massachusetts* (Boston, 1919–64), I, 265; II, 63, 361.

21. *MPCR,* IV, 47–9, 64–6.
22. Daniel Neal: *The History of New England* (2nd edn., London, 1747), II, 113.
23. Petition from seven men of York to Governor Dudley, October 15, 1711, "Fogg Collection" (Mss., Me. Hist. Soc.), IX.
24. James Savage: *A Genealogical Dictionary of the First Settlers of New England* (Boston, 1860–2), IV, 54–6.
25. *PPNH,* II, 102.
26. *PPNH,* II, 105.
27. *PPNH,* II, 119–21.
28. *PPNH,* II, 124, 147.
29. *MPCR,* IV, 50–1.
30. *MPCR,* IV, 42–3, 50–1, 60–1; Bridenbaugh: *Cities in the Wilderness,* pp. 6, 113. The estimate of the Kittery population is in Fairchild: *Pepperrell,* p. 22.
31. *MPCR,* IV, liv, 38.
32. *MPCR,* V, xxxii, 143.
33. See, e.g., *MPCR,* IV, 46, 364, 367.
34. *MPCR,* IV, 288–9.
35. Parkman: *Half-Century of Conflict,* I, 41.
36. Fairchild: *Pepperrell,* p. 24.
37. *MPCR,* IV, 424.

Chapter VI · The Conquest Bears Fruit, 1600–1732

1. William D. Williamson: *History of the State of Maine* (Hallowell, Me., 1832), I, 419.
2. *MPCR,* II, 80–1.
3. *MPCR,* II, 101.
4. Sidney K. Perkins: "The Churches and Ministers of the Town of York," in James Phinney Baxter: *Agamenticus, Bristol, Gorgeana, York* (York, Me., 1904), p. 123.
5. Nathaniel Adams: *Annals of Portsmouth* (Portsmouth, N.H., 1825), p. 51.
6. George Bishop: *New-England Judged by the Spirit of the Lord* (London, 1703), pp. 361–8; *PPNH,* I, 238–40, 243–4.
7. *MPCR,* II, xxxvii.
8. Bishop: *N.E. Judged,* pp. 386–98; William Edmundson: *A Journal of the Life, Travels, Sufferings, and Labour of Love in the Work of the Ministry of . . . William Edmundson* (London, 1715), pp. 78–9; Calvin M. Clark: *History of the Congregational Churches in Maine* (Portland, 1935), II, 38; *MPCR,* II, xxxviii–xxxix.
9. *MPCR,* II, xxxiv–xxxviii.

10. See Everett S. Stackpole: *History of New Hampshire* (New York, 1916), I, 74–5, for a summary of witchcraft cases in New Hampshire, none of which resulted in convictions within the province. A very few references to witchcraft, which seems to have caused neither excitement nor punishment except, in one case, for "blasphemy," may be found in *MPCR*, II, 56, 82, and 86. Some of the legal documents connected with the Fuller affair are in *PPNH*, I, 415–19.

11. *Laws of New Hampshire*, Vols. I and II ed. Albert S. Batchellor (Concord, 1904–22), I, 560–1; II, 143–4.

12. Frederick Lewis Weis: *The Colonial Clergy and the Colonial Churches of New England* (Lancaster, Mass., 1936), pp. 247, 249, 251, 253, 256, 267, 277, 280; *Sibley's Harvard Graduates*, IV, 179–81.

13. *Sibley's Harvard Graduates*, II, 448–54.

14. *Sibley's Harvard Graduates*, III, 2–5.

15. Rufus M. Sawyer: "Agamenticus, Gorgeana, or York, Maine," *Congregational Quarterly*, VIII, 267.

16. Frank D. Marshall: "Historical Sketch of York," in Baxter: *Agamenticus*, p. 42.

17. York County Probate Records (York County Court House, Alfred, Me.), I, 19.

18. York County Probate Records, I, 20.

19. York County Probate Records, I, 128.

20. *Sibley's Harvard Graduates*, IV, 356–7.

21. Sawyer: "Agamenticus," p. 276.

22. Sawyer: "Agamenticus," pp. 272, 275.

23. Samuel Moody: *The Vain Youth Summoned to Appear at Christ's Bar* (3rd edn. enlarged, New London, 1760), p. 47.

24. Clifford K. Shipton provides a list of Moody's works, with their editions, in *Sibley's Harvard Graduates*, IV, 364–5. In addition to fourteen published titles, Shipton includes a Ms. sermon book for 1728 deposited in the Congregational Library in Boston. See also Clifford K. Shipton and James E. Mooney: *National Index of American Imprints Through 1800 —The Short-Title Evans* (Worcester, Mass., 1969), I, 533–4.

25. *Sibley's Harvard Graduates*, IV, 361.

26. Samuel Moody: *Discourse to Little Children* (Boston, 1770), pp. 21–2.

27. *New-England Weekly Journal*, February 10, 1736.

28. York town records quoted by Marshall in Baxter: *Agamenticus*, pp. 53–4.

29. Cotton Mather: *A Letter to Ungospellized Plantations* (Boston, 1702), p. 15.

Chapter VII · The Oligarchy Prospers, 1700–1730

1. Howard T. Oedel: "Portsmouth, New Hampshire: The Role of the Provincial Capital in the Development of the Colony, 1700–1775" (un-

published dissertation, Boston University, 1960), pp. 800–9; Charles W. Brewster: *Rambles about Portsmouth* (Portsmouth, N.H., 1859), I, 21; *Strawbery Banke in Portsmouth, New Hampshire—Official Guidebook and Map* (2nd rev. edn., Portsmouth, 1968), pp. ix, 17.

2. Oedel: "Portsmouth," p. 809. The figure for vessels is for 1697, when Lord Bellomont reported eleven ships, five brigantines, four ketches, and four sloops owned at Piscataqua. William G. Saltonstall: *Ports of Piscataqua* (Cambridge, Mass., 1941), p. 18.

3. Oedel: "Portsmouth," pp. 486–8; Geoffrey P. Moran: "A Survey of the Domestic Architecture of Portsmouth, New Hampshire, in the Colonial Period" (unpublished M.A. thesis, University of New Hampshire, 1967), pp. 59, 73.

4. I. S.: "Piscatway River" (c. 1662?), map in A. B. Hulbert: *The Crown Collection of Photographs of American Maps* (Cleveland, O., 1904–8), I, 23.

5. Hugh T. Morrison: *Early American Architecture* (New York, 1952), p. 17, and cuts, p. 18; John M. Howells: *The Architectural Heritage of the Piscataqua* (New York, 1937), pp. xvi–xvii; Strawbery Banke, Inc.: *Architecture Near the Piscataqua* (Portsmouth, 1964), p. 9.

6. Moran: "Domestic Architecture of Portsmouth," p. 35.

7. See *MPCR*, I, II, *passim*.

8. *Strawbery Banke Guidebook*, pp. 26–30; Moran: "Domestic Architecture of Portsmouth," p. 28; Brewster: *Rambles*, II, pp. 45–6. I am also indebted to Mr. Moran for an instructive guided inspection of the Sherburne house and other buildings in the vicinity in the summer of 1968, during his tenure as a member of the staff of Strawbery Banke, Inc., which is completing an important preservation project in this section of Portsmouth.

9. Moran speculates, on little basis except for an informed and intelligent guess, that this building may have been based on the typical English country manor house of the period. "Domestic Architecture of Portsmouth," pp. 18–20.

10. Morrison: *Early American Architecture*, p. 22.

11. Thomas T. Waterman: *The Dwellings of Colonial America* (Chapel Hill, 1950), pp. 251–3; *Bull. Metr. Mus.*, XXXIII (January 1938), 21.

12. *PPNH*, II, 325–31.

13. *Bull. Metr. Mus.*, XXXIII, 22; John Wentworth: *Wentworth Genealogy* (Boston, 1878), I, 72–99, 113.

14. Wentworth: *Genealogy*, I, 178, 180; *Bull. Metr. Mus.*, XXXIII, 21–3; *PPNH*, I, 608, 636, 640; Saltonstall: *Ports*, p. 62 *n*.

15. Oedel: "Portsmouth," p. 252.

16. See Francis Parkman: *Half-Century of Conflict* (Boston, 1902), I, Chap. XI, for a dramatic and careful account of this famous incident.

17. Daniel Neal: *The History of New England* (2nd edn., London, 1747), II, 210, 213–14.
18. Neal: *Hist. N.E.*, II, 210–11.
19. Neal: *Hist. N.E.*, II, 211; Saltonstall: *Ports*, p. 23; Carl Bridenbaugh: *The Colonial Craftsman* (New York, 1950), p. 112.
20. Joseph J. Malone: *Pine Trees and Politics* (Seattle, 1964), p. 66.
21. Saltonstall: *Ports*, p. 18; Charles M. Andrews: *The Colonial Period of American History* (New Haven, 1934–8), IV, 102.
22. Robert G. Albion: *Forests and Sea Power* (Cambridge, Mass., 1926), pp. 241–2.
23. Albion: *Forests and Sea Power*, p. 243; Andrews: *Col. Period*, IV, 102–3; Malone: *Pine Trees and Politics*, p. 29.
24. For a severe assessment of Bridger's character and accomplishments, see Malone: *Pine Trees and Politics*, pp. 28–81, esp. 29; for a more sympathetic treatment, see Albion: *Forests and Sea Power*, pp. 243–9.
25. Malone: *Pine Trees and Politics*, pp. 57–81.
26. Malone: *Pine Trees and Politics*, pp. 47, 49–50, 127–8; Saltonstall: *Ports*, p. 67.
27. *PPNH*, III, 366; Malone: *Pine Trees and Politics*, p. 66; Oedel: "Portsmouth," p. 117.
28. Albion: *Forests and Sea Power*, pp. 248–50.
29. Albion: *Forests and Sea Power*, pp. 255–67. See also Clifford K. Shipton's sketch of Elisha Cooke in *Sibley's Harvard Graduates*, IV, 349–56, for the effect upon Massachusetts politics of the struggle between Cooke, a "patriot" leader and extensive speculator in Maine timber lands, and Governors Shute and Belcher.
30. Malone: *Pine Trees and Politics*, pp. 82–123, 142–3.
31. *PPNH*, III, 718–19.
32. Eleanor L. Lord: *Industrial Experiments in the British Colonies of North America*. John Hopkins University Studies in Historical and Political Science, XVII (Baltimore, 1898), pp. 107, 142.
33. *Calendar of State Papers, America and West Indies, 1716*, quoted in Saltonstall: *Ports*, p. 64 *n*.
34. Saltonstall: *Ports*, p. 62 *n*.
35. William Douglass: *A Summary, Historical and Political, of the First Planting, Progressive Improvements, and Present State of the British Settlements in North-America* (London, 1760), I, 538, 539; II, 50, 99, 162, 259, 294.
36. Howells: *Architectural Heritage of the Piscataqua*, p. 205.
37. William G. Wendell: *Jonathan Warner (1726–1814), Merchant and Trader, King's Councillor, Mariner, Jurist* (Newcomen Society pamphlet, New York, 1950), pp. 10–12.
38. Wendell: *Jonathan Warner*, pp. 14–16.

39. Howells: *Architectural Heritage of the Piscataqua,* pp. 66–9.
40. Howells: *Architectural Heritage of the Piscataqua,* p. 113; Wendell: *Jonathan Warner,* p. 18.
41. See William B. Weeden: *Economic and Social History of New England* (Boston and New York, 1890), II, 540.
42. Oedel: "Portsmouth," pp. 268–71; *SPNH,* XXXII, 114–21.
43. Bridenbaugh: *Col. Craftsman,* pp. 109–12; Oedel: "Portsmouth," pp. 271–86; Brewster: *Rambles,* I, 133–8.
44. Brewster: *Rambles,* I, 159.
45. Brewster: *Rambles,* I, 127–8.
46. Oedel: "Portsmouth," p. 23.
47. Adams: *Portsmouth,* pp. 189–90; Oedel: "Portsmouth," pp. 751–5.
48. Isaiah Thomas: *The History of Printing in America* (Worcester, Mass., 1810), I, 432–3.
49. Brewster: *Rambles,* I, 78–84.
50. Adams: *Portsmouth,* pp. 50, 56.
51. Oedel: "Portsmouth," pp. 24–5.
52. Anon.: *A Short Account of the Present State of New-England* (n.p., 1690), p. 5.

Chapter VIII · Expansion, 1713–1744

1. William G. Saltonstall: *Ports of Piscataqua* (Cambridge, Mass, 1941), pp. 21–4, 62 *n.*; Byron Fairchild: *Messrs. William Pepperrell, Merchants at Piscataqua* (Ithaca, N.Y., 1954), pp. 44–7. For discussions of wartime profiteering in the larger colonial ports, see Carl Bridenbaugh: *Cities in the Wilderness* (New York, 1964), pp. 143, 175.
2. See, e.g., Robert G. Albion: *Forests and Sea Power* (Cambridge, Mass., 1926), pp. 269–72; Robert E. Pike: *Tall Trees, Tough Men* (New York, 1967), pp. 45–9; and Charles M. Thompson: *Independent Vermont* (Boston, 1942), pp. 38–51, where one can find a succinct, readable summary of the "New Hampshire Grants" episode.
3. William Willis: *The History of Portland* (Portland, Me., 1831), II, 11; *Journals of the Reverend Thomas Smith and the Reverend Samuel Deane, Pastors of the First Church in Portland,* ed. William Willis (Portland, Me., 1849), p. 10.
4. See Francis Parkman: *Half-Century of Conflict* (Boston, 1902), Chap. X.
5. William S. Southgate: *The History of Scarborough, from 1633 to 1783* (n.p., 1853), pp. 140–2.
6. Roy P. Fairfield: *Sands, Spindles, and Steeples* (Portland Me., 1956), p. 12; George Folsom: *History of Saco and Biddeford* (Saco, Me., 1830), p. 200.
7. I am indebted for this observation and for other facts and insights con-

cerning Wells to one of my graduate students at the University of New Hampshire, Mr. Robert Woodbury, who has presented his findings in a paper, "The Defense of Wells, Maine, During the Indian Wars" (1968).

8. Parkman: *Half-Century*, I, 48.
9. M.H.S. *Collections*, IV (1795), 90–1.
10. Daniel Neal: *The History of New England* (2nd edn., London, 1747), II, 212.
11. M.H.S. *Collections*, III (1794), 9.
12. Evarts B. Greene and Virginia D. Harrington: *American Population before the Federal Census of 1790* (New York, 1932), p. 29.
13. Raymond McFarland: *A History of the New England Fisheries* (New York, 1911), pp. 70–7.
14. William Douglas: *A Summary, Historical and Political, of the First Planting, Progressive Improvements, and Present State of the British Settlements in North-America* (London, 1760), I, 538.
15. *Laws of New Hampshire*, II (ed. Albert S. Batchellor, Concord, N.H., 1913), 301–2.
16. *New-England Weekly Journal*, June 19, 1727.
17. *New-England Courant*, December 2, 1723.
18. Jeremy Belknap: *The History of New-Hampshire* (Dover, N.H., 1812), III, 112.
19. *New-England Weekly Journal*, November 28, 1738.
20. Ms. certificates dated October 22, 1735, "Andrew Hawes of Stroudwater Collection, 1682–1855" (Mss., Me. Hist. Soc.).
21. Belknap: *N.H.*, III, 112.
22. *Acts and Resolves . . . of the Province of Massachusetts Bay*, II (Boston, 1874), 185, 383, 600.
23. *Laws of N.H.*, II, 259–60; III, 215–16.
24. *Laws of N.H.*, II, 260–1, 270–2. See also *MPCR*, IV, 37, for a presentment of the town of Kittery for failure to have a pound in 1695.
25. *Laws of N.H.*, II, 726–8.
26. *Sibley's Harvard Graduates*, IV, 349–56.
27. Diary of Thomas Fayerweather of Boston (typewritten copy in Me. Hist. Soc. of Ms. in Bangor, Me., Public Library), pp. 1–4, 6–8.

Chapter IX · Resettlement:
The Massachusetts Colonial System, 1713–1750

1. William D. Williamson: *History of the State of Maine* (Hallowell, Me., 1832), II, 29–32, 81; *Doc. Hist. Me.*, IX, 94.
2. Williamson: *Me.*, II, 81–3.
3. *Journals of the House of Representatives of Massachusetts* (Boston, 1919–64), I, 19. See also *Sibley's Harvard Graduates*, IV, 209–14, 260–4.

4. *Acts and Laws of Massachusetts Bay* (Boston, 1726), pp. 240–1.
5. *Doc. Hist. Me.,* IX, 361–2.
6. *Doc. Hist. Me.,* IX, 387–8, 423–4.
7. From Vol. I, p. 32, of a collection of manuscripts entitled "North Yarmouth Maine Papers" in the Maine Historical Society. The bulk of the following account of the resettlement of North Yarmouth has been reconstructed from the first two of the five volumes that comprise this collection, which was assembled by the Reverend David Shepley during his pastorate of the First Parish Church in North Yarmouth from 1829 to 1849. Documents in the collection will be cited hereafter as N. Yar. Mss., followed by the volume and page numbers.
8. *Doc. Hist. Me.,* IX, 386–7.
9. William H. Rowe: *Ancient North Yarmouth and Yarmouth, Maine, 1636–1936* (Yarmouth, Me., 1937), p. 58.
10. N. Yar. Mss., I, 36.
11. Rowe: *North Yarmouth,* p. 60; *Sibley's Harvard Graduates,* IV, 349–56. *Cf.* list of proprietors in Rowe: *North Yarmouth,* pp. 68–9.
12. N. Yar. Mss., I, 34; Rowe: *North Yarmouth,* p. 60.
13. N. Yar. Mss., I, 38, 40, 45, 48.
14. N. Yar. Mss., I, 49, 60
15. N. Yar. Mss., I, 52, 53.
16. N. Yar. Mss., I, 50.
17. N. Yar. Mss., I, 55, 56.
18. N. Yar. Mss., I, 50.
19. N. Yar. Mss., I, 54.
20. N. Yar. Mss., I, 69.
21. N. Yar. Mss., I, 69.
22. Rowe: *North Yarmouth,* p. 69.
23. Rowe: *North Yarmouth,* p. 70.
24. N. Yar. Mss., I, 87.
25. Rowe: *North Yarmouth,* p. 70.
26. N. Yar. Mss., I, 78.
27. N. Yar. Mss., I, 87.
28. N. Yar. Mss., I, 81.
29. N. Yar. Mss., I, 92.
30. N. Yar. Mss., I, 109.
31. N. Yar. Mss., I, 71.
32. N. Yar. Mss., I, 79.
33. N. Yar. Mss., I, 111.
34. N. Yar. Mss., I, 111.
35. N. Yar. Mss., I, 114.
36. N. Yar. Mss., I, 112.
37. N. Yar. Mss., I, 112.
38. N. Yar. Mss., I, 115.

39. N. Yar. Mss., I, 117.
40. N. Yar. Mss., I, 118.
41. N. Yar. Mss., II, 7.
42. N. Yar. Mss., II, 19.
43. *Sibley's Harvard Graduates,* VII, 503–4.
44. N. Yar. Mss., II, 2.
45. N. Yar. Mss., II, 10.
46. N. Yar. Mss., II, 18.
47. N. Yar. Mss., II, 22–6.
48. *Journals of the House of Representatives of Massachusetts,* XI, 19.
49. N. Yar. Mss., II, 74.
50. *The Acts and Resolves, Public and Private, of the Province of Massachusetts Bay* (Boston, 1869–1922), II, 616–17; *New-England Weekly Journal,* November 15, 1731.
51. N. Yar. Mss. I, 81, 85.
52. N. Yar. Mss., I, 115.
53. Rowe: *North Yarmouth,* pp. 71–2.
54. N. Yar. Mss., I, 115.
55. N. Yar. Mss., I, 117.
56. N. Yar. Mss., I, 119.
57. Rowe: *North Yarmouth,* p. 71.
58. Rowe: *North Yarmouth,* p. 75.
59. *Journals of the House of Representatives of Massachusetts,* XI, 176.
60. Rowe: *North Yarmouth,* pp. 82–3.
61. *Journals of the House of Representatives of Massachusetts,* XI, 383, 384, 401, 411.
62. *Journals of the House of Representatives of Massachusetts,* XII, 200.
63. *Journals of the House of Representatives of Massachusetts,* XVI, 104–5, 139–40.
64. Rowe: *North Yarmouth,* pp. 73–4.
65. N. Yar. Mss., II, 113.
66. N. Yar. Mss., II, 79.
67. N. Yar. Mss., II, 62, 98.
68. Records of the First Parish Church of North Yarmouth (Ms., Me. Hist. Soc.), I.

Chapter X · Moses Pearson and Old Falmouth, 1727–1764

1. *Journals of the Reverend Thomas Smith and the Reverend Samuel Deane, Pastors of the First Church in Portland,* ed. William Willis (Portland, Me., 1849), p. 67.
2. William Willis: *The History of Portland* (Portland, Me., 1831), II, 97.
3. Willis: *Portland,* II, 15–18.

4. Willis: *Portland,* II, 21.
5. Willis: *Portland,* II, 24–5; *Smith and Deane Journals,* p. 77. See also several petitions of the Old Proprietors to the General Court in *Doc. Hist. Me.,* X, 420–8.
6. *Doc. Hist. Me.,* X, 428.
7. *Smith and Deane Journals,* p. 66 *n.*; Ernest R. Rowe: *Highlights of Westbrook History* (Portland, Me., 1952), pp. 13–19; William Goold: *Portland in the Past, with Historical Notes of Old Falmouth* (Portland, Me., 1882), pp. 204–5.
8. Willis: *Portland,* II, 39 *n.*
9. *Smith and Deane Journals,* p. 10.
10. *Smith and Deane Journals,* p. 66 *n.*; Rowe: *Westbrook,* p. 17.
11. Willis: *Portland,* II, 24 *n.*; Henry Cole Quinby: *New England Family History,* II (New York, 1908–9), 164.
12. Willis: *Portland,* II, 22–3; "Falmouth Papers and Plans" (Mss., Me. Hist. Soc.), II, 10. The following documents, all in "Andrew Hawes of Stroudwater Collection, 1682–1855" (Mss., Me. Hist. Soc.), I, contain Moses Pearson's signature as proprietors' clerk: Warrant for new proprietors' meeting dated April 28, 1730; Notice for proprietors' meeting dated May 3, 1731; Notice for proprietors' meeting dated September 11, 1731. An application for a proprietors' meeting dated October 31, 1732, was addressed to Pearson as proprietors' clerk.
13. Quinby: *N.E. Family Hist.,* II, 167.
14. In "Documents relating to Old Falmouth, Portland, given to the Maine History Society by D.A.R., Elizabeth Wadsworth Chapter" (Mss., Me. Hist. Soc.).
15. Willis: *Portland,* II, 112.
16. Quinby: *N.E. Family Hist.,* II, 167.
17. Quinby: *N.E. Family Hist.,* II, 168.
18. Pepperrell to Pearson, February 8, 1744[/5], "Andrew Hawes Collection," I.
19. "Falmouth Papers and Plans," II, pp. 27–61 *passim.*
20. Evarts B. Greene and Virginia D. Harrington: *American Population before the Federal Census of 1790* (New York, 1932), p. 23 *n.*
21. Willis: *Portland,* II, 40–2.
22. Willis: *Portland,* II, 97.
23. Willis: *Portland,* II, 42; *Smith and Deane Journals,* p. 139 *n.*
24. Willis: *Portland,* II, 42.
25. Willis: *Portland,* II, 43, 45.
26. Willis: *Portland,* I, 205 *n.*
27. York County Probate Records (York County Court House, Alfred, Me.), IV, 49–51.
28. *Smith and Deane Journals,* p. 138 *n.*; Willis: *Portland,* II, 115.

29. *Smith and Deane Journals*, pp. 45, 46.
30. *Smith and Deane Journals*, pp. 52, 66.
31. Ms. Plan of Portland, Me. Hist. Soc.
32. Willis: *Portland*, II, 44.
33. Enoch Freeman's Diary (Ms., Portland, Me., Public Library), February, 1744; *Smith and Deane Journals*, p. 96.
34. See *Smith and Deane Journals*, pp. 76–7, 85, 86, 87, 96, 103, 132, 133, 151.
35. William B. Weeden: *Economic and Social History of New England* (Boston and New York, 1890), II, 578.
36. Weeden: *Ec. & Soc. Hist. N.E.*, II, 578.
37. Joseph J. Malone: *Pine Trees and Politics* (Seattle, 1964), pp. 147–8.
38. William Douglass, *A Summary, Historical and Political, of the First Planting, Progressive Improvements, and Present State of the British Settlements in North-America* (London, 1760), II, 54.
39. Goold: *Portland in the Past*, p. 199.
40. Sheriff's execution in favor of Samuel Waldo, quoted in Goold: *Portland in the Past*, p. 204.
41. Goold: *Portland in the Past*, p. 202.
42. Rowe: *Westbrook*, p. 11.
43. Malone: *Pine Trees and Politics*, pp. 70–1.
44. Leonard B. Chapman: "The Mast Industry of Old Falmouth," Me. Hist. Soc. *Collections*, 2nd Ser., VII (1896), 394–5.
45. Chapman: "Mast Industry," p. 395.
46. Chapman: "Mast Industry," p. 396; Goold: *Portland in the Past*, p. 203.
47. Chapman: "Mast Industry," pp. 397–8.
48. Douglass: *Summary*, II, 53.
49. *Smith and Deane Journals*, p. 79.
50. "Andrew Hawes Collection," II.
51. *Smith and Deane Journals*, p. 128.
52. *Smith and Deane Journals*, pp. 181–2. See Willis: *Portland*, II, 333, and map, II, 156–67, for an indication of the comparative size and value of Mayo's house.
53. See, e.g., Carl Bridenbaugh: *Cities in Revolt* (New York, 1964), p. 348; and *Peter Harrison: First American Architect* (Chapel Hill, 1949), pp. 27–8 n.
54. *New-Hampshire Gazette*, October 28, 1756.
55. *Smith and Deane Journals*, p. 169; *New-Hampshire Gazette*, November 4, 1756. For arrangements concerning an earlier masting convoy, this one forming at Portsmouth in 1741, see *New-England Weekly Journal*, September 15, 1741.
56. *Smith and Deane Journals*, p. 190.
57. Rowe: *Westbrook*, p. 18; Goold: *Portland in the Past*, pp. 204–6; Charles

Singer, E. J. Holmyard, A. R. Hall, and Trevor I. Williams, eds.: *A History of Technology* (Oxford, Eng., 1957), III, 412, and cut, p. 414.

58. *Smith and Deane Journals,* pp. 79, 81.

59. Willis: *Portland,* II, 104–5.

60. Willis: *Portland,* II, 105.

61. Willis: *Portland,* II, 106; *Smith and Deane Journals,* p. 51.

62. *Smith and Deane Journals,* p. 132. See deposition by Conant in "General Samuel Waldo Papers" (Mss., Me. Hist. Soc.) for an account of his activities at Saccarappa and his difficulties in maintaining his mill when his house was requisitioned for use as a garrison house in the early 1740's.

63. Willis: *Portland,* II, 106, and map, II, 156–7.

64. *Smith and Deane Journals,* pp. 76–7, 85, 86, 87, 96, 103, 132, 133, 151; *New-England Weekly Journal,* May 3, 1737.

65. Enoch Freeman's Diary, *passim;* there are several references to rentals of the gundalows during 1747.

66. Willis: *Portland,* II, 102.

67. Enoch Freeman's Diary, August 18, 1758.

68. "Account Book, Waterford and Falmouth, 1748–1755" (Ms., Me. Hist. Soc.), *passim.* Pearson's account is on p. 21.

69. "Account Book," p. 41.

70. See Willis: *Portland,* II, 283–4, for a brief description of the clothing and manners of the Falmouth "quality," as he called them.

71. *Smith and Deane Journals,* pp. 16–18.

72. Enoch Freeman's Diary, February, 1744.

73. York County Probate Records, IV, 49–51.

74. York County Probate Records, VI, 102–6; Willis: *Portland,* II, 297–8.

75. York County Probate Records, V, 95–6.

76. York County Probate Records, V, 50–1.

77. York County Probate Records, VIII, 250–1.

78. York County Probate Records, VII, 243–4.

79. Willis: *Portland,* II, 98.

80. Thomas Chute's Account Book (Ms., Me. Hist. Soc.), p. 153.

81. Bill of sale, Noyes to Pearson, "Andrew Hawes Collection," I.

82. *Sibley's Harvard Graduates,* VI, 403, 409.

83. *Smith and Deane Journals,* p. 231 *n.*

84. "Andrew Hawes Collection," I.

85. "Andrew Hawes Collection," I.

86. "Andrew Hawes Collection," II.

87. "Andrew Hawes Collection," I.

88. Mary Brown to Moses Pearson, February 28, 1763; George Stacey to Moses Pearson, March 24, 1763; David Sewall to Moses Pearson, May 21, 1763; William Greenleaf, Jr., to Moses Pearson, August 6, 1763. All in "Andrew Hawes Collection," II.

89. "Andrew Hawes Collection," II.

90. Willis: *Portland,* II, 64–5.
91. *Smith and Deane Journals, passim,* See, e.g., pp. 113, 168.
92. Willis: *Portland,* II, 67–70; *S.P.G. Sermons and Abstracts, 1765 Proceedings,* pp. 49–50.
93. Willis: *Portland,* II, 46.
94. "Andrew Hawes Collection," I.
95. Willis: *Portland,* II, 47–50.
96. *Smith and Deane Journals,* p. 69.
97. Willis: *Portland,* II, 287–8.
98. George Stacey to Moses Pearson, "Andrew Hawes Collection," II.
99. Willis: *Portland,* II, 69, 97–8.

Chapter XI · Into the Back Parts, 1719–1750

1. Roy Hidemichi Akagi: *The Town Proprietors of the New England Colonies* (Philadelphia, 1924), pp. 175–88.
2. Robert G. Albion: *Forests and Sea Power* (Cambridge, Mass., 1926), pp. 269–71.
3. *New-England Courant,* July 23, 1722.
4. *TPNH,* XI, 352–3; XIII, 174, 381–2.
5. Ava H. Chadbourne: *Maine Place Names* (Portland, 1955); Howard T. Oedel: "Picket Sentinels—Seven Proprietary Townships Established in Maine 1733–1759," Ms., 1951, Me. Hist. Soc.
6. *The History of the Colony and Province of Massachusetts-Bay,* ed. Lawrence Shaw Mayo (Cambridge, Mass., 1936), II, 252.
7. *Sibley's Harvard Graduates,* IV, 209–14, 260–4.
8. *Journals of the House of Representatives of Massachusetts* (Boston, 1919–64), II, 65.
9. *Journals of the House of Representatives of Massachusetts,* II, 293–4; Edward L. Parker: *The History of Londonderry, Comprising the Towns of Derry and Londonderry, N.H.* (Boston, 1851), pp. 36–9, 52–5.
10. *TPNH,* XII, 429–30.
11. Akagi: *Town Proprietors,* pp. 248–50; *DAB,* s.v. "Waldo, Samuel"; Jasper J. Stahl: *History of Old Broad Bay and Waldoboro* (Portland, Me., 1956), I, 92–4, 138–9.
12. *TPNH,* XIII, 332.
13. *TPNH,* XI, 146; Everett S. Stackpole: *History of New Hampshire* (New York, 1916), I, 244.
14. *Journals of the House of Representatives of Massachusetts,* VII, 148, 261–2.
15. *Journals of the House of Representatives of Massachusetts,* XII, 128.
16. *Journals of the House of Representatives of Massachusetts,* XII, 137.

17. Samuel Eliot Morison: *The Proprietors of Peterborough, New Hampshire* (Peterborough, 1930), pp. 6–8.

Chapter XII · From Wilderness to Country Town, 1720–1760

1. John Farmer: "Historical Sketch of Amherst, N.H.," N.H.H.S. *Collections*, V (1837), 82. For locations of some proprietors' meetings, see advertisements in *New-England Weekly Journal,* April 14, 1729; June 16 and 23, 1729; November 30 and December 7, 14, and 21, 1730; January 27 and February 10, 1736; July 20, 1736; October 12 and 19, 1736; February 17 and 24 and March 3, 1741.
2. Farmer: "Amherst," p. 82.
3. Misc. records of Gorhamtown proprietors, "Andrew Hawes of Stroudwater Collection, 1682–1855" (Mss., Me. Hist. Soc.), II.
4. *Journals of the House of Representatives of Massachusetts* (Boston, 1919–64), X, 366–8; XI, 230.
5. Advertisements in *New-England Weekly Journal,* October 12 and 19, 1736.
6. George M. Bodge: *History of Windham, Maine* (arr. Nathan Goold, in 1910 from several numbers of the *Maine Genealogical Recorder,* IV, 1887), pp. 13–15.
7. George Abbot Morison: *History of Peterborough, New Hampshire* (Rindge, N.H., 1954), I, 29–42.
8. Jeremy Belknap: *The History of New-Hampshire* (Dover, N.H., 1812), III, 57.
9. Salma Hale: "Annals of the Town of Keene, From its First Settlement, in 1734, to the Year 1790," N.H.H.S. *Collections,* II (1827), 79–80.
10. Belknap: *N.H.,* III, 58–9.
11. Edward L. Parker: *The Settlement of Londonderry, N.H.* (Old South Leaflet No. 93), pp. 3–7, 11.
12. Londonderry Town Records (Mss., N.H.H.S.), II, 50.
13. Edward L. Parker: *The History of Londonderry, Comprising the Towns of Derry and Londonderry, N.H.* (Boston, 1851), p. 47.
14. *TPNH,* IX, 480.
15. William B. Weeden: *Economic and Social History of New England* (Boston and New York, 1890), II, 674.
16. *Records of the Proprietors of Narragansett, No. 1, Now the Town of Buxton,* ed. William F. Goodwin (Concord, N.H., 1871), pp. 101–2.
17. *Records of Prop., Narra. No. 1,* p. 103.
18. *Records of Prop., Narra. No. 1.,* pp. 46–7.

19. Howard T. Oedel: "Picket Sentinels,—Seven Proprietary Townships Established in Maine 1733–1759" (Ms., 1951, Me. Hist. Soc.), pp. 18–22.
20. Farmer: "Amherst," p. 87.
21. Samuel T. Dole: *Windham in the Past,* ed. Frederick H. Dole (Auburn, Me., 1916), p. 340.
22. Dole: *Windham,* pp. 292, 311, 324–5.
23. Dole: *Windham,* pp. 481–2; Thomas Chute's Account Book (Ms., Me. Hist. Soc.), p. 172.
24. Dole: *Windham,* pp. 56–7.
25. Dole: *Windham,* pp. 63–84.
26. Massachusetts Archives, LXXIII, 348, printed in Bodge: *Windham,* p. 58.
27. Massachusetts Archives, LXXIII, 354, printed in Bodge: *Windham,* p. 63.
28. Bodge: *Windham,* p. 68.
29. Dole: *Windham,* p. 60; Bodge: *Windham,* p. 54.
30. Bodge: *Windham,* pp. 25–7.
31. See, e.g., *Journals of the House of Representatives of Massachusetts,* XI, 177, 179; *Doc. Hist. Me.,* XI, 140; Moses Long: "Historical Sketches of the Town of Warner, N.H.," N.H.H.S. *Collections,* III (1832), 182.
32. Hugh T. Morrison: *Early American Architecture* (New York, 1952), pp. 67–8.
33. Harold R. Shurtleff: *The Log Cabin Myth* (Cambridge, Mass., 1939), pp. 171–2; Jasper J. Stahl: *History of Old Broad Bay and Waldoboro* (Portland, Me., 1956), I, 114–15.
34. Shurtleff: *Log Cabin Myth,* p. 10, and illustration, p. 11.
35. Dole: *Windham,* pp. 271–2.
36. Parker: *History of Londonderry,* p. 47.
37. This anecdote was printed for the first time, after being handed down by Morison's descendants for a century and a quarter, in John H. Morison: *Life of the Hon. Jeremiah Smith* (Boston, 1845), p. 11 *n.* It is quoted in Shurtleff: *Log Cabin Myth,* p. 177, and in Parker: *History of Londonderry,* p. 70.
38. Shurtleff: *Log Cabin Myth,* p. 178 *n.*
39. Parker: *History of Londonderry,* p. 45.
40. Parker: *History of Londonderry,* p. 47 and plate opp. p. 275.
41. Massachusetts Archives, LXVII, 481, copied in Bodge: *Windham,* pp. 25–7.
42. Charles Bell: "Facts Relating to the Early History of Chester, N.H.," N.H.H.S. *Collections,* VII (1863), 347.
43. Dole: *Windham,* pp. 29–31.
44. Dole: *Windham,* p. 41.
45. Shurtleff: *Log Cabin Myth,* pp. 184–5 *n.*
46. Clifford K. Shipton: "The New England Frontier," *New England Quarterly,* (March 1937), 32. Douglas Edward Leach quotes it with approba-

tion in his generally excellent *Northern Colonial Frontier* (New York, 1966), p. 174.

Chapter XIII · The Country Town
Takes Shape, 1725–1760

1. Charles J. Fox: *History of the Old Township of Dunstable* (Nashua, N.H., 1846), pp. 10–18.
2. Londonderry Town Records (Mss., N.H.H.S.), I, 1.
3. Sumner Chilton Powell: *Puritan Village: The Formation of a New England Town* (Middletown, Conn., 1963), pp. 88, 96.
4. Londonderry Town Records, I, 37–41.
5. Jacob B. Moore: "Historical Sketch of Concord, in the county of Merrimack, N.H.," N.H.H.S. *Collections,* I (1824), 153–4, 156.
6. Windham Proprietors or Grantees Book (Ms., Me. Hist. Soc.), pp. 13–14; Samuel T. Dole. *Windham in the Past,* ed. Frederick H. Dole (Auburn, Me., 1916), p. 15.
7. *Records of the Proprietors of Narragansett No. 1, Now the Town of Buxton,* ed. William F. Goodwin (Concord, N.H., 1871), p. 105.
8. Windham Prop. or Grantees Book, pp. 13–18, 25.
9. Londonderry Town Records, I, 4.
10. Londonderry Town Records, I, 4.
11. Londonderry Town Records, I, 12.
12. Windham Prop. or Grantees Book, pp. 15, 17, 30.
13. Windham Prop. or Grantees Book, pp. 31–2.
14. Windham Prop. or Grantees Book, p. 39; Dole: *Windham,* pp. 29–30.
15. *Records of Prop., Narra. No. 1,* p. 105.
16. *Records of Prop., Narra. No. 1,* p. 125.
17. *Records of Prop., Narra. No. 1,* p. 51.
18. *Records of Prop., Narra. No. 1,* p. 162.
19. Moses Long: "Historical Sketches of the Town of Warner, N.H.," N.H.H.S. *Collections,* III (1832), 185–8.
20. Salma Hale: "Annals of the Town of Keene, From its First Settlement in 1734, to the Year 1790," N.H.H.S. *Collections,* II (1827), 76.
21. Edward L. Parker: *The History of Londonderry, Comprising the Towns of Derry and Londonderry, N.H.* (Boston, 1851), p. 48.
22. Londonderry Town Records, I, 28.
23. Londonderry Town Records, II, 51.
24. Windham Prop. or Grantees Book, pp. 31–2, 66–7.
25. Powell: *Puritan Village,* Fig. 10 following p. 60, and p. 74.
26. Powell: *Puritan Village,* Fig. 13 following p. 76.
27. Charles M. Andrews: *The River Towns of Connecticut (Johns Hopkins University Studies in Historical and Political Science,* 7th Ser., VII–VIII–IX [July–September, 1889]), 42–71, and map of Wethersfield, p. 6.

28. James G. Leyburn: *The Scotch-Irish: A Social History* (Chapel Hill, 1962), pp. 263–4.
29. Parker: *History of Londonderry,* p. 119.
30. Parker: *History of Londonderry,* p. 82. Londonderry Town Records, I, 10; II, 58.
31. Parker: *History of Londonderry,* p. 82.
32. Londonderry Town Records, II, 50.
33. Londonderry Town Records, I, 37–41.
34. Londonderry Town Records, II, 67; *TPNH,* IX, 502–3; Parker: *History of Londonderry,* pp. 92–3, 147. For a fuller discussion, see Chap. XVI, below.
35. *History of Bedford, New Hampshire, Being Statistics, Compiled on the Occasion of the One Hundredth Anniversary of the Incorporation of the Town, May, 19, 1850,* comp. Peter P. Woodbury, Thomas Savage, and William Patten (Boston, 1851), p. 110.
36. Samuel Eliot Morison: *The Proprietors of Peterborough, New Hampshire* (Peterborough, 1930), pp. 8–9.
37. Parker: *History of Londonderry,* p. 184. See also map of Peterborough in 1819 in George Abbot Morison: *History of Peterborough, New Hampshire* (Rindge, N.H., 1954), following p. 148.
38. Dole: *Windham,* pp. 292–3.
39. Dole: *Windham,* pp. 56–7, 99–100.
40. Dole: *Windham,* p. 95.
41. George M. Bodge: History of Windham, Maine (arr. by Nathan Goold in 1910 from several numbers of the *Maine Genealogical Recorder,* IV, 1887), p. 56.
42. Dole: *Windham,* p. 80.
43. Dole: *Windham,* pp. 83–5.
44. Dole: *Windham,* p. 58.
45. Windham Prop. or Grantees Book, p. 92.
46. Windham Prop. or Grantees Book, pp. 101, 106, 109, 129.
47. Massachusetts Archives, LXVII, 481, copied in Bodge: *Windham,* pp. 25–7.
48. Windham Prop. or Grantees Book, *passim.*
49. Curtis Chute's wedding date is in Dole: *Windham,* p. 340.
50. Dole: *Windham,* pp. 481–2.
51. Dole: *Windham,* p. 173.
52. Dole: *Windham,* pp. 35–7.
53. Dole: *Windham,* pp. 480–1.
54. Dole: *Windham,* p. 46.
55. Dole: *Windham,* p. 292.
56. Dole: *Windham,* p. 44.
57. Dole: *Windham,* p. 47.
58. Dole: *Windham,* p. 42.

59. Dole: *Windham,* pp. 146–8; Windham Prop. or Grantees Book, p. 43.

60. Record of meeting of the Proprietors of Sebago Township, March 2, 1754, "Andrew Hawes of Stroudwater Collection, 1682–1855" (Mss., Me. Hist. Soc.), II.

61. Windham Prop. or Grantees Book, p. 129.

62. Windham Prop. or Grantees Book, pp. 130–1.

63. Windham Prop. or Grantees Book, pp. 138–9.

64. Windham Prop. or Grantees Book, pp. 145–6.

65. Windham Prop. or Grantees Book, pp. 154–5; Dole: *Windham,* pp. 151–5.

66. Rev. Peter Thacher Smith's Church Record Book (Ms., Me. Hist. Soc.), Contents page prior to p. 1.

67. Evarts B. Greene and Virginia D. Harrington: *American Population Before the Federal Census of 1790* (New York, 1932), p. 38.

68. Windham Prop. or Grantees Book, p. 148; Windham Town Record Book (Ms., Me. Hist. Soc.), p. 1.

69. Long: "Warner," pp. 188–9.

70. John Farmer: "Historical Sketch of Amherst, N. H.," N.H.H.S. *Collections,* V (1837), 83.

71. Mitford M. Mathews: *A Dictionary of Americanisms* (Chicago, 1951), I, 512; *A Dictionary of American English* (Chicago, 1940), II, 801.

72. Parker: *History of Londonderry,* p. 88.

73. See frontispiece, *The Diary of Matthew Patten of Bedford, New Hampshire* (Concord, N.H., 1903).

74. Harold Donaldson Eberlein: *The Architecture of Colonial America* (Boston, 1929), pp. 44–6; Abbott Lowell Cummings, ed.: *Rural Household Inventories, 1675–1775* (Boston, 1964), p. xv.

75. Diaries of the Reverend Timothy Walker, N.H.H.S. *Collections,* IX (1889), 169–70. See photograph of house and comment in *Historical New Hampshire,* XXII (Autumn 1967), 8.

76. John Mead Howells: *The Architectural Heritage of the Merrimack* (New York, 1941), pp. 220–1.

77. *New-England Weekly Journal,* July 5, 1737.

78. Salma Hale: "Annals of the Town of Keene, From its First Settlement, in 1734, to the Year 1790," N.H.H.S. *Collections,* II (1827), 80–1.

79. Hale: "Keene," pp. 85–6.

80. "Journal of Captain Phineas Stevens' Journey from Charlestown, N.H., to Canada, 1752," in Newton D. Mereness, ed.: *Travels in the American Colonies* (New York, 1916), p. 319.

81. Martha McD. Frizzell et al.: *Second History of Charlestown, N.H.* (Littleton, N.H., 1955), p. 218; Francis Parkman: *Half-Century of Conflict* (Boston, 1902), II, 219.

82. Stevens' Journal, in Mereness: *Travels,* pp. 319–20; *Oxford English Dictionary,* s.v. "Score."

83. Stevens' Journal, in Mereness: *Travels,* pp. 320–1.

84. Fiske Kimball: *Domestic Architecture of the American Colonies and of the Early Republic* (New York, 1927), pp. 21–30.

Chapter XIV · Making Good, and
Three Who Did, 1725–1763

1. Edward L. Parker: *The Settlement of Londonderry, N.H.* (Old South Leaflet No. 93), pp. 49–51.
2. Samuel T. Dole: *Windham in the Past,* ed. Frederick H. Dole (Auburn, Me., 1916), pp. 173–4.
3. Memoirs and Journal of the Reverend Paul Coffin, Me. Hist. Soc. *Collections,* IV (1856), 284.
4. Jeremy Belknap: *The History of New-Hampshire* (Dover, N.H., 1812), III, 97.
5. Belknap: *N.H.,* III, 98–9.
6. Percy Wells Bidwell and John I. Falconer: *History of Agriculture in the Northern United States, 1620–1860* (New York, 1941), p. 125.
7. See Bidwell and Falconer: *Hist. of Agriculture,* pp. 123–4, for descriptions of eighteenth-century plows and plowing. The authors quote extensively from Charles L. Flint: *A Hundred Years' Progress in American Agriculture* (11th Annual Report, Maine Board of Agriculture, 1874), pp. 111, 119.
8. Bidwell and Falconer: *Hist. of Agriculture,* pp. 124–5; *The Diary of Matthew Patten of Bedford, New Hampshire* (Concord, N.H., 1903), p. 87.
9. Dole: *Windham,* p. 275. See also references to various crops in the mid-eighteenth century in Jared Eliot: *Essays Upon Field Husbandry in New England and Other Papers,* ed. Henry J. Carman and Rexford G. Tugwell (New York, 1934), *passim.*
10. A description of the methods of eighteenth-century flax culture and one phase of linen manufacture may be found in *Select Essays: Containing: The Manner of raising and dressing Flax, and Hemp. Also, the whole Method of Bleaching or Whitening Linen-Cloth* . . . (Philadelphia, 1777), pp. 1–37, 87–139.
11. James G. Leyburn: *The Scotch-Irish: A Social History* (Chapel Hill, 1962), p. 164 *n.*
12. Parker: *Settlement of Londonderry,* p. 49.
13. Dole: *Windham,* p. 275.
14. George Woodbury: *John Goffe's Legacy* (New York, 1955), pp. 70–1.
15. *New-Hampshire Gazette,* October 21, 1756. This was the third number of the newspaper.
16. Thomas Chapman: *The Cyder-Maker's Instructor, Sweet-Maker's Assistant, and Victualler's and Housekeeper's Director* (Boston, 1762), pp. v–vi, 9–15.

17. Diaries of the Reverend Timothy Walker, N.H.H.S. *Collections,* IX (1889), 166.

18. *Diary of Matthew Patten,* p. 62.

19. Memoirs and Journal of Coffin, pp. 282–3.

20. *The Philosophical Transactions of the Royal Society of London, . . . Abridged,* VI (1809), 458–9 (abridged from Royal Society of London, *Philosophical Transactions,* XXXI [1720], 27).

21. Belknap: *N.H.,* III, 85.

22. *Phil. Trans., Abridged,* VI, 459; Belknap: *N.H.,* II, 86.

23. Salma Hale: "Annals of the Town of Keene, From its First Settlement, in 1734, to the Year 1790," N.H.H.S. *Collections,* II (1827), 78.

24. Dole: *Windham,* p. 276.

25. Londonderry Town Records, I, 26–7; Dole: *Windham,* p. 272.

26. *A Journal for the Years 1739–1803 by Samuel Lane of Stratham, New Hampshire,* ed. Charles Lane Hanson (Concord, N.H., 1937), pp. 26–30, 33–7, 39.

27. *Cf.* Bidwell and Falconer: *Hist. of Agriculture,* p. 131, which contains similar comments on Yankee versatility and the quotation by Livingston from "American Agriculture" in *Edinburgh Encyclopedia* (1st Amer. edn., 1832), I, 338.

28. William H. Brown: *Colonel John Goffe* (Manchester, N.H., 1950), pp. 21–4.

29. Brown: *Goffe,* pp. 24–7.

30. Brown: *Goffe,* pp. 49–53.

31. Brown: *Goffe,* pp. 53–5.

32. Brown: *Goffe,* pp. 57–70.

33. Brown: *Goffe,* p. 76.

34. Brown: *Goffe,* pp. 77–8.

35. *TPNH,* XII, 25.

36. Brown: *Goffe, passim;* Belknap: *N.H.,* II, 305–6.

37. Brown: *Goffe,* p. 206.

38. Brown: *Goffe,* pp. 207, 222.

39. *Diary of Matthew Patten,* p. 266.

40. *Diary of Matthew Patten,* pp. 94–5.

41. *Diary of Matthew Patten,* p. 95.

42. *Diary of Matthew Patten,* pp. 8–15.

43. *Diary of Matthew Patten,* p. 27.

44. *Diary of Matthew Patten,* p. 25.

45. *History of Bedford, New Hampshire, Being Statistics, Compiled on the Occasion of the One Hundredth Anniversary of the Incorporation of the Town; May 19th, 1850,* comp. Peter P. Woodbury, Thomas Savage, and William Patten (Boston, 1851), p. 205.

46. *Diary of Matthew Patten,* p. 111.

47. *Diary of Matthew Patten,* p. 113.

48. *Diary of Matthew Patten*, p. 51.
49. *Diary of Matthew Patten*, p. 87.
50. *Diary of Matthew Patten*, p. 112.
51. *Diary of Matthew Patten*, pp. 48, 82.
52. *Diary of Matthew Patten*, pp. 140–1.
53. *Lane Journal*, pp. 32–3.
54. *Hist. of Bedford*, pp. 214–16.
55. *Diary of Matthew Patten*, p. 3.
56. *Diary of Matthew Patten, passim.* See esp. p. 129.
57. *Diary of Matthew Patten*, p. 123. See also p. 62.
58. "Captain Thomas Chute's Account of Bayonets supply'd his Company" in "Autographs of Special Note" (Ms. Collection, Me. Hist. Soc.), I; Dole, *Windham*, pp. 65–6.
59. Dole: *Windham*, pp. 34, 94.
60. Thomas Chute's Account Book (Ms., Me. Hist. Soc.), pp. 1–47.
61. Chute's Account Book, pp. 148–65.
62. Chute's Account Book, p. 153.
63. Chute's Account Book, pp. 166–217, but see esp. pp. 168, 170; George M. Bodge: Index to Chute's Account Book (Ms., Me. Hist. Soc.), Introduction.
64. Chute's Account Book, pp. 176–8.
65. Chute's Account Book, p. 153.
66. Chute's Account Book, p. 181; Dole: *Windham*, pp. 41, 225–6.
67. Chute's Account Book, pp. 207, 217.
68. Bodge: Index to Chute's Account Book, Introduction.
69. Bodge: Index to Chute's Account Book, Introduction; Chute's Account Book, p. 169.
70. Chute's Account Book, pp. 166–7, 171, 173; Bodge: Index to Chute's Account Book, Introduction.
71. Chute's Account Book, p. 168.
72. Chute's Account Book, p. 173.
73. Chute's Account Book, p. 177.

Chapter XV · The Life of the Country Town, 1725–1763

1. "Manners and Customs of Olden Time," N.H.H.S. *Collections*, V (1837), 225–6.
2. "Journal of Captain Phineas Stevens' Journey from Charlestown, N.H., to Canada, 1752," in Newton D. Mereness, ed.: *Travels in the American Colonies* (New York, 1916), pp. 319, 321.
3. John Farmer: "Historical Sketch of Amherst, N.H.," N.H.H.S. *Collections*, V (1837), 86.

4. Moses Long: "Historical Sketches of the Town of Warner, N.H.," N.H.H.S. *Collections,* III (1832), 192–3.

5. *New-England Weekly Journal,* February 17, 1729.

6. Memoirs and Journal of the Reverend Paul Coffin, Me. Hist. Soc. *Collections,* IV (1856), 242–3, 247.

7. "A Record of the Transactions of the annual Convocation of Ministers in the Province of N: Hampshire, began July 28th, 1747," N.H.H.S. *Collections,* IX (1889), 2, 25.

8. "Record of Transactions," pp. 55–8.

9. Memoirs and Journal of Coffin, p. 244.

10. *Sibley's Harvard Graduates,* IV, 146–53.

11. Jacob B. Moore: "Historical Sketch of Concord, in the county of Merrimack, N.H.," N.H.H.S. *Collections,* I (1824), 154–63; Diaries of the Reverend Timothy Walker, N.H.H.S. *Collections,* IX (1889), *passim; Sibley's Harvard Graduates,* VII, 603–14; Joseph B. Walker: *Chronicles of an Old New England Farm—The Farm of the First Minister* (Concord, N.H., 1906), pp. 7, 17, 23; *DAB,* s.v. "Cotton, John."

12. "Manners and Customs," p. 225; Farmer: "Amherst," p. 84.

13. "Manners and Customs," pp. 226–7.

14. "Manners and Customs," p. 227; Farmer: "Amherst," p. 84.

15. See Ola Elizabeth Winslow: *Meetinghouse Hill* (New York, 1952), pp. 150–70.

16. Edward L. Parker: *The History of Londonderry, Comprising the Towns of Derry and Londonderry, N.H.* (Boston, 1851), pp. 74–5.

17. Parker: *History of Londonderry,* pp. 76–7.

18. *The Diary of Matthew Patten of Bedford, New Hampshire* (Concord, N.H., 1903), p. 69.

19. *Diary of Matthew Patten,* p. 16.

20. *Diary of Matthew Patten,* p. 119.

21. Parker: *History of Londonderry,* pp. 77–8; "Manners and Customs," p. 227.

22. Long: "Warner," p. 191.

23. Long: "Warner," p. 191.

24. Advertisement in *New-Hampshire Gazette,* October 13, 1758.

25. *Diary of Matthew Patten,* p. 100.

26. Parker: *History of Londonderry,* p. 91.

27. Parker: *History of Londonderry,* pp. 93–4, 120–2.

28. Samuel T. Dole: *Windham in the Past,* ed. Frederick H. Dole (Auburn, Me., 1916), p. 276.

29. Dole: *Windham,* p. 35.

30. Thomas Chute's Account Book (Ms., Me. Hist. Soc.), p. 172.

31. Nathaniel Bouton: *The History of Concord* (Concord, N.H., 1856), pp. 18–20; Daniel F. Secomb: *History of the Town of Amherst* (Concord, N.H., 1883), pp. 97–8; Benjamin Read: *The History of Swanzey, New*

Hampshire (Salem, Mass., 1892), p. 11; S. G. Griffin: *A History of the Town of Keene* (Keene, N.H., 1904), pp. 32–3.

32. Joseph Fullonton: *The History of the Town of Raymond, N.H.* (Dover, N.H., 1875), pp. 16–18.

33. Robert Earle Moody: "The Maine Frontier, 1607–1763" (unpublished dissertation, Yale University, 1933), pp. 350–2, 351 *n*.

34. Massachusetts Archives, XXIX, 335–59 (Ms. copy in Me. Hist. Soc.).

35. John S. C. Abbott: *The History of Maine* (Boston, 1875), pp. 319–23.

36. *New-England Weekly Journal*, June 19, 1727.

37. Jaazaniah Crosby: "Annals of Charlestown, in the County of Sullivan, New-Hampshire," N.H.H.S. *Collections*, IV (1834), 121; "Journal of Captain Phineas Stevens' Journey from Charlestown, N. H., to Canada, 1752," in Newton D. Mereness, ed.: *Travels in the American Colonies* (New York, 1916), p. 319.

38. *New-Hampshire Gazette*, July 1, 1757; June 16, 1758.

39. Kenneth Scott: "Colonial Innkeepers of New Hampshire," *Historical New Hampshire*, XIX (Spring 1964), 7–8, 30–1.

40. Salma Hale: "Annals of the Town of Keene, From its First Settlement, in 1734, to the Year 1790," N.H.H.S. *Collections*, II (1827), 82–3. See also pp. 91–2 for Ferry's treatment after an Indian raid on the settlement eight years later.

Chapter XVI · The Great Awakening and the Great Crusade, 1727–1745

1. See p. 159.

2. See p. 117.

3. *Journals of the Reverend Thomas Smith and the Reverend Samuel Deane, Pastors of the First Church in Portland*, ed. William Willis (Portland, Me., 1849), pp. 63–4; *New-England Weekly Journal*, March 27, 1727; Calvin M. Clark: *History of the Congregational Churches in Maine* (Portland, 1935), II, 84; C. C. Goen: *Revivalism and Separatism in New England, 1740–1760* (New Haven, 1962), p. 12; Jeremy Belknap: *The History of New-Hampshire* (Dover, N.H., 1812), III, 227.

4. *Smith and Deane Journals*, p. 79.

5. *Smith and Deane Journals*, p. 81.

6. Jabez Fitch: *The Work of the Lord in the Earthquake, to be duly Regarded by us* (Boston, 1728), pp. 10, 17.

7. *The Christian History . . . For the Year 1743* (Boston, 1744), p. 383.

8. *Sibley's Harvard Graduates*, III, 418–20.

9. *Christian History, 1743*, p. 384.

10. [Jabez Fitch]: *An Account of the Numbers that have Died of the Dis-*

temper in the Throat, Within the Province of New-Hampshire (Boston, 1736), pp. 4–5.

11. [Fitch]: *An Account*, pp. 1–6.

12. Belknap: *N.H.*, II, 97.

13. *Smith and Deane Journals*, pp. 82–3.

14. *Smith and Deane Journals*, p. 86.

15. *Smith and Deane Journals*, pp. 85 *n.*, 102 *n.*

16. Jabez Fitch: *Two Sermons on Occasion of the Fatal Distemper* (Boston, 1736): see esp. pp. 26–7.

17. [Fitch]: *An Account*, pp. 3–4, 6.

18. Fitch: *Two Sermons*, p. 27.

19. *Smith and Deane Journals*, pp. 86–9.

20. Nicholas Gilman's Diary (Ms., N.H.H.S.), December 20 and 23, 1741; January 13, 1741/2.

21. Belknap: *N.H.*, II, 97.

22. Londonderry Town Records (Mss., N.H.H.S.), II, 32–63, 67, 84–5; Frederick Lewis Weis: *The Colonial Clergy and the Colonial Churches of New England* (Lancaster, Mass., 1936), p. 203.

23. Edward L. Parker: *The History of Londonderry, Comprising the Towns of Derry and Londonderry, N.H.* (Boston, 1851), p. 92. MacGregor must have been ordained by the Boston Presbytery, which was organized at least as early as 1727. (Parker: *History of Londonderry*, p. 131.)

24. Weis: *Col. Clergy*, p. 69.

25. *TPNH*, IX, 495–500.

26. *TPNH*, IX, 502–3.

27. Parker: *History of Londonderry*, pp. 147–51.

28. William Willis: *The History of Portland*, (Portland, Me., 1831), II, 58; Clark: *Congregational Churches in Maine*, II, 131–2.

29. George Whitefield: *The Two First Parts of his Life, with his Journals* (London, 1756), pp. 398–9.

30. Whitefield: *Journals*, pp. 400–1.

31. *Smith and Deane Journals*, p. 95.

32. *Christian History*, 1743, pp. 383–94.

33. *An Abstract of the . . . Proceedings of the Society for the Propagation of the Gospel in Foreign Parts, from the 19th of February, 1741–42, to the 18th of February, 1742–43*, appended to *A Sermon Preached before the Incorporated Society . . . February 18, 1742–43* (London, 1743), p. 42; S.P.G. Transcripts, p. 16a, quoted in Howard T. Oedel: "Portsmouth, New Hampshire: The Role of the Provincial Capital in the Development of the Colony, 1700–1775," (unpublished dissertation, Boston University, 1960), p. 386.

34. For an account of the visit of Tennent to Portsmouth in January 1741, see *New-England Weekly Journal*, January 20, 1741.

35. Goen: *Revivalism and Separatism*, pp. 105–6.

36. *Smith and Deane Journals,* pp. 102–4.

37. *Smith and Deane Journals,* pp. 116–17; Goen: *Revivalism and Separatism,* p. 12.

38. *Smith and Deane Journals,* p. 119.

39. *Smith and Deane Journals,* pp. 119, 121.

40. *S.P.G. Sermons and Abstracts, 1742/3 Proceedings,* p. 40.

41. Parker: *History of Londonderry,* p. 148.

42. [John Newmarch]: *The Result of a Council of Ten Churches, Conven'd at Exeter, Jan. 31, 1743* (Boston, 1744); Goen: *Revivalism and Separatism,* p. 319.

43. *A Journal for the Years 1739–1803 by Samuel Lane of Stratham, New Hampshire,* ed. Charles Lane Hanson (Concord, N.H., 1937), p. 17.

44. *Lane Journal,* pp. 30–1.

45. Gilman's Diary, February 25–October 3, 1740, *passim.* Biographical data is from *The Native Ministry of New Hampshire* (Concord, N.H., 1906). See also *New-England Weekly Journal,* May 17, 1737.

46. Gilman's Diary, December 20, 1741–January 15, 1741/2 *passim.*

47. Gilman's Diary, March 4–April 14, 1742.

48. Quoted in Goen: *Revivalism and Separatism,* pp. 181–2.

49. Gilman's Diary, March 24, 1741/2; May 9, 1742; March 3, 1742/3.

50. Gilman's Diary, June 17, 1742; Goen: *Revivalism and Separatism,* p. 104.

51. See Backus Papers, Andover-Newton Theological School Mss. My attention was directed to Backus's connections with Durham by Professor William G. McLoughlin.

52. Everett S. Stackpole and Lucien Thompson: *History of the Town of Durham, New Hampshire* (Concord, N.H., 1913), I, 197; N.H.H.S. *Collections,* IX (1889), 1, 5–8, 9–10.

53. Stackpole and Thompson: *Durham,* I, 194.

54. Belknap: *N.H.,* II, 159–60. See also Usher Parsons: *The Life of Sir William Pepperrell, Bart.* (Boston, 1856), and Francis Parkman: *Half-Century of Conflict* (Boston, 1902), II, 74–7.

55. Belknap: *N.H.,* II, 160.

56. Parsons: *Pepperrell,* p. 57.

57. Belknap: *N.H.,* II, 165; Henry S. Burrage: *Maine at Louisbourg in 1745* (Augusta, Me., 1910), pp. 19–20.

58. "Andrew Hawes of Stroudwater Collection, 1682–1855" (Mss., Me. Hist. Soc.), I.

59. Burrage: *Maine at Louisbourg,* p. 20.

60. Burrage: *Maine at Louisbourg,* p. 22.

61. *Smith and Deane Journals,* p. 116.

62. Parkman: *Half-Century,* II, 77.

63. Belknap: *N.H.,* II, 165–72; Parsons: *Pepperrell:* pp. 57–100; *DAB,* XIV, 456–7.

64. *Sibley's Harvard Graduates*, IV, 363–4.
65. *Smith and Deane Journals*, pp. 119–20.
66. *Extraordinary Events the Doings of God, and marvellous in pious Eyes* (Edinburgh, 1746), pp. 34, 37–8.
67. Parsons: *Pepperrell*, p. 109; Burrage: *Maine at Louisbourg*, p. 47.
68. Belknap: *N. H.*, II, 174; Thomas Hutchinson: *The History of the Colony and Province of Massachusetts-Bay*, ed. Lawrence Shaw Mayo (Cambridge, Mass., 1936), II, 322 and *n*.

Chapter XVII · Religion, Society, and Politics, 1730–1752

1. Jeremy Belknap: *The History of New-Hampshire* (Dover, N.H., 1812), I, 167–9; Nathaniel Adams: *Annals of Portsmouth* (Portsmouth, N.H., 1825), p. 99.
2. Adams: *Portsmouth*, pp. 129–32; *Sibley's Harvard Graduates*, III, 379–82, 418–20; IV, 201–6; *New-England Courant*, October 7, 1723.
3. Belknap: *N.H.*, II, 98–9; Thomas Hutchinson: *The History of the Colony and Province of Massachusetts-Bay*, ed. Lawrence Shaw Mayo (Cambridge, Mass., 1936), II, 292.
4. Adams: *Portsmouth*, p. 162; Robert 'Hayes Dunn: "A History of the Diocese of New Hampshire, 1802–1952," *The New Hampshire Churchman*, V, (June, 1952), p. 5; Howard T. Oedel: "Portsmouth, New Hampshire: The Role of the Provincial Capital in the Development of the Colony, 1700–1775 (unpublished dissertation, Boston University, 1960), pp. 378–9.
5. S.P.G. Transcripts (Mss., Portsmouth, N.H., Public Library), pp. 6–8, 30; Robert Hayes Dunn: *Old St. John's at Portsmouth* (Newcomen Society pamphlet, New York, 1947), pp. 13–15.
6. *An Abstract of the . . . Proceedings of the Society for the Propagation of the Gospel in Foreign Parts, from the 17th of February 1737–38, to the 10th of February 1738–39*, appended to *A Sermon Preached before the Incorporated Society . . . February 16, 1738–39* (London, 1739), p. 42.
7. *An Abstract of the . . . Proceedings of the Society for the Propagation of the Gospel in Foreign Parts from the 20th of February, 1740–41, to the 19th of February, 1741–42*, appended to *A Sermon Preached before the Incorporated Society . . . February 19, 1741–2* (London, 1742), pp. 43–4.
8. Quoted in Mary Cochrane Rogers: *Glimpses of an Old Social Capital* (Boston, 1923), p. 23.
9. *Sibley's Harvard Graduates*, IV, 44.
10. Quoted in Rogers: *Social Capital*, pp. 22–3.
11. *An Abstract of the . . . Proceedings of the Society for the Propaga-*

tion of the Gospel in Foreign Parts, from the 17th of February 1743, to the 15th of February 1744, appended to *A Sermon Preached before the Incorporated Society* . . . *February 15, 1744* (London, 1744), p. 44.

12. Browne to the Rev. Dr. Thomlinson, S.P.G. Transcripts, Doc. 30.

13. Adams: *Portsmouth*, p. 185.

14. *TPNH*, IX, 712–14.

15. *PPNH*, V, 136.

16. Belknap: *N.H.*, II, 143.

17. *Sibley's Harvard Graduates*, VI, 132.

18. *Sibley's Harvard Graduates*, VI, 113–14. John Wentworth's will is in "Wentworth Mss.," Box 1, Folder 1, N.H.H.S.

19. John F. Looney: "The King's Representative: Benning Wentworth, Colonial Governor, 1741–1767" (unpublished dissertation, Lehigh University, 1961), pp. 1–3.

20. Looney: "King's Representative," p. 6; *Sibley's Harvard Graduates*, VI, 114.

21. *Sibley's Harvard Graduates*, VI, 115.

22. *Sibley's Harvard Graduates*, VI, 115–16; Looney: "King's Representative," pp. 9–12.

23. *Sibley's Harvard Graduates*, VI, 116–18; Looney: "King's Representative," p. 14.

24. *Sibley's Harvard Graduates*, VI, 118.

25. *PPNH*, V, 136–7.

26. *Sibley's Harvard Graduates*, VI, 119.

27. *PPNH*, V, 139–40, 143, 145–6.

28. *PPNH*, V, 148.

29. Looney: "King's Representative," pp. 33–4.

30. Belknap: *N.H.*, II, 133; Evarts B. Greene and Virginia D. Harrington: *American Population Before the Federal Census of 1790* (New York, 1932), p. 71; *PPNH*, V, 134–5.

31. Greene and Harrington: *American Population*, p. 72.

32. Belknap: *N.H.*, III, pp. 226–43 (tables).

33. John M. Howells: *The Architectural Heritage of the Piscataqua* (New York, 1937), p. 161; Geoffrey P. Moran: "A Survey of the Domestic Architecture of Portsmouth, New Hampshire, in the Colonial Period" (unpublished Master's thesis, University of New Hampshire, 1967), pp. 104, 106.

34. Howells: *Architectural Heritage of the Piscataqua*, p. 165.

35. *PPNH*, V, 626.

36. Howells: *Architectural Heritage of the Piscataqua*, pp. 112–13.

37. Howells: *Architectural Heritage of the Piscataqua*, pp. 140–6.

38. Howells: *Architectural Heritage of the Piscataqua*, pp. 120–1.

39. The Boston newspapers between 1720 and 1740 frequently filled their front pages with reprints of European correspondence from the British

press. See esp. the *New-England Courant* and the *New-England Weekly Journal*, both of which are available in microprint from the Readex Corporation.

40. *New-Hampshire Gazette,* November 18, 1756.
41. Included among the advertisements from the Piscataqua region were several announcing runaway Negro slaves and, more frequently, Irish indentured servants. See, e.g., *New-England Weekly Journal,* November 10, 1729, November 8, 1737, June 5, 1739, and July 8, 1740.
42. *New-England Courant,* August 7, December 18, and December 25, 1721, January 22, 1722; *Laws of New Hampshire,* II, ed. Albert S. Batchellor (Concord, N.H., 1913), 355–8.
43. The Library Society is discussed more fully in Chapter XVIII.
44. See the discussion of this point as to the American colonies as a whole by Leonard W. Labaree in *Royal Government in America* (New York, 1958), pp. 174–9, 426–63.
45. *Sibley's Harvard Graduates,* V, 653; Belknap: *N.H.,* I, 221; Adams: *Portsmouth,* p. 191.
46. *Sibley's Harvard Graduates,* V, 654–5.
47. Looney: "King's Representative," p. 62; *PPNH,* V, 134–5.
48. Nicholas Gilman's Diary (Ms., N.H.H.S.), January 11–February 1, March 20, 1739/40; May 14, October 3, October 28–November 10, December 13, 1740; February 26, 1740/1; April 23, May 5, June 20–July 1, November 3, 1741; April 8, July 13, November 3, December 21–5, 1742; January 8–13, 1742/3; May 9, August 31, 1743; April 5, April 22, 1744.
49. Looney: "King's Representative," pp. 44–5.
50. *PPNH,* V, 260–4; Looney: "King's Representative," pp. 45–6.
51. *PPNH,* V, 286–301
52. *PPNH,* V, 305.
53. *PPNH,* V, 306.
54. *SPNH,* XVIII, 220.
55. *SPNH,* XVIII, 220–2. The reply signed by Rogers, which expressed the same sentiments in somewhat less abandoned language, is in *PPNH,* V, 306–8.
56. *PPNH,* V, 308–9.
57. Looney: "King's Representative," pp. 47–9; *PPNH,* V, 320–2.
58. Looney: "King's Representative," p. 49; *PPNH,* V, 322, 337–8.
59. Looney: "Benning Wentworth's Land Grant Policy: A Reappraisal," *Historical New Hampshire,* XIII (Spring 1968), 5; Jere R. Daniell: "Politics in New Hampshire under Governor Benning Wentworth, 1741–1767," *William and Mary Quarterly,* 3rd Ser., XXIII (January 1966), 87–8.
60. Belknap: *N.H.,* II, 200–7.
61. *PPNH,* V, 611; *SPNH,* XVIII, 397.

62. Looney: "King's Representative," pp. 64–5; Daniell: "Politics in N. H.," 101–2. Waldron's correspondence with Royall and Belcher, covering the period September 7, 1747, to March 10, 1748/9, is reproduced in *PPNH*, VI, 39–63.
63. Looney: "King's Representative," p. 66; *SPNH*, XVIII, 339–40.
64. *PPNH*, VI, 70–93.
65. *PPNH*, VI, 65–7.
66. Labaree: *Royal Government*, p. 182; *PPNH*, VI, 123.
67. Labaree: *Royal Government*, pp. 183–4; Looney: "King's Representative," pp. 73–4; *PPNH*, VI, 128–43.
68. *Sibley's Harvard Graduates*, V, 657; VIII, 493–4.
69. *PPNH*, VII, 116, quoted in *Sibley's Harvard Graduates*, VI, 132.

Chapter XVIII · Cultural Beginnings, 1750–1760

1. John M. Howells: *The Architectural Heritage of the Piscataqua* (New York, 1937), pp. 92–5.
2. Nathaniel Adams: *Annals of Portsmouth* (Portsmouth, N.H., 1825), p. 204.
3. Adams: *Portsmouth*, p. 195.
4. Adams: *Portsmouth*, p. 195.
5. *New-Hampshire Gazette*, March 11, March 18, March 25, and April 1, 1757; *PPNH*, VI, 363, 456, 546–7, 614–15, 672, 715; Adams: *Portsmouth*, p. 199.
6. Howard T. Oedel: "Portsmouth, New Hampshire: The Role of the Provincial Capital in the Development of the Colony, 1700–1775" (unpublished dissertation, Boston University, 1960), pp. 307–9.
7. Oedel: "Portsmouth," pp. 486–90.
8. Howells: *Architectural Heritage of the Piscataqua*, p. 96; see also plates, pp. 97–9.
9. Adams: *Portsmouth*, p. 199.
10. William G. Saltonstall: *Ports of Piscataqua* (Cambridge, Mass., 1941), pp. 35–6.
11. *New-Hampshire Gazette*, November 18, 1756; February 18 and April 1, 1757. See also advertisement of John Nelson, *New-Hampshire Gazette*, February 9, 1759.
12. *New-Hampshire Gazette*, November 25, 1757.
13. *New-Hampshire Gazette*, June 10, 1757. See Percy Wells Bidwell and John I. Falconer: *History of Agriculture in the Northern United States, 1620–1860* (New York, 1941), pp. 143–4 for a discussion of the dependence of New England, and northern New England in particular, upon the Middle Colonies for grain throughout the eighteenth century.

14. *New-Hampshire Gazette*, February 25, August 12, and October 8, 1757.

15. Quoted in Saltonstall: *Ports*, p. 35.

16. *New-Hampshire Gazette*, December 24, 1756, and March 18, 1757.

17. *New-Hampshire Gazette*, January 21 and October 28, 1757.

18. *New-Hampshire Gazette*, December 2, 1756.

19. *New-Hampshire Gazette*, July 22, August 5, and August 12, 1757.

20. See Carl Bridenbaugh: *Cities in the Wilderness* (New York, 1964), p. 458, and *Cities in Revolt* (New York, 1964), p. 181.

21. "The First Book of the Records and Proceedings of the Library Society of Portsmouth in the Province of New Hampshire . . ." (Ms., Portsmouth Athenaeum), pp. 1–3, 20.

22. "Library Society," p. 1.

23. "Library Society," p. 2.

24. For a summary of the incident that precipitated Fowle's moving to Portsmouth and an assessment of his unusual enterprise, see C. E. Clark: "Science, Reason, and an Angry God: The Literature of an Earthquake," *New England Quarterly*, XXXVIII (1965), 342–7.

25. Charles Evans: *American Bibliography* (12 vols., Chicago, 1903–1934), entries 7608, 7694, 7746, 7827, 7832, 7841, 7856, 7857, 7965, 8034, 8051, 8052, 8074, 8095, 8113, 8161, 8166, 8202, 8272, 8314, 8389, 8427, 8428, 8450, 8562, 8616, 8617, 8632, 8679.

26. *New-Hampshire Gazette*, October 21 and 28, 1756.

27. *New-Hampshire Gazette*, November 18, 1756.

28. Jeremy Belknap: *The History of New-Hampshire* (Dover, N.H., 1812), III, 217.

29. Belknap: *N.H.*, III, 217–18.

30. See p. 166.

31. Adams: *Portsmouth*, pp. 202–3.

32. *Boston Weekly Newsletter*, January 17, 1760.

33. See pp. 279–82.

34. N.H.H.S. *Collections*, IX (1889), 14.

35. See Carl Bridenbaugh: *Mitre and Sceptre: Transatlantic Faiths, Ideas, Personalities, and Politics, 1689–1775* (New York, 1962), esp. Chaps. II–IV: and, for a detailed examination of the Torrey–MacSparran case, C. E. Clark: "A Test of Religious Liberty: The Ministry Land Case in Narragansett, 1668–1752." *A Journal of Church and State*, XI (Spring 1969), 295–319.

36. N.H.H.S. *Collections*, IX, 16.

37. N.H.H.S. *Collections*, IX, 18–20.

38. N.H.H.S. *Collections*, IX, 22.

39. N.H.H.S. *Collections*, IX, 50.

40. Bridenbaugh: *Mitre and Sceptre*, Chap. I; Alan Heimert: *Religion and the American Mind from the Great Awakening to the Revolution* (Cambridge, Mass., 1966), pp. 157, 369–78.

41. N.H.H.S. *Collections*, IX, 50.
42. *New-Hampshire Gazette*, March 4, 1757.

Chapter XIX · Northern New England in 1760

1. Francis Parkman: *Montcalm and Wolfe* (Boston, 1898), II, 80.
2. Evarts B. Greene and Virginia D. Harrington: *American Population Before the Federal Census of 1790* (New York, 1932), pp. 70, 72; Jeremy Belknap: *The History of New-Hampshire* (Dover, N.H., 1812), III, 226–48.
3. Greene and Harrington: *American Population,* pp. 10, 16, 50, 63.
4. Belknap: *N.H.,* II, 235–6; John G. Palfrey: *History of New England* (Boston, 1890), V, 191–2.
5. William Douglass: *A Summary, Historical and Political, of the First Planting, Progressive Improvements, and Present State of the British Settlements in North-America* (London, 1760), I, 467.
6. *New-Hampshire Gazette*, February 24, 1758.
7. Lois K. Mathews: *The Expansion of New England* (New York, 1962), pp. 97–8.
8. Douglass: *Summary,* I, 466.
9. Nathaniel Adams: *Annals of Portsmouth* (Portsmouth, N.H., 1825), pp. 204–5; George F. Marlowe: *Coaching Roads of Old New England* (New York, 1945), p. 159.
10. M.H.S. *Proceedings,* XVI (1878), 7–8.
11. Carl Bridenbaugh, ed.: *Gentleman's Progress: The Itinerarium of Dr. Alexander Hamilton, 1774* (Chapel Hill, 1948), pp. 124–5.
12. John Adams's Diary, quoted in Robert S. Rantoul: "Some Notes on Old Modes of Travel," *Essex Institute Historical Collections,* XI (1872), 33.
13. Me. Hist. Soc. *Collections,* 1st Ser., IV (1856), 275–8.
14. *Acts and Laws, of His Majesty's Province of the Massachusetts-Bay in New-England* (Boston, 1726), pp. 375–6, 620–1.
15. *Laws of New Hampshire,* II (ed. Albert S. Batchellor, Concord, N.H., 1913), 380–2.
16. Londonderry Town Records (Mss., N.H.H.S.), I, 220.
17. *Laws of New Hampshire,* III (ed. Henry H. Metcalf, Bristol, N.H., 1915), 75.
18. *Laws of N.H.,* III, 340–2.
19. *Laws of N.H.,* II, 585–6; III, 172–5.
20. Londonderry Town Records, II, 259.
21. Samuel T. Dole: *Windham in the Past,* ed. Frederick H. Dole (Auburn, Me., 1916), p. 273.
22. Belknap: *N.H.,* III, 121.
23. *Laws of N.H.,* III, 128–9.

24. *New-Hampshire Gazette,* December 17, 1756; April 1, 1757.

25. *New-Hampshire Gazette,* March 23, 1759.

26. *Laws of N.H.,* III, 72, 220–1.

27. *New-Hampshire Gazette,* March 18, 1757.

28. *New-Hampshire Gazette,* October 28, 1756.

29. *Laws of N.H.,* III, 514–15.

30. *Laws of N.H.,* II, 339; *Acts and Laws of Massachusetts Bay,* pp. 215–18. See also the general New Hampshire law of 1716 regulating taverns, providing for their inspection by "Tything-men," and fixing a limit on the number of taverns in each town. *Laws of N.H.,* II, 196–8.

31. *Laws of N.H.,* II, 358.

32. *Laws of N.H.,* II, 719–20.

33. Londonderry Town Records, II, 5; *Laws of N.H.,* III, 169–70.

34. *Laws of N.H.,* III, 225–6.

35. Kenneth Scott: "Colonial Innkeepers of New Hampshire," *Historical New Hampshire,* XIX (Spring 1964), p. 45.

36. See, e.g., Nicholas Gilman's Diary (Ms., N.H.H.S.), May 4, 1740; *A Journal for the Years 1739–1803 by Samuel Lane of Stratham, New Hampshire,* ed. Charles Lane Hanson (Concord, N.H., 1937), p. 37.

37. Adams: *Portsmouth,* p. 187; Carl Bridenbaugh: *Cities in Revolt* (New York, 1964), p. 129.

38. *New-Hampshire Gazette,* November 18, 1757.

39. Adams: *Portsmouth,* p. 207; Bridenbaugh: *Cities in Revolt,* p. 129.

40. *Lane Journal,* p. 38.

41. Howard T. Oedel: "Portsmouth, New Hampshire: The Role of the Provincial Capital in the Development of the Colony, 1700–1775" (unpublished dissertation, Boston University, 1960), pp. 768–9; Adams: *Portsmouth,* p. 196; *Laws of N.H.,* III, 177–9.

42. *New-Hampshire Gazette,* May 19, 1758.

43. Adams: *Portsmouth,* p. 203.

44. *Laws of N.H.,* III, 227–9.

45. Belknap: *N.H.,* III, 21–2; Memoirs and Journal of the Reverend Paul Coffin, Me. Hist. Soc. *Collections,* IV (1856), 273–4.

46. Thomas Bailey Aldrich: *Old Town by the Sea* (Boston and New York, 1893), p. 79.

47. Gilman's Diary, June 15, 1741.

48. *MPCR,* IV, 34–5.

49. *Laws of N.H.,* II, 292.

50. See, e.g., *New-Hampshire Gazette,* August 5, August 19, and September 30, 1757; Samuel Waldo, Jr., to Moses Pearson, July 26, 1757, "Andrew Hawes of Stroudwater Collection," Mss., Me. Hist. Soc., II.

51. *Laws of N.H.,* II, 152.

52. Greene and Harrington: *American Population,* p. 72.

53. *New-Hampshire Gazette,* August 4, 1758.

54. *New-Hampshire Gazette,* January 21, May 18, and April 1, 1757; February 24, 1758; February 2 and February 9, 1759.

Chapter XX · The Breaking of the Dike, 1760–1775

1. Lois K. Mathews: *The Expansion of New England* (New York, 1962), pp. 91–5, 103, and maps opp. pp. 70, 98; Herman R. Friis: *A Series of Population Maps of the Colonies and the United States 1625–1790* (New York, 1968), p. 16, and maps between pp. 12 and 13.
2. John M. Bumsted: "Transplantation of New England Settlement to Nova Scotia, 1759–1770," paper presented to Pacific Coast Branch, American Historical Association, at San Diego, Cal., August 27, 1969.
3. Mathews: *Expansion of New England,* pp. 34, 52–6, 66–9, 95–7, 117–28.
4. Stephen Hosmer: *A Peoples Living in Appearance* (New London, 1720), p. 10, quoted in Clifford K. Shipton: "The New England Frontier," *New England Quarterly,* X (March 1937), p. 31.
5. Carl Bridenbaugh: *Cities in the Wilderness* (New York, 1964), pp. 253, 259; *Cities in Revolt* (New York, 1955), pp. 138–9, 152.
6. Mathews: *Expansion of New England,* pp. 111–12; George P. Baker: "New Hampshire Frontier 1760–1795" (unpublished Bachelor's thesis, Harvard University, 1953), pp. 31–2.
7. Jack M. Sosin: *The Revolutionary Frontier 1763–1783* (New York, 1967), pp. 21, 47; Mathews: *Expansion of New England,* p. 115; Evarts B. Greene and Virginia D. Harrington: *American Population Before the Federal Census of 1790* (New York, 1932), p. 86.
8. Charles B. Fobes: "Path of the Settlement and Distribution of Population in Maine," *Economic Geography,* XX (1944), 66–7; Mathews: *Expansion of New England,* pp. 113–15; Greene and Harrington: *American Population,* pp. 39–40.
9. Greene and Harrington: *American Population,* pp. 10, 36–40, 74–9; Sosin: *Revolutionary Frontier,* p. 47. The figure of 150,000 (20,000 for Vermont, 80,925 for New Hampshire, and 47,279 for the three Maine counties) is the most modest of several widely varying estimates.
10. U.S. Bureau of Census: *A Century of Population Growth* (Washington, 1909), pp. 4–9, cited in Baker: "N.H. Frontier," p. 30.
11. See esp. Sosin: *Revolutionary Frontier,* pp. 23–6; and, with respect to the settlement of Bennington, Mathews: *Expansion of New England,* pp. 116–17.
12. Sosin: *Revolutionary Frontier,* pp. 39–40; Mathews: *Expansion of New England,* p. 112.
13. Ray Allen Billington: *Westward Expansion: A History of the American Frontier* (3rd edn., New York, 1967), p. 96.
14. See the perceptive and detailed treatment of this pattern of settlement in

New Hampshire in Baker: "N.H. Frontier," pp. 31–7.

15. Photostat of Colonial Office 5/942 in Wentworth Mss., N.H.H.S., Box 1, Folder 3, pp. 115–17.

16. Edna Scofield: "The Origin of Settlement Patterns in Rural New England," *The Geographical Review*, XXVIII (1938), p. 663, and plan of Meredith, N.H., p. 662.

17. Me. Hist. Soc. *Collections*, IV (1856), 278, 284, 286.

Essay on Authorities and Sources

The reader who contemplates further investigation into northern New England in the seventeenth and eighteenth centuries will find no book other than this one which deals exclusively and extensively with this topic as a unit. However, two excellent recent studies in the *Histories of the American Frontier* series, under the general editorship of Ray Allen Billington, provide relatively compact but highly informative treatments of the life of this region within a broader geographic context, and from the perspective of the entire history of American "westward" expansion. Each of these books, Douglas Edward Leach's *The Northern Colonial Frontier, 1607–1763* (New York, 1966) and Jack M. Sosin's *The Revolutionary Frontier, 1763–1783* (New York, 1967), offers interpretations in the "frontier" tradition based on the most recent scholarship. The reader ought to supplement these two studies by a much earlier one in the same general tradition, Lois Kimball Mathews (Rosenberry): *The Expansion of New England* (Boston, 1909; New York, 1962). This minor historical classic deals with the migration of New Englanders and the spread of New England institutions and influence northward, southward, and westward from 1620 to 1865. It has not been superseded in the sixty years since its first appearance, though a new treatment of the same theme, and of similar scope, might now be undertaken profitably.

For standard treatments of somewhat more specialized topics which give further insight into the colonial history of the region, the reader might then look into: Alden T. Vaughan: *New England Frontier: Puritans and Indians, 1620–1675* (Boston, 1965), which treats the relationships between the Puritan settlers of New England and the Indians in the period before King Philip's War and provides as a side benefit a convenient description of the Indian tribes of New England, including those of northern New England; Roy Hidemichi Akagi: *The Town Proprietors of the New England Colonies* (Philadelphia, 1924), which has long been recognized as a distinguished monograph on the township proprietary system; and Sumner Chilton Powell: *Puritan Village: The Formation of a New England Town* (Middletown, Conn., 1963), not because it deals with northern New England but because in undertaking a close analysis of the settlement, the land system, and the institutional and political development of Sudbury, Massachusetts, the author demonstrates handsomely the riches that are to be gained from a detailed community study and provides suggestive conclusions that cannot help but be of value in considering other American colonial communities, especially in western and northern New England. Two books by Darrett B. Rutman, *Winthrop's Boston: A Portrait of a Puritan Town, 1630–1649* (Chapel Hill, 1965) and *Husbandmen of Plymouth* (Boston, 1967), offer provocative revisions of the social history of seventeenth-century Boston and the Plymouth colony; in his methodology and in his findings, Rutman offers a suggestive point of departure for other community studies and bases of comparison of interest to the prospective student of northern New England. For the intercolonial wars and their effect on the northeastern frontier, the best sources are two of Francis Parkman's volumes in *France and England in North America,* which have been reprinted in so many forms since the first appearance of the series between 1865 and 1892 that it is superflous to designate editions. The portions of that magnificent work that are most relevant to eighteenth-century northern New England are *A Half-Century of Conflict* and *Montcalm and Wolfe.* Both books are sources not only of detailed and authoritative information but also of salutary inspiration for the aspiring historical craftsman.

A number of regional and state histories have proved to be among the more valuable reference works during the making of this book, and should be consulted by anyone who wants to look further into the colonial history of northern New England. Some of the eighteenth-century histories, especially Cotton Mather's great *Magnalia Christi Americana* and its accompanying map (London, 1702), Daniel Neal's *The History of New England* (I used the second edition, 2 vols., London, 1747, because Neal added much important material on New Hampshire not included in the first edition), and William Douglass's *A Summary, Historical and Political, of the First Planting, Progressive Improvements, and Present State of the British Settlements in North-America* (2 vols., London, 1760) were of special value.

Jeremy Belknap's classic *The History of New-Hampshire* (3 vols., Dover, N.H., 1812) provides a straightforward account of the settlement and political development of New Hampshire until after the Revolution, but its usefulness goes beyond that. The appendices of all three volumes contain an extensive collection of letters, documents, tables, and chronologies, and in Volume III is located a table containing the date of incorporation, all ministers and their dates of settlement, and other data for every town. This proved to be a most valuable reference. For a more modern treatment of the history of New Hampshire, I have used Everett S. Stackpole's *History of*

New Hampshire (4 vols., New York, 1916), which clarifies especially well the period from the founding of the four original towns to the assumption of jurisdiction by Massachusetts.

William D. Williamson's *History of the State of Maine* (Hallowell, Me., 1832) survives as the standard authority on the first two centuries or so of Maine history, supplementing and in most respects surpassing in thoroughness James Sullivan's earlier *History of the District of Maine* (Boston, 1795). I made occasional use of John S. C. Abbott: *The History of Maine* (Boston, 1875), which, because of the author's preoccupation with the scenic wonders of his native state and what he fancied to be the uncommon achievements of its people in the nineteenth century, is on the whole inferior to Williamson. A comprehensive treatment of the expansion of settlement in Maine during the colonial period, with particular attention to Indian relations and the role of the great speculative tracts in and beyond the region of the Kennebec, may be found in Robert Earle Moody's unpublished Yale University dissertation, "The Maine Frontier, 1607–1763" (1933). To check political facts during the period of the study, I had recourse to one of the best possible references for that purpose, Thomas Hutchinson's *The History of the Colony and Province of Massachusetts-Bay,* ed. Lawrence Shaw Mayo (3 vols., Cambridge, Mass., 1936).

Perhaps the most exciting, certainly the most romantic phase of the region's history is its discovery, exploration, and first settlement—a phase that reaches back into the fog-shrouded final decades of the sixteenth century and finally emerges into the light of day soon after 1600. Certain and detailed knowledge of what the first permanent fishing and trading posts along the coast of Maine and New Hampshire were like must await the patient work of anthropologists and archeologists. However, there is a literature of exploration and settlement that provides a good basis for further investigation. For early exploration of the region, the most useful printed works by contemporary authors include: Sir Humphrey Gilbert's *A Discourse of a Discoverie for a new Passage to Cataia* (London, 1576); Richard Hakluyt's *The Principal Navigations, Voiages, Navigations, Traffiques, and Discoveries of the English Nation* (3 vols., London, 1598–1600); James Rosier's *A True Relation of the most prosperous voyage made this present yeere 1605, by Captaine George Waymouth, in the Discovery of the land of Virginia* (London, 1605); Christopher Levett's *A Voyage into New England Begun in 1623 and ended in 1624* (London, 1628); Captain John Smith's *New England's Tryalls* (London, 1622) and *The Generall Historie of Virginia, New-England, and the Summer Iles* (London, 1632); and three modern compilations of original accounts of significant voyages: David Beers Quinn, ed.: *The Voyages and Colonising Enterprises of Sir Humphrey Gilbert* (London, 1940); George Parker Winship, ed.: *Sailor's Narratives of Voyages along the New England Coast 1524–1624* (Boston, 1905), which includes Verrazano's log of 1524; and Charles Herbert Levermore, ed.: *Forerunners and*

Competitors of the Pilgrims and Puritans (2 vols., Brooklyn, N.Y., 1912), which includes the journal of Samuel de Champlain's remarkable exploratory and mapping cruise southwestward from Port Royal to Cape Cod in 1604. Descriptive sources for early settlements are less profuse, but there is a wealth of information relating to the operation of one of the most successful fishing and trading stations of the 1630's in the "Trelawney Papers," edited by James Phinney Baxter and published as Volume III of *Documentary History of Maine* (Portland, 1884). John Josselyn's *An Account of Two Voyages to New-England* (London, 1674) is a colorful and richly detailed description of day-to-day life on the Maine coast in the seventeenth century; and Samuel Maverick's *A Briefe Discription of New England*, written in 1660 and published in Boston in 1885 with a preface by John Ward Dean, offers a more general view of the state of economic and political development of the same region in the same period. The accounts of both Josselyn and Maverick are colored by their royalist sympathies and their opposition to the growing independence and apparent arrogance of Massachusetts Bay, but Josselyn is likewise offended by the state of near-anarchy that he found in some of the Maine settlements during the period that Massachusetts was attempting to exert her influence eastward. *A Short Account of the Present State of New-England* (n.p., 1690), published anonymously, is useful for a somewhat later period.

For convenient secondary treatments of the earliest settlements and related topics, the reader should consult: Raymond McFarland: *A History of the New England Fisheries* (New York, 1911); Charles Knowles Bolton: *The Real Founders of New England* (Boston, 1929); R. V. Coleman: *The First Frontier* (New York, 1948), which is designed for the general reader; Henry S. Burrage: *The Beginnings of Colonial Maine* (Portland, 1914), which is both thorough and scholarly; and Philip L. Barbour's fascinating biography of an equally fascinating figure, *The Three Worlds of Captain John Smith* (Boston, 1964). Discussions of the legend of Norumbega may be found in Benjamin F. da Costa: "Norumbega and Its English Explorers," in *Narrative and Critical History of America,* ed. Justin Winsor (Boston and New York, 1884), III, 167–218, and Sigmund Diamond: "Norumbega: New England Xanadu," *The American Neptune,* XI (April 1951), 95–107.

The best summaries of the absorption of New Hampshire and Maine by Massachusetts Bay in the seventeenth century—the political side of what I have called the "Puritan conquest"—are to be found in the general histories of Maine, New Hampshire, and Massachusetts mentioned above. These might be supplemented by Charles M. Andrews's readable and still reliable colony-by-colony institutional history in the relevant portions of *The Colonial Period of American History* (4 vols., New Haven, 1934–8). One can become well acquainted with John Wheelwright, the founder of Exeter, New Hampshire, through: Charles H. Bell: *John Wheelwright, His Writings . . . and a Memoir* (Prince Society Publications, Boston, 1876);

Edmund M. Wheelwright: "A Frontier Family," *Publications of the Colonial Society of Massachusetts*, I (March 1894), 271–303; and Emery Battis: *Saints and Sectaries* (Chapel Hill, 1962).

Two pamphlets by Cotton Mather, *A Letter to Ungospellized Plantations* (Boston, 1702) and *The Fisher-mans Calling* (Boston, 1712), supply concrete evidence of at least one Puritan's ambition to convert the eastern parts; and the printed sermons of Samuel Moody of York demonstrate the evangelical fervor with which the most successful of the frontier missionaries went about his task. I have used especially *The Doleful State of the Damned; Especially Such as Go to Hell from Under the Gospel* (Boston, 1710), *The Vain Youth Summoned to Appear at Christ's Bar* (3rd edn. enlarged, New London, 1760), and *Mr. Moodey's Discourse to the Little Children* (Boston, 1770). One by-product of the Puritan conquest, a rash of Quaker persecutions in New Hampshire, receives vivid (and biased) treatment in the works of three Quakers: George Bishop's *New-England Judged by the Spirit of the Lord* (London, 1703), and the *Journals* of William Edmundson (London, 1715) and James Dickinson (London, 1745). Edmundson and Dickinson, besides describing the persecution of members of their sect in New England, supply valuable glimpses of life along the northeastern coast in the seventeenth century.

The town of Portsmouth, New Hampshire, mercantile and social capital of northern New England during the eighteenth century as well as the political capital of the province, has received extensive treatment at the hands of historians, antiquarians, and biographers. The bulk of this considerable body of literature, however, is marred by filiopiety and an uncritical use of sources. Not even the most scholarly recent general work on this community in the eighteenth century, Howard T. Oedel's "Portsmouth, New Hampshire: The Role of the Provincial Capital in the Development of the Colony, 1700–1775" (unpublished dissertation, Boston University, 1960), is entirely free from the admiring tone of some of the less professional studies. Oedel's dissertation did provide me with much useful information and guided me to many sources. It is especially strong on Portsmouth architecture, but is longer than it needs to be. Most of the general works on Portsmouth use as starting points two meaty studies by nineteenth-century antiquaries. These are: Nathaniel Adam's *Annals of Portsmouth* (Portsmouth, 1825), an extremely comprehensive local history which suffers from a primitive chronological organization; and Charles W. Brewster's *Rambles about Portsmouth* (2 vols., Portsmouth, 1859 and 1869), an eccentrically arranged series of articles organized by neighborhood, street, or building. Despite their drawbacks in organization and the need to apply a healthy dose of scholarly skepticism to their findings, both authors' thorough absorption in Portsmouth lore make these two repositories of fact and legend indispensable tools for the student of early Portsmouth.

The economic and maritime history of Portsmouth and its neighboring towns is covered competently and professionally in William G. Saltonstall's *Ports of Piscataqua* (Cambridge, Mass., 1941), which is well documented, well written, and handsomely illustrated, and in Byron Fairchild's excellent *Messrs. William Pepperrell: Merchants at Piscataqua* (Ithaca, N.Y., 1954). One might supplement these absorbing accounts with a nineteenth-century biography of the hero of Louisbourg, Usher Parsons's *The Life of Sir William Pepperrell, Bart.* (Boston, 1856), and with William G. Wendell's little study of the second occupant of the Macpheadris house, *Jonathan Warner (1726–1814), Merchant and Trader, King's Councillor, Mariner, Jurist* (Newcomen Society pamphlet, New York, 1950).

"Strawbery Banke, Inc.," which sponsors an important restoration project on the Portsmouth waterfront and has thus helped to rescue a large segment of that community's astounding collection of eighteenth-century dwellings from destruction or decay, provides a useful introduction to the architecture of Portsmouth with two small publications: *Architecture Near the Piscataqua* (Portsmouth, 1964) and *Strawbery Banke in Portsmouth, New Hampshire—Official Guidebook and Map* (2nd rev. edn., Portsmouth, 1968). The most scholarly monograph on Portsmouth buildings is Geoffrey P. Moran's brilliant "Survey of the Domestic Architecture of Portsmouth, New Hampshire, in the Colonial Period" (unpublished M.A. thesis, University of New Hampshire, 1967), which constitutes a worthy supplement to John M. Howells's lavishly illustrated *Architectural Heritage of the Piscataqua* (New York, 1937).

Two general books on Portsmouth of only limited usefulness are: Thomas Bailey Aldrich's *Old Town by the Sea* (Boston and New York, 1893); and Mary Cochrane Rogers's *Glimpses of an Old Social Capital* (Boston, 1923), which purports to describe Portsmouth but has as its principal concern the glorification of the Reverend Arthur Browne and his descendants.

For the period after its appearance in 1756, the *New-Hampshire Gazette* of Portsmouth—northern New England's first newspaper—is a source of supreme importance. The Portsmouth Athenaeum holds a complete file.

The student of the other principal seaport of the region, old Falmouth, Maine (modern Portland), cannot escape indebtedness to William Willis, whose careful and exhaustive scholarship resulted in two indispensable works that have not lost their great usefulness after well over a century. Willis's *The History of Portland* (two parts in one volume, Portland, 1831) remains the standard history of that community, and a very good one. It may be supplemented with William Goold: *Portland in the Past, with Historical Notes of Old Falmouth* (Portland, 1882). No one undertaking even a cursory study of eighteenth-century Falmouth can count his task finished until he has looked into the diary of the Reverend Thomas Smith, the town's first minister. The manuscript, unfortunately, was expurgated many years before Willis combined it with the diary of a later minister and published it with extensive and useful notes under the title *Journals of the Reverend*

Thomas Smith and the Reverend Samuel Deane, Pastors of the First Church in Portland (Portland, 1849). Another useful diary is that of Enoch Freeman, which is in manuscript at the Portland Public Library. Though not as comprehensive a source as Parson Smith's *Journal,* it supplements the minister's record with good evidence relating to the economic life of Falmouth. By far the richest collection of miscellaneous manuscripts that I encountered during this study was the "Andrew Hawes of Stroudwater Collection, 1682–1855" in the library of the Maine Historical Society, of which Volumes I and II pertain to the period covered by this book. The collection consists primarily of documents illustrating the history of old Falmouth and Portland. Its greatest virtue from my point of view was the vast quantity of material relating to Moses Pearson, the central character of Chapter X; its greatest weakness is the fact that the documents are neither indexed nor numbered. Other collections held by the Maine Historical Society and containing a variety of manuscripts, some of considerable interest and many relating to Falmouth, are: the "Fogg Collection," Vol. IX; "Documents relating to Old Falmouth, Portland, given to Maine Historical Society by D.A.R., Elizabeth Wadsworth Chapter"; "Falmouth Papers and Plans"; and "Autographs of Special Note," Vol. I. Useful details about Moses Pearson may be found in a genealogical study in Henry Cole Quinby: *New England Family History,* Vol. II (New York, 1908–9).

To illustrate the process of resettling abandoned eastern communities after the Peace of Utrecht under the supervision of the Massachusetts General Court, I used the example of North Yarmouth, for which ample documentary evidence is available. The "North Yarmouth Maine Papers," collected in five volumes by David Shepley and deposited with the Maine Historical Society, contain either the original or certified copies of hundreds of town and proprietors' records and form the basis of Chapter IX of this book. The Records of the First Parish Church of North Yarmouth, also in manuscript at the Maine Historical Society, completed the documentary evidence necessary to the study contained in that chapter, and William H. Rowe's good town history, *Ancient North Yarmouth and Yarmouth, Maine, 1636–1936* (Yarmouth, 1937), proved a valuable supplement.

For exploring further into the expansion of settlement into the back country of northern New England and the rural society that emerged from the "frontier" stage of that movement, two articles on frontier and rural life are useful starting points. Clifford K. Shipton's "The New England Frontier," *New England Quarterly,* X (March 1937), was an early analysis of the "frontier experience" that accompanied the expansion of the Puritan settlements to western and northern New England. It is a perceptive article and should be read by anyone interested in the topic, even though I believe that it is necessary to qualify Shipton's central assertion that "The frontiersmen of New England . . . continued without much change the social institutions of their fathers." The other fundamental article is Carl Bridenbaugh's "The New England Town: A Way of Life," *Proceedings of the American Antiquarian Society*, LVI (April 1946), which, though not concerned specifically with northern New England, addresses itself to life in the rural New England town—a concern which is of central importance in this book.

Treatments of expansion and rural settlement from the geographer's point of view may be found in: Edna Scofield's "The Origin of Settlement Patterns in Rural New England," *The Geographical Review*, XXVIII (1938); Charles B. Fobes's "Paths of the Settlement and Distribution of Population in Maine," *Economic Geography*, XX (1944), 65–7, which includes interesting maps; Glenn T. Trewartha's "Types of Rural Settlement in Colonial America," *The Geographical Review*, XXXVI (1946), 568–96; F. Grave Morris's "Some Aspects of the Rural Settlement of New England in Colonial Times," in L. Dudley Stamp and S. W. Wooldridge, eds.: *London Essays in Geography* (Cambridge, Mass., 1951), pp. 219–27; and Herman R. Friis's *A Series of Population Maps of the Colonies and the United States 1625–1790* (New York, 1968).

Two unpublished undergraduate theses, both dating from the early 1950's, furnish excellent surveys of separate phases of the eighteenth-century expansion process. One is Howard T. Oedel's "Picket Sentinels—Seven Proprietary Townships Established in Maine 1733–1759" (Boston University, 1951), a copy of which is in the library of the Maine Historical Society; the other is George F. Baker, Jr.'s, "New Hampshire Frontier, 1760–1795" (Harvard University, 1953), a copy of which is in the library of the New Hampshire Historical Society.

The richest source for rural life in eighteenth-century northern New England is *The Diary of Matthew Patten of Bedford, New Hampshire* (Concord, N.H., 1903), which was rescued from oblivion by the town of Bedford nearly seventy years ago and without which my own quest for the day-to-day details of the upcountry farmer's life would have been considerably less rewarding. Charles Lane Hanson has performed a similarly valuable service to the student of this topic by editing and making available to the public *A Journal for the Years 1739–1803 by Samuel Lane of Stratham, New Hampshire* (Concord, N.H., 1937). The extensive diaries of the Reverend Timothy Walker, minister of Penacook, have been edited and annotated by Joseph B. Walker and published in Volume IX (1889) of the *Collections* of the New Hampshire Historical Society, providing intimate glimpses into the life of a clergyman who also operated a successful farm in a community at the edge of civilization. Mr. Walker's journals are well supplemented by Joseph B. Walker: *Chronicles of an Old New England Farm—The Farm of the First Minister* (Concord, N.H., 1906). Other diaries and journals useful for studying pioneering and rural life in northern New England include: "Memoirs and Journal of the Reverend Paul Coffin" in the *Collections* of the Maine Historical Society, IV (1856); and "Journal of Captain Phineas Stevens' Journey from Charlestown, N.H., to Canada, 1752" in *Travels in the American Colonies,* ed. Newton D. Mereness (New York, 1916). The business dealings of Thomas Chute, the pioneer settler of New Marblehead, Maine, are made readily apparent by his unusually comprehensive "Account Book" (Ms., Maine Historical Society), the utility of which is enhanced by an introduction and index by George M. Bodge. An anonymous article, "Manners and Customs of Olden Time" in the *Collections* of the New Hampshire Historical Society, V (1837), consists of boyhood reminiscences describing food, drink, clothing, amusements, diseases, agriculture, and transportation in the rural towns in the middle or late eighteenth century. *Rural Household Inventories, 1675–1775* (Boston, 1964), edited by Abbott Lowell Cummings, and Eloise Hubbard Linscott's *Folk Songs of Old New England* (New York, 1939) helped me in my effort to flesh out the country life of the eighteenth century, and provide rewarding reading.

James G. Leyburn gives a good introduction to the immigrants to America from Ulster—a small portion of whom settled the Merrimack Valley of New Hampshire early in the eighteenth century—with *The Scotch-Irish: A Social History* (Chapel Hill, 1962). There are two treatments of one of the most colorful and forceful leaders of the Merrimack Valley settlements (not one of the Scotch-Irish himself): William H. Brown's *Colonel John Goffe* (Manchester, N.H., 1950) and George Woodbury's *John Goffe's Legacy* (New York, 1955)—of which Brown's book is the more useful and Woodbury's the more entertaining.

In every part of this book, but especially in those sections which deal with the settlement and development of the rural communities of the interior, I have made extensive use of local histories. The New England town history of the nineteenth century, whose publication generally was occasioned by the observance of the local centennial or bicentennial, is a fascinating genre. Compounded of filial pride, antiquarian detail, endless genealogies, countless anecdotes introduced by "It is said," a Civil War roster if published after 1865, and usually at least one temperance essay, the town history nevertheless provides the modern researcher with an abundance of useful material. Its biographical sketches and genealogies are the most convenient, and often the only available source for determining settler's places of origin and routes of migration. Its listing of farms and houses provides the data for determining patterns of settlement. The extensive extracts of documents and correspondence that are often supplied are of obvious value. It would be superfluous to list all of the town histories I have consulted. They are cited in the footnotes, and one can be reasonably confident that nearly every community has at one time or another had its history published in some form. For specific listings, the reader might consult: O. G. Hammond: *Checklist of New Hampshire Local History* (Concord, 1925); D. B. Hall: "Reference List on Maine Local History," New York State Library *Bulletin* No. 63 (1910); and A. J. Huston: *A Check List of Maine Local*

Histories (Portland, 1915). In a somewhat different category from the standard kind of town history just described are the "historical sketches" or
"annals" of specific communities found in the *Collections* of the various state
historical societies, usually during the first half of the nineteenth century.
These normally lack the lists and extended quotations found in the more
comprehensive histories that are characteristic of the period roughly from
1850 to 1915, but contain much anecdotal information that is often intensely
interesting although it is usually difficult or impossible to check its authenticity. Several of the earlier full-fledged town histories, such as Willis's
Portland and George Folsom's *History of Saco and Biddeford* (Saco, Me.,
1830), are on the whole less strident and more scholarly than some of the
later ones. There is also a handful of local histories of varying quality by
modern scholars and antiquaries. Foremost among them, though I regret
that my area of principal interest did not admit of my using it more extensively, is Jasper J. Stahl's monumental and scholarly *History of Old Broad
Bay and Waldoboro* (2 vols., Portland, 1956). Roy P. Fairfield's *Sands,
Spindles, and Steeples* (Portland, 1956) is a good study of Saco, but his
primary interest is in a later period than this one. Samuel Eliot Morison
sacrificed nothing of his scholarship and charm to write *The Proprietors of
Peterborough, New Hampshire* (Peterborough, 1930).

For the technical aspects of agriculture in the colonial period, one may
glean many insights from the diaries of Matthew Patten and Timothy
Walker, but any serious student of this topic ought to consult Percy W.
Bidwell and John I. Falconer: *History of Agriculture in the Northern United
States, 1620–1860* (Washington, D.C., 1925, or New York, 1941). Two
works by contemporary authors are also indispensable. One is Jared Eliot's
*Essays upon Field Husbandry in New England and Other Papers, 1748–
1762*, ed. Harry J. Carman and Rexford G. Tugwell (New York, 1935).
The other is *American Husbandry* (London, 1775), whose author analyzed
the social structure as well as the agricultural habits of the New England
countryside. Though I was fortunate to have access to the original edition,
the work is more widely available in an edition edited by Harry J. Carman
(New York, 1939). In addition to these general works, contemporary technical essays such as Paul Dudley's "An Account of Making Sugar from
. . . Maple Trees" in *The Philosophical Transactions of the Royal Society
of London, . . . Abridged*, VI (1809), 458–9 (which appeared originally
in the *Philosophical Transactions* for 1720, Vol. XXXI); Thomas Chapman's
*The Cyder-Maker's Instructor, Sweet-Maker's Assistant, and Victualler's
and House-Keeper's Director* (Boston, 1762); and *Select Essays: Containing: The Manner of raising and dressing Flax, and Hemp. Also, The Whole
Method of Bleaching or Whitening Linen-Cloth . . .* (Philadelphia, 1777)
provide exact descriptions of how certain tasks of farming and home industry were performed. Joseph Seccombe's *Business and Diversion inoffensive to God* (Boston, 1743) offered to the fishermen who gathered at Amos-

keag Falls on the Merrimack in 1739 a religious justification of fishing for pleasure or profit.

Carl Bridenbaugh's *The Colonial Craftsman* (New York, 1950) offers a compact, sprightly introduction to the various trades and crafts of the period and the men who practiced them. More extended and detailed treatments of the whole realm of manufacturing and technology are provided by: Charles Singer, E. J. Holmyard, A. R. Hall, and Trevor I. Williams, eds.: *A History of Technology* (Oxford, 1957), of which Volume III is pertinent to the period of this study; T. K. Derry and Trevor I. Williams: *A Short History of Technology from the Earliest Times to* A.D. *1900* (New York, 1961); and Eleanor L. Lord: *Industrial Experiments in the British Colonies of North America* (Johns Hopkins University Studies in Historical and Political Science, XVII; Baltimore, 1898), which places particular emphasis on the naval stores industry.

Robert G. Albion's fascinating *Forests and Sea Power* (Cambridge, Mass., 1926) not only deals graphically with the materials and problems of building wooden ships but also with the intricacies of the British woodlands policy, its reasons, and its effects. For further illumination of the political side of this topic, one should consult, as I did with profit, Joseph J. Malone's slim monograph, *Pine Trees and Politics* (Seattle, 1964). Leonard B. Chapman's "The Mast Industry of Old Falmouth," *Collections of the Maine Historical Society,* 2nd Ser., VII (1896), 390–404, is a useful essay on the technical and economic aspects of masting.

There are many books on American colonial architecture, but one ought to match every hour spent with them with another hour spent viewing and touching surviving buildings themselves. I used as my principal authorities: Hugh Morrison, without whose *Early American Architecture* (New York, 1952) I should have spent a great deal of time in basic research in this area and emerged immeasurably less enlightened; Harold R. Shurtleff, whose findings in *The Log Cabin Myth* (Cambridge, Mass., 1939) contributed substantially to some of my conclusions about the country town; and Geoffrey P. Moran, whose contributions I have already acknowledged. The collections of illustrations in John M. Howells: *The Architectural Heritage of the Piscataqua,* previously cited, and his *The Architectural Heritage of the Merrimack* (New York, 1941) were of immense value; and Abbott Lowell Cummings's *Architecture in Early New England* (Old Sturbridge Village Booklet Series, 1958), Thomas T. Waterman's *The Dwellings of Colonial America* (Chapel Hill, 1950), Harold D. Eberlein's *The Architecture of Colonial America* (Boston, 1929), and Fiske Kimball's *Domestic Architecture of the American Colonies and of the Early Republic* (New York, 1927) were important supplements.

The religious life of northern New England sprang into prominence with the Great Awakening, for which the most convenient secondary sources are Edwin S. Gaustad: *The Great Awakening in New England* (New York,

1957) and C. C. Goen: *Revivalism and Separatism in New England, 1740–1800* (New Haven, 1962). The most significant recent intellectual and cultural interpretation of that movement is Alan Heimert's *Religion and the American Mind from the Great Awakening to the Revolution* (Cambridge, Mass., 1966), which sheds new light upon and offers a revised argument about the dispute between the "evangelical" and "liberal" wings of the Congregational clergy of New England in that era. Contemporary sources that are particularly relevant to the revivals in New Hampshire and Maine are: *The Christian History . . . For the Year 1743* (Boston, 1744); George Whitefield: *The Two First Parts of his Life, with his Journals* (London, 1756); "A Record of the Transactions of the annual Convocation of Ministers in the Province of N: Hampshire, began July 28th, 1747" in the *Collections* of the New Hampshire Historical Society, IX (1889); and especially the diary of Nicholas Gilman, Durham revivalist (Ms., New Hampshire Historical Society), which records both the exterior life of a town caught up in the flames of an extraordinary revival and the private development of an unusual spiritual pilgrim. There is reason to hope that this last may soon be published, as it surely ought to be. From sermons on "remarkable providences" by Jabez Fitch of Portsmouth—*The Work of the Lord in the Earthquake, to be duly Regarded by us* (Boston, 1728) and *Two Sermons on Occasion of the Fatal Distemper* (Boston, 1736)—one can become saturated in the sort of religious "improvement" of these events to which Mr. Fitch's parishioners were exposed and with which they were prepared for the Great Awakening. His *Account of the Numbers that have Died of the Distemper in the Throat, Within the Province of New-Hampshire* (Boston, 1736) is the standard source on the epidemic in northern New England. In modern times, Dr. Ernest Caulfield has offered a physician's account and analysis of the epidemic under the title *A True History of the Terrible Epidemic Vulgarly Called the Throat Distemper Which Occurred In His Majesty's New England Colonies Between the Years 1735 and 1740* (New Haven, 1939). Dr. Caulfield draws a cautious connection, with which I agree but Gaustad does not, between the epidemic and the ensuing revivals.

The student of institutional and biographical aspects of the religious history of the region will find convenient references in: Frederick Lewis Weis's *The Colonial Clergy and the Colonial Churches of New England* (Lancaster, Mass., 1936); *The Native Ministry of New Hampshire* (Concord, 1906); Jeremy Belknap's table in Volume III of *The History of New Hampshire*, previously cited; Calvin M. Clark's *History of the Congregational Churches in Maine* (Portland, 1935); and Robert Hayes Dunn's *Old St. John's at Portsmouth* (Newcomen Society pamphlet, New York, 1947). By far the most pleasurable method of investigating into the lives of specific New England clergymen of the period is to profit from the research and craftsmanship of John Langdon Sibley, and more especially of his successor, Clifford K. Shipton. It is impossible to conceive how a serious writer on colonial New England could fail to become indebted to these two scholars for their *Biographical Sketches of Graduates of Harvard University* and *Biographical Sketches of Those Who Attended Harvard College* (14 vols., Cambridge, Mass., 1873–1968). Shipton's colorful and scholarly sketches of Harvard men provided me with most of the important facts about most of the magistrates and merchants as well as nearly all of the ministers whom I encountered in this study.

Among the documents relating to the New Hampshire activities of the Society for the Propagation of the Gospel are the annual *S.P.G. Sermons and Abstracts* for the years between 1738 and 1765 and a manuscript collection in the Portsmouth Public Library entitled "S.P.G. Transcripts."

The struggle for political power in New Hampshire, and especially the personality and policies of Benning Wentworth, have attracted the attention of a number of recent historians. The insights about the New Hampshire situation that are recorded by Leonard W. Labaree in his *Royal Government in America* (New York, 1958) were very useful to me; and I found that John F. Looney clarified many points in his slender but well-presented "The King's Representative: Benning Wentworth, Colonial Governor, 1741–1767" (unpublished dissertation, Lehigh University, 1961). Looney portrays Wentworth's "New Hampshire grants" from an unusually sympathetic point of view in "Benning Wentworth's Land Grant Policy: A Reappraisal," *Historical New Hampshire*, XIII (Spring 1968). One of the leading students of New Hampshire provincial politics in the period is Jere R. Daniell, who has summarized some of his findings in "Politics in New Hampshire under Governor Benning Wentworth, 1741–1767," *William and Mary Quarterly*, 3rd Ser., XXIII (January 1966), 76–105.

The records of provincial legislatures and courts, town proprietors, and churches are essential tools for virtually every colonial historian. The standard collections of Massachusetts and New Hampshire laws are *The Acts and Resolves, Public and Private, of the Province of Massachusetts Bay* (21 vols., Boston, 1869–1922) and *Laws of New Hampshire* (Vols. I and II edited by Albert S. Batchellor, Concord, N.H., 1904–13; Vol. III edited by Henry H. Metcalf, Bristol, N.H., 1915). Occasionally I found it more convenient to refer to contemporary official law books; in those few cases, the edition used is cited in the notes.

For the official records of Massachusetts, two published collections are indispensable: *Records of the Governor and Company of the Massachusetts Bay* (ed. Nathaniel B. Shurtleff, 5 vols., Boston, 1853–54) and *Journals of the House of Representatives of Massachusetts* (36 vols., Boston, 1919–64). For New Hampshire, the principal collection is *Provincial and State Papers of New Hampshire*, edited by Isaac Hammond and Albert S. Batchellor. Both the arrangement and the titling of this series are confusing in their complexity, but the contents are rewarding in the extreme, since the collection contains correspondence, petitions, court records, and a variety of other documents as well as legislative journals. I have used principally: Volumes II–VI, entitled *Provincial Papers of New Hampshire* (Concord, 1868–72); Volume X, entitled *Provincial and State Papers of New Hampshire* (Concord, 1877); Volumes XI–XIII, entitled *Town Papers of New Hampshire* (Concord, 1882–4); and Volumes XVIII and XIX, entitled *State Papers of New Hampshire* (Concord, 1890–1).

By far the most entertaining and, to the social historian, one of the most useful collections of documents from northern New England is *Province and Court Records of Maine* (Vols. I and II edited by Charles Thornton Libbey, Portland, 1928–31; Vol. III edited by Robert E. Moody, Portland, 1947; Vols. IV and V edited by Neal W. Allen, Jr., Portland, 1958–60). These thoroughly annotated court records have provided me with much material with which to illustrate the kind of life that was lived in the tiny Maine communities of the seventeenth century and very early eighteenth century. The Probate Records of York County are deposited in manuscript form in the York County Court House in Alfred, Maine.

Like *Provincial and State Papers of New Hampshire*, the *Documentary History of Maine* goes far beyond a mere collection of official documents. Comprising Volumes I–XXIV (Portland, 1869–1916) of the second series of the *Collections* of the Maine Historical Society, this series includes correspondence relating to settlement and countless affairs of state as well as official records. The student of the region is also likely to find much of value, as I did, in other series of the *Collections*, as well as in the *Publications* of the Colonial Society of Massachusetts and in the *Collections* of the Massachusetts Historical Society and the New Hampshire Historical Society.

The earliest town records of Portsmouth are published in Frank W. Hackett's *1645–1656 Portsmouth Records* (Portsmouth, 1886). The records of Londonderry are also published, but I used the original town records deposited in the library of the New Hampshire Historical Society. The town records of both Scarborough and Windham are to be found in the library of the Maine Historical Society; but in the case of Windham, since the town was not incorporated until 1762, the most useful source for me was the "Windham Proprietors or Grantees Book," which contains the proceedings of the proprietors of New Marblehead from the beginning. Other proprietors' records of special value are published as *Records of the Proprietors of Narragansett, No. 1, Now the Town of Buxton*, ed. William F. Goodwin (Concord, N.H., 1871). Among the church records which I found useful were the Records of the First Parish Church of North Yarmouth and the Reverend Peter Thacher Smith's Windham Church Record Book, both at the Maine Historical Society.

The following maps, though some of them date from a later period than I should have preferred for purposes of this study, proved to be of great value to me and might profitably be consulted by other students of the region: several maps of the Piscataqua region and the Maine coast in the late seventeenth century in Volume I of Archer Butler Hulbert, ed.: *The Crown Collection of Photographs of American Maps* (Cleveland, Ohio, 1904); several excellent pilotage charts and a view of Portsmouth in Volume I of Joseph F. DesBarres: *The Atlantic Neptune* (London, 1780); D. F. von Sotzmann: *New Hampshire* (Hamburg, 1796); and a map of New England based on Jeffrey's Map (London, 1774) in John G. Palfrey: *History of New England* (Boston, 1890), V, following p. 2.

Useful guides for locating manuscripts and contemporary printed materials are: Elizabeth Ring: *A Reference List of Manuscripts Relating to the History of Maine* (3 vols., Orono, Me., 1938–41); Harriette M. Forbes: *New England Diaries, 1602–1800* ([Topsfield, Mass.], 1923); Edward G. Cox: *A Reference Guide to the Literature of Travel*, Vol. II, "The New World" (Seattle, 1938); and Charles Evans: *American Bibliography* (12 vols., Chicago, 1903–34).

Index

A Note About the Author

Charles Edwin Clark was born in Brunswick, Maine, in 1929. He received his A.B. from Bates College in 1951, his M.S. from the Graduate School of Journalism, Columbia University, in 1952, and his Ph.D. in American Civilization from Brown University in 1966. In the 1950's he served in the U.S. Navy as an air intelligence officer and as a reporter for *The Valley News,* West Lebanon, New Hampshire, and *The Providence Journal* and *Evening Bulletin,* Providence, Rhode Island. From 1965 to 1967 he was an assistant professor of history at Southeastern Massachusetts Technological Institute. He has taught at the University of New Hampshire since 1967, and is presently an associate professor there.

A Note on the Type

This book was set on the Linotype in Old Style No. 7. This face is largely based on a series originally cut by the Bruce Foundry in the early eighteen-seventies, and that face, in its turn, appears to have followed in all essentials the details of a face designed and cut some years before by the celebrated Edinburgh type founders Miller and Richard. Old Style No. 7, composed in a page, gives a subdued color and an even texture that make it easily and comfortably read.

This book was composed, printed and bound by
The Colonial Press Inc., Clinton, Massachusetts.
Typography and binding design by
Bonnie Spiegel.

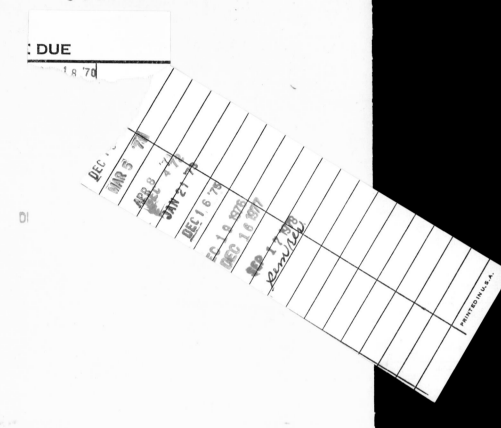